The Forgotten

The Forgotten

Canadian POWs, Escapers and Evaders in Europe, 1939–1945

Nathan M. Greenfield

HarperCollins*PublishersLtd*

The Forgotten

Published by HarperCollins Publishers Ltd

First published in Canada in a hardcover edition by HarperCollins Publishers Ltd: 2013
This trade paperback edition: 2014

Map of RCAF Pilot/Officer Sydney P. Smith's Evasion Route is reproduced from *Lifting the Silence: A World War II RCAF Bomber Pilot Reunites with His Past* (Toronto: Dundurn Press, 2010), by Sydney Percival Smith and David Scott Smith. Map of Bonaparte Beach is reproduced from *The Evaders: True Stories of Downed Canadian Airmen and Their Helpers in World War II* (Whitby: McGraw-Hill Ryerson, 1992), by Emerson Lavender and Norman Sheffe.

HarperCollins books may be purchased for educational, business, or sales promotional use through our Special Markets Department.

HarperCollins Publishers Ltd
2 Bloor Street East, 20th Floor
Toronto, Ontario, Canada
M4W 1A8

www.harpercollins.ca

Library and Archives Canada Cataloguing in Publication
information is available upon request

ISBN 978-1-44340-490-7

Printed and bound in the United States
RRD 9 8 7 6 5 4 3 2 1

To Micheline,
who walked the steps of many of these camps with me
and who shares the steps of her days with me.

And to Julie and Eric, now grown,
who follow their own paths through life.

A prisoner of war is a public enemy armed or attached to the hostile army for active aid, who has fallen into the hands of the captor, either fighting or wounded, on the field or in the hospital, by individual surrender or capitulation.

A prisoner of war is subject to no punishment for being a public enemy, nor is any revenge wreaked upon him by intentional infliction of any suffering or disgrace, by cruel imprisonment, want of food, by mutilation, death or any other barbarity.

Prisoners of war shall be fed upon plain and wholesome food whenever practicable, and treated with humanity.

*Honourable men, when captured, will abstain from giving to the enemy information concerning their own army, and the modern law of war permits no longer the use of violence against prisoners, in order to extort the desired information, or to punish them for having given false information.**

**Articles 49, 56, 76 and 80 of General Orders, no. 100 of the Armies of the United States, 24 April 1863, authorized by President Abraham Lincoln, which formed the basis for subsequent international conventions that deal with prisoners of war.*

CONTENTS

NOTE TO READERS

The original plan for this book called for it to tell the stories of the POWs, escapers and evaders, how their families dealt with their absence, and how the government in Ottawa and organizations such as the Red Cross responded to the ongoing needs of the soldiers, sailors, airmen and merchant mariners who had fallen into Germany's hands. The richness of the POWs', escapers' and evaders' stories combined to push most of the second and third parts of the book onto the "cutting-room floor." For those interested in the mechanics of how the Canadian government responded to the legal and material needs of the POWs, I can do no better than point toward Jonathan Vance's *Objects of Concern* and his "Men in Manacles: The Shackling of Prisoners of War, 1942–1943," which explain the complicated diplomatic manoeuvring between Germany and Britain, and Britain and Canada vis-à-vis the shackling of the survivors of Dieppe. Of great interest also is Serge Durflinger's *Fighting from Home.*

For ease of reading, I have rendered most telegrams in sentence case and time in as a.m. or p.m. form. Since the POW camps in areas that are now in Poland or Lithuania were then either annexed to the Reich or in conquered areas, I have used German spellings for towns: thus Posen and not Poznań, as it is properly known today. Since my focus is on these men's experience as prisoners, I have not always indicated the names of the regiments or the numbers of their squadrons.

To keep from littering the pages with references, I have not cited quotations from official reports or unpublished memoirs. Quotations from men I interviewed are signalled by using the present tense—for example, "Reid remembers"—whereas those in past tense—"Prouse recalled"—come from either published or unpublished memoirs. Locutions such as "Father Goudreau wrote" signal that the words come from a memoir, letter or report. I have grouped together citations to published sources, usually following the first quote in the entry. Translations from French have been provided by my wife, Micheline R. Dubé.

I determined the dates in the subheadings in various ways. Some are the date a POW wrote the letter or when it was received in Canada; in the latter case, I have made that clear in the narrative. Some are the dates mentioned in published and unpublished memoirs. In a few cases, I have had to make an educated guess as to when the events occurred. Several of the memoirists write chapters that deal with life in the POW camps during the winter. I have assigned information, such as the first time a POW saw a Klim-tin blower, to the first winter he spent as a POW; any misassignment of generic events to the wrong year does not, I believe, materially affect these men's stories.

POW CAMPS IN GERMANY AND OCCUPIED EUROPE

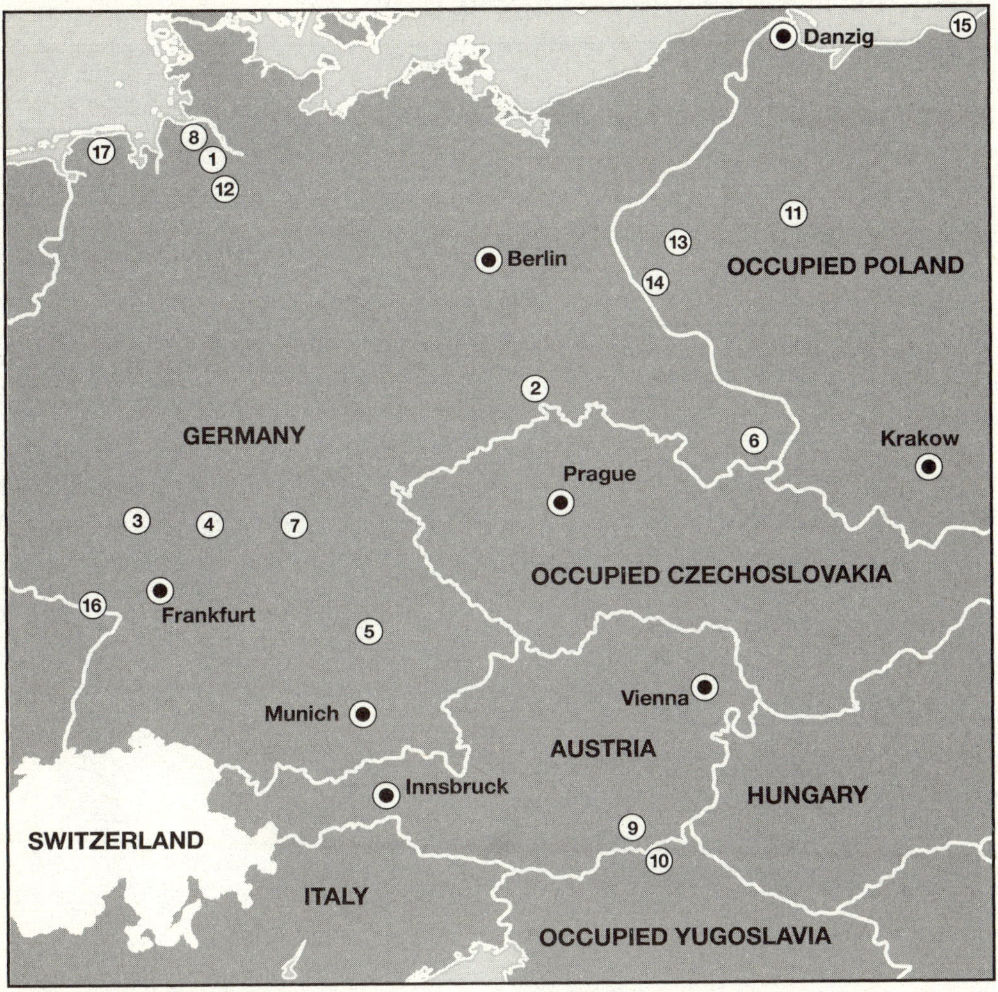

1. Marlag und Milag Nord (Westertimke)
2. Oflag IV-C (Colditz)
3. Oflag IX-A/H (Spangenberg)
4. Oflag IX-A/Z (Rotenberg)
5. Stalag VII-A (Moosberg)
6. Stalag VIII-B (Lamsdorf)
7. Stalag IX-C (Bad Sulza)
8. Stalag X-B (Sandbostel)
9. Stalag XVIII-A (Wolfsberg)
10. Stalag XVIII-B/Z (Marburg)
11. Stalag XX-A (Thorn)
12. Stalag XI-B (Fallingbosel)
13. Stalag XXI-D (Posen)
14. Stalag Luft III (Sagan)
15. Stalag Luft VI (Heydekrug)
16. Dulag Luft (Frankfurt am Maim)
17. Dulag Nord (Wilhelmshaven)

RCAF PILOT/OFFICER SYDNEY P. SMITH'S EVASION ROUTE FROM SERBONNES, FRANCE, TO GIBRALTAR, SPAIN

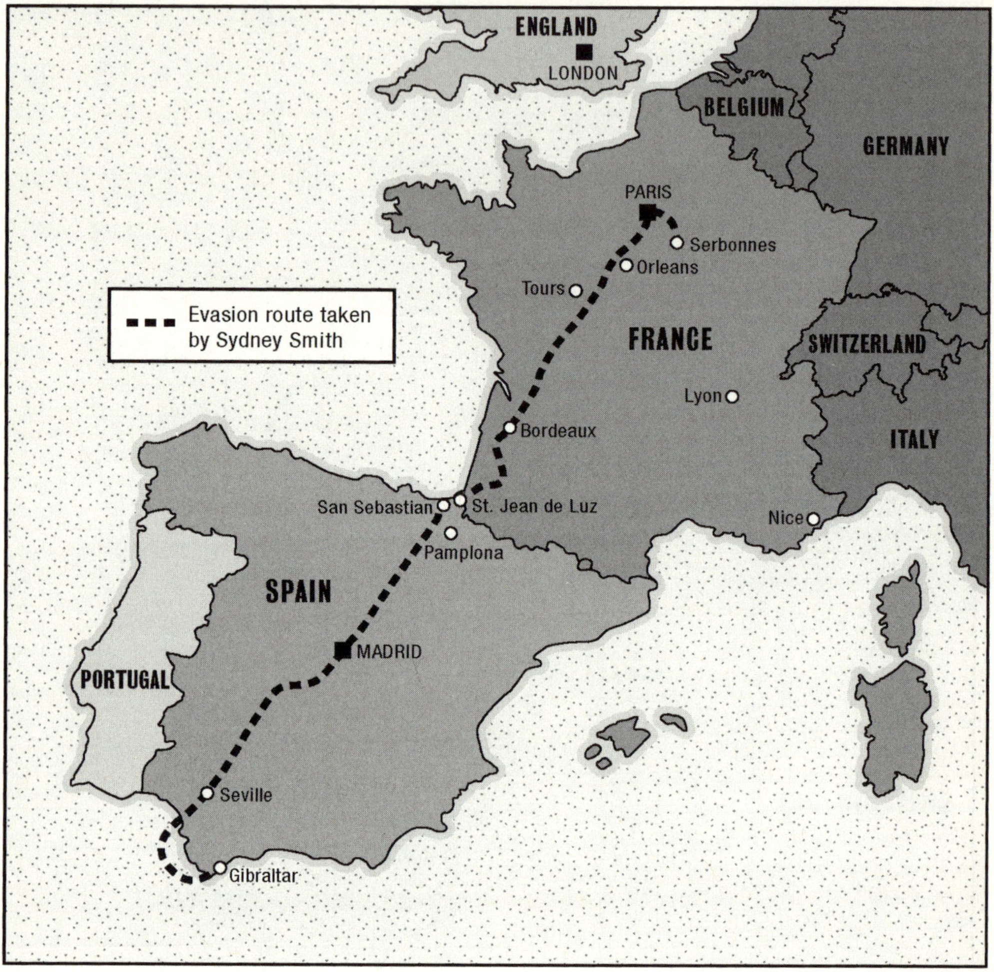

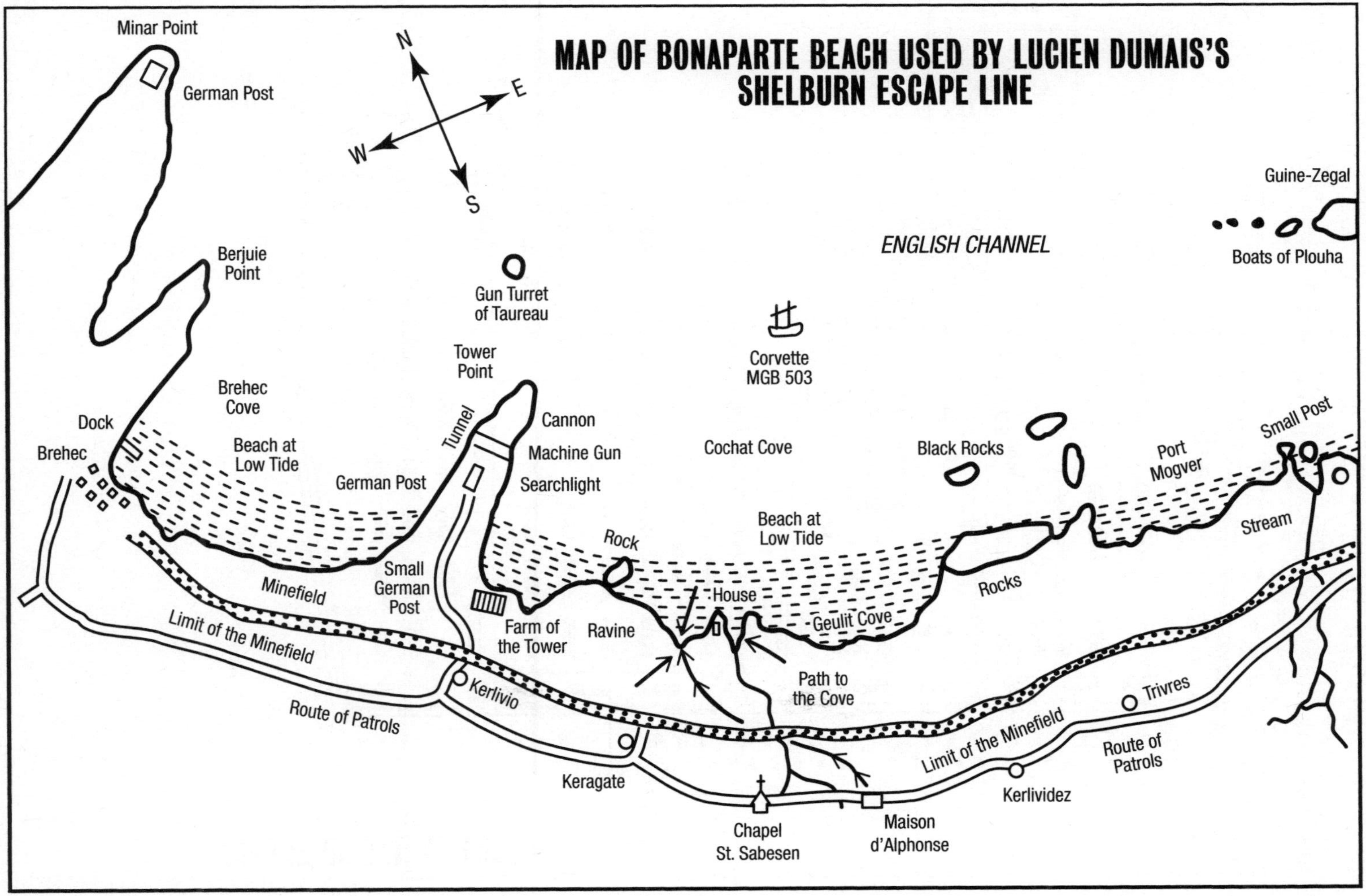
MAP OF BONAPARTE BEACH USED BY LUCIEN DUMAIS'S SHELBURN ESCAPE LINE
N
E
W
S
Minar Point
German Post
Berjuie Point
Brehec Cove
Dock
Brehec
Beach at Low Tide
German Post
Minefield
Small German Post
Limit of the Minefield
Route of Patrols
Gun Turret of Taureau
Tower Point
Tunnel
Cannon
Machine Gun
Searchlight
Farm of the Tower
Kerlivio
Ravine
Rock
Keragate
House
Corvette MGB 503
Cochat Cove
Beach at Low Tide
Geulit Cove
Path to the Cove
Chapel St. Sabesen
Maison d'Alphonse
ENGLISH CHANNEL
Black Rocks
Rocks
Limit of the Minefield
Kerlividez
Port Mogver
Trivres
Route of Patrols
Small Post
Stream
Guine-Zegal
Boats of Plouha

LAYOUT OF STALAG LUFT III

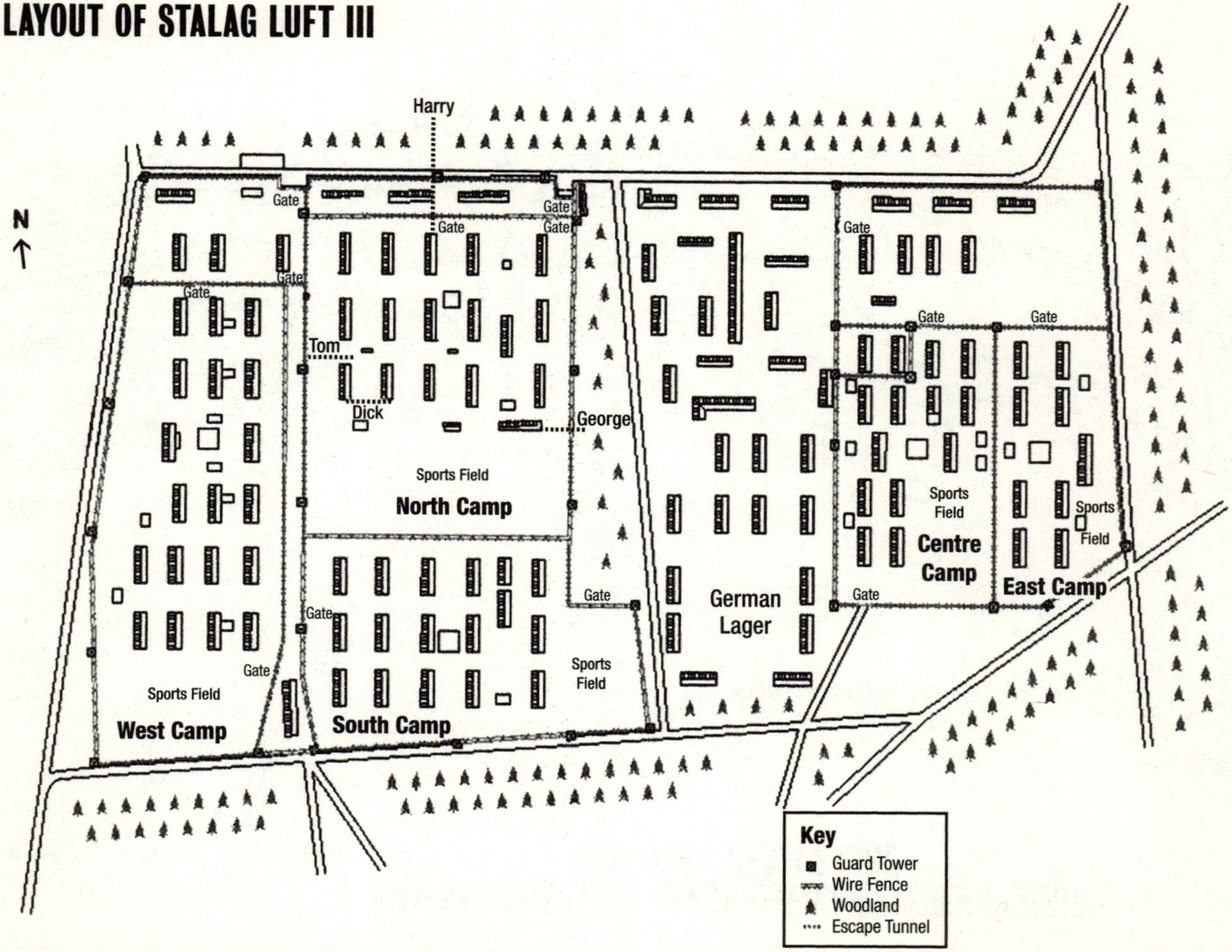

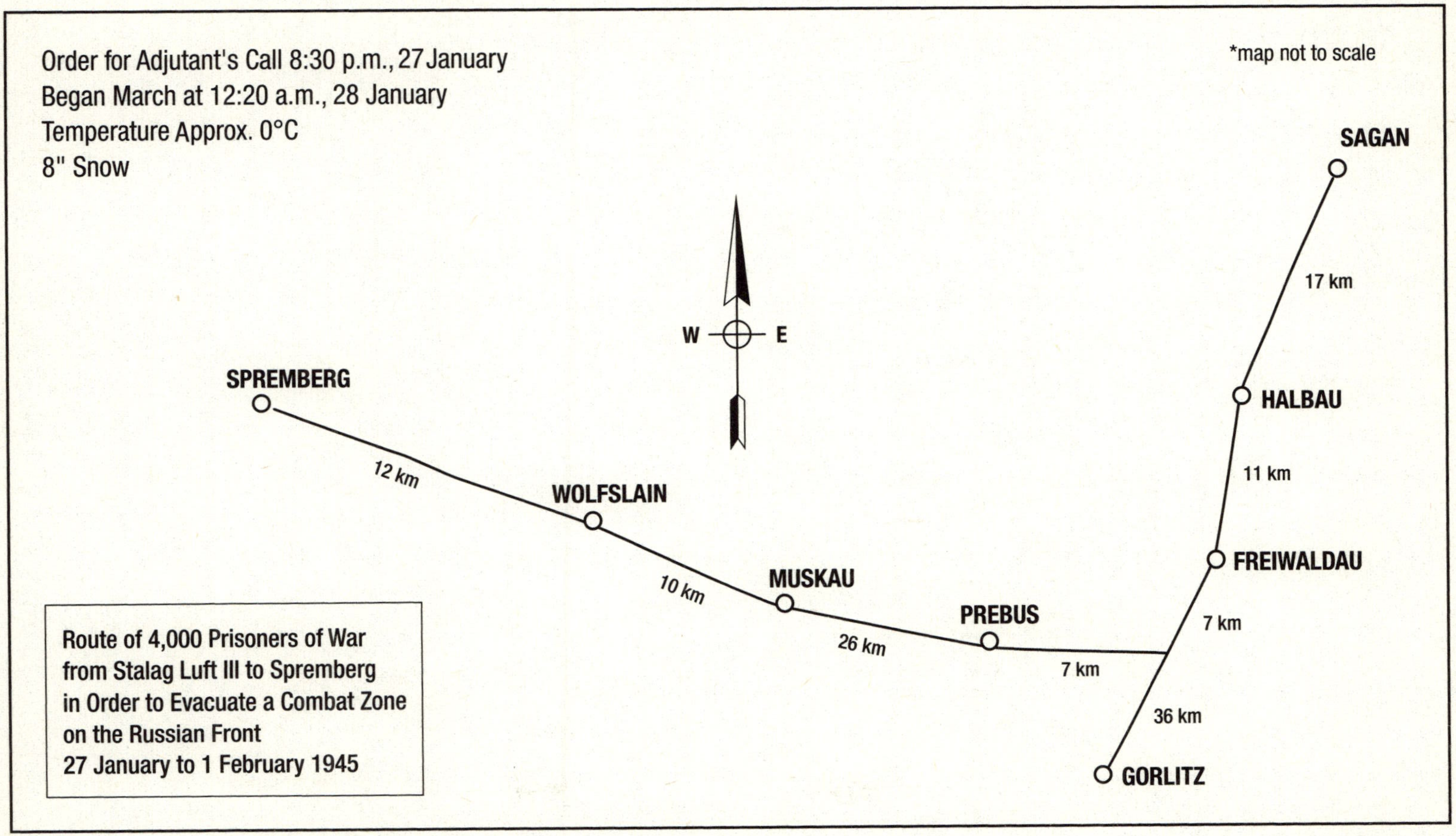

Order for Adjutant's Call 8:30 p.m., 27 January
Began March at 12:20 a.m., 28 January
Temperature Approx. 0°C
8" Snow
*map not to scale
SAGAN
17 km
HALBAU
11 km
FREIWALDAU
7 km
36 km
GORLITZ
7 km
PREBUS
26 km
MUSKAU
10 km
WOLFSLAIN
12 km
SPREMBERG
W
E
Route of 4,000 Prisoners of War
from Stalag Luft III to Spremberg
in Order to Evacuate a Combat Zone
on the Russian Front
27 January to 1 February 1945

INTRODUCTION

For Ian MacDonald's parents, who lived in Lourdes, Nova Scotia, the moment they had hoped to be spared arrived on 17 April 1943. The news was not borne for them (as it was for tens of thousands of other Canadians) by a telegraph boy, wearing the iconic blue cap and uniform, bicycling to the door of their house. Rather, it came via the familiar voice of Miss Mable MacLean, the town's telegraphist, who immediately after transcribing the telegram from the War Office called the house that stood across the laneway from her own to tell her neighbours that "SERGEANT IAN ROSS MACDONALD IS REPORTED MISSING AIR OPERATION OVERSEAS APRIL FIFTEENTH STOP."

Neither William nor Mary MacDonald had a military background so were unused to the peremptory orders. However, like everyone else on the east coast, they had seen posters with the words "Careless Words May Cause Disaster!" superimposed upon the track of a torpedo heading for a merchant ship. In fact, the posters had special meaning for them because their eldest son, Alexander, and Leo, the one after Ian, were both serving in the Royal Canadian Navy. Thus, the MacDonalds were not surprised that the telegram ended by saying that, to protect Ian, they were to "withhold information from press or radio until name appears official casualty list five weeks hence. Stop."

A few days later, the MacDonalds received a letter from the commander of MacDonald's Royal Canadian Air Force 408 Bomber Squadron. Mary and "Billy B.," as William was known to his family, learned that Ian's comrades "looked upon [him] as a good fellow" and that he did not return from a raid on Stuttgart on the night of 14/15 April. But they latched onto the possibility that Ian "may be a prisoner of war." A subsequent letter explained the prohibition on speaking to the press: "It is possible that he has landed in enemy territory and[,] in that event, publicity at this time might imperil his chances of escape."

The MacDonalds were not alone in their shock and grief: the next of kin of MacDonald's six crewmates received identical letters. Indeed, after four and a half years of war, thousands of Canadian families with sons, husbands and brothers in the RCAF, Royal Air Force, RCN and merchant marine had received similar letters. So too had almost 4,000 families of soldiers captured at Hong Kong in December 1941 or at Dieppe in August 1942.

The MacDonalds' extended family rallied to their support. Hoping that because he was a soldier his words carried the stamp of military reason, William's nephew, John Keay, then stationed in Montreal, wrote that he believed Ian was "safe but possibl[y] a prisoner." Keay then slipped easily into the venerable words of prayer recited, sometimes silently, by the thousands of men who, after bailing out of their aircraft, trusted their lives to the gossamer weave of silk—and, of course, by the hundreds of thousands more who faced battle on land and sea. From Yonkers, New York, William's sister, Eunice wrote, "If it is 'His Will' that Ian shall survive—he will survive," and arranged for her priest to say mass for Ian so that she could take communion for him.

The MacDonalds' hope rose and fell, though not to the beat of the headlines, which in the second quarter of 1943 told of victory in North Africa, the Red Army's push through the Caucuses, huge bombing raids on Germany, the joint American-Canadian victory in the Aleutians and victory in the Battle of the Atlantic. A letter written at the end of April by Mrs. M. Parkinson of Toronto (mother of "Parky" Parkinson, a crewmate of Ian's) that told that a crewmate, Sergeant Walter Reed, was a prisoner of war was like a life preserver. But another, written that same day in London, England, darkened the mood in the small white house that still stands just before the first rise on Emmanuel Street, a street that in those days had no numbered addresses. The Air Council expressed "grave concern" about Sergeant MacDonald's fate. Then came word that Harry Jay, the plane's rear gunner, was also a prisoner.

As the last letter his mother had written Ian, now stamped "Reported Missing," made its way back to Nova Scotia, other letters arrived. On 7 June, by which time the MacDonalds knew that a third crewmate, Sergeant R. Dressler, had been captured, Mrs. Parkinson wrote again, this time with the news that Pilot Officer Lee Usher had been seen at a POW camp. Her son, Parky; John Courtney, the plane's navigator; and MacDonald were still unaccounted for.

Two weeks later, an envelope with a return address the MacDonalds had never seen arrived from Moncton, New Brunswick. Before Mrs. MacDonald even read the letter, tears streaked her face. For enclosed with the letter was a photograph of Ian and Ernest Moore, another RCAF NCO, taken a few days before MacDonald's second and last mission. In September, Mrs. Parkinson wrote with the good news that her son was a POW and in good shape.

The letter the MacDonalds most feared was written on 19 October. Given the lapse of time since Ian had been shot down and in the absence of any further information, the "Air Ministry now propose[d] to take action to presume his death for official purposes" such as releasing his personal effects and bank account to his family. The letter did not, however, have the expected horrifying effect: two days earlier, Mrs. Parkinson had called with the news that she had heard from her son that Ian was indeed alive and a prisoner of war.

Three months later (on 10 January 1944), the mailman brought a postcard postmarked in Germany and in which MacDonald told his parents that he "was two months trying to escape, caught and held prisoner in ----- Paris for four months" but that he was "feeling fine and entirely unwounded so that there was no need to worry."[1]

* * *

Each airman, soldier, sailor and merchant mariner that we will meet below was a volunteer.* Some, like Pilot Officer Alfred Burke "Tommy" Thompson, who was shot down even before Canada formally declared war on Nazi Germany, flew in the RAF Royal Navy. Others, like MacDonald and Sergeant Edward Carter-Edwards, belonged to the RCAF. Among the 41 merchant mariners who survived the sinking of the Canadian freighter *A.D. Huff* were a number of Canadians, who, like their crewmates, spent four years in Milag Nord, the prisoner-of-war camp near Bremen run by the Kriegsmarine for merchant sailors. In May 1944, the survivors of HMCS *Athabaskan*, sunk off France the previous month, arrived at Marlag Nord, the navy camp adjacent to Milag Nord. The largest group of Canadians captured at one time were the almost 2,000 men who survived the cauldron of Dieppe but were unable to escape Hitler's Europe on that fateful August 1942 afternoon. By the end of the war, in addition to these men, the Germans held some 2,290 men belonging to the RCAF, scores of Canadians flying for the RAF, and more than 5,016 captured in Italy, North Africa, Normandy and northwest Europe.

* The stories that follow could have been organized thematically, with chapter headings such as "The Terror of Surrendering," "I've Never Been So Homesick" or "The Stench of Death." Such "silos" would have meant tracing the war years a number of times. Instead, I have opted for a longitudinal organization that begins on the second night of the war and carries through to its end. We meet each of these 45 men at a moment of high drama—when they are shot down, captured or on the run, or when they find themselves in a POW camp—and then follow them through to the end of the war. Issues such as hunger, fear, boredom, daring escapes or longing for mail appear as part of their daily lives rather than being summoned to the fore by this historian's plan. Following these POWs, escapers and evaders through time and place enabled me to build up a picture of their experiences across the length and breadth of Europe and approximate their experience of time.

None of these men expected to hear the words "*Für Sie ist der Krieg zu Ende*" or its English equivalent, "For you, the war is over," and then feel the wave of humiliation born of a profound sense of failure wash over them. Yet they expected that, were they to raise their hands in surrender, the Germans would accord them the protections laid out in the Geneva Convention. And many, including the men who surrendered with Lieutenant Colonel Douglas Catto on the hills above Dieppe, were. So too was Pilot Officer Brian Hodgkinson, who was so badly injured when he bailed out of his bomber in October 1941 that he was immediately taken to a well-equipped hospital.

By contrast, at Dieppe, some Germans refused to give the defeated Canadians water, and on the beach that Jack Poolton's Royal Regiment of Canada attacked, one officer walked among the wounded, shooting them. Just under two years later, within hours of the Canadians landing at Juno Beach and storming ashore, SS-Brigadeführer Kurt Meyer's men killed the first of more than 150 Canadians who would be murdered in Normandy.

Less lethal violations of Geneva included long train trips without food and water, the cessation of Red Cross parcel delivery and grossly inadequate rations of about 1,400 calories a day, about half of what a man of soldiering age required, and sometimes as few as 800. Leo Panatelo, who was captured at Dieppe, recalls one day what fats and protein the soup had had come from a "boiled horse's cock." The humiliation of being shackled did not violate Geneva, though being made to stand for hours with your nose against a wall and the rifle butts to the small of the back for those who moved did. The enforced labour—slave labour—extracted from men like RCAF Squadron Leader Edward Blenkinsop also violated Geneva.

The Geneva Convention applied to uniformed servicemen only. Thus, from the moment the six men who successfully escaped from trains taking the soldiers captured at Dieppe to POW camps donned civilian clothes, they placed themselves outside the convention's famed protections—at least until the Gestapo recognized that they were, in fact, soldiers. By placing themselves in the hands of the Resistance and exchanging their uniforms for civilian clothes, evaders—like MacDonald, who was on the run after being shot down—also placed themselves outside Geneva, which explains why when they were captured they were held by the Gestapo until Heinrich Himmler's minions had satisfied themselves that (1) these men were airmen and not secret agents and (2) they could get no more information about the Resistance cells that helped them evade capture.

As the Allies closed in on Paris in August 1944, the Gestapo moved 168 captured Allied airmen, including John Harvie and Edward Carter-Edwards and 25 other RCAF officers, from Fresnes Prison to a concentration camp, where the air was tinged with oily human smoke. Geneva did not, perforce, apply to Frank Pickersgill, Kenneth Macalister and Romeo Sabourin, three Canadians who were agents belonging to the Special Operations Executive and who were executed in Buchenwald, not far from the hut where their fellow Canadians suffered.

The Germans had no doubt that the 86 men captured after the Great Escape came under Geneva, which both allowed for escapes and laid down penalties for those men who were recaptured. Yet with the full knowledge that a year earlier Korvettenkapitän Wolfgang Heyda, who had escaped from the POW camp in Bowmanville, Ontario, was simply returned to the camp after being recaptured on the shores of the Baie des Chaleurs, the Germans on Hitler's orders, executed 50 of the escapers, including six Canadians.

Central to my telling of the story of these men of the Second World War is another group of volunteers that has been completely forgotten. The sinking of the SS *Zamzam* in April 1941 delivered into German hands 17 Canadian civilians: 12 French-Canadian Oblate priests and brothers, and 5 Sacred Heart Brothers. *Les religieux* were missionaries on their way to South Africa and thence to Basutoland (the present-day Kingdom of Lesotho). Also on board and bound for Basutoland were some 150 American Protestant ministers and their families; some of these were Lutherans from the

Midwest who were going to Africa to replace German Lutheran missionaries who had been interned by the British.[2]

Ironically, given that during the war the Germans repatriated a number of British padres and the Nazi state's abjuration of Christianity, the Germans interned the priests and brothers because they were churchmen, though, as became clear, the Nazis did not understand the difference between a priest and a religious brother. While no records have been found in German archives to explain why the Canadian Catholics were held while the American missionaires were repatriated, an extraordinary (and hitherto all but unused) cache of letters, memoirs and other documents in the Archives Deschâtelets at Saint Paul University in Ottawa allows us to piece together the story.

Though the Nazis had neutered the Catholic Church in the 1930s, they did not trust Germany's Catholic priests enough to allow them to minister in the Reich's POW camps. However, the Germans were cognizant of Article 16 of the Geneva Convention, which states that POWs "shall be permitted complete freedom in performance of their religious duties, including attendance at the services of their faith," for Catholics this requires the presence of a priest both for confession and communion.

Sent first to Stalag X-B and then to Milag und Marlag Nord (as the two camps were known together) before a number of them were sent on to other camps in Germany, Poland and Austria, the priests and brothers were not treated as regular POWs. Like the officers they were housed with, some were allowed parole walks—walks on one's "word" or promise to return—outside the barbed wire. At Stalag Luft III, Father Philippe Goudreau had a private room. However, since *les religieux* were civilians, the Germans did not follow the Geneva requirement to pay them as either ordinary soldiers or officers (military padres hold honorary officer rank), though the priests were paid for conducting specific services. This money, along with their share of the money officers pooled from the pay provided by the Germans, went to purchasing materials for saying mass.

Early in their captivity, the priests and brothers were restricted to the same three letters and ten postcards that other POWs were allowed to write per month; in some camps later in the war, this number was doubled. At least three priests were allowed to use typewriters. Even more interestingly, alone among all POWs, *les religieux* were exempted from the rule that prevented prisoners in different camps from writing to each other; presumably their letters were transhipped via Stalag Luft III, where most of the censors were. These letters and memoirs allow us to chart much more than the succour the padres (for that is what the priests and brothers became) are supposed to provide for the men: the Oblates and Sacred Heart Brothers stood up to German authorities, risked their lives in secret religious meetings both inside and outside the camps; their experiences behind the barbed wire pushed at least two priests to question important parts of the Church doctrine, including the miracle of transubstantiation.

Also forgotten are the stories of the "home runs" by evaders, men who (at least for a while) avoided capture after being shot down, and men like Robert Prouse, who was captured at Dieppe and escaped a number of times. His career as an evader after being shot down in January 1943 may have lasted only a few hours, but that did not dampen RCAF Pilot Officer Andrew Carswell's ardour to escape, which he too did more than once. Other home runs were more successful, taking men to freedom in Spain, through Vichy France or Sweden and, for at least one Canadian, the Vatican. Some men, MacDonald included, evaded for weeks before being captured; others slipped by Hitler's noose entirely. Most of the evaders and a few of the escapers owed an unpayable debt to the civilians in the French Resistance and MI9 escape lines.

The triumph of the victory campaign has largely obscured the story of the Hunger Marches. For 45 days in one case, more than 60 in another, beginning just after New Year's Day 1945, thousands of Canadians were among the hundreds of thousands of Western POWs being force-marched through a terribly cold and snowy winter. Weeks of sleeping in the open or in unheated barns, rations so poor that one man was reduced to stealing oats meant for horses, trudging through high snowdrifts and shivering in temperatures that reached -40°C combined to break spirits, and sicken and kill thousands. The ostensible reason for these marches that zigzagged away from the American, British, Canadian and Russian armies that by early 1945 were crushing the Reich was to protect the POWs from battle (and thus appeared to accord with Geneva). In reality, the Germans sought to hold on to the POWs for two reasons: to prevent them from adding their strength to the armies and air forces pummelling Germany, and to serve as bargaining chips for some imagined future peace treaty.

On the frozen roads and fields of Germany, men fought to retain what heat they could and to keep as dry as possible while they tended to the sick—and watched their comrades die, their bodies to be left in the snow. Even in their reduced state, they felt shame for their inability to do anything for those who were, incredibly, even more unfortunate than themselves. Private John Grogan's elegy for an elderly man, this one with a Star of David sewn onto his threadbare coat and who "half lay, half sat on the tongue of an abandoned wagon, one naked foot stuck up from the snow, no bullet wasted on him—brown stains down his gray beard and on his striped pajamas, blood congealing and frozen from a jagged wound in his throat," is but one of the many that testify to the human drama these men lived through in those terrible days.[3]

For most of the "Kriegies" (the name the men gave themselves, from the German word for prisoner of war, *Kriegsgefangener*) liberation did not resemble the end of battle, accompanied by unaccustomed silence or, as Sergeant Major Lucien Dumais recalled, on the beach before Dieppe with the throwing down of one's gun. Rather, it came with the unexpected arrival of a small Russian, British, American or Canadian detachment at a POW camp or, in some cases, on a road or field in France, Poland or Germany.

Chapter One

September 1939–December 1940

I alone
Prepare'd myself the conflict to sustain
Both of sad pity, and the perilous road,
Which my unerring memory shall retrace.

—Dante, "The Inferno"

9–10 SEPTEMBER 1939, BERLIN

RAF Pilot Officer "Tommy" Thompson Meets a Very Important Person

In the years that followed, he smiled at the memory of the meeting that occurred two days after bailing out of his plane on the seventh night of the war. And in 1944, when threatened with death, he was saved by the promise the fat, thick-necked man had made under a tree on 10 September 1939.

For Tommy Thompson, there would be nothing phony, or *drôle*, as the French called it, about the war that had begun months before the Blitzkrieg knifed through Holland, Belgium and France in the spring of 1940. Yet, as he climbed into his two-engine bomber, Thompson could not help but think that this was a funny way to fight a war. In place of 14 bombs, his Whitley Mk III was loaded with thousands of leaflets that, in the strongest language British prime minister Neville Chamberlain's government could muster, told the Germans to stop making war. A few moments after dropping the leaflets, an engine overheated, forcing Thompson and his navigator, Squadron Leader Phillip Murray, to bail out near Weimar.

Although hundreds of others who over the next six years "hit the silk" would report being struck by the silence, Thompson was engulfed in sound as his 25,000-pound bomber—one engine still roaring—spiralled toward him not once but twice before veering off and crashing not far from where he himself landed. After catching his breath, Thompson rushed to the wreck and destroyed its radio, just before a group of civilians captured him and Murray, who had landed nearby.

The police who soon picked them up quickly transferred them to the Luftwaffe. One German officer made alarming comments about "last wishes."[4] However, nothing more threatening than several high-ranking Luftwaffe officers and a "sumptuous repast" awaited them at the small hospital outside Berlin that had been pressed into service as a POW camp.[5] Later in the war, the Luftwaffe would have scores of specially trained officers devoted to tricking downed airmen into divulging operational and technical information. But on their second night in Germany, Thompson and Murray faced only a couple of officials who woke them several times during the night to ask about their mission, plane and squadron.

The next morning, the two prisoners were on the move, first through a forest on the far side of which lay a railway siding; then, in what seemed like something out of British music hall comedy, into and out of a passenger carriage; then to a clearing. There through their bloodshot eyes they saw seated in a stout chair on a platform a figure of Falstaffian bulk who held almost as many titles as he wore medals: Reichsminister for forestry, Reichsstatthalter of Prussia and head of the police among them. Hermann Göring was also Reichsminister of aviation. As commander of the Luftwaffe, he merited a salute, though only Murray remembered to afford him this courtesy.

After speaking to Murray alone for a few moments, Göring motioned Thompson over, saying that they had cost him a good night's sleep. Their flight had caused an air-raid alert that had sent him to a shelter outside the capital, Göring told them, which explained why the second most powerful man in Germany was now conducting an interview beside a railway siding. The Red Baron's successor commiserated with their loss of "the freedom of the skies" but found Thompson's presence perplexing, since, for at least a few more hours, Canada and Nazi Germany would (officially) be at peace. More concerned with the propaganda value of pictures of downed airmen looking well-cared-for than with the intricacies of the Statute of Westminster (which in 1931 granted Canada independence in foreign policy) and the Canadian prime minister's pledge that (even though the Royal Canadian Navy was already operating with the Royal Navy) Parliament would decide if Canada was going to declare war on Germany, Göring skipped over his 1937 meeting with Prime Minister William Lyon Mackenzie King.[6]

Instead, Göring discussed ice hockey, predicting that Thompson would have a complete Canadian team by Christmas. And, with his Luftwaffe destroying cities, slaughtering civilians and shredding the Polish army, Göring promised Murray and Thompson that they'd be well-treated and would survive what he assured them would be a short war.

The Air Ministry in London stole a march on Joseph Goebbels's propaganda plans by announcing on 10 September that Thompson had been "interned in Belgium after having been forced down there" a day earlier. Presumably, being an internee in still-neutral Belgium was substituted for being a POW in Germany to prevent pictures of Thompson in newspapers or newsreels from amounting to a recruiting image for becoming a POW.

13 JUNE 1940, TRONDHEIM, NORWAY

Royal Navy Fleet Air Arm
Captain Vernon Howland Is Shot Down

The bullet's nose was slightly flattened as it cut through the metal skin of Vernon Howland's Skua dive-bomber at almost three times the speed of sound before the 1.3 oz. piece of lead ripped into Howland's leg with the force of a mule's kick. The Skua had none of the dash of Junkers Ju-87 and may have flown "like a bathtub," but it had, Howland recalled, one redeeming feature: "It could take an awful lot of punishment." Something it proved as machine-gun blasts from two Messerschmitts chipped pieces off its wings when Howland was still ten miles from his target, the battle cruiser *Gneisenau*, then undergoing repairs in Trondheim, Norway. Although the flak thrown up by *Gneisenau*'s gunners so badly damaged the plane that when he dropped his bombs, instead of lurching upward, the plane continued diving, finally levelling off close to the water, the Skua remained airborne.

Struggling to return to the aircraft carrier HMS *Ark Royal*, the pilot from Fort Qu'Appelle, Saskatchewan, gambled that he'd be safer over the town than the open water and so coaxed his shuddering plane around, only to hear the sound of bullets fired from machine gunners on the rooftops tearing into the plane's belly. A few moments later, just beyond the town, the Skua's engine seized and the plane "seemed to stand on its tail and then just slammed into a clearing in a farmer's field," luckily from only treetop height.

Weak from loss of blood, Howland couldn't, as his gunner did, make a run for Sweden, a dozen miles away. But he remained conscious long enough to see his crewmate return, a German soldier holding a gun at his back.

8 SEPTEMBER 1940, HAMBURG

RAF Warrant Officer 1st Class Andrew Cox Is Told "We Shoot You in the Morning"

With his plane on fire 8,000 feet above Hamburg, Andrew Cox reached for his parachute. He was worried, but not about getting out of the burning four-man Hampden bomber; his radioman's position put him just seconds from the escape hatch. Rather, the proud Bluenose worried about the integrity of his parachute. On a previous raid, battery acid had spilled onto the chute's canvas cover, eating through it and damaging the small pilot chute, whose job was to pull out the main chute.

Mercifully, the chute deployed, but then, by the light cast by the searchlights, Cox could see he was heading for the Elbe River. To avoid it and the likely fate of drowning, he pulled on the lines on one side of his chute, which caused it to partially collapse, dangerously increasing the speed but changing the angle of his descent. As soon as he let go, the chute blossomed, but he still slammed into the ground so hard he was knocked out.

When he came to, Cox mistook a bright light and the shaking ground for an oncoming train but soon realized that the light was the moon and the thunder in the ground was caused by the pounding hoofs of cattle frightened by the anti-aircraft shells exploding 10,000 feet above them. Spotters, he knew, would be watching for where he landed, so he had to get away quickly. He jumped to his feet and started for a nearby hedge but didn't get many steps before ending up on his back looking up at the sky, which glowed orange from the burning oil refineries ten miles away. After unclipping his harness, Cox darted for the hedge at the far end of the field.

A short time later, he climbed up the drain pipe of a farmhouse, where he hoped to steal some food, but quickly jumped down when a woman inside opened the window and started to yell. He then avoided a group of drunken soldiers and slipped around the back of another house. Transfixed by the fireworks over Hamburg, the occupants of that house didn't notice Cox. But their neighbours did; just as he was about to try to open the back door they came rushing out of theirs. Cox ran, but the men soon caught up to him. As they yelled at him in German, he screamed "Englishman, Englishman" until one understood and spat at him. Cox dodged the spittle and landed a fist on the German's face; an older man then parried Cox's next punch with his shotgun.[7]

The men subdued Cox and took him back to the house, where the family looked at him with curiosity. While allowing him to wash and giving him some porridge, the farmer who had blocked his punch kept his gun at the ready until a policeman arrived.

Revolver in hand, the policeman asked Cox questions in broken English. When Cox refused to answer, he shoved the pistol into his stomach, saying, "Now will you tell." Cox feigned bravery by keeping silent. "What does it matter, anyway? We shoot you in the morning," said the policeman before bundling Cox into a car.

9–10 SEPTEMBER 1940, HAMBURG AND DULAG LUFT, FRANKFURT

Cox Discovers He Is a Good Poker Player

For the first few minutes after waking, Cox thought that the Luftwaffe planned to execute him. Instead, he was marched onto a bus that already held the other members of his crew. It took them to an interrogation centre in Hamburg, where the crew members were isolated. After some time, Cox was brought into a room, where two German officers played the roles British intelligence had warned airmen to expect. One German gave Cox a cup of ersatz coffee as he and another officer, sitting in armchairs, spoke in English, pausing now and again to include Cox in their discussion, which included the latest news about the ongoing Battle of Britain. Cox may have dismissed the grandiose claims he heard and the predictions that England's morale would crack, both standard fare in Goebbels's propaganda. But that same day, following an attack by 500 bombers that killed 370 Londoners, including many in an East End public shelter, destroyed when a bomb dropped down its ventilation shaft, and wounded more than 1,400 others, even the Home Intelligence report warned, "The population is showing visible signs of nerve cracking from constant ordeals."[8]

After Cox complained about his treatment when he was captured, one of the officers picked up the phone and made a show of berating some underling. Later, in an attempt to find out what type of plane Cox flew and about his course, they appealed to his serviceman's pride, telling him they needed to ensure that the men who shot him down would get their due recognition. Cox said that since he wasn't the navigator, he didn't know the course.

A few hours later he was reunited with his crewmates for a bus ride to the airport, where they boarded a small plane. Each sized up the situation: six of them, three armed German aircrew and one armed guard sitting at the back of the plane. Wordlessly, they agreed that, once airborne, they would make their move. But the Luftwaffe had their measure. Just before taking off, the plane came to an abrupt halt and the door opened to admit six armed guards. One sat next to each POW for the short flight to Hannover. From there they were transferred to a truck for the five-hour drive to Dulag Luft, the interrogation and transit camp near Frankfurt am Main.

There, the psychological operations (psych-ops) game began and included being separated, but given a bed with clean sheets. The Luftwaffe officer who woke Cox the next morning seemed friendly and concerned: "Don't get up, old chap. I know you must be very tired after what you have been through; however, I have to ask you certain questions."[9] After giving him a Player's cigarette, which Cox assumed came from British stores captured at Dunkirk, the officer produced a form that he said would be sent to the Red Cross, which would then inform Cox's family that he was a POW. Cox wrote his name on it but abruptly put the pen down when he realized that many of the questions asked for personal and military information.

Cox's interlocutor changed tactics, taking out a thick book filled with names and a great deal of information about pilots who had been shot down—designed to underscore the futility of any further resistance. The German overplayed his hand. "We know you were in a Blenheim bomber," he said, which told Cox they had not found the wreckage of his Hampden. Cox won the poker game a few minutes later when the officer left the room in anger. A few hours later, the Canadian was released into the camp's general population.

By the time his wife received a letter from the Red Cross confirming that Cox was a prisoner of war, it was old news. For even before Cox left Dulag Luft, in one of his addresses designed to weaken British morale, William Joyce (Lord Haw-Haw) named him as one of several airmen who had recently been shot down and captured.

LATE 1940, STALAG LUFT I, NEAR STETTIN, GERMANY

Cox Blows out a Candle to Survive

Cox arrived at Stalag Luft I and soon learned that the number 270 stamped on his metal POW identity tag was pronounced *zweihundertsiebzig*. Two days later, his barracks' leader told him of the tunnel Vernon Howland and others were digging beneath a pot-bellied stove. The tunnel had to be about 150 feet long. To keep excavation to a minimum, the tunnel was a mere two-and-a-half-feet high by two-and-a-half-feet wide, which still produced 950 cubic feet of earth that had to be hid from the "ferrets," guards charged with finding tunnels.

The tunnel was lit by electric lights, powered by a surreptitious splice into the hut's electric lines. Boards taken from the bunks supported the tunnel's roof; to keep their mattresses from collapsing through the gaps, the men stiffened them with more straw. Each charcoal briquette pressed into the damp earth walls to strengthen them was one fewer to burn in the quixotic attempt to heat the icy barracks.

One day as he was excavating, the roof caved in, trapping Cox at the tunnel's face, 70 feet from the entrance. Unless he was dug out within minutes, Cox would suffocate. To conserve air, he blew out his candle. As the minutes ticked by in the tomb-like darkness, Cox stopped himself from panicking, which would only use up more air. As deathly drowsiness began to overtake him, he felt a hand on his boot and then a stream of damp, heavy air.

CHRISTMAS 1940, OFLAG VI-B, DÖSSEL, GERMANY

Thompson's Second Kriegie Christmas

A year earlier, the memories of Christmas at Georgian Bay were fresher. Then, Thompson could still believe that Göring was right that the war would be short—though, of course, in Thompson's version, the Allies would be holding the victory parades. Now, as Thompson found himself in his fifth POW camp, Hitler's writ ran from Calais through half of Poland. Thompson's memories of Christmas focused on dinner at his aunt's and skiing down mountains and across snow-covered fields, where he first experienced something like the freedom he lost the night before he met Göring. Even more important were the memories of All Saints' Anglican Church, where for generations his family had sat in the first pew. His father, Penetanguishene's Member of Provincial Parliament, was a fine lay reader who gave his voice to the Nativity story, which echoed against a number of stained-glass windows that commemorated Thompson's family

The one for his late mother showed the Presentation of Jesus at the Temple, while the one for the grandfather for whom he, Alfred Burke Thompson, was named, depicted sunlit Jesus holding a shepherd's crook and a baby lamb.

CHAPTER TWO

1941

I have been in danger at sea.
I have suffered shipwreck.
I have been in hunger and thirst often starving.

—2 CORINTHIANS 11: 24[10]

JANUARY 1941, OFLAG IX-A, SPANGENBERG, GERMANY

Vernon Howland Is Punished in an Underground Cell

The month started badly. First, there was the cold, not the dry cold of a Prairie winter, but the cutting raw cold of the north German coast. Were it not for their Red Cross parcels that arrived every couple of weeks, the prisoners would have been weak from hunger. Despite what Geneva said about POWs receiving the same rations as garrison troops, and the hundreds of thousands of tons of grain and thousands of tons of other foodstuffs that poured into Hitler's Germany under the Nazi–Soviet Pact and huge requisitions of food from the occupied countries, Howland received only two slices of dark and sour German bread, a small piece of sausage, watery cabbage or turnip soup and a cup of burned acorn coffee.

Then, the ferrets discovered the tunnel, and sent Vernon Howland and 50 other men to the *Führerlager*, a hut outside the main camp but still surrounded by barbed wire. Though disappointed by the discovery of the tunnel, when he arrived at the *Führerlager*, Howland practised the skills needed to break out of a POW camp. While the guards searched the other men, he sidled up to the table and pocketed a pair of wire cutters presumably seized from another prisoner. During the night, as he hoped, the camp's lights were extinguished when an RAF bomber stream passed nearby and he and RAF Wing Commander Joe Hill dropped through a hole in the floor they'd cut that afternoon.

Equipped with the wire cutters and a board, and heartened by Howland's bravado—"I'm from the Prairies, I'm used to barbed wires; there's not too much problem here"—their nerve held even as, once at the fence, they could hear guards leading snarling attack dogs and their snip of the first wire "sounded like a rifle shot." Using the board, Howland pushed the next wire up to enlarge the hole and was beginning to climb through it when the "All Clear" prompted him to slide back through the wire. Just as they started to dash back to the *Führlager*, the lights came back on. Caught unawares, the guards shouted and in their confusion fired a few wild shots, giving the two inexperienced escapers time to slip behind a garbage can, then safely run to the hut. A few days later, Howland and Hill were transferred to Oflag IX-A, in a 13th-century Spangenberg castle now ringed by machine guns and a dry moat home to three wild boars.

The gloom, compounded by the stench of rotten potatoes that hit them as they entered the underground prison, lifted slightly when the British prisoners served the new arrivals a fortifying stew. Only later did Howland learn that the stew was made from rations the Tommies had saved by going three days without food. His unheated, windowless, lice-infested cell was retribution for the conditions endured by captured U-boat men imprisoned in Fort Henry in Kingston, Ontario.

22 FEBRUARY 1941, 600 MILES OFF CAPE RACE, NEWFOUNDLAND

GNEISENAU SINKS THE CANADIAN MERCHANT SHIP *A.D. HUFF*

The outcome was never in doubt.

On the one side steaming toward Halifax at 8 knots was the 6,000-ton, 410-foot-long freighter, her holds half-filled with crushed stone for ballast, armed with an old 4-inch gun. On the other, a 38,000-ton warship capable of making 30 knots, bristling with guns, including nine that fired 11-inch shells. The short battle began when Nova Scotia–born Preston Ross's captain, ignoring the message "Heave To," ordered his gunner to fire on the battle cruiser and his engine room to squeeze another knot from *A.D. Huff*'s two-decades-old boilers. The gunner's target was almost 800 feet long. But the mists above the Gulf Stream can be dense, and he could barely make out *Gneisenau*, the very ship Vernon Howland had tried to bomb 7 months earlier. Realizing how little his gun could do against 14-inch-thick armour, the gunner refused to fire and, along with Ross and other crewmates, watched the awe-inspiring flash and heard the thunderous report of shells straddling their ship.

The gunners found their range with the shell that hit the windlass just behind *Huff*'s bow. The force of a 600-pound shell smashing into the Canadian ship at two and half times the speed of sound was enough to pierce her half-inch-thick steel deck. The explosion of 300 pounds of amatol staggered the ship and blew the heavy windlass on which was bolted the ship's anchor chain into the sky. As the chain and wreckage rattled down on the mangled deck, Ross saved himself by ducking behind an open steel hatch. Nothing could save the fourth engineer and oiler, who were enveloped in scalding steam—or the ship when another shell blew up in the engine room.

As the man-of-war closed in, the *Huff*'s 41 remaining crew members took to the lifeboats. The captain planned to guide the lifeboats 600 miles north to Newfoundland. But, to prevent merchant mariners from signing on with another ship and thus working to carry much-needed supplies across the Atlantic, *Gneisenau*'s captain ordered Ross and his crewmates aboard the warship, where they were jammed into a small, airless room—the "air was so bad you couldn't light a match, before the brimstone would burn, it would go out," recalled Ross.[11]

17 APRIL 1941, 600 MILES FROM CAPE TOWN, SOUTH AFRICA

After the Sinking of the *SS Zamzam*, 17 French-Canadian Priests and Brothers Are Captured

Even as the phosphorescence of the South Atlantic enchanted them, the 17 Canadian Oblates and three Sacred Heart Brothers wondered whether the German navy would recognize the SS *Zamzam*, their Egyptian-flagged ship steaming toward Cape Town, South Africa, as neutral. Near 6:30 a.m., as shells started exploding on the ship, they knew the answer.

As Father Herménégilde Charbonneau struggled in the darkness to get dressed and put on his life vest, the passageways filled with steam and panicked men, women and children. Charbonneau reached the dining room seconds before another shell detonated, showering him and three other priests with broken glass. Fearing that the next explosion would kill them, the four Quebec-born Oblates of Mary Immaculate gave each other mutual absolution. A shell that exploded near Brother Léo Parent, then making his way toward the bow, sent a splinter from a metal beam hurtling onto his ankle. The faith of *les religieux* helped them keep calm while, all around them, women, children and the other men rushed to the lifeboats, some discovering that theirs had been destroyed.

The tons of water pouring into *Zamzam*'s blasted hull caused her to settle, but her keel remained even, so the undamaged lifeboats could be launched. At Father Pierre-Paul Pellerin's lifeboat station, order began to break down, and though he was willing to give his place to the Protestant missionaries' wives and children, he was no weakling. As grown men pushed forward, Pellerin claimed his place by grabbing a cable and swinging into his assigned boat. The situation was calm enough at Father Louis Larivière's lifeboat station that he had time to return to his cabin to retrieve his forgotten crucifix and still board his boat before it was lowered. Holding to his "precious companion," he could do no more than watch and pray as the overloaded boat avoided the people bobbing in the water below.[12]

After seeing that his lifeboat had been destroyed, Charbonneau made his way to the bridge—just in time to see the *Zamzam*'s killer emerge from the mist. During those long moments, he feared that the commerce raider *Atlantis* (which was disguised as a Norwegian freighter named *Tamesis*) would fire again. Lost in the din were voices from Father Barsalou's lifeboat that urged on those trying to free the oars from their stowage positions at the bottom of the boat. Unable to do so, the people in the boat then tried to push it away from the cargo that had been blasted out of *Zamzam*'s hold and which, driven by the swells, crashed against the sides of the fragile craft. As water rose in the lifeboat, someone screamed, "Where's the plug?"—moments later another 25 souls were adrift when it sank.

While the Germans boarded the *Zamzam* and allowed Charbonneau and the others on the bridge to go to their cabins to retrieve personal items, Barsalou, buoyed by his lifebelt, swam for his life. After ten exhausting minutes, he neared a Carley float on which four young Protestants were singing "a hymn that showed their faith in the Lord." He thought he'd been saved as he grasped a line trailing from the float, but it disintegrated in his hands. Somehow he managed a few strong strokes, reached the float and, despite being weighed down by his wet clothes, lifted himself onto it. He gained only a moment's respite before others trying to climb onto the square float caused it to flip over, throwing everyone back into the sea.

Over the next 45 minutes, German motor launches plucked men, women and children out of lifeboats and from the water, which was warm enough so that none died of hypothermia. By the time Charbonneau and the other passengers and crew still aboard *Zamzam* were transferred to Kapitän zur See Bernhard Rogge's ship, he knew that, although the United States might object to the sinking, it would not set off a crisis that could bring America into the war. For not only had *Zamzam* been sailing blacked out and zigzagging, but her captain and engineer were British. In her hold were trucks destined for the British 8th Army, then slugging it out with General Erwin Rommel's Afrika Korps. And, most importantly, Rogge had in his hands papers that proved she was sailing under Admiralty orders.

EARLY MAY 1941, OFLAG IX-A, SPANGENBERG, GERMANY

Vernon Howland Sees the Sun,
and Hints of the German Attack on Russia

Berlin's acceptance of a Red Cross report that German POWs in Fort Henry were not, in fact, living in dungeons resulted in an immediate improvement in Howland's rations, in the form of Red Cross parcels and an end to his troglodyte existence, at least for an hour a day.

Howland welcomed the air, sunshine and exercise. Evidence of the buildup of German arms in the east, foretelling an attack on Russia, also heartened him. So did the talkative guard who predicted that once Germany was fighting the Bolshevik hordes, Britain would become Germany's ally—though Howland knew Britain would not switch sides. An attack on Russia would, however, embroil Germany in a two-front war it could not win.

Since Spangenberg is hundreds of miles west of Germany's eastern border, Howland was surprised when he saw the construction of anti-tank traps. The sight of the old men, women and children digging it being lashed by a guard with a 15-foot whip made him vomit.

19 MAY 1941, ATLANTIC OCEAN AND FRANCE

Les missionaires errants de l'Atlantique:
Wandering Missionaries of the Atlantic[13]

The exhausted and frightened Zamzamers, as they would come to call themselves, were welcomed aboard Kapitän zur See Walter

Jäger's supply ship, *Dresden*, by lines of marines, their bayonet-topped rifles at the ready. From her deck, they watched the doleful sight of their liner, her keel blasted open by charges, slip beneath the waves.

The move to the German supply ship improved their living conditions. On *Atlantis/Tamesis*, more than 230 men, women and children were crammed into a fetid hold on the ship's fourth deck. Mothers with children soon called out in vain for milk, and to everyone's dismay, men, women and children shared the single bathroom. The knowledge that, since they were below the ship's water line and locked behind a watertight door, none of them would likely survive were the commerce raider to be attacked, underscored the urgency of the prayers in English, French and, by *Zamzam*'s Egyptian crew, Arabic. Aboard *Dresden*, most of the 80 women and 34 children slept on mattresses laid out in what had been the ship's smoking salon. More than 200 men slept on the canvas-covered floor of a 54-by-54-foot hold, without portholes, ventilators or light bulbs.

The presence of more than 200 unexpected mouths to feed forced Jäger to put the Zamzamers on half rations, feeding them "a swill of rice, small pieces of meat, a flour paste, bread without butter, weak tea, while the Germans ate ham and eggs, beef, potato salad, oranges, coffee."[14] It didn't take long for dysentery and constipation to manifest themselves. Still, Jäger tried to make life as comfortable as he could for his prisoners. Married men could visit their families, for example. Despite the Nazis' ban on "decadent Negro American" music, Jäger allowed the playing of jazz records. The Quebecers sang French folk songs, including "Un Canadien Errant" (The Wandering Canadian), a mournful song about *un canadien* banished from his homeland who sits by a river and asks it to tell his friends, family and country that he remembers them.

Even more important for the Oblates and Sacred Heart Brothers was Jäger's decision to allow the priests to use the wardroom as a chapel for Sunday mass. To prepare the wardroom, *les religieux* removed the board to which were affixed pictures of Hitler and Großadmiral Erich Raeder. The discovery of a crucifix on the bulkhead delighted them, as did its position between the two pictures, for it recalled Jesus's position between the two thieves on Golgotha.

By 1941, many Lutheran churches had been folded into the (Nazified) Deutsche Christen Church, which denied that Jesus was Jewish and glorified war. Broadly speaking, under the Concordat of 1933 between the Vatican and Berlin, the Nazis agreed to leave the Catholic Church alone as long as it stayed out of politics. The Oblates unknowingly crossed this line toward the end of the mass when they recited the last line of the Lord's Prayer, "Deliver us from evil," which led Jäger to deny them further use of the wardroom, though he did allow services under a tarp on deck.

Weeks later, as the *Dresden* steamed into the North Atlantic, prayers took on greater urgency, as did the lifeboat drills, for now they were in waters heavily patrolled by the British. Just after sunrise on 18 May, Father Gérard Boulanger saw a lighthouse and knew that Spanish neutrality now shielded them from British bombs, torpedoes and bullets. A few days remained until they would reach France, the home of their order founded in 1826. The brothers planned to undertake a pilgrimage to Lourdes to thank the Blessed Virgin for her protection, until Jäger told them that because they were British subjects they would not be freed when *Dresden* docked in France. By contrast, since the Americans belonged to the still-neutral United States, they would be freed. This greatly disappointed British secretary of state for foreign affairs Anthony Eden, who had hoped that the attack on a ship carrying American missionaries, many from the Midwest, would provide President Franklin Roosevelt with an argument to counter midwestern isolationists. Jäger assured the Canadian Catholics that since they were civilian missionaries and not military padres, they would be repatriated soon.

When they walked off *Dresden*'s gang plank, the priests and brothers found themselves in a cordon of heavily armed guards, who marched them to a barbed-wire enclosure.

19 MAY 1941, OTTAWA

Canada Learns That the Priests and Brothers Have Been Captured

Concern for the Oblates' and Sacred Heart Brothers' well-being had been growing since 2 May, when, having heard nothing of them since a telegram sent from Brazil almost a month earlier, the Provincial in Ottawa (the head of the order's national office) sent a night letter to Thomas Cook travel agency asking for news. The company that arranged the missionaries' passage to South Africa responded curiously: "Several sources leave us to believe that they have arrived safe and sound in Cape Town."[15]

L'Action catholique broke the news on 19 May under the headline "*Zam-Zam* sunk in the Atlantic: Catholic Missionaries Aboard." Later that day, Radio Canada reported that among the missionaries were 17 French-Canadian Oblates and Brothers of the Sacred Heart.

After an anxious 24 hours, officials in Canada picked up a Radio Berlin broadcast to the effect that the passengers and crew had landed in Occupied France.[16] A month later, *Life* magazine published "The Sinking of the 'Zamzam,'" written by Charles J.V. Murphy with pictures by David E. Scherman, two American journalists who had been on the ship. Before releasing Scherman, the Germans had developed and approved the pictures of people in lifeboats and of the sinking ship that later ran in *Life*. The Germans knew nothing of another roll that, with seven-year-old Peter Levitt on his knee, Scherman surreptitiously shot of *Atlantis/Tamesis* and then hid in the bottom of his toothpaste tube. Hundreds of copies of the ship's silhouette were printed and placed in the wardroom of every Royal Navy ship of the line, allowing the battle cruiser HMS *Devonshire* to identify and sink her six months later.

LATE MAY 1941, ON A TRAIN TO GERMANY

RCN Surgeon Lieutenant Charles M. Fisher Faces Down an Arrogant Prussian

The ten days he spent on the prison ship after being transferred from the commerce raider *Thor*, which sank his ship, HMS *Voltaire,* on 4 April 1941, Charles Fisher's rank of surgeon lieutenant merited him a berth in a cabin with some Swedish officers. Though the Kriegsmarine had sunk their neutral ship, the Swedes were not prisoners of war and hence were provided with a liberal supply of the liquor aquavit, which did little to dull the memories of the days Fisher spent in *Thor*'s hold. There, the physical conditions were bad enough, with three wooden decks, each supplied with an oil drum that served as a latrine, around which formed stinking sludge. But what really riled the doctor on loan from the RCN was the Germans' decision to ignore cases of gonococcal conjunctivitis, pulmonary tuberculosis and diphtheria.

Conditions barely improved once the prisoners were landed in La Rochelle and marched to the same former cavalry barracks that Ross and the other survivors of *A.D. Huff* had passed through before they were sent via Holland to prison in Germany.[17] Fisher's most vivid memory of this POW camp was the free-for-all that followed the dumping of a huge pile of used clothing, which he suspected came from interned political prisoners. Remembering the chilly night just passed, Fisher did not care if the clothing matched, only whether it would pass the test of the officer who, shortly after Fisher took the navy oath, advised him, "Never be cold."

From the prison camp at Saint-Médard-en-Jalles, where they

detrained four days later, Fisher could see Bordeaux's famous vineyards. Prisoners, including a 75-year-old British woman, slept on rough-hewn floorboards. After hearing that 90 men had escaped from the last train to take prisoners to Germany, Fisher concluded that the diet of "weak flour soup with a trace of vegetable" was designed to debilitate them; the men quickly lost weight and, more importantly, "wounds refused to heal." An epidemic of chills, fever and general lassitude suggested dengue fever, sandfly fever or encephalitis.

For the trip from Saint-Médard-en-Jalles to Sandbostel, the site of Stalag X-B, the Germans herded the men into the same sort of cattle cars that took the 1st Canadian Division to the front in 1915. The cars were built to hold "*40 hommes ou 8 chevaux*"; the car was so crowded and dirty that the men felt like they were sharing the car with 40 horses—although that would have at least provided some warmth as they shivered in the unheated car during the cold nights. Geneva requirements notwithstanding, the Germans did not provide any water during the trip; indeed, when the train was stopped and a Frenchman upon hearing shouts of "*eau*" brought a water jug to Fisher's car, the German guards smashed it. A day later, Fisher learned just how little his rank meant to the "huge, fat-faced, beady-eyed, brush-cut Prussian madman" who led a group of guards into the stinking boxcar after the Germans realized that several men had escaped through loosened sideboards.

In an effort to stop the guards who were punching, kicking and slapping—with the flat part of their bayonets—his shipmates as other guards pointed pistols and rifles at the bedraggled men, the 22-year-old educated at the University of Toronto, who was the Senior British Officer present, loudly objected to his men's treatment. As the Prussian turned toward the surgeon lieutenant, so did the other guards, whose guns and obvious drunkenness made Fisher fear of his life. The Prussian, however, had something less lethal but still demeaning in mind; he whipped his riding crop down toward Fisher's head a number of times.

LATE MAY 1941, STALAG LUFT I, NEAR STETTIN, GERMANY

Andrew Cox Is Hungry and Embarrasses the Kommandant

The diet of one-tenth of a loaf of black bread, two small potatoes, a spoonful of "goon jam" (wood pulp and artificial flavour), a little margarine, ersatz coffee and the odd stolen potato that Andrew Cox had to eat each day left a gnawing hunger that was lessened only slightly by the foodstuffs in regular deliveries of Red Cross and personal parcels. The welcome taste of home was hardly an extravagance; from the point of view of weight and bulk, the chocolate, sent by Cox's wife, for one, was the most efficient way of delivering badly needed fats and calories. In the harsh world of a German POW camp, the warm clothing, shaving equipment, toothpaste, soap and cigarettes she sent were anything but "luxury items," as Cox jokingly called them. Cigarettes not only satiated nicotine addiction and suppressed appetite, they served as currency and as a means to suborn guards.

The Geneva Convention required the Detaining Power to attend to the "intellectual and moral needs of prisoners of war," in part to deal with the crushing boredom of incarceration. Equally important for the Detaining Power was the reality that time spent reading, painting, in class, studying or rehearsing a play was time not spent disrupting the camp's routine or planning home runs. By the end of the war, the Red Cross alone had sent POWs almost 240,000 books, while, at the behest of individual families, publishers sent hundreds of thousands more in five-pound packages.[18] Reading, one POW recalled, was "probably the greatest morale factor in the camp next to the Red Army."[19] Even books the men didn't like were important, for they too took up time, and their minds out of their camps.

By the time Cox arrived at Stalag Luft I, the "POW University" was up and running. Kriegies could take courses from Oxford or McGill. The Red Cross arranged for their exams to be proctored by local German professors.[20] In the weeks before the Oblates arrived at Milag Nord in late June, George Shaker, another Canadian who had been aboard the *A.D. Huff*, took shorthand, and studied Spanish and Chinese. Hundreds of servicemen became thespians and stagehands. In May 1941, on a windup record player, Cox heard the words and music of Bing Crosby, Deanna Durbin and Noël Coward, which transported him part of the long way home.

In late May, however, Cox's preferred activity involved flies and hornets. After capturing large ones, he would tie a thread around one of each bug's legs. Attached to the thread was a cigarette-sized paper cylinder with such messages as "Germany kaput" or "Hitler nicht goot." [21] To the Kommandant's great embarrassment, a number of these messages reached the nearby village.[22]

4 JULY 1941, STALAG X-B, SANDBOSTEL, GERMANY

Les Religieux Are Sent to Germany

For the ten days they were in the same transit camp that Fisher and the men from the *A.D. Huff* passed through, *les religieux* hoped that what they saw as their Babylonian captivity would be short.[23] Despite the rigours of the camp, which, as Father Barsalou learned on the second night there, included being shot at for leaving the barracks after dark, the priests were allowed to minister, with the honour of saying the first mass behind barbed wire falling to Father Charbonneau. Other masses were said for a somewhat surprising group, Catholic lascars. On 30 May, the joy they felt at the conversion of a British soldier evaporated when a local Oblate official told them that, despite official entries, they were going to be sent to POW camps in Germany.

It is a measure of how powerful the experience of being in a POW camp is that, after being in one for only a week, the everyday world of the train station seemed alien. As they "glanced about at the neatly, well-dressed Bordeaux citizens milling about the station carrying their baggage here and there, munching on large sandwiches, drinking wine, conversing enthusiastically on the events and their plans for the day and the days after," *les religieux* felt as if they had come from another world, recalled Brother George-Aime Lavalée.

The Germans piled so many other men into the cattle cars that there was not enough room to lie down. A pail served the office of a latrine. The priests and brothers were given only two small bottles of water. In an overloaded cattle car filled with stinking, unwashed men jostling against each other, setting up even a makeshift altar was impossible. Accordingly, each recited a "*messe blanche*," a mass said while reading their missals, observing the silences, as reminders of their communion.

The wooden Crosses tucked into their belts meant nothing to the guards at Stalag X-B, in Sandbostel, who met the exhausted priests and brothers with bayonets at the ready. The few who had been able to take their belongings from *Zamzam* found the heavy suitcases strained arms and bent backs, causing them to stumble as they marched the five miles to the POW camp enclosed by two high barbed-wire fences that ran parallel to each other, separated by a couple of yards called No Man's Land. At every 100 yards stood a 15-foot-high guard tower equipped with spotlights and machine guns.

Like the hundreds of other barracks at the camp, through which a million prisoners would pass (and where some 50,000 died), Barracks No. 63 was a 140-by-40-foot wood-framed, uninsulated hut. Both the pillows and paillasses were filled with straw and wood chips, and were more solid than the three-level bunks themselves. "On the very first night, one broke and the sleeper below it was shocked to receive in this rather impolite fashion his companion in his arms," Brother Roland Cournoyer later recalled with a smile. "Imagine the noise and the mess, not to mention the weight of the sleeper." This happened many times over the years, "and it was hard for the witnesses to avoid laughing and teasing the stunned victims."[24]

Used to thinking in symbolic and Christological terms in which daily life imitates Christian mystery, the Oblates and Sacred Heart Brothers saw the sand-swept camp as symbolic, as a modern-day Valley of Humiliation. Being forced to stand naked for hours while being deloused after arriving at the camp Brother Georges-Aimé Lavallée recalled as being "treated as non-humans." Showers were welcome, but since there were no dividers in the room, they were uncomfortably immodest.

For their German captors, the photographing of each man with a small blackboard on which his POW number was written hanging around his neck was a mere bureaucratic moment. For *les religieux* it seemed an inversion of both baptism and the solemn ceremonies in which the priests and brothers received their religious names. Brother Antoine Lavallée coped with the indignity of being reduced to a number by mocking the metal identity disks that aped the crucifix and symbolized the barbed wire ringing the camp: "Oh number 104 452! / You will now stand for me for my family, my friends, my surname and my given name. . . . / And, if I die, Oh! Little piece of tin, / You will not lie with me in the cold bier, / But half of your lifeless face will be put on the cover of my tomb, / And the other sent to my loved ones in Canada."[25]

Even for men used to the regimented life of a religious order, lining up three times a day to be counted was humiliating. So were the meals. Breakfast consisted of two sardines or a couple of prunes, while lunch was watery soup with a few potatoes and traces of sausage, or a "stew" containing bits of dried fish. Fisher, who was in the camp at the same time, forced himself to eat this revolting dish until "one day a full-blown glassy fish eye swam into my spoon and stared fixedly" at him. What meat—horse meat—they were given was often crawling with maggots. The cutting of the loaf of coarse black bread into pieces—each man was entitled to three thin slices—was another humiliating ritual. Growling stomachs pushed aside thoughts of convivial breaking of bread and, even, the symbolism of the Last Supper as they watched the cutting of the bread with eagle eyes and stooped to pick up crumbs from the floor.

The decision to send *les religieux* to a Stalag instead of interning them in a civilian camp in Vichy France or Germany, or granting them the honorary rank of captain, accorded to padres, and thus sending them to an *Oflag* (an officers' camp), meant that they would be treated like regular soldiers and as such were required to work. In and of itself, this was not a humiliation. But their nauseating job involved shovelling excrement from the latrine into "Smelly Nelly"—and then pulling it from the camp to a farmer's field.

There were moments when the warm summer breezes blew, when if they closed their eyes, *les religieux* could almost forget they were in a POW camp. Or when they ministered to some of the 6,000 men held in Sandbostel, many of whom had not heard the gospel in years. The night of 18 June was not one of those times. "The alarm sounded as soon as the explosions began. . . . Outside the sky was set ablaze and all we heard was the dull revving of the engines and the rattle of machine guns. Everything was punctuated by the sinister sound of the bombs. 'Had our last hour come?' we asked ourselves. If you could have seen each of us, you would have seen terrified and panicked faces, and men praying," Father Pellerin wrote in a letter.[26]

MID-AUGUST 1941, STALAG X-B, SANDBOSTEL, GERMANY

Father Pâquet Explains the Difference between a Priest and Brother

What surely was one of the strangest meetings in the history of the Third Reich started with an order for the Oblates and Sacred Heart Brothers to come to Kommandant Spiess's office. After the formulaic apology for their capture and imprisonment, Spiess handed a paper to Father Gérard Pâquet, the group's de facto leader. The

Oblate wasted little time objecting to the names on the list, of those who were to be sent to minister at other POW camps. The problem, he explained, was not that several of the men Berlin had chosen were British subjects by convenience; indeed, the Germans knew that the Sacred Heart Brothers were Americans who had taken British citizenship to expedite the paperwork so that they could get on with their missionary duties in Basutoland, which was part of the British Empire. Rather, the problem was that they were teaching brothers and not priests and, hence, were incapable of performing the sacraments or saying mass.

Whatever Spiess's thoughts about the Nazi state he served were, likely it was his background as a Lutheran that explained his "difficulty in understanding the difference between a priest and a teaching brother."[27] One can almost imagine him looking quizzically through a monocle and asking in a heavy German accent, "What is this, this ordination?" At all events, he looked embarrassed and agreed to let Pâquet draw up a new list, which included Fathers Goudreau, Larivière, Charbonneau, Boulanger and Pellerin.

MID-SEPTEMBER 1941, STALAG XXI-B, THURÉ, POLAND

Father Goudreau's Nightmare

Father Phillipe Goudreau went to sleep concerned. He'd expected the search of his suitcase to be perfunctory, for he was spending only one night at Stalag XX-A while on his way to Stalag Luft III. But the guards, envious of his kid gloves and alarmed by his Sesotho-English dictionary, looked further and found a hacksaw blade he'd forgotten about. Once asleep, concern gave way to terror as he dreamt that the Gestapo fired questions at him—Where had it come from? What was he going to do with it?—and responded to his answer that he'd bought it in Baltimore and then forgotten about it by savagely whipping him.

Reality was more prosaic, though no less dangerous. After being woken from the nightmare, he was asked by the guards the kind of questions he'd dreamt about. Mercifully, the real-life guards were more accepting than his imagined ones of the answer that he had brought the hacksaw blade from America because such items were not easily available in Africa and that he did not expect to have his voyage to South Africa interrupted. The guards seized the blade, of course, as well as his gloves and dictionary, this last, presumably, because they thought it was a code book.

As he lay in bed, Goudreau thanked Jesus that the guards who interrogated him knew nothing about the founder of the Oblate order, for between 1809 and 1811, while still a novitiate, Eugène de Mazenod smuggled letters between Napoleon's prisoner, Pope Pius VIII, and the College of Cardinals. For had the Gestapo agents looked a little deeper in his bag, they would have found that he was smuggling letters to officers at Stalag Luft III, which, since he was not covered by the Geneva Convention, could have branded him as a spy and possibly cost him his life.[28]

LATE OCTOBER/EARLY NOVEMBER 1941, PRISON HOSPITAL, SAINT-OMER, FRANCE

RCAF Pilot Officer Brian Hodgkinson Meets Another Kanadischer Pilot

In their retelling, the moments seemed almost scripted.

The instrument panel exploding as a stream of 15-mm bullets rip through the Spitfire. The fire searing his leg and burning his right hand stiff. The plane's death spiral making bailing out seem all but impossible. The moments during the parachute jump when the oncoming Messerschmitt 109 seems to be closing in for the kill and Brian Hodgkinson finds himself reciting the Lord's Prayer. That plane's last second banking turn, followed by a salute. The German Leutnant finding him on the ground and saying, "My, your name is—how do you say in English—a mouth-ful, yes?" before adding, "It is my duty to inform you that you are now a prisoner of war in the custody of the German Wehrmacht." Regaining consciousness in a hospital, where the doctor says in perfect American English, honed during his eight-year medical residency in Milwaukee, "You're chewed up pretty badly, son," and who adds after Hodgkinson says he is from Winnipeg, "I know it well. Been there on a couple of medical conventions. Nice city, very nice city. But awful cold in the wintertime." And the visit a few days later of a Luftwaffe officer named Gunther Langendorf, who learned English working in the tourist industry in Vienna and tells Hodgkinson, "I give you my solemn word, the Luftwaffe does not shoot enemy fliers out of their parachutes."[29] They were all too real, however, and lived by Hodgkinson in the last few days of October and the first few days of November after his Spitfire was hit over Calais.

The hospital ward in Saint-Omer, France, where Hodgkinson awoke after Dr. Meinhoff operated on his leg, was filled with other Allied airmen. Their meals were enough to live on— a "bowl of hot water with just a whiff of chicken. . . . A thin slice of sun-baked leather, one small scoop of rice, and a smaller something called a potato."[30] But the ward's window provided a ringside seat from which to watch their war. The day after his visit, Langendorf likely battled the swarm of Allied planes, which were cheered on by the men in the ward. Bound to his bed by his wounds, the 26-year-old, whose baritone voice had been a fixture on the CBC in the days before his RCAF Squadron No. 1 (later 401) was rushed across the sea to help fight the Battle of Britain, had to content himself with the blow-by-blow account shouted out by more ambulatory men.

The next day, after they parsed the *Völkischer Beobachter*'s version of the battle, Hodgkinson heard the words "*Kanadischer Pilot, schwer verwundet*" as an orderly wheeled in a seriously wounded Canadian pilot, his face swathed in bandages. Later, the quiet of the night was broken by a wail, followed by the pathetic words "My face! My face! Where am I? My face? My face?" It took a few minutes for the nurse to arrive and a few more for her to sedate the agony-stricken man.

Some days earlier, after Hodgkinson blanched upon seeing that most of RAF pilot Sandy MacRae's torso was heavily bandaged, the British officer bucked him up by saying that German machine guns "have a way of rearranging a man's anatomy." And, of course, Hodgkinson's own terrible burns showed him what fire could do to human flesh. Nothing, however, prepared him for the hideous sight he could not break away from when an orderly removed the bandages from the head of the Canadian pilot who had been engulfed by flames. "It was swollen to at least three times its normal size, and so puffed up and inflated were the cheeks and forehead, bloated with poison and pus, that the poor soul's eyes were barely visible. . . . his mouth was no more than a slightly flexible gash, which you wouldn't have thought was capable of forming the sounds of the language." When the orderly had finished removing the bandages and saw that the pilot's cheeks were "so bulbous [that] they protruded beyond the tip of his nose," he cried "*Mein Gott!*" and fled the room.[31]

As Hodgkinson bit down on his pillow to keep from vomiting, another Allied officer asked the Canadian what had happened. His story of escaping from his burning plane was similar to Hodgkinson's. When Hodgkinson asked him his name, he startled everyone by rising from his bed like Lazarus, "his arms outstretched before him and his poor bloated head swinging from side to side," and calling out "Hodge! Hodge! Is that you, Hodge?"

"Yes! Yes! I'm Hodge. Sergeant Brian Hodgkinson! Who are you?"

"It's Scruffy, Hodge. Scruffy Weir. Don't you recognize me?"[32]

Ignoring the pain of his own wounds and orders to remain in bed, Hodgkinson struggled to embrace Weir. Through his tears, he apologized for not recognizing his friend.

24 NOVEMBER 1941, STALAG X-B, SANDBOSTEL, GERMANY

Father Pâquet's "Dark Night of the Soul"

By noting that he was writing on the Fête de Saint Jean de la Croix, Father Pâquet does more than indicate the banal fact that he remembers the calendar of the saints.[33] Rather, he telegraphed to Father Labrecque how *les religieux* understood their trials and provided what amounts to a spiritual diary. *Les religieux* saw themselves as re-enacting St. John of the Cross's passion. In December 1577, Carmelites opposed to the reforms advocated by St. Teresa of Ávila (1622) kidnapped her supporter, John. After a trial before a kangaroo court, he was imprisoned in a cell scarcely large enough to hold him, repeatedly brutally beaten in public and fed only water, bread and bits of salted fish.

While Labrecque knew that his brethren's conditions were immeasurably better, he would have understood that St. John's struggles to read his breviary by the light that came from an adjoining cell served as a metaphor for the priests' and brothers' struggle to live their faith under the Nazis' heel. Just as St. John was dependent on a kindly friar to provide him with paper, on which he wrote his famous poems, Pâquet and his brethren were dependent on their captors for the materials necessary for the mass and for a place to say it—and, indeed, for the very paper he was writing on. St. John's escape prefigured not his brethren's physical escape but, rather, the triumph of their faith over the naked force that kept them behind the barbed wire.

Pâquet also knew that his friend would understand how the 16th-century Spanish mystic's poems, especially his most famous "Dark Night of the Soul," charted his and the other missionaries' spiritual lives. "Dark Night of the Soul" opens with the frank admission that, beset by doubts, in the middle of the night the poet (the "soul") leaves the house of God "by a secret ladder" and finds himself seemingly alone in the world. For the fathers and brothers who have been cast into the Nazis' hands, "night" is more than the moment of doubt that such important Catholic thinkers as Augustine and Thomas Aquinas admitted to. Whether it occurred in the stinking hold of a German warship, while hungry on a train, when finding one's self able to offer only prayers—which seemingly go unanswered—when watching Russian POWs starve to death or when alone at night in a cold hut far from home, listening to the rumble of your empty stomach, the "night" of being a prisoner of war is one that, if it admits of God's presence, keeps the Holy Spirit well hidden. As Labrecque knew, St. John sings that deep in the night, redolent of sin and death, the soul finds that darkness itself is an ember that "guided me/ more surely than the light of the noon/ to where he was awaiting me / —him I knew so well."[34]

By alluding to the poem, Pâquet shows how in the light of their faith, their humiliations and the pain they feel at their own and others' sufferings gather.

LATE NOVEMBER 1941, STALAG LUFT I, NEAR STETTIN, GERMANY

Cox Mistakes a Dead Man for a Pile of Potato Sacking

Cox was struck by the remnants of humanity, the Russians reduced by the Germans far below simply being the shards of Soviet armies smashed by Wehrmacht. Given the Nazis' concept of the *Untermensch*, it is an open question how the Germans would have treated the millions of Russian prisoners who had fallen into their hands had Stalin signed the Geneva Convention. Since he hadn't, the Germans felt free to march the three million POWs captured on the battlefields of Poland and Russia with little food or water, and no protection against the elements to POW camps; marches during which hundreds of thousands died. Free to ignore outbreaks of dysentery that killed thousands more in camps in which Russian POWs received less and worse food than did the Western POWs, and little medical attention. In some camps, the death rate of Soviet

POWs reached 2 per cent *per day.* Free to let them shiver in the cool of autumn and die in the cold of winter, clad only in the rags left from their summer uniforms. Over the course of the Ostkrieg, three-quarters of the four million Russian POWs died; in the first year, fully two million died, some collapsing where they stood, in sight of the missionaries and other Allied POWs.

The thousands of gaunt bodies that somehow still walked in the compound that abutted Stalag Luft I testified to the lengths that the Nazis would go to work their will on Europe. The cold wind that came through the chinks in the wall of Cox's barracks, which was barely heated by the pot-bellied stove, ripped through the Russians' thin tents. At the risk of being punished if caught and knowing that they were increasing their own hunger, Cox and the other Allied pilots threw loaves of bread over the barbed wire, and, for a few moments, saw "a glimmer of what had been a human being."[35]

But those loaves, a dozen or even a hundred dozen, could do nothing against typhus, which broke out among the lice-ridden Russians. It didn't take long for infected lice to bring the disease into Cox's compound. Typhus, the Germans well knew, was the scourge of many an army, killing thousands of Napoleon's men as they trooped toward Moscow. Accordingly, the Germans allowed the Senior British Officer in the camp to contact the Red Cross for a supply of anti-typhus serum, which was quickly administered to the British POWs, albeit painfully since German medics used only one needle for each line of men.

Those Russians whom the Germans chose to form a slave labour force survived to do the Nazis' bidding because were allowed to shower to rid themselves of lice. They used the same shower room Cox and his comrades used. One day, the change room was especially crowded, and Cox had to undress next to a three-foot-high pile of what he took to be potato sacking, perhaps worn by a Russian POW. When he inadvertently stepped on the rough cloth, Cox felt something strange. He looked down and saw to his horror that he had stepped on the head of a dead Russian, one of the 11,000 souls to perish in that typhus epidemic.

EARLY DECEMBER 1941, DULAG LUFT, FRANKFURT

Hodgkinson Enters a World without Civilians

Dr. Meinhoff was a puzzle.

When a sadistic orderly increased Weir's pain by leaving his wounds open to the air, Meinhoff threatened to transfer the man to the Russian Front. While escorting Hodgkinson to Frankfurt, Meinhoff, who was on his way to Stuttgart on leave, bought the Canadian lunch and protected him from an angry crowd, in the Cologne train station.

These acts made it all the more difficult to comprehend that this cultured man was indeed a Nazi. One day, Meinhoff asked Hodgkinson why he was even involved in the war: "[You Canadians are] 3,000 miles from this war, for God's sake. . . . Why should you bother your head about it, let alone pay the price you guys are paying in this hospital?" Meinhoff dismissed the argument another pilot made, that everyone knew that Germany would not stop should Rommel be successful in conquering North Africa and if Russia collapsed: "Did it ever occur to you people that the world needs a new order? A system for governing itself, a more efficient method of production and organization, which only we Germans can provide?" A Scottish officer had the last word. "That bullshit you're peddling is making me sicker than your bullets!" Some weeks later, however, in the Cologne train station, Meinhoff provided a coda of sorts after Hodgkinson took the top off his sandwich and winced when he saw the filling: "Now then, aren't you sorry you didn't mind your own business and stay at home in Canada like a good boy?"[36]

At Dulag Luft, after the obligatory stint in solitary confinement, Colonel Gustave Metterling played the usual game of placing cigarettes within reach without offering them, and softening Hodgkinson up by telling him that he'd learned his English in New York, where he sold forgeries to "the gullible rich."[37] Hodgkinson took the cigarette, guessed that saying he had been a radio announcer before the war wasn't revealing anything Metterling didn't already know and agreed with the intelligence officer that Germany would never be able to compete with American production lines.

8 DECEMBER 1941, STALAG LUFT I, NEAR STETTIN, GERMANY, AND STALAG X-B, SANDBOSTEL, GERMANY

The Kriegies Learn That the United States Has Entered the War

The radio was like ones bought across Canada at stores such as Canadian Tire. The power came not from an electrical connection but from the "cat's whisker," a thin, fine piece of wire lightly touching a piece of crystalline stone, the wire and the earphone coming from stolen telephone parts. Unlike the ones teenaged boys built on boards so they could be proudly shown off to family, the crystal radio at Stalag Luft I could be taken apart in seconds, so its parts could be hidden. On 7 or 8 December, with one ear pressed to the receiver, the camp's shorthand expert copied down the news that the Japanese had attacked Pearl Harbor, and that as a result the United States had entered the Second World War. [38]

At Sandbostel, Fisher learned of the Japanese attack from a German guard on 8 December, and immediately recognized it was a strategic mistake. What *les religieux* learned about Pearl Harbor went unrecorded, but if he learned of it on the night of 7 December, Brother Antoine Lavallée played it safe, writing of his concern for the souls of the hundred Russians for whom they gave the rites *in articulo mortis*, which the Germans would have dismissed as feminine Christian weakness.[39]

MID-DECEMBER 1941, STALAG LUFT I, NEAR STETTIN, GERMANY

Making Homebrew for Christmas

As December wore on, the men in Cox's barracks readied to celebrate Christmas. They melted Red Cross chocolate to dip peanuts in, which, in the holiday spirit, were placed in decorative dishes made from the foil that had wrapped their cigarettes. The Germans supplied wheat flour, which the enterprising cooks stretched with homemade potato flour, for a cake.

The joyous ornaments of the season heightened the POWs' feelings of loneliness. Howland's memories of his family back in Fort Qu'Appelle, of the Christmas scenes in the windows of the red-brick Hudson's Bay store, were magical. Memories of the crèches in church and at home were at the same time a balm and a source of great pain. The soothing rituals of carols and the expectation of a Christmas meal were double-edged swords, pale imitations of the holiday cheer the POWs once knew.

Perhaps because they knew that behind the convivial singing, which would reach its high point on Christmas Eve, was real pain, in mid-November the guards at Stalag Luft I had given Cox's barracks a large wooden barrel in which to make homebrew. The POWs started the fermentation using yeast and dried fruit. When their Red Cross supplies of fruit ran out, they added scraps of vegetables, including frostbitten turnip, which, Cox discovered, was surprisingly sweet.

A few weeks before Christmas, the brewmaster decreed that the mash was cooking nicely and that, instead of adding to it, they now had to skim off the fermentation foam. [Because they were brewing in a barrel and not a still, where the alcohol is boiled off and collected in copper tubing, skimming off the foam in which particles were suspended would remove these unwanted particles from the brew.] As Christmas drew closer, two pints of brew per man were ready.

25 DECEMBER 1941, STALAG X-B, SANDBOSTEL, GERMANY, AND STALAG LUFT III, SAGAN, POLAND

Christmas Day

Many POWs recall that, no matter how hungry they were the rest of the year, by skimping and saving from their Red Cross parcels (and, in some cases, because of extra rations from the Germans), they were able to have an acceptable Christmas dinner. Their cake may have been as heavy as lead, but Cox's Christmas dinner measured up. He attributed the gusto with which he and his comrades sang carols to the homebrew. Packing the punch of rotgut whisky, it ensured that they would be hungover. But it also lowered their emotional guard, tightening their bonds to each other, and made the war, at least for that evening, seem something outside the clapboard barracks in which their decorations made from foil spread the light of a weak bulb.

Of the 450 or so Canadians taken prisoner in the previous 12 months, *les religieux* were the best prepared to celebrate Christmas in their enclaves, in a country that despite its long Christian history was even less accepting of Christ than were the "heathen lands" they were sent to evangelize. Though their letters spoke of the pain of being separated from the Basutos in their time of famine, the missionaries remained *les bons pasteurs*; "If Jesus were to walk the ground today," they believed "he would be in a POW camp."[40] With supplies given to them from the Red Cross, on Christmas Eve the Oblates at Sandbostel conducted masses in a small room that had been set aside as a chapel, where they improvised a crèche. Despite one being at 9 p.m. and the other at 11 p.m., both were "midnight masses," the French Canadians taking special joy in the first, which was *en français*.

Late that night, a few hundred miles to the east, in Poland, Father Goudreau sat at his desk writing, knowing that as he did, the sky was beginning to lighten above Canada's most eastern shore. It had been four months since he'd been separated from his brethren and had passed through two other camps, and the strain of being alone was beginning to show as he compared himself to, of all things, the Wandering Jew before continuing, "It's Christmas! It's cold outside, the white flakes touch for the first time the soil of Pomerania. It is indeed a little cold in my heart . . . I am warm tonight, the play of warm friendships of old. . . . It seems that I will stay here until the end. I have lost faith in being released." Alone in his little room in Stalag Luft III, despite the joy of the Nativity and his heartfelt best wishes to the Oblates back in Canada, Goudreau could not help but write that he found himself "at the zero point of hell."

Chapter Three

January–July 1942

Behind the barbed wire, it is not only the most vigorous who survive, but those who carry fire.

—Alfred Fabre-Luce, *Double Prison*

EARLY JANUARY 1942, STALAG VII-A, MOOSBURG, GERMANY

Brian Hodgkinson Sees Russian POWs Die

Near midnight, having managed to blot out the torment of the cold drops of water that fell on him—the men's breath having condensed on the ceiling—and the vermin that crept from his paillasse into the warmth of his clothes, the report of three high-powered rifle shots jolted Brian Hodgkinson awake. As he climbed down from his bunk, another inmate rubbed the frost from the window, revealing a Russian POW on the ground near the fence. The "gut-wrenching moans" of another hanging on top of the barbed wire that divided the Russian from the Allied compound provided a ghastly undertone to the POW, who said in horror, "They're leaving them to die in the cold!" A few minutes later, another recent arrival asked why the Russians headed into their compound rather than out of the camp. The answer: "The poor bastards are starving, and they know if they can get into our compound we'll feed them. Trouble is they never make it."[41]

EARLY FEBRUARY 1942

The six coal-dust briquettes provided to the barracks each day did so little against the cold spilling into the hut through the ill-fitting windows and door that Hodgkinson dreamt of burning his bunk to create a fire strong enough to warm his feet. The Germans provided only black bread (made from barely edible rye husks, potatoes and sawdust) and, three days a week, wretched-tasting, thin Swede soup. Without the Red Cross–supplied can of Spam, sardines or salmon; powdered milk; a bar of chocolate; prunes or raisins; and the hardtack and marmalade they ate for breakfast, starvation would have stalked the British side of the camp too.

Several weeks earlier, a couple of hundred officers—from the RAF, RCAF and other Commonwealth air forces—cursed Colonel Manfred Fitzleben. They did not blame the Kommandant for the execrable food or cold barracks. What riled them was the order to fall out on the camp's *Sportplatz* for close-order drill, something most hadn't done since flight-training school and which the avoiding of was a mark of honour among airmen. Fitzleben's first attempts at company-major English were credible: "Com-panee, Atten-shun." But the language he studied at Oxford before the last war and practised after being captured at Vimy Ridge couldn't stand the strain. "Not a single man jack of you move now," he ordered, "or I'll shoot you with a ball of your own shit."[42] The men's laughter hung in the cold air that reminded Hodgkinson of home, but under Fitzleben's eye, they practised their marching four more times that day. And the next, and the next.

The food did not improve, the cold lingered and, despite a few recreational activities, the crushing boredom remained. Yet after a few weeks, the men noticed a change in themselves. From mocking the drills, they began looking forward to the order to fall out. The better they marched, the straighter they walked, and soon their morale improved. And that, the Kommandant told Hodgkinson, was the point.

Fitzleben's claim that he wanted to reawaken the prisoners' esprit de corps and pride, which soon shone through their scruffy clothes and increasingly gaunt faces, set Hodgkinson back on his heels. For a moment, the war symbolized by the swastika flag in

Fitzleben's office and the picture of his Führer opened like a scrim in a theatre, and Hodgkinson found himself standing in front of man whom he could respect, and he reached to shake his jailor's hand.

27 FEBRUARY 1942, STALAG XXI-D, POSEN, POLAND

Father Herménégilde Charbonneau's Secret Life

For some months after arriving at Stalag XXI-D, in a fort built a century before to deter a Russian invasion, he'd been allowed to meet with Fathers Pellerin and Larivière, who were in camps nearby. But save for one recent visit with Larivière, that privilege ended at Christmas. Even if Father Herménégilde Charbonneau had suspected it, he could have never written that the visits were stopped because of the Gestapo, which, in its effort to bend the priests to its will, isolated them to prevent them from giving each other mutual absolution.

Charbonneau's 27 February letter is a masterpiece of fact and indirection. He writes of the morale-sapping effects of hunger, augmented by the incessant cold that because of hunger made the winter even more of an enemy than it was in Canada. He writes of the humiliation he felt witnessing POWs trade £15, watches or wedding rings for a single piece of bread.

German censors, he knew, would read "the present situation—a young priest among 750 soldiers—is not without worry" not as a reference to his physical safety but as referring to the difficulty of maintaining his morale in sacerdotal isolation. True, his roommate, Dr. Davidson, shared clothing and, more importantly, the chocolate and other foods sent from the United States. But he was a Protestant, and neither he nor any of the Catholics could provide the intellectual life the priest not long out of the seminary was used to. Worse, the prison camp was denuded of religious life. The soldiers' way of coping—cursing; singing obscene songs; having shouting matches; boxing; engaging in meaningless conversations, often about women—were alien to the gentle, bespectacled priest.

Toward the end of the letter, Charbonneau's emotions fairly spilled out. His characterization of Monsignor Johannes Pietsch's letter as "the first, very comforting words, from my congregation" is a *cri de coeur*; Pietsch had evangelized around James Bay. A few lines later, after writing in his own hand the dehumanizing words "British POW" Charbonneau realized that he'd allowed something like despair to rear its head and ended the letter "*Je m'excuse, T.R. Père.*"

Charbonneau's ministry, if not his life (as well as others') required that the censors buy the picture of the anguished priest, for it hid a truly remarkable story.

Upon arriving in Posen, where, he knew, the Germans had murdered priests, including numerous Oblates, Charbonneau asked a workman in the camp to carry a letter, written in Latin, to one of the few Oblates remaining in the area, thus beginning a clandestine correspondence with Father Jean Woziwodski. Carried into the camp by another workman or various young women, Woziwodski's letters, which were written in excellent French, detailed the Nazis' persecution of the Church and thus had to be burned immediately after Charbonneau read them. In an effort to protect his life and Woziwodski's, Charbonneau wrote in such a way as to hide both his and his reader's identity; if discovered, the lives of the couriers, all involved knew, were beyond earthly protection.

EARLY APRIL 1942, ON A TRAIN TO STALAG LUFT III, SAGAN, POLAND

Andrew Cox Doesn't Believe an Explanation

After four days of the four-hours-standing/four-hours-sitting regimen the men packed into the cattle car imposed on themselves, Andrew Cox's arms, legs and back ached. Yet he counted himself lucky. For while he could do nothing about the fetid smell of the unwashed men around him, at least he wasn't next to the excrement-filled metal bins, the foul contents of which slopped over onto the hapless men near them.

Locked in the cattle car, the men could not see the sky above the marshalling yard, but the drone of bomber engines told them that the night was relatively clear. When the roar of bombs exploding close enough to rock the train drowned out the men's prayers, Cox knew that that afternoon, through the blue haze of cigarette smoke, his comrades in Bomber Command had seen the marshalling yard he was now in, on the maps tacked to briefing-room walls.

The next day, before it reached Stalag Luft III, in Sagan, Poland, Cox's train pulled into a station, where the guards allowed the POWs to disembark and stretch their legs. Across the platform, Cox saw a long line of cattle cars loaded with men, women and children who, a guard said, were being relocated to the east. Though unaware of the unfolding "Final Solution to the Jewish Question," the "anxiety, dread and haunted eyes of these people left [the POWs] with a feeling that the guards were not telling [them] the truth."[43]

6 APRIL 1942, MILAG UND MARLAG NORD, NEAR BREMEN, GERMANY

Father Robert Barsalou Sends a Secret Message in a Letter about Easter

At 9:30 p.m. on Easter Monday, Father Barsalou looked back with satisfaction on the observance of Easter, which began with the baptizing of a 22-year-old British soldier on what in his Scottish homeland is called Black Saturday, the only full day during which Jesus was dead. His German censors would have been pleased that he wrote of having enough tobacco to enjoy a smoke now that Lent was over, and that he wrote in glowing terms of the makeshift chapel, the Cross of which was blackened with shoe polish.

What they almost certainly missed was a secret message in the sentence that praises Father Raoul Bergeron for building the chapel. Barsalou could be sure that his readers back in Canada would recognize that the sentence "*Le Père Bergeron avait élevé un magnifique reposoir*" would be understood both as praise for Bergeron's carpentry skills and as an echo of Genesis 33:20, when, after he reached safety in the land of Sechem, Jacob "raised a magnificent altar." Barsalou had no way of saying that even at these highest of masses, in order to stretch their supply of wine, the priests used a pipette to place into the chalice four minute drops of wine, which after transubstantiation was turned into the blood of Christ.

21 APRIL 1942, MILAG UND MARLAG NORD, NEAR BREMEN, GERMANY

THE SS TRIES TO BREAK THE PRIESTS' COMMUNION

The improving weather and the priests' transfer from bleak Sandbostel to Milag und Marlag Nord moved Brother Roland Cournoyer to lyricism when describing their new camp: "Half is on a small grove where the small birds come at all hours to entertain us with their gentle songs."

In a letter to an old classmate, Father Barsalou was more serious and makes clear something all POWs felt as they write to their loved ones: that letters, be they the ones that were once in the hands of a wife, mother or religious brother back in Canada or the ones written on paper stamped *Kriegsgefangenenpost*, dissolve space and time, uniting the sender and recipient through the act of reading. "Contact! . . . This paper had actually been in my home in Montreal! It had been touched, handled, folded by loving compassionate hands . . . . Touching it was touching them, an invisible embrace, a reunion, a banishing of all the grime and horror and ugliness," explained another Canadian POW upon receipt of his first letter.[44]

It may have taken Brother Roland Courtemanche's letter months to reach Milag Nord, but what he said about their common vocation dissolved not just time but distance. For, Barsalou wrote, their lives, one in a prison camp in northern Germany and the other as a missionary to the "*Esquimaux*" on the shores of Hudson's Bay share much besides the cold. Is a year behind barbed wire all that different from "*le* Barren Land *et le grand silence blanc?*" wrote the priest, who knew that even when profoundly alone, they were united in communion with each other.

The SS had a finer understanding of this communion than their abjuration of Christianity might suggest, as *les religieux* learned after Fathers Barsalou and Bergeron were moved to separate compounds. To stop the fathers, who were a mere 60 yards apart, from taking part in the sacrament of confession, they were prevented from meeting. When the SS saw that the fathers would stand at the fence and shout to each other, the SS wove straw into the fence so they would not be able to see each other. However, this didn't keep the fathers from standing at the fence and shouting "mysterious words (presumably in Latin), which had significance only to people in the know."[45]

LATE APRIL 1942, OFLAG VI-B, DÖSSEL, GERMANY

VERNON HOWLAND ESCAPES

The camp's barbed wire ran up each end of the building's rear wall. Set in the middle of that wall was Vernon Howland's first goal, a window that faced out of the camp. Ironically, because that window looked into the corridor on either side of which were punishment cells, reaching it required first getting sent to the cooler, which he and five other men arranged by swapping identities (exchanging clothes and identity disks) with men who had committed such minor infractions as failing to salute a passing German officer. The second and more difficult step occurred a few days later during the 9 p.m. latrine run when a staged disturbance distracted the guard while a POW slipped open the bolt on the cell's door.

A short time later, just before jumping to the ground, Howland, the last of the men to escape, gingerly closed the window behind him so that the Germans would waste time trying to figure out how he had escaped through a corridor's locked door. Despite the moonlight and reflection from the searchlights, Howland reached the woodpile but could not find the food and water that dragooned Polish workers had promised to leave. A few hours later, while making his way for a rail yard, he saw a bank of snow and dug out a mouthful to quench his thirst. He was soon doubled over, retching his guts out, for the snowbank was in fact "an old manure pile covered in snow."

At dawn, realizing he wouldn't reach the marshalling yard, he hid under a low tree branch, crawling to a clump of bushes when children started playing nearby. In the afternoon, the soldiers walking by worried him less than did the police dog, which, perhaps because of Howland's rank odour, turned up its nose at him.

That night, Howland hopped a train heading west, jumping off it shortly before dawn. After barking dogs warned him off from an attempt to steal food, he boarded another train. By this time, his dehydration was so severe that he began hallucinating an escape partner.

His imaginary consort did not argue when Howland pointed out that the situation was so desperate that travelling during the day was worth the risk. When he tried to move to a train heading toward Holland, Howland hoped that the presence of French workers milling about would hide him. He hadn't gone more than a few steps before a guard stopped him. The delusional Canadian forgot that he was wearing another man's identity disk and gave his real name, which put him outside the Geneva Convention's protections and almost landed him in the arms of the Gestapo. Fortunately, a few phone calls established his identity. A few days later, Howland arrived at Stalag Luft III.

28 APRIL 1942, STALAG VII-A, MOOSBURG, GERMANY

Hodgkinson Watches a Messy Explosion

The "Biblical nudity" that distressed Father Goudreau and the "incredibly crude language" that shocked Brother Georges-Aimé Lavallée was for Hodgkinson simply a fact of life.[46] Hodgkinson could accept the 30-holer *sans* partitions with equanimity but not the ten-inch worms—worms that kept the contents of the tank liquid enough so that it could be pumped into a honey wagon—which could slither onto the seats. Somewhat less bothersome was Dominique Fiouloir, who didn't shy away from talking during "one of man's most compelling moments of concentration."[47]

On 28 April, just as Hodgkinson buttoned his fly, the French POW provided some unintended excitement when, after lighting a cigarette, he tossed the still-burning match into the latrine. A moment later a sound resembling "a dozen tympani" began rolling through the ground as the methane gas trapped beneath the latrine caught fire. The ensuing explosion shot flames and then jets of excrement through every hole. Through the stinking, stygian miasma, Hodgkinson heard the astonished Fiouloir call out, "*Sacre bleu! . . . Putain de Dieu! . . . Jésus Christ! . . . Mére de Dieu!*" phrases Hodgkinson found fit the slapstick-like moment but would have made *les religieux* blush.[48]

MAY 1942, STALAG XXI-D, POSEN, POLAND

Father Louis Larivière Wants *Les Religieux* to Become Royal Navy Officers

After almost a year in captivity, the Oblates were unsure of their legal ecclesiastical status or who their Ordinary, or superior, was. In the Roman Catholic Church, bishops have jurisdiction of a diocese, thus the Bishop of Calgary or Bishop of Gatineau. Since the

Oblates belonged to a congregation, they came under the jurisdiction of the Oblate Provincial, Monsignor Leo Deschâtelets. Had they reached Basutoland, their Ordinary would have been Monsignor Joseph Bonhomme, who was headquartered in Basutoland but because of the war, was stranded in Ottawa. By this logic, the Oblates in Germany should have been under the authority of the Provincial in Germany and those in Poland under the Polish Provincial. The Germans, however, would never have allowed this. In Poland, for example, their war against the Church cost the lives of 3,000 Polish priests, including 34 of 35 Oblates sent to concentration camps.[49]

Since *les religieux* were being held as British POWs, Father Larivière, on 1 May, told Monsignor Johannes Pietsch in Rome that he had recently written to "Bishop Dey, Roman Catholic Chaplain to H.M. Forces, whom I take to be my Ordinarie)." Larivière was incorrect.

To be under Dey's authority, Larivière and the other priests and brothers would have had to be in the British Armed Forces. A request to be breveted as officers in the Royal Navy ran up against bureaucratic inertia in London. On 7 June, Father Barsalou enlisted the aid of Lady Encombe, patron of the Catholic Truth Society, to submit his request for "a temporary appointment as an RN Roman Catholic Chaplain in H.M. Fleet for the duration of captivity" directly to Archbishop Arthur Hinsley. Pushed by the facts on the ground in Marlag Nord, Captain F.W. Wilson Graham, the Senior British Officer, took it upon himself to appoint Barsalou the Roman Catholic chaplain of the prisoners in the Royal Navy camp. Barsalou took this appointment to mean that he came under Hinsley's authority. Barsalou too was mistaken.

The Germans were equally confused about the priests' and brothers' status. In many ways, they treated them like officers, allowing some of them parole walks, and housing them with officers or in private rooms. The Germans did not, however, pay them either as officers or enlisted men, though they did pay the priests

14 reichsmarks for saying mass, which allowed them to purchase, from outside the camps, the materials necessary to say mass. Alone among inmates of POW camps, the priests and brothers in one camp were allowed to write to their brethren in Christ in other camps. When, later in the year, Father Paul Juneau was sent to Stalag XVIII-A, in Austria, the Kommandant considered him the chaplain for the English Catholics, housed him with the officers, and gave him an orderly.

MID-JUNE 1942, MILAG UND MARLAG NORD, NEAR BREMEN, GERMANY

Months of Captivity Wear on *les Religieux*

German rations—a thin piece of cheese for breakfast, vegetable soup devoid of vegetables for lunch and two pieces of stinking headcheese for dinner—left the Sacred Heart Brothers, who were suffering from extremely bad colds and diarrhea, believing that they'd never see Canada again. The Red Cross parcels were so important to Kriegies' survival that the fathers would have overlooked the somewhat blasphemous way of reckoning time recalled by Surgeon Lieutenant Fisher, who soon would be joining them at Milag und Marlag Nord: "BRC" and "ARC," Before Red Cross and After Red Cross.

Wearying too were the long months of inactivity. "If you have never experienced it," wrote one veteran of the Colditz POW camp, "you can never imagine what it is like to get up in the morning to face a long empty day with nothing whatever to do except what you do yourself."[50]

The POWs suffered psychologically from the indeterminacy of their sentence. Unlike prisoners who have been convicted and sentenced, prisoners of war have no idea when their incarceration—by an unfriendly power, it must always be remembered—will end. Through clandestine radios and the camps' jungle telegraphs, the

Kriegies knew that in February *Gneisenau* and two other capital ships had humiliated the Royal Navy by dashing through the Channel to the North Sea and thence to Germany and that the Wehrmacht stood at the gates of Moscow and was closing in on Stalingrad. They also knew of the military disasters in the Far East.

Yet in a real sense, the POWs were out of time, living with images of the past made present by acts of memory or via the fleeting joy of a letter, which, because it could be six months old, often raised more questions than it answered: "Has a favourite cousin recovered from an illness?" "Does my young son or daughter even remember me?" "Do you remember the feel of my arms around you?" Or, as Father Goudreau wonders in a letter written that August, has that problem in James Bay been solved? In a letter he wrote in June, Father Bernard Desnoyers shifted the time scheme forward by asking his parents to send him his brother's and sister's final grades.

Les religieux at Milag Nord were surprised to find that their communal life did not transfer well to life in the camps. Indeed, given the differences between their sense of propriety and the crudeness of camp life, their community may have been under special pressures. "Eight, ten, twelve men eat, sleep, read, write, think and suffer inside the same four walls," wrote Brother Cournoyer. At times they suffered from insomnia and depression, which became worse during periods of bombings. While their faith never broke, bad news, hunger and the "insalubrity of the barracks" affected them as it did other POWs. "It was miraculous that in these conditions . . . men of the cloth were not tempted to come to blows."[51]

On 14 June, Goudreau assured his superior in Ottawa that despite having been separated from his brothers for the past six months, he was well in body and mind. In addition to ministering to 150 Catholics, he filled his days by teaching philosophy, French and Greek to three officers, including one from Mont-Joli, Quebec. What lay behind his note of concern about Father Charbonneau remains unclear, but he clearly was worried about the priest who had been ordained only a year before they set sail for Africa.

17 JUNE 1942, STALAG XXI-D, POSEN, POLAND

Father Charbonneau Spends the Night at an Oblate Residence

The letter Father Charbonneau wrote the Provincial in Ottawa three days later would scarcely have assuaged Father Goudreau's worries.

The red flag wasn't Charbonneau's decision to use the powers Pope Pius XII gave priests in war zones to give general absolution but, rather, the letter's distressed tone. The assertion that God has shown him that it is a man's "personality that is the one thing that allows him to overcome the obstacles of life" shows his anguish. Even more worrisome is the letter's close: "May I repeat myself, it takes a great deal of prayer by us and for us because ours is a hard experience. And when we think of the millions of prisoners who are in continuous moral danger."

Neither the German nor the Canadian censors could guess the whole truth behind this sentence in the middle of the letter: "German authorities are very good to me." It is impossible to pin down how much the Kommandant learned of the clandestine correspondence Charbonneau was by then conducting with Oblates outside the camp. Shortly before the Gestapo arrested Father Woziwodski, whom they would murder, he put Charbonneau in touch with Father Théodore Nandzik, who, because of his advanced age, was left alone by the Gestapo. One day, after visiting another camp (with the Kommandant's knowledge), Charbonneau's guard led him to the small Oblate residence where Nandzik lived. After spending the evening speaking with the old Oblate, who reminisced about being a missionary in Keewatin, as much of northwestern

Ontario was once known, Charbonneau slept in a real bed in a private room.

In the morning, after Charbonneau experienced the joy of celebrating mass in a consecrated chapel, the guard returned and escorted him back to his camp, where once, in the middle of the night, the Kommandant, who "opposed the Nazis . . . did not fear to come on his knees in his uniform and with medals hanging on his chest before a British prisoner to celebrate the Mass."[52]

17 JULY 1942

IAN MACDONALD FLIES OVER NIAGARA FALLS

Ian MacDonald had already travelled a long way from small-town Nova Scotia since shipping out for flight-training school six months earlier.

Six weeks training in Lachine, Quebec, was followed by six more in Montreal East, and then he was off to Belleville, Ontario, before going to Jarvis, Ontario, where he learned how to be a bomb aimer. Through days filled with geometry and gunnery classes, learning emergency evacuation procedures and target-identification drills, he looked forward both to going into action and to weekends when a friend invited him off base for a home-cooked meal.

MacDonald knew his family wanted to hear his voice, so he told them he'd just received the picture of Kathleen in the lilac tree, and of his memory of his father and uncle painting the garage. He had not, he assured his father, forgotten his birthday, though admitted to failing to find the gift he was looking for in "the little one-horse town" in which he was stationed.

Having written the words parents wanted to read, he then told them about "not doing so hot" on his first bomb-sighting exercise because the pilot, who was on his first bomb training run, had difficulty levelling off the Fairey Battle trainer, and also MacDonald had forgotten to engage the bomb selector switch. Concerned about him though they were, his parents knew Ian had always wanted to fly and, thus, when they read his letter could hear the relish in his voice as he told them the following day that the pilot let him take control of an Avro Anson for a few minutes. For a couple whose idea of excitement was taking the train to New Glasgow, their Ian circling over Niagara Falls at 2,000 feet seemed like something out of a Hollywood movie.

26 JULY 1942, STALAG LUFT III, SAGAN, POLAND

Father Goudreau Loses Hope

The reason Father Goudreau was still at Stalag Luft III impressed RCAF bomber pilot Kingsley Brown, who had arrived there in early July after being shot down over northwest Holland. Not long after the priest arrived at the camp, arrangements were made for the repatriation of several British chaplains captured in North Africa. On the appointed day, Goudreau refused to pack his bags, telling the Kommandant, "I have no instructions from the superior of my order. . . . I must obey my own conscience. I shall remain here to serve my fellow prisoners."[53] Perhaps unsurprisingly, though surely unbureaucratically, Friedrich Wilhelm von Lindeiner-Wildau accepted the Oblate's decision.

The pilot was equally impressed with the thin, dark-eyed priest's common touch and "intellectual honesty." Despite never having fired a shot, dropped a bomb or worn a uniform, Goudreau spent endless hours "sitting in on bull sessions," a phrase the priest never would have used. Goudreau welcomed questions about Catholicism from the largely Anglican and Protestant officers. He refused, however, to conduct conversions, telling prospective communicants that their lives in the POW camp were "abnormal and artificial" and thus the camp was not the milieu in which a reasoned decision to accept the doctrines of the Catholic Church could be made.

If Goudreau wrote of his decision to refuse to leave the camp for a train to Sweden, the letter is lost. Yet it is impossible that he did not replay this scene in his mind when he wrote in a late July letter, "I am always alone, *sans espoir* [without hope] *de délivrance*."

Chapter Four

August–September 1942

Wir haben viele Verwundete,
wir kommen mit zurück, bringen Sie Ihren Feldwebel
(We have many wounded, we are bringing them back,
get your sergeant.)

—Company Sergeant Major Lucien Dumais
to the German who took his surrender at Dieppe

19 AUGUST 1942, MID-MORNING, PUYS, FRANCE

Private Jack Poolton Surrenders and Sees War Crimes

The fighting continued a mile or so to the east, on the beaches before Dieppe and a half mile further east at Pourville. At Puys, where 606 men belonging to Lieutenant Colonel Douglas Catto's Royal Regiment of Canada had landed at 5:35 a.m., the battle was over almost before it began; most, Jack Poolton included, never got off what was code-named "Blue Beach." A stream of lead poured into Poolton's boat before its ramp even touched down, killing several men but missing the mortar operator, weighed down by his pack, a mortar launcher, a dozen mortar bombs, hand grenades and hundreds of rounds of ammunition in addition to his rifle.

The sergeant major who taught Poolton how to handle a mortar would have been pleased that, even though caught in a brutal maelstrom that shocked veteran CBC journalist Ross Munro "almost to insensibility," the recruit with no battle experience noted the pattern the German mortar operators used.[54] One bomb exploded near the seawall, knocking out stretcher-bearer Bill McLennan and tearing the head off another soldier, whose body, still pumping blood, fell on McLennan. Poolton heard the dull thump of bullets hitting bodies around him and counted himself lucky that one only knocked the rim of his helmet, for scant inches away lay his haversack filled with a dozen mortar bombs. Closer to Dieppe, a bullet hit a sapper's backpack, turning the man into a human torch.

At 9:50 a.m., as hand grenades fell from the cliff above, and others that failed to reach the top of the cliff fell back and blew up among the Canadians who had thrown them, Poolton saw the landing craft sent to withdraw them driven back by a terrible fusillade.

The 31-year-old would never forget the wave of humiliation that swept over him, having dreamt from boyhood of being a soldier. "You can train a soldier to fight and you can train a soldier to accept death," he later wrote, "but there is no way to prepare a soldier to be taken prisoner." As one of the few unwounded men on Blue Beach, Poolton was set to work by the Germans as a stretcher-bearer. Three times he thread his way over sand turned brown and blood-slickened stones to pick up men, most of them buddies, some with arms and legs blown away, others with their intestines hanging out. Each time, he passed "corpses with the whites of their eyes transfixed on the heavens." On one trip, as he knelt to speak to a man who could not move, he saw "a German officer walking from place to place shooting the worst of the wounded in the head."[55]

19 AUGUST 1942, EARLY AFTERNOON, DIEPPE

The Germans Take Company Sergeant Major Lucien Dumais's Surrender Correctly

The forlorn sight of tanks, their tracks thrown, and pockmarked by mortar explosions on the beach before Dieppe was framed by the burned-out landing craft shoved onto the shore at oblique angles or drifting lifeless on the tide. Scores drowned in capsized landing craft. To Private Al Richards, who swam for shore after being thrown from a landing craft, the steel helmets still attached to bodies that floated upright looked "like turtles on the water."[56] In one sector of the beach lay a group of Fusiliers Mont-Royal that Major René Painchaud railed at for hitting the dirt—before he realized that every one of them was dead or wounded. Even as the cutting smell of cordite blew away where the blood was fresh, the air was sickeningly sweet and, where men's abdomens had been ripped open, the thick stench of shit hung heavy.

Just after 1 p.m., the destroyer that held the headquarters for Operation Jubilee, HMS *Calpe*, her decks slick with the blood of hundreds of wounded, hove into view. Braving mortar fire, she sped toward the beach, getting close enough that some men ripped off their boots and stripped off their pants to increase their odds of swimming the 250 yards to the ship. Sergeant Major Lucien Dumais was not a strong swimmer and had already cheated the sea once (when the wash from the propellers of the landing craft he'd been attempting to board drove him, unconscious but alive, onto the beach), so he remained on shore and watched *Calpe* steam away.

Small white flags fluttered above tanks that sheltered wounded men to their lee. Neither Dumais and the men with him behind a landing craft beached some distance up the beach nor the Germans took these flags as a sign of general surrender. Thus, when a medical officer told Dumais that the incoming tide had begun lapping at the wounded down the strand, the Montrealer gave greater weight to the possibility that, since the landing craft was on fire and the ammunition within it was exploding, the Germans thought his command was larger than it was and was firing at them, than he did to the moon's effect on the oceans. A short time later, the medical officer said, "Well, Sergeant Major? It'll soon be too late." The proud soldier, who later, in describing a standoff that had occurred a few hours earlier in the old casino that dominated the beach, wrote, "I drew faster than he did, so I was alive and he was dead," reluctantly agreed to lay down his arms.[57]

The formal structure of the Geneva Convention suggests that the moment a soldier raises his hands or waves a white flag, the victorious side, in the manner of a battlefield accountant, records his surrender according to established rules; on the battlefield, reality is much more complicated. The soldier who surrenders is torn by the desire to keep fighting and washed over by humiliation, while the soldier who is asked to accept the surrender is torn by fear that he is being duped (once he lowers his rifle would some unseen shooter do him in?); fuelled by the adrenaline of battle augmented by the exhilaration of victory and, we must never forget, driven by blood lust. Thus, it is not surprising that the first reaction to Dumais's surrender flag was a burst of rifle fire, which almost caused him to pull his rifle back to his shoulder and begin shooting.

A nearby German motioned to Dumais to drop his rifle and raise his arms. He slowly lowered his gun, untied the yellowed flag he'd waved and threw the rifle down toward the shingle. "The bayonet dug itself in and the rifle stuck, butt end up: the way we mark the spot where a soldier lies wounded or dead," Dumais later wrote. "It seemed to symbolize the fact that my military life was over."[58]

19 AUGUST 1942, AFTERNOON, DIEPPE

Canadian Prisoners March through Dieppe, and the Germans Deny Them Water

Three hours after *Calpe* slipped over the horizon, Captain George A. Browne, a Forward Observation Officer attached to the Royal Regiment of Canada, followed Catto out of a small wood they and some 20 other men had taken shelter in after destroying six machine guns on a hill above the beach. After almost 11 hours, Operation Jubilee was over, some 1,400 men were dead or wounded and 1,975 Canadians were prisoners of war.

How the prisoners were treated varied greatly. Hauptmann Richard Schnösenberg recalled the moment of Catto's surrender as "the last knightly encounter with the enemy on the field of battle." Those who took his surrender of the South Saskatchewans and the Cameron Highlanders behaved correctly. Once the Germans who had fired at Dumais realized how many wounded men he had, they provided medical care. And even on Blue Beach, a medical officer gave Captain Robert Robertson, a Royal Regiment doctor, dressings to bind up wounds.[59]

In places, the victors gave the vanquished water and, in at least one case, some beer. In others, in contravention of Geneva, the Germans did more than refuse to give the exhausted, shocked and desperately thirsty men water. While *les dieppoises* did not spirit men away under their skirts, they were an enterprising bunch. Some placed buckets of water on the streets on which the POWs, some singing "La Marseillaise" or whistling "The Maple Leaf Forever," Canada's unofficial anthem (and a surprisingly martial tune), were marched into captivity. Others ignored the Germans on horseback; one woman ran up to one man and whispered that the POWs should start cursing in French and shaking their fists at her. Word quickly spread down the line, and when they did as she said, she feigned anger and threw tomatoes at them. By laughing and congratulating the woman for "flinging tomatoes at the *Engländer Schweine*," the Germans enjoyed what appeared to be a violation of Geneva's prohibition against public insults and missed the fact that the woman provided the Canadians with some much-needed food.[60]

Other violations of Geneva occurred, including the pilfering of watches, pens and money. Luckily, the Germans didn't find Dumais's penknife, which he soon used to cut up his and other POWs' Mae Wests to fashion foot coverings for the many men who had lost their boots.

19 AUGUST 1942, LATE AFTERNOON, NEAR DIEPPE

Just-Married Madame Dupuis Cries upon Seeing the Defeated Canadian Soldiers

She woke early, near 3 a.m., but not because she was nervous that after the church service that day would come her first night with her husband. Since the French Revolution, civil weddings had preceded church weddings, which meant she was already Madame Paul Dupuis, and he lay sleeping beside her in their marital bed. Rather, what woke her was the roar of German and Royal Navy guns, the rumble of which could still be heard during the church ceremony. In the late afternoon, as the wedding party made its way back toward Dieppe under skies no longer stained by anti-aircraft fire and the condensation trails of fighter planes, the revellers met with a column of Canadians being marched from Dieppe to Envermeu, where the officers were herded into the very church in which the Dupuises' marriage had been solemnized.

To Madame Dupuis, resplendent in her white wedding dress, and Monsieur Dupuis, dressed in his finest suit, and the other members of the wedding party, the halting column of haggard men must have seemed like a gruesome scene out of a medieval fresco. The hobbled were not allegories of moral failings, however, but real men, soldiers from across the sea, some now held up by shaking legs or by the near failed strength of a comrade's shoulder. For the barefoot, each step on the rocky road was a physical reminder of their defeat. All were thirsty and hungry.

They were a beaten army, but to the Germans' surprise, when they saw the wedding party, the Canadians showed that loss in battle did not equal defeat of spirit. Some who had hidden money from the Germans' sticky fingers threw it to Madame Dupuis, causing her to cry. The shout "Long live the lovely bride" both saluted her and thumbed the POWs' noses at the Germans because it echoed the toast to King George VI, "Long Live the King." She ignored the bills fluttering to her feet, picking up only a single bronze penny to hold as a tribute to them.[61]

As Private Stan Darch drew close to young Jean-Claude Robillard, who was holding his father's hand as he watched the procession of the lame, the private realized that this would be the last time for who knew how long that he'd be able to hug a child. Jean-Claude sensed something of this and held his father's hand tighter. What grabbed his father's attention, however, was Darch's bloody feet. As the rest of the wedding party threw cigarettes, Robillard quickly bent down, unlaced his shoes and handed them to the Canadian from Hamilton, Ontario, who knew only one word of French: "*Merci.*"

19 AUGUST 1942, LATE EVENING, ENVERMEU, NEAR DIEPPE

German Soldiers Deny the POWs Water, Again

At the church, the officers were separated from their men, who were marched some miles further to a disused brick factory. The priest, who had earlier presided over the Dupuises' marriage, was surprised at the number of French-speaking Canadians and provided straw to soften the pews and floor the exhausted men were to sleep on. Before collapsing into sleep, Major Brian McCool realized that although he had surrendered his revolver, he had forgotten about the cartridges in his pocket. Risking sacrilege, but to keep the Germans from finding them, McCool removed the plug from the baptismal font and dropped the cartridges down the drain.

Captains John Foote and Wes Clare also spent the night in the church. Because of the insignia on their shoulders, they'd been picked up to be interrogated by intelligence officers. Clare, a Royal Regiment medical officer, knew little and said less. Foote, his Presbyterian ministry notwithstanding, had used a Lewis gun on the beaches of Dieppe, and dissembled more than a padre should when he told his interlocutor that as a chaplain he "didn't know anything about the technical part of the war." Foote, who ignored one order by going to Dieppe and who earned a Victoria Cross for refusing another by staying with the wounded men on the beach, enjoyed saying that morale in England was "just fine."[62]

At the brick factory, some men were fed, Dumais receiving a hunk of German black bread that even in his famished state he found revolting. The disgusting smell and taste of rubber *Kaffe* heartened him. For, he reasoned, if this "is what they were reduced to for coffee, they must be in a poor way."[63] Others, like Darch, had had nothing to drink since the morning and did not get water until the next day because by the time it was their turn to go to the water pipe, Hitlerjugend, who ignored Geneva and shut the valve, had replaced the Wehrmacht troops standing guard. Poolton was so desperate to relieve his thirst that he scraped a hole in the factory's hard dirt floor and pressed his tongue and parched lips to the damp earth.

As he drifted off to sleep on the floor, Darch had no way of knowing that Monsieur Robillard was passing his first night in a dank prison cell in Envermeu, punishment for his act of kindness.

20 AUGUST 1942, NEAR DIEPPE

DUMAIS ESCAPES AND WHISTLES "UN CANADIEN ERRANT"

The ever-decreasing rumble of the train and sound of shots told him two things: the train carrying the bulk of the Canadians to a POW camp was heading into the gathering night, and the guards suspected that someone had jumped from it. Then he recognized the French voice calling out "Sergeant Major Dumais." He was about to call back when he saw a railway patrol. Some minutes later, as he walked along the embankment hoping to find his countryman, Dumais whistled a song he knew that no German or Frenchman would know but any French Canadian would: "Un Canadien Errant," one of the songs the Oblates sang aboard the *Dresden*.

23 AUGUST 1942, VERNEULLES, FRANCE

Canadians Captured at Dieppe Suffer Numerous Violations of Their Geneva Convention Rights

On the 20th, ever the sticklers for rank, the Germans put the officers in third-class compartments. Poolton and Darch were two of the more than 1,000 "ordinary ranks" shoved, 70 at a time, into cattle cars, but at least they'd been given some water and a hunk of black bread, which, they noticed, had been augmented by sawdust. Whatever fillip the Canadians got from seeing peasants flash furtive V signs vanished when they reached Verneulles, an old military base 100 miles from Paris, and saw the gallows adjacent to the railway siding.

Nothing at Verneulles evinced the Germans' reputation for order or concern for their Geneva responsibilities. The huts provided protection from the elements—and dirty floors on which to sleep without blankets. Worse, despite knowing that scores of men were wounded, some with suppurating wounds, the Germans provided no medical services. The best efforts of the Canadian doctors could not save several men from dying in the five days they were at Verneulles.

What interested the Germans was information. Impressed with the maps they'd seized and remembering the Canadian Corps' prowess in the final hundred days of the last war, when it defeated the Germans at several battles, the Germans wanted to know how Canadian generals could think that a single division lacking even field artillery, let alone the support of heavy naval guns, could make a lodgement against a well-defended port. The obvious senselessness of the raid led to the question, which bemused Captain John Runcie, "Had [it] been ordered by Stalin?"

Hitler sent Dr. Paul Schmidt, who in 1937 had translated at his meeting with Prime Minister William Lyon Mackenzie King, to interview the Canadians.[64] Blocked by military intelligence from asking probing questions, Schmidt lapsed into clichés about "huge, hearty backwoodsmen with . . . jolly laughs which revealed their perfect teeth."[65]

In his memoir, Schmidt inadvertently promoted Captain Antoine Masson two ranks, but he remembered the gist of the conversation in which *le canadien* ignored what he and his men were going through and took the occasion to complain about Germany's treatment of the Polish Catholics, which prompted Schmidt to say, "Nazism and Christianity could not be reconciled." After admitting that many Germans listened to the BBC, Schmidt predicted that Stalingrad would soon fall, a point Masson disputed. With ultimate cheek, Masson told Schmidt not only that he would soon escape but also that he would "answer Dr. Schmidt on the radio."

Perhaps because before the First World War, Germany's foreign minister, Joachim Von Ribbentrop, had lived in Canada, working first on the Quebec Bridge and later as a dealer in fine wines in Ottawa, the Germans knew enough about Canada to try to suborn the hundreds of French Canadians. First they told them that, since they were French and Germany was not at war with France, they were not at war with Germany and offered them the opportunity to broadcast home via Radio Calais. Knowing how important letting families in Canada know that their loved ones were alive, the officers told their men to record the broadcasts and include as many names as they could.

The second effort to suborn the French Canadians involved food, and goes some distance in proving that the decision to provide scant rations at Verneulles had nothing to do with being surprised by having "so many 'guests.'" Rather, the Canadians understood their poor rations as an attempt to soften them up. After three days of only two bowls of watery soup each a day and a small ration of hard bread (augmented by some handfuls of grass), the Fusiliers Mont-Royal were ordered to gather round a truck, where an official from Vichy France called them "brothers" and offered them fresh fruit, cigarettes and chocolate. At first, the fusiliers refused, but then their officers told them to accept the gifts. The Vichy and German authorities were shocked when *les Canadiens français* turned around and shared their largesse with their English compatriots, saying to their captors, "We are one nation of Canadians and that is why we fought so well."[66]

24 AUGUST 1942, LE MANS, FRANCE

Dumais Finds Help on His Home Run

Among the 400 or so people filing out of the church in Le Mans, 130 miles south of Dieppe, following Sunday mass on 22 August, some would help, others might turn him in. Perhaps the old woman over there would be like the lone woman who, turning pale when she saw the Canada patches on Dumais's shoulders and being unable to help herself, pointed to another house, saying, "Try her." Or maybe that couple would be like the Collais, who ignored the freshly posted notices threatening death for anyone "who helps, shelters or fails to reveal the presence of an Allied soldier." While Madame Collai fed him, her husband, Robert, replaced the nails in his boots (which would have given him away) with cement before leading him to a shelter in a clay quarry, where Dumais spent a dry night despite the heavy rain. The next morning, Madame Collai brought him food, civilian clothes, a map of France ripped from a school book and some money, then walked him to the train station. Even the presence of a German soldier a short way down the corridor could not prevent Dumais from waving a discreet goodbye to this helpful and courageous woman.

Some in the crowd leaving church may have already seen him, for he'd arrived in Le Mans the day before. Then, the need for food forced his hand and, after walking some distance out of town, he approached a farmer and explained who he was. The farmer was gruff and suspicious but, perhaps because Dumais's accent, which for reasons the farmer and Dumais almost certainly did not know seemed more familiar than the French of either Paris or Vichy, the farmer gambled that the man in front of him was not an *agent provocateur.*[67] The farmer and his wife gave him food and let him sleep in their stable. The next morning, Sunday, they again fed the mysterious stranger, then gave him a bacon sandwich and some hard-boiled eggs before ushering him on his way.

When he'd approached the Collai farmhouse and spoke to the farmer, Dumais risked being recaptured. But at least, had an alarm gone up from the house, he could run, and if the farmer had turned on him . . . well, Dumais was a trained soldier. Neither option was feasible in the crowd that, after church, gathered in the market area of the town famous for its 24-hour motor race. Risking being noticed because he was not known, Dumais listened for any stray word that would reveal the speaker's allegiance. Amid the gossip and jabber about shopping, he heard a woman complain to a man about yet another German requisition of foodstuffs and, even more importantly, say a few words "on the possible meaning of the Dieppe raid."[68] When, a few minutes later, the man was alone, Dumais went up to him and asked for his help.

The man took Dumais to a restaurant, the owner of which was suspicious of Dumais until he was unable to give her the correct number of meal tickets for a glass of cognac. Before he left, she gave him 500 francs. At the train station, Dumais hid himself in plain sight by carrying a woman's heavy luggage onto the train. Several hours later, he arrived in Poitiers at 3:30 a.m.

25 AUGUST 1942, ON A TRAIN TO GERMANY

"Churchill's Second Front"

It was more than another train made up of stinking cattle cars crammed with men. It was a propaganda statement.

Aware of the clamour for a Second Front by such unlikely allies as Stalin and Lord Beaverbrook, not to mention rallies in London, New York and Toronto calling for one, the Germans painted "Churchill's Second Front" on the sides of the cars carrying the remnants of the 2nd Canadian Division to Stalag VIII-B in Lamsdorf, in Upper Silesia. At some stops and railway crossings, the men heard soft cheers. At a stop outside Brussels, the schoolgirls the Germans had brought to see the sad state of the girls' hoped-for deliverers refused their part in the drama by singing "Will ye no come back again," until they were silenced by rifle butts.

25 AUGUST 1942, NEAR LUSSAC-LES-CHÂTEAUX, VICHY FRANCE

Dumais Crosses the Demarcation Line

The Promised Land lay on the other side of the railway line. Holding in check the impulse to run across it, Dumais stealthily moved a 100 yards first to his right, then to the left of his original position, all the while sniffing the air for a whiff of a guard's cigarette. Only when he was sure that there was "no movement, sound or smell" did he jump over the fence, cross the tracks and leap another fence before diving into some bushes.[69]

The relief of being in Vichy France almost did him in. While walking down a road as if he "hadn't a care in the world," he suddenly heard the dread word "*Halt!*" and saw through the darkness a guard raising his rifle. In the few seconds it took the guard to pull back the bolt of the rifle and call out "*Halt*" again, Dumais had taken a few steps backwards, putting just enough distance between them that when the guard fired and missed, Dumais could jump into the ditch on his right and start running down it. He disappeared into a copse of trees and then ran into the thick undergrowth on the other side of the road. After running through a field heavy with ripe artichokes and across another field, Dumais found a haystack in which he "bedded down, warm and safe."[70]

Woken at 8 a.m. by the sound of a truck, Dumais started down the road. Under bright sunshine, he slipped into a reverie in which the sound of an RAF plane coming to pick him up drowned out the sound of the very real car that slowed down just as it reached him. Though ready to run for it, Dumais tried to look unconcerned as the driver asked if he was going to Lussac-les-Châteaux. "Yes, I'm going there," he replied and, when offered a lift, warily climbed into the car.

Though the woman in the car was chatty, Dumais could see the driver keeping watch on him in the rear-view mirror. Keeping the conversation going became difficult when the woman's questions became personal. The tension lessened when Dumais saw the sign for the village and the car slowed down in front of a garage. It rocketed up when the man asked, "Would you be going to the Hôtel de la Gare?"—the hotel the old blacksmith who had given him directions on where to cross the demarcation line had told him to go and ask for Père La Classe. Trying to sound nonchalant, Dumais replied, "Not particularly, unless the cooking is good." The driver said, "The cooking is exceptionally good; you should try it," and pointed down the road to the hotel. It took Dumais a moment to realize that the woman and driver were part of a "conspiracy" orchestrated by the blacksmith who had helped him a few days earlier to ensure that the Canadian soldier ended up in the hands of a Resistance cell that would, three weeks later, bring him to Marseilles.[71]

26 AUGUST 1942, PARIS

PRIVATES ROBERT VANIER, CONRAD LAFLEUR AND GUY JOLY REACH PARIS

None of the three French Canadians knew which Resistance cell they lucked into on 25 August, the day after they too leaped from the train carrying the Dieppe survivors. Whichever it was, it was efficient. After feeding and giving them clothing, the farmer they revealed themselves to went to get a doctor to dress their wounds and photograph them so that fake identity papers could be produced.

The next day, armed with bogus work passes signed by the mayor of another town, they were driven to Amiens by the doctor, who took the time to point out an ammunition dump so that the Allies could bomb it. By 4 p.m., accompanied by a member of the doctor's family and carrying more than 2,000 francs and knapsacks filled with food, they were on a train for Paris.

For months after the war started, feeling safe behind the Maginot Line, the three French Canadians found Paris to still be the "City of Light." Then came the disaster of May 1940. By 23 June, Hitler himself was there. At noon each day, German troops goose-stepped down Champs Élysées, while Parisians learned to fear the knock on the door in the middle of the night. More important even than the humiliation of the swastika hanging from the Arc de Triomphe was the requisitioning of huge quantities of food, including almost all the food available in Paris, and 80 per cent of the country's cattle. In 1941, hungry Parisians turned to their cats, causing the authorities to issue warnings about eating cat stew. By 1942, malnutrition led to a 41 per cent rise in deaths in Paris; the 13.5 million food parcels sent by families elsewhere in France allowed the 2.5 million Parisians to stave off starvation.

Paris had been "reduced to a sham," wrote Jean-Paul Sartre, the streets of the famed Latin Quarter, which had bustled with students since the Middle Ages, empty, while the Folies Bergère and cafés were filled with German soldiers.[72] The cacophony of the Parisian night, with its motorcycles and horns, had been replaced by "rifle shots; the sudden pepper of a machine-gun" and the sound of powerful cars in which, it was always feared, was another Parisian arrested by the Gestapo.[73] Still, for the three French Canadians, the names were almost enough: Gare du

Nord, Montparnasse, Notre Dame, the Métro, the Louvre (which, they did not know, was empty). The little hotel their guide took them to stood next to the rambling, art deco department store Samaritaine, its shelves and cases uncommonly bare. And, even though the presence of German patrols meant that at any moment they might hear the dread words "*Eins, zwei, drei, halt!*" privates Robert Vanier, Conrad Lafleur and Guy Joly "did a little discreet sightseeing."

28 AUGUST 1942, NEAR PARIS

Captains Browne and Masson Are Fed and Given a Place to Sleep

Conditions aboard the train carrying the Dieppe survivors to Germany had deteriorated greatly. The few medical supplies Ron Beal and other stretcher-bearers had saved had long since run out. So had the food. The sleep-deprived, cold men, still struggling with the ignominy of surrender, felt also the degradation of their reeking filthy bodies, which hadn't seen water, save for perhaps the bloody saltwater at Dieppe, in more than ten days.

The link between cleanliness and a soldier's self-esteem, the spit and polish for which company sergeant majors are so derided by their charges, demonstrates an army's organization and is a physical manifestation of esprit de corps as well as, of course, protection against diseases like typhus. By depriving the survivors of Dieppe of the opportunity to clean the terrible marks of battle and their own filth from their bodies, the Germans struck directly at the Canadians' pride as free men. Primo Levi, who survived Auschwitz, wrote that a prisoner must do anything possible "to stay clean in order not to debase yourself in your own eyes" and thereby do the dirty work of the Germans for them.[74]

In one cattle car, exhaustion, hunger and thirst unhinged at least one Canadian. Lieutenant Frederick Woodcock hallucinated that the Germans had bent him "backwards over this pile of barbed wire and they were wrapping wire all around [his] right shoulder."[75]

The third-class compartments in which the officers rode were more comfortable, but since their windows were nailed shut, they were stifling. Near 1 a.m., Masson left his compartment and, after bribing a guard with a cigarette, stood near an open window. Just east of Paris when the train slowed in a tunnel, Masson jumped out the window. The side of the tunnel was closer than he realized, and he hit his head on the wall, luckily falling between the train and the wall. By the time the train had left the tunnel, Masson could see four figures—in fact other Canadians who had also jumped from the train—leave the tunnel in the direction from which it had come. Then, the flash of a light, a challenge in French and the sound of the men being arrested.

About an hour later, as he neared a small village, Masson passed a man whose decidedly un-French "*Bonsoir*" caused Masson to look back over his shoulder. Only then did he notice what he'd missed in the darkness: the man's Canadian battle dress. It took only a moment for Masson and Captain George A. Browne, who had also jumped from the train, to establish their identities and decide to start walking away from Paris.

About a half mile down a small path, they saw some workers' houses. As Browne hid in the shadows waiting to see how Masson was received, the French-speaking officer knocked on the door of a house. When a man came to the window, Masson explained that he and another soldier had been on the raid on Dieppe and had just escaped from a German POW train. Their rank smell, dirty faces and greasy hair notwithstanding, the family fed them and, after giving them water to wash, put them to bed.

29 AUGUST 1942, STALAG VIII-B, LAMSDORF, GERMANY

The Dieppe POWs March Smartly into the POW Camp

Once the train entered the Reich, the Canadians had little idea where they were, but not because they couldn't read German. Rather, the names of the stations had been removed. At one station, the SS kicked to the ground the food and water civilians tried pushing through the slats of the befouled cattle cars. In Private Danny MacDonald's legs, the bacteria that had seeped into the wounds caused by machine-gun bullets bred uncontrollably, producing copious amounts of foul-smelling puss. "Churchill's Second Front" completed its journey when it reached the railway siding on the road that led to the prison camp near Lamsdorf, in far eastern Germany.

As the gaunt, exhausted, famished and desperately thirsty men climbed down from the train and, as gently as they could, took their wounded comrades down on stretchers, they noticed the beautiful day and the thousands of plump cherries hanging from the trees, within easy reach on either side of the road. The guards barked that they'd shoot any man who touched one.

Unbeknownst to the Germans, as they arranged the POWs in four columns for the march to the camp a mile away, Regimental Sergeant Major Harry Beesley, the senior officer present, prepared a bit of theatre that signalled the Canadians' implacable resistance. Given what they'd been through on the beaches of Dieppe, at Verneulles and on the train, Ron Beal and the others could hardly believe Beesley when he said, "You've had it pretty good. You've had one action. You're prisoners of war now [but] there are men in that camp that have been prisoners for two and a half to three years who were taken at Dunkirk, some in North Africa, some in Crete, some in Greece . . . their spirits are broken. We've got to show them that there is still a British army and an Allied force."

To the guards' dismay, the men, many of whom were so stiff and weak when they climbed off the train that they stumbled around like drunkards, formed up and began marching as if on parade. The NCOs lifted their heads and swung their arms. Barefoot or not, and irrespective of the condition of their uniforms or whether they even still wore one, the men marched in step. Not even the sight of a cemetery in which they saw maple leaves etched into grave stones, indicating that Canadians had died in that very prison camp during the First World War, broke their march. As they neared the gates, the British POWs, who looked relatively healthy, responded with cheers and shouted, "Good old Canada!"[76]

After days without food, the Canadians expected to be fed when they were stopped between the camp's inner and outer wire. Paperwork, however, took precedence and, instead, each man was photographed, fingerprinted and given a disk with his *Kriegsgefangenennummer* (POW number) stamped into it: "Mine was *zwei, fünf, zwei, drei, acht*—25238," recalls Darch. So many men answered the question about their occupation the same way that one German officer was heard saying, "My, they have an awful lot of farmers in Canada."[77]

Although the Canadians had been expected for at least a week and the camp was already feeding thousands of POWs, no excuse was offered by the Germans for failing to fulfill the Geneva requirement to feed POWs the same rations as garrison troops. Accordingly, the men saw the German failure to feed them as psychological warfare designed to break their spirit. Indeed, even when they were finally given food—which, they later found out, came not from the camp larder but from the British POWs who gave up their daily ration of watery cabbage soup—the Germans ensured that the very act of eating underlined the POWs' subservient status. Instead of handing them cups and spoons, the Canadians were allowed to go to a garbage pit to retrieve dirty cans. Poolton ate the putrid soup from his boot.

29 AUGUST 1942, SAINT-AMAND-MONTROND, VICHY FRANCE

VANIER, LAFLEUR AND JOLY ESCAPE TO ENGLAND

Their papers were good, but the gendarmes in the small town in the south of France where Lafleur, Joly and Vanier got off the train were better.

Had Lafleur and Joly (Vanier, still troubled by a wound, remained in the train station) known that the small town's most famous resident was Maurice Papon, who since July had been responsible for deporting Jews from Vichy and seizing their property, the two Canadian soldiers might have gone through with their plan to overpower the gendarmes who stopped them on the street and make a run for it. Instead, after diplomatically bringing up Dieppe and seeing the gendarmes' favourable response, Lafleur and Joly told the gendarmes who they were.

To their relief, the gendarmes said that the police commissioner would be sympathetic. Aware that the Deuxième Bureau regularly tested local officials' rectitude, the commissioner carefully questioned the three Canadians (Vanier having been picked up) before loading them into his car and driving them to the home of a wealthy American, who hid them until MI9 spirited them to safety via Marseilles and then Toulouse, eventually taking them to Perpignan, where the Royal Navy picked them up.

EARLY SEPTEMBER 1942, STALAG VIII-B, LAMSDORF, GERMANY

THE CANADIANS LEARN THE KRIEGIE LIFE

"After five days in a cattle car, even barracks seemed almost human—at least there was place to lie down and sleep," recalls Darch, who occupied the middle of a three-tier bunk bed on the right side of the almost 200-foot-long clapboard building. "When you walked in to it from each end, there was an area where there were two tables that sat about eight men, a washstand and a stove. It was still warm in September, so we did not notice that this stove would provide precious little heat when the winter winds began to blow. There were three sets of bunks down the length of the hall. Twelve men to a section, bunks around a central post . . . six on one side and six on the other. The paillasses were infested with lice and bedbugs, and so were we."

The men washed in the barracks. "We had soap," says Darch, "but it was hard and full of pumice. It allowed us to clean our hand and faces and take a sponge bath, which, at least for a short time, did something about the lice. [But] the cold water and hard soup were no match for the lice in the seams of our uniforms. Nor could the cold water and foamless soap clean the blood stains off our uniforms." Each man's uniform was a memento mori of sorts, a symbol of their defeat.

Few Canadians spoke German, but it didn't take them long to learn the essential words. Each day started with a guard slamming open the barracks' door and yelling, "*Raus! Raus!*" meaning "Get up and out of the barracks!" Rain or shine, at 8 a.m. and again at 5 p.m., the Kriegies made their way to the camp's *Appellplatz*, where they were counted. Like Poolton and Beal, Darch still wore his uniform. "Others didn't. They came off the beach with nothing." Although the men did not know the extent of Germany's requisitions of the countries it had conquered, the well-kept German towns they had seen through the slats of the cattle car told them something of Germany's resources. They were therefore surprised—and enraged—that the Germans left the men without clean clothes until Red Cross supplies arrived some weeks later.

The stench of the 40-holer that served 1,500 men was overwhelming. "From time to time a horse-drawn wagon—the 'Honey Wagon'—came to pump out the latrine, which made shit go down but did nothing about the population of rats. Seeing their eyes peering up at you before you sat down to do your business gave you added incentive to be quick about it," recalls Darch.

Of even greater concern were the rations. They came near noon, but there was never enough to fill the POWs' stomachs. A pint or so of cabbage soup that was supposed to contain their meat ration almost never did, unless worms and bugs counted. "Dividing the solid food was more complicated. Groups of ten men were given a bunch of potatoes, which were boiled with skins on. Then they were placed in rows according to size, and then we drew cards to see which you got," says Darch. A group of ten divided into two groups of five for the division of the hard loaf of sour black bread, which was often covered in green mould. "Cutting the loaf was a ritual each of us watched eagerly," recalls Darch. "Every crumb mattered." Each man was supposed to receive 350 grams, or just over 12 ounces. "Normally, this worked out to six pieces for each of us 'muckers'—'muckers' was the name for the men in a food group. Two for lunch, two for dinner, and you had to save two for breakfast, which, if you were lucky, you smeared with some ersatz jam. If you didn't save your pieces for breakfast, you went hungry." They would have starved were it not for the Red Cross parcels that started arriving in early October. John Grogan and three other members of the Royal Regiment shared two parcels twice a week.

6 SEPTEMBER 1942, HÔPITAL DE LA SALPÊTRIÈRE, PARIS

CAPTAIN JOHN RUNCIE'S HOME RUN BEGINS

For the last four days, he'd had it pretty good.

Before that, he'd been at Verneulles. Then, with the connivance of Canadian medical officers, Captain John Runcie convinced a German medical officer that he was suffering from acute appendicitis and that he should be sent to Paris for an X-ray. Perhaps because the staff at the Hôpital de la Salpêtrière were French, they placed him in a private room, the ward on the other side of the wall being filled with Germans wounded on the Russian Front. Runcie was a decent actor, for while the X-ray showed nothing, the German doctor prescribed a special diet and a few more days' hospital rest, days the Canadian put to good use.

Just over two weeks earlier he'd put his faith in machine guns, mortars, radios, 6-inch naval guns, fighter planes and the other accoutrements of modern warfare. Now, late on the night of 5 September, he put his faith in 17th-century aesthetics, specifically, the French window (that opened outward like two doors) and the low wall that enclosed the grounds of the hospital designed by one of Louis XIV's favourite architects. The window opened, and the healthy Runcie quickly climbed the rain-slickened stone wall. He found the Resistance fighter who'd promised to be there waiting in the shadows of a nearby church, holding civilian clothes and shoes for the pyjama-clad, barefoot army officer. Because of the curfew, he had about an hour to get Runcie to a safe house.

Unlike Dumais, Lafleur and the other fusiliers on home runs, the English-speaking Runcie had to be even more careful about being overheard. Still, for the ten days that he stayed with a family in Montmartre, accompanied by the man who had met him by the church, Runcie "moved freely about Paris during the daytime, mingling with parties of German sightseers in the streets and entering cafés and places of entertainment."

Runcie does not say and likely did not know how his hosts procured the food they gave him, or the ration tickets needed in restaurants. Given the limited official rations available, it's almost certain that his allotment came from the flourishing black market. A month earlier, the police officials prosecuted 42 cases of trading on *le marché noir*, a phrase that appeared for the first time in the Larousse dictionary published that year.

15 SEPTEMBER 1942, NEAR THE DEMARCATION LINE

BROWNE'S AND MASSON'S HOME RUN FAIL

Led by a 12-year-old boy carrying a fishing rod, Browne and Masson neared the Allier River, on the other side of which lay Vichy France. Stuffed in Masson's pockets were forged demobilization papers and an identity card with a believable photograph that stated he was Alsatian, which, he and Browne hoped, would explain Masson's accent. Browne also carried demobilization papers; to explain why he didn't speak, he was listed as being deaf.

The presence of German guards forced Masson's party to walk further down the river than originally planned. After fording it, they found a taxi that took them to the town of Sancoins. The two Canadians and their young guide were shocked when the taxi driver stopped at the police station and told them that because he picked them up so close to the Demarcation Line, they had to report to the police.

It took only a moment for the gendarme who interviewed Masson to know that he was not an Alsatian, for he was, and Masson couldn't understand a word of his. Masson countered the accusation that he was a Polish Jew by saying he was from Toulouse and was travelling alone to visit his sick mother. The suspicious official then called in Browne, who played deaf while the official accused him of having a false photo on his identity card, which was ironic, since it was the one true part of their cover story.

With their stories in tatters, Masson went for broke and told the official they were Canadian officers and promised that if they were let through, 100,000 francs would be forwarded to him as soon as they reached England. The officer's demeanour changed and after telephoning his superior indicated that he would help them. Keeping most of their money and papers in his possession, the official ordered another policeman to take them to a hotel.

The boy smelled a rat and, once they were alone in the hotel, persuaded the Canadians to take advantage of the cover of night to push on, by foot, toward Saint-Amand-Montrond. Assuming that the police were now looking for them, every time they heard a car, all three dove into the nearest ditch. Toward morning, near the village of Saint-Pierre-les-Étieux, the poor condition of Browne's feet (he had been walking barefoot for days because the shoes given to him in Paris were too small) forced them to board a gasoline trolley, only to find themselves face to face with the policeman who had taken them to the hotel.

According to Browne, the policeman told them that by running away from the hotel they "had complicated things" and must now be kept out of sight until arrangements could be made for them to continue their journey. Masson recalled a more frightening moment: the flashing of a revolver and the policeman saying "he would handle the whole thing unofficially."

For the next few days, they believed this promise. True, they were in a cell in the gendarmerie in Châteauroux. However, the men there who claimed to be Deuxième Bureau agents were friendly, as were the guards who brought them their food. And, always a hopeful sign, cigarettes were plentiful. They assumed that their handcuffing before going to the train station was part of an agitprop drama designed to pre-empt questions from any official they might meet along the way, an assumption seemingly confirmed when they were on the train. Even having to spend the night of 14 September in a cell in the gendarmerie in Lyons did not alarm them, for again they were very well-treated, and timing their disappearance, they knew, was a delicate operation.

Their hopes were dashed the next morning when the truck they'd been hustled onto stopped at the forbidding Fort de la Duchère.

FALL 1942, STALAG VIII-B, LAMSDORF, GERMANY

THE IMPORTANCE OF CRIBBAGE

Pictures of poorly shaven, dishevelled soldiers playing cards while smoking an endless number of cigarettes paint a decidedly unmartial portrait of POWs, who, though ever more hungry, remained, after recovering from the shock of defeat and the Germans' treatment of them, fit men in their prime. In the years to come, a number of men would experience depression or, as they called it, fall victim to "wire happiness," the most obvious sign of which was a vacant stare. The greatest enemy was boredom. To fight it, hundreds bashed the circuit—that is, walked endless times around the inside perimeter of the barbed-wire fence, which both kept them in shape and familiarized them with the camp's layout and security, as well as with areas beyond the camp—essential information for a successful escape.

Games like bridge and, for Darch, cribbage, were vital ways to keep their spirits up and their competitive instincts honed. And the games did more than simply take up time, as important as that was. In a world where they were powerless, where a guard nicknamed "Ukrainian Joe" sadistically bullied and physically pushed around men who could not respond, card games and cribbage reminded the Kriegies that, elsewhere, rules governed everyone equally. The games provided and transported players from the drab surroundings of the prison camp to a place that all knew from before the war. "You forgot you were in a miserable hut in Germany when you were playing; you had to concentrate on the cards and think about strategy," explains Darch, who found that, as did writing and receiving letters, cribbage took him out of the prison camp.

Chapter Five

October–December 1942

"Anyone stepping over this trip-wire will be shot"

—Sign in POW camps

4 OCTOBER 1942, MILAG NORD, NEAR BREMEN, GERMANY

Father Louis Larivière Uses Special Wartime Priestly Powers

On 4 October, Father Larivière did something not covered in any of the theology or canon law courses he took while studying to become a priest. So that the celebrants at the second (5 p.m.) mass he conducted could have communion, which he was required to have with them, he made recourse to the special powers Pope Pius XII had given priests in war zones. Larivière gave himself special dispensation from the rule of Eucharist Fasting, a rule that no longer exists. The rule that communicants must fast for five or six hours before consuming the Eucharist was meant to ensure that the body and blood of Christ would not be mixed with ordure or urine.

The Protestant padres required only Bibles when preaching to or comforting the men; the Anglicans, The Book of Common Prayer; but Catholic priests required more than their missals, Hosts and communion wine. Presumably the German censors, who earlier in the year pondered letters asking for titles such as *Apologia Pro Vita Sua*, were relieved to find in a June letter a less technical list: New Testaments and hymnals; catechisms; and pamphlets on the Church, the sacraments and mass, social questions and married life.[78]

Larivière likely referred to this last in early October. For though the details are lost, he had to deal with the morale-crushing receipt of one or more "Dear John" letters. "There is nothing more demoralizing for a soldier, especially if he is a prisoner, than the infidelity of the other," he wrote to Monsignor Joseph Bonhomme. "I hope that young Canadian wives are made to realize how odious this injustice is toward a conscript."[79]

EARLY OCTOBER 1942, MARSEILLES, VICHY FRANCE

DUMAIS SEEKS HELP FROM THE AMERICAN CHARGÉ D'AFFAIRES

He expected a warmer welcome from his fellow North American.

A day earlier, just before Dumais left for the station where he was to take the train to Marseilles, the hotelier who risked his life hiding him grasped, then dropped, the Canadian's hand before hugging and kissing the foreigner who had come to fight for France's liberty. Now, having just explained to the American consul in Marseilles who he was and that the two Free French soldiers with him wanted to escape to fight under General Charles de Gaulle, Dumais stood dumbfounded as the consul said, "The United States is a neutral country. . . . There's nothing I can do for you."[80] Although the United States had been at war for almost a year, it maintained diplomatic relations with Vichy France, as did Canada.

A short while later, believing that they were the reason he'd been given the cold shoulder, Dumais's companions persuaded him to try again, this time alone. The consul saw Dumais as soon as he entered the consulate but didn't have time to speak before Dumais said, "You're American and I'm Canadian. Does that frontier really make so much difference?"[81] Set back on his heels, the consul asked, "Where are your French friends?" Dumais told him that he'd left them in a café. Legally this changed nothing, but it changed everything. "Go to this address. There you will find a doctor. Tell him you have a sore throat and a sore right foot. Go at once, and don't tell your friends. Good-bye and good luck."

8 OCTOBER 1942, STALAG VIII-B, LAMSDORF, GERMANY

The Dieppe Survivors Are Shackled

The ripping sound of the Schmeisser submachine-gun bolts being pulled back seemed but the stuff of another post-Dieppe nightmare. Then, through the pre-dawn darkness, came Sergeant Major Beesley's call: "Everybody up!" Just a few moments later, the guttural "*Raus! Raus!*" of armed guards as they slammed doors open could be heard.[82] In Grogan's hut, the goon nicknamed "Dog Man" led five Doberman pinschers, while another guard walked down the aisle with his rifle's bayonet ominously locked in place.

As the Canadians were marched to the furthest end of Stalag VIII-B, the thought that they had survived the beaches of Dieppe only to be massacred on a field in the middle of a cool German night seemed too horrible to be true, but nothing else seemed to make sense.

Once assembled beyond the barracks, instead of the staccato sound of gunfire drowning out the thud of bullets hitting human flesh, the Canadians heard an interpreter read in halting English a statement that caused equal measures of bewilderment and derision: "The German Government has always shown the utmost clemency to prisoners of war and accorded them the treatment due honourable men captured in battle."

The machine guns would not be silent much longer, the Canadians feared, when they heard that both at Dieppe and during a later raid on a Channel island, German soldiers had been found shot with their hands tied behind their backs and that, since the British government refused to provide assurance that such inhumane treatment would not be repeated, Germany had "no alternative but to take reprisals against all the members of the Dieppe Force!"[83]

The Canadians knew nothing, of course, about the raid on the island of Sark on 3 October. Some may have known that when the commander of the Royal Hamilton Light Infantry, Lieutenant Colonel Robert Labatt, had asked Major General Hamilton Roberts, the commander of Operation Jubilee, what to do about prisoners who could not be taken back to England, Roberts is reputed to have reminded his men that they carried revolvers. Roberts's orders were that prisoners were to be kept in pens if captured before being loaded onto landing craft so they could be taken to England and interrogated. Morever, he also ordered that this written order not be taken ashore. But Brigadier William Southam had brought a written copy ashore, and the Germans had found it. Ron Beal heard one German say that the Canadians were going to be treated like pigs because on the beaches of Dieppe they had taken German POWs to a "Schweinerstall," a tendentious translation of "pig pen."

In any event, what mattered now were the machine guns, the curious sight of the guards standing in front of them holding two-and-a-half-foot-long strands of rope and the order for ten men to step forward. Determined to show the Germans that the Canadians were better soldiers than they were, Beesley called out "Marker" and Remi Leroux stepped forward.[84] The Germans took no chances and marched Leroux and the nine men who followed him into a building at bayonet point. Once inside, each was ordered to cross his arms in front so hands could be tied together.

Over the next few hours, as groups of men were marched away so that their hands could be tied, the Dominion soldiers quickly found ways to mock the Germans. Some laughingly compared the punishment to childhood games of cowboys and Indians. Others had comrades untie them so they could get back in line, to be tied up all over again.

After the last Canadian hands at Lamsdorf had been tied, the officer leading the operation again spoke through the interpreter.

As part of the reprisal, the Canadians were forbidden both from leaving their barracks during the day, except to go to the latrine, and from lying down on their bunks during the day. The cutting off of their Red Cross parcels violated Geneva and, more importantly, threw the Canadians back onto the inadequate German rations. Sentries at Lamsdorf were ordered to shoot anyone outside the barracks who was not in a group of ten tied or shackled men accompanied by a "sanitator," a medical orderly identified by a white arm band, whose hands were not tied because they were needed to help the shocked men use the latrine. As well, the attack guard dogs that normally patrolled the outside perimeter of the camp at night would now patrol inside the compound during the day.

Shackling struck at the heart of their honour as soldiers. According to the laws of war, POWs are not criminals. Rather, they are prisoners because they belong to a military enemy; they are incarcerated because of international politics, that is, because Canada was at war with Nazi Germany and each of them represented Canada. Even more than the difficulties shackling caused for eating or drinking, shackling was a symbolic attack, making men who had voluntarily signed their attestation papers that made them soldiers in King George's Canadian Army appear like men on a chain gang and thus as unfree men *tout court*.

The men were deeply humiliated by the indelicacy of the latrine arrangements. Being unable to unbutton their own trousers meant that several times a day another man had to perform this intimate act. "Worse, both for the 'sanitator' and us, was the need to clean us. We did not have toilet paper. Instead, he had to use pages ripped from a softcover pocket book. Before using it, he had to rumple it up and then, of course, clean us in the most degrading manner. And each of us had to stand there while he did this to nine other men," recalls Darch, who more than seven decades later still cringes at the memory.

MID-OCTOBER 1942

Dumais Reaches "The Rock"

The cut to half a biscuit and half a cup of water a day was not unexpected after Gibraltar signalled it could not spare a ship to meet the trawler that had picked up Dumais and 64 other men from a beach near Canet-Plage, a small village on the Mediterranean Sea. As he sweated under the hot sun while his thirst mounted and stomach growled, Dumais could not help but think of the few days he'd spent at the doctor's in Marseilles, where he became a "parcel" in the care of Patrick Albert O'Leary, the *nom de guerre* of Albert-Marie Guérisse.

There he'd had his first bath in weeks, slept between starched sheets, been given clean clothes and, before the doctor even came home, had afternoon tea with his wife. During the days he stayed in his room reading, spending the evenings talking with his hosts.

Had Dumais known that O'Leary, who after escaping at Dunkirk returned to France to run an escape line, had said he was a Canadian airman to explain his accent, the real Canadian would have understood why O'Leary confirmed Dumais's identity by quizzing him on obscure details about Quebec and Montreal. A few days later, Dumais was surprised when O'Leary led him into a train compartment filled with rough-looking men—and flabbergasted when he started speaking in English to the men, who were also on home runs.

At Canet-Plage, O'Leary placed the French-speaking Dumais in a hotel and the others in a three-room cottage. Four nights later, at 1 a.m., O'Leary led them single file down to the beach, where they waited, scanning the sea, not for a light but for a dark spot that would grow larger as the boat moved closer. After hours of shivering in the darkness, as the first hint of light appeared on the horizon, O'Leary led them back to the cottage. The next night was equally disappointing, as was the next after that. MI9's standard operating procedure could be summed up in baseball lingo: "Three strikes and you're out." O'Leary's radioman, however, convinced London to try again. Late that night, unsure whether he'd really seen a patch of blackness in the darkness, Dumais shut his eyes for several seconds. When he opened them, "the dark spot was still there and was definitely bigger."[85]

Bigger, but not big. Instead of boats like the landing craft that took the Fusiliers de Mont-Royal onto the beaches at Dieppe or like the more than 30-foot-long voyageur canoes that could hold three tons of cargo and 12 men, Dumais saw a couple of dinghies. Concerned about the stability of a dinghy designed for two holding eight standing men, Dumais "gingerly bent down to hold onto the side" of the small craft, only to find about an inch of freeboard.

A few days earlier, Dumais had imagined an escape involving a Royal Navy destroyer whisking him to Gibraltar at 30 knots. Reality was much more prosaic: the dinghies took them to a small trawler, crewed by ex-pat Poles, capable of making only six knots. The heat could be alleviated by a swim, but nothing could be done about the cut in rations, which, when some men were caught queuing up for seconds, the captain enforced with the threat of throwing the miscreants into the sea.

Since the trawler had to look like a working fishing boat, whenever a boat and aircraft came near, Dumais and the others had to scramble under upturned lifeboats or reeking fishing nets. One night, woken abruptly by the sound of shells straddling the trawler, Dumais ran for his lifeboat station and heard from the dark sea a voice calling out through a loud-hailer, "What ship are you?" Since the men knew that the British gunners had their range, each moment seemed endless, until the captain called out the name of his boat. Dumais had speculated about the ship's allegiance but never imagined that "the smelly old trawler" belonged to the Royal Navy.[86]

19 OCTOBER 1942, STALAG LUFT III, SAGAN, POLAND

Father Goudreau Asks for Something from Home

Although his days were filled with ministering to some 500 men or reading philosophy and theology, time and separation from his confrères wore heavily on Father Goudreau. Letters helped, though the seemingly random sequence in which some arrived made logical exchange difficult. Back in August, he tried to put his best face forward when he told Father Gilles Mousseau that just seeing his "patriarchal beard" in the photo he'd enclosed in a letter made him smile. But the strain soon broke through as Goudreau echoed the psalmist, writing, "Thus, the days pass. . . . but the months are long. When will our sacrifice end?" In September, an exchange with Father Terragon, in which Goudreau urged his friend to start editing the book he was writing as soon as he could, even though "university presses take such a long time" to publish, took Goudreau beyond the barbed wire.

Just how much life behind the barbed wire influenced Goudreau is evident in a mid-October letter to his sister. "You would not believe the happiness that flashes in our eyes with the receipt of a letter," he writes before going on to a simile that owes less to Matthew 5:14 ("You are the light of the world") than it does to what he'd heard from hundreds of downed airmen: "It is like a jet of burning crude oil."

At the end of the letter, Goudreau turns to a more banal concern. Since he doubts that the latest fix of his watch's main spring will last, he asks that his brother-in-law contact the Tacy Watch Company for a replacement spring. For without the watch, time moved even more slowly.

EARLY NOVEMBER 1942, STALAG VIII-B, LAMSDORF, GERMANY

Hungry Canadians Watch Helplessly as Russian POWs Die

As colder weather set in, morale plummeted.

The Canadian prisoners had not yet received any mail, neither had their families. Indeed many, including Darch's, did not know if their loved ones were alive. Family lore says that when Darch's mother learned he was a POW, she fainted.

With their hands tied, everyday tasks became impromptu ballets for the POWs. Rolling a cigarette required three men: one each to hold the paper, pour the tobacco and provide a wet tongue against which to rub the gummed side of the rolling paper.

Neither the daily rations nor the twice-weekly restaurant-sized pat of margarine or one-ounce slice of stinking fish or cheese filled stomachs, though they did cause hundreds of cases of dysentery, which both the men and the sanitator faced with admirable stoicism. Sometimes the meat in the soup was easily identified by the rat's skeleton found in the broth. Yet despite their hunger, the Canadians would stand by the fence that divided their compound from the Russians' and throw their emaciated allies what food they could.

Nothing the Canadians could do, however, could stem the typhus epidemic that killed hundreds of Russians. Every morning, human skeletons, barely able to walk themselves, somehow summoned up the strength to carry dead comrades on anything that would serve as a stretcher out of the camp. The soldiers, universally known as Ivans, took step after exhausting step until, without a word from a minister let alone the traditional volley for a soldier, they dumped their comrades, not yet stiff from rigor mortis, into an open pit.

MID-NOVEMBER 1942, ARBEITSKOMMANDO 1049, NIEDERORSCHEL, GERMANY

Provost Marshal A. Robert Prouse Learns to Cut Wood

The doctor in Rouen told Private Robert Prouse that even though his legs were numb, he must keep them moving, so he spent hours sweeping the floor and bringing food to those more badly wounded than he was. One day, he graduated to being an "anaesthetist"—one of four who held a patient down while a German doctor operated without the aid of anaesthesia. In early September, he was among those shipped to the hospital at Stalag IX-C, 150 miles southwest of Berlin, arriving just in time for the typhus epidemic.

In an effort to staunch the outbreak of diseases carried by lice and fleas, the POWs were shaved from head to toe; Prouse never forgot the moment that a German orderly held his penis in one hand and with a straight razor swiped away his pubic hair. Mercifully, the doctor at the nearby hospital used anaesthesia when he operated on Prouse's infected calf. The hospital staff were less fastidiousness about the ward's toilet, "a filthy mess, with the floor, walls and seat completely soiled."[87]

Prouse arrived at the POW camp to find his comrades' hands tied with cord used to bind Red Cross parcels. The camp authorities knew he was Canadian but ignored this, and the fact that, since he was an NCO, he could not be made to work. Assuming that because he was a Canadian he was also a lumberjack, Prouse was assigned to Arbeitskommando 1049, a plywood factory. For piling and cutting logs with a power saw (something he'd never seen before) and later as a carpenter's helper, reichsmarks were credited to his account, which he could have spent at the camp's canteen had there been one.

While camp authorities could and did issue orders directly to POWs, most of the time orders were transmitted through a chain of command, at the top of which was the camp's Man of Confidence, who was either elected by the POWs or chosen by the senior officer to liaise with the Kommandant or the Senior British Officer. At the work camp, the factory's manager and effectively its Kommandant had been well-treated during his stint as a POW in England during the last war and was amenable to the Man of Confidence's requests for wood and other supplies to winterize the drafty bunkhouse.

POWs, however, have their own code of honour. Thus, as they lined their bunkhouse's walls, ceiling and floor, they built in secret trapdoors, providing secret storage spaces. The Germans knew Prouse built a small suitcase but not that it had a secret bottom. Not until a stool pigeon inserted into the barracks reported it did the Germans know that bunkhouse boards were being used to shore up an escape tunnel.

22 NOVEMBER 1942, ON THE ROADS OF FRANCE

John Runcie Escapes

After a few nights of dodging patrols and skirting roadblocks, Runcie decided to risk travelling by day. On the roads from Paris through Fontainebleau to Orléans, Blois, Tours and beyond, he found to his surprise bridges and other natural places for road-blocks unguarded. His beret and heavily accented French provided enough cover for two German truck drivers to each give the "Basque worker" a lift. The French were not fooled but were willing to help, though some farms were so stripped of food that all the farmer could offer was his barn to sleep in.

Some 500 miles from Paris, the very terrain of France seemed to turn against the escaper. In the forest of Landes, between Bordeaux and Bayonne, he could find neither people to help him nor shelter from the cold of night. Though hunger made him light-headed, he knew he could go weeks without eating. Water, however, was vital, and as his thirst worsened, he looked desperately for any sign of water where once the ground was so wet peasants used stilts to get around. But the French hydrologists and agronomists who designed the man-made pine barrens did their job well, and as each breath expelled more water, Runcie's thirst gave way to dry mouth, headaches and exhaustion.

Runcie's report does not say where he found water. But he did, for he made it through the forest and into Biarritz, where a friendly waiter sketched out the map of the French-Spanish frontier, which he crossed on 22 November. The intelligence officer who briefed Runcie after he arrived in Britain wrote how impressed he was with Runcie's solo home run.

2 DECEMBER 1942, STALAG VIII-B, LAMSDORF, GERMANY

The Importance of Sardine-Can Keys

The Canadians at Stalag VIII-B did not know that, after he had been "selected for 'escape'" by a pliable Vichy official in Fort de la Duchère, Captain Masson had reached freedom in Spain. Nor did they know of the public debate that exploded after word of their shackling reached Canada. After a few days of calls to shackle the 16,000 German POWs in Canada, cooler heads prevailed, with the *Globe and Mail* ultimately declaring on 14 October, "Let us not . . . embark upon a contest which we cannot hope to win." Still less did the Canadians POWs know of the toing and froing between Ottawa and the Dominion Office in London, of Churchill's direct appeal to Mackenzie King to approve shackling German POWs or of the riot that ensued when Canadian guards tied to shackle U-boat men in Bowmanville, Ontario.[88]

What they did know was that the guards in front of them were carrying handcuffs to replace the rope that had been used to tie their hands. Though heavier, the handcuffs were somewhat more comfortable than the ropes, though many found the stamp "Made in Birmingham, England" rudely ironic.

Just before Appell, the cry "Chains Up!" would ring out and

the men would line up, a guard putting the handcuffs on them. They did not, however, stay on long. For the men realized that the key that opened a Klim (powdered milk) or sardine can did the same for the handcuffs, which meant that the cuffs could be surreptitiously taken off when in the barracks.

One day, the men in Jack Poolton's barracks used their ability to open the handcuffs to get back at their Blockführer, the hated "Spitfire" who once kicked a pot of water Poolton was boiling for tea over onto a prisoner, scalding him. After being shackled, each man would unlock the cuffs, place them back in their box, go to the back of the line, and then appear again in front of Spitfire for cuffing. After some four hours, a not-too-happy officer arrived and asked what Spitfire had been doing. His sputtered answer, "Chaining up the prisoners," amused the Canadians but not Spitfire's superior officer. Another time, Spitfire saw a man washing himself outside the barracks unchained and naked. "How did this man remove his clothing?" the hapless guard demanded. "He's a magician," someone called out.[89]

Spitfire, however, got his revenge. The penalty if caught without your hands cuffed was having them cuffed behind your back and being made to stand with your nose and toes against an outside wall for eight hours, no matter what the weather. "If you moved," says Darch, "you got a rifle butt in the back."

7 DECEMBER 1942, NEAR L'ALBENC, VICHY FRANCE

George Browne Wonders Whom He Can Trust

Fifteen days in solitary confinement after an unsuccessful attempt to break out of Fort de la Duchère did little to dull George Browne's ardour to escape.

He had Operation Torch to thank for the fact that the guards on the buses taking him and the other internees to Grenoble were

Italian and not French; in response to the Allied invasion of North Africa, Germany occupied Vichy, though Hitler allowed Mussolini to grab a piece of southeast France. The guards may have been insensitive to the POWs' bladders, but they couldn't ignore the need to fill the buses' radiators and so stopped on a bridge in a village about 40 miles northwest of Grenoble to do so. To provide light, the drivers arranged the buses in a semicircle, which gave Browne his chance to slip out the back door of his bus.

A guard noticed something, for just moments after Browne bolted into a nearby street, he heard yelling and saw flashlights. The street turned out to be a cul-de-sac, and upon reaching the dead end, Browne turned right. After jumping two fences, he reached the river, which he ran through for about 30 yards before climbing back onto the same side of the bank he'd started from, then hid in a row of hops. Twice, flashlight beams shone mere inches away. When the searchers moved on, he crossed the river and went through some parkland to the main road so that he was now behind the convoy.

Browne was by no means the only man on the roads of southern France. But demobilized Vichy soldiers and even tramp workers had papers; Browne didn't. And they weren't wearing RAF battle dress under their civilian clothes, which he was. Nor did they speak French with an English accent. Browne could do nothing about this last, but with some help, he might cover the other two bases.

Had he known that the man who would answer the door was the engineer of the local power station, Browne might have sought help elsewhere. Despite being a civil servant, the engineer accepted Browne's battle dress in exchange for food and a much-needed pair of dry socks before sending him off with explicit directions on how to pass checkpoints on his way to Sassenge, where he could expect to find sympathetic railwaymen.

In the darkness, Browne erred by staying to the right at a fork in the road and near dawn found himself near the village of l'Albenc, once again not knowing whom he could trust.

10 DECEMBER 1942, PARIS

RCAF Pilot Officer Sydney Smith Hides among German Uniforms

The farmer's dog sniffed around the haystack Sydney Smith had burrowed into around at 5 a.m., after parachuting from his Vickers Wellington bomber. The farmer looked kind, but Smith decided to wait before revealing himself. By dusk, thirst and hunger forced his hand, and when the farmer again came close to the haystack, Smith slid down from the top. The unexpected appearance of a man in flying dress stunned the farmer, but he quickly recovered, asking, "*Anglais?* RAF?"[90] before taking Smith's arm and walking him briskly to his house, where he was fed and given a clean bed.

The next day, 11 December, the farmer took him to Madame Brunel de Serbonnes's house. A few hours later, as the aroma of what de Serbonnes called "habbet stew" filled the ornate house, a doctor working for the Resistance arrived bearing news that the police had captured three of Smith's crewmates. The doctor decided Smith would be safer in Paris, where he could be hidden by de Serbonnes's daughter, Catherine Janot.

Smith, whose idea of excitement when he was growing up was going to Sudbury for a movie and a lunch at Woolworths, was smitten by the radiant Parisian blonde with an aquiline nose and smouldering eyes who arrived the next day. Janot's accented English as she repeated his name, "Sydney Percival Smith," enchanted him.

The next day, after dropping into the river his watch, the metal buttons from his uniform (which had been burned) and anything else that would tell the Germans that a Canadian airman had been near the village 20 miles southwest of Paris, Janot and he boarded a train for the city. During the 45-minute ride, he ached to ask why she was ignoring the sign that stated women who helped downed Allied airmen would be sent to concentration camps in Germany. Later, he learned that Janot's husband had suffered the fate she was determined to keep Smith from: being a prisoner in Germany.

In Janot's apartment, Smith found himself, as if in a dream, looking out the window at the Seine, the Eiffel Tower and the rest of Paris, defaced as it was by the huge swastikas. At about the same time that the RCAF casualties officer in Ottawa sent a telegram telling Smith's family that he was missing, Janot got Smith past a row of Waffen-SS troops by the simple expedient of walking haughtily, as if she were reviewing the troops. Later he joined Janot, who played her cover as an *haute bourgeoise* to the hilt, at a performance of *Macbeth* in French, in an audience studded with German officers in dress uniform.

16–22 DECEMBER 1942, IN THE PYRENEES

BROWNE ENTRUSTS HIMSELF TO SMUGGLERS

A century earlier, escaped slaves knew to "follow the drinking gourd," for the Big Dipper pointed to the North Star and freedom in Upper Canada. For Browne, who was freezing while walking above Pic de Peyrot's snow line of 8,500 feet, on the French-Spanish border, seeing Polaris in front of him beckoned disaster. He had taken a wrong turn and was heading north, away from Spain.

Five days earlier, after missing the turn to Sassenge, he'd been lucky. The farm family he gambled on fed him, gave him a bed and put him in contact with a Gaullist, who took him to Grenoble, where he was given money, an identity card and a train ticket to Toulouse. Through six more towns and villages, one person after another helped him. The man on the road to Auzat warned Browne that the village he planned to stop in before making his way into the Pyrenees was full of Germans and suggested another, where a farmer fed him and urged him to find a guide to lead him over the mountains. Browne didn't miss his watch or the 3,000 francs he paid the three young men he met on the road to Goulier-et-Olbier to lead him to the top of the mountain. As the sub-zero wind whisked away precious body heat, Browne regretted having paid his guide with his extra set of clothes.

By the light of the quarter moon, he saw a half-constructed dam and a deserted hut. His boots soaking by this time, he entered the hut. But since neither the building waste he crawled under nor the little bit of dry and cold bread he ate could break what he recognized to be a dangerous shivering, Browne soon left the hut. A few minutes later he saw another cabin, its lights signalling both the promise of not freezing to death and the threat of being captured.

The benumbed Canadian didn't feel the sting of knocking on the door. Through chattering teeth, he told the engineers who opened it that he was an escaped POW, and with blue fingers took out his fake identity card. Recognizing his desperate state, they gave Browne food and hot red wine, then covered him with blankets.

The next morning, the engineers placed Browne's life in the hands of smugglers who carried contraband wireless sets to a village about two miles from the border of the postage stamp–sized principality of Andorra. A few days later, a second group of smugglers took him from the neutral principality's capital, Andorra la Vella, to the village of Martinet, five miles north of the Spanish border, from where he contacted the British consul in Barcelona. The consul arranged for Browne's transport to Madrid and thence to Gibraltar; Browne reached London on 26 January 1943.

20–22 DECEMBER 1942, ON FRENCH TRAINS

Smith Reaches Bordeaux

As he boarded the train from Paris to Bordeaux, accompanied by the pretty Janine De Greef and Tante Dédée, the *nom de guerre* of Andrée de Jongh, co-organizer of the famed *Comet Line*, Smith could not help but note the irony of an officer and a gentleman putting his life in the hands of women between 18 and 25. Yet despite numerous warnings from German officers about feminine wiles, Wehrmacht soldiers were routinely befuddled by these women. As their train clattered toward the southwest, Smith's home run unfolded with cinematic order. Smith, Janine, Dédée, two Belgian soldiers and a British one had their own compartment; the British soldier was forbidden to speak and Smith, the mute grocer, "couldn't." At Bordeaux, they transferred to the train to Bayonne.

When they stepped onto the platform in Bayonne, a young woman came running up to Dédée and kissed her on the cheeks. Like her father, the teenaged Lucienne was part of the *Comet Line*, and that afternoon her task was to bring word of German movements in the town. German boots were on the bridge they had to cross, she whispered to Dédée, which prompted Dédée to play the envy card. She took one man in each arm, sent one with Janine and Smith with Lucienne, telling the two other women, as she was going, to make a show of intimacy with their "parcels." Just before starting off, Dédée told the escapers that, since they were taller than the average Bayonnoise, they should bend a bit, one of the many examples Smith remembered of her life-saving attention to detail. This was in stark contrast to his momentary lapse on the Paris Métro when after jostling a woman he said "Excuse me" instead of "*Excuse-moi*"—and just feet away from two SS guards who mercifully didn't notice.[91] Like other "parcels," he surely would have been told as well to, when in a restaurant, keep his fork in his left hand even when lifting food to his mouth.

A few hours later, after a short train ride to a town ten miles southwest of Bayonne, Smith's party was met by a couple of women who replaced Janine and Lucienne. As the sun began to set, the four Allied servicemen and their three guides reached a large white farmhouse, where Madame Usandizaga welcomed them warmly. Smith's question of how the escapers were going to climb the rugged Pyrenees was lost in the excitement generated by the arrival of the guide, Floretino Goicoechea, a smuggler who had turned his skills over to the Allies. A short while later, Dédée said her goodbye and, despite her "ever-present intensity," Smith heard in her voice the emotion of the moment in her words: "*Prenez garde*"—Be careful—"my brave boys."[92]

LATE DECEMBER 1942, STALAG VIII-B, LAMSDORF, GERMANY

The Lead Up to Christmas

The days before Christmas were especially difficult, recalls Darch. "We put up some silver paper that our cigarettes had been wrapped in, but it didn't help much. The barracks were dismal and lit only by a few weak bulbs, so the silver paper didn't twinkle much." Memories of Christmas dinners amid the warmth of families and roaring fires made the ever-present cold and gnawing hunger all the more difficult. Nor did singing Christmas carols help; the absence of women's and children's voices underlined the men's distance from home.

At his *Arbeitskommando*, Prouse too found Christmas depressing because it "started me thinking too much of loved ones and home."[93] The arrival of Christmas crackers brightened the mood. Prouse doesn't record if anyone thought it strange that these crackers came from an organization other than the Red Cross, but once they started eating them, they quickly realized that the crackers were not their only Christmas present. Because the food contained in Red Cross parcels was so important for survival, MI9 never used those parcels to send escape gear such as the rice-paper maps of Germany and adjoining countries that were baked into the Christmas crackers.

22–23 DECEMBER 1942, IN THE PYRENEES

Smith Reaches Andorra

None of the four evaders had any doubt what their guide, Goicoechea, meant when he "pressed his slab of a hand over his mouth" moments after they walked out the door and started toward the Pyrenees. A short time later, as they climbed in almost pitch blackness "over narrow overgrown paths and at an almost vertical incline," and made their way along ledges just a few inches from drops several hundred feet high, the Canadian from Ontario's mining country found the cold bearable.[94] As the sky to the east began to lighten, they began climbing down, which required finding handholds to keep from falling down the mountain.

Goicoechea didn't allow any rest until they staggered into a safe house several hours from the border. Yet Smith breathed easier as he shivered while wading across the river Bidassa, during which he could not help comparing the former smuggler to Moses leading his people out of bondage.

25 DECEMBER 1942, THE POW CAMPS

Christmas Day

"The Germans were human after all," Poolton wrote acidly decades later about the order that allowed the Canadians to remain unshackled for two days, beginning on Christmas Eve.[95] Prime Minister Mackenzie King's Christmas message neither inspired nor warmed the hearts of men like Fusilier Jacques Nadeau, who had been captured at Dieppe and desperately wanted word from his family, not Ottawa. The delivery of British Red Cross parcels, albeit one for every four instead of two men, was, however, welcomed.

After weeks of living on filthy food—the Germans didn't waste water washing the cabbage before making the weak soup, which caused hundreds of cases of dysentery—chocolate, Spam, sugar, tea and coffee made for a feast. "The making of sauce for Christmas pudding from the butter in the can took us out of the moment and transported us back to . . . to our mother's kitchens or where we first tasted it," says Darch.

It is difficult to overstate the importance of the Christmas services organized at Stalag VIII-B by Chaplain John Foote, and by the Oblates in seven different camps. Armies grant padres special powers; for example, they can conduct funeral rites in religions other than their own. On this holy night, Foote conducted a joint service with the Anglican padre. A week earlier, Father Juneau had celebrated the Feast of the Immaculate Conception with "pomp" and assisted by several Protestants.

The year before, *les religieux* conducted Christmas services in a makeshift chapel. This year would be different. Just a few weeks earlier, Father Bergeron rejoiced in telling his Provincial that the very letter he was writing was "from the feet of *Jesus-Hostie*. Because, thank the Lord, our camp now has its own modest chapel."[96] *Les religieux* credited Mary with ensuring that they received the materials necessary to build the chapel, Étoile de la mer or Stella Maris (Star of the Sea), which they dedicated to the Virgin Mother. Bergeron told his family that the toil with tools and brushes was worth it, for it provided them with a holy place to host Milag Nord's Catholics for services during the year and, especially, the commemoration of Jesus's birth.

In a letter written home after Christmas, Juneau told of celebrating Christmas mass in Stalag XVIII-A's theatre. That midnight mass was held five hours early mattered less than the gathering of the faithful in the chapel, complete with a crèche, the statues of Mary, Joseph, the three kings and the shepherd boy made from plaster of Paris.

At the POW camp near Blechhammer, in south-central Poland, Father Charbonneau conducted mass in a sanctuary that was a feast for the eyes. With the help of materials smuggled into the camp, he turned a 25-by-12-foot corner of the barracks into what a Red Cross official called "the most beautiful chapel in a prison camp."[97] A Gothic arch, made from Red Cross boxes, framed the altar. Both were painted to look like stone. On each side of the arch were pieces of stained glass, one with Mary's monogram framed in flowers and one with Joseph's, a sleigh handmade of paper and cardboard by an English soldier.

Mass began with the familiar Latin words that not only told the believers that their faith and Church lived on but also connected them to their families back home, as they too soon would be hearing the same words and praying the same prayers. The two paintings and a memorial that decorated Charbonneau's humble chapel were the manifestation of the Church in the milieu of the prison camp. "One is of Calvary, the other of Christ coming to the prisoners, with this inscription: 'I will refresh you (sic), *je vous referai.*'"[98] To the left of the altar, in another Gothic arch, was a memorial for the soldiers who had disappeared.

Chapter Six

January–April 1943

[Courage] is a cold choice between two alternatives, the fixed resolve not to quit; an act of renunciation which must be made not once but many times by the power of the will.

—Lord Moran, *The Anatomy of Courage*

MID-JANUARY 1943, STALAG VIII-B, LAMSDORF, GERMANY

The Return of the Dieppe Prisoners' Red Cross Parcels

The decision to again distribute Red Cross parcels to the Dieppe POWs provided more than desperately needed calories and nutrients via the familiar tastes of Spam, chocolate, condensed milk, raisins and canned peaches. They provided a sensory experience that took the POWs out of their drab surroundings. "It felt real good to have those tastes again. They brought back the good times, of life back in Canada," says Stan Darch, who still remembers the sizzle of Spam and hot tea cooked on the Klim-tin blower.

In contrast to the huts' stoves, in which the fuel was placed at the bottom, the result being that much of the heat radiated out of the bottom and sides of the stoves, the Klim-tin blowers worked like a forge. A stream of air, generated by a blower cut from a cookie tin or can, linked by a belt made from shoelaces or strips of leather, supercharged the air in the small combustion chamber at the bottom of the Klim can. A few wood chips or a bit of coal sufficed to boil a pot of tea. "We learned how to make [the Klim-tin blowers] from the men who were already in Lamsdorf," recalls Darch. "They were wonderful. Just a few bits of wood or charcoal and we could brew up tea, cook the few potatoes they gave us or even the little bit of bacon we got every now and then."[99]

The parcels also provided fodder for some much-needed entertainment in the form of what amounted to a bazaar. Some exchanges were relatively straightforward: bramble jelly from a Canadian parcel for marmalade from a British one. Muslim British soldiers held in another compound at Lamsdorf were eager to exchange cans of bacon for tea (which, like cigarettes, served the purpose of currency) or cans of salmon. Canadian Klim was highly prized, as were soap and sugar.

Charles Fisher recalled Stalag X-B as having a thriving black market, in which the law of supply and demand was nakedly apparent. "Two ounces of coffee bought two eggs one day, three the next." The eggs, like white bread, sausage and even whisky, came from Germans who were willing to risk execution for real coffee and cigarettes. Cigarettes, the default currency, differed from real currency in that, over time, they literally went up in smoke, causing the black market economy to seize up. Unfreezing it required the injection of more cigarettes. At times this new "currency" came from newly arrived Red Cross parcels. Other times, to entice those men who'd held on to their cigarettes to part with them, men wrote IOUs on their banks in England, sometimes at the price of five dollars per cigarette. Letters home recorded these IOUs and "relatives transferred money to the home accounts of prison sellers," wrote Fisher.

From both a psychological and a nutritional point of view, it would have been better for the POWs to have husbanded the Red Cross supplies. When Fisher was at Stalag X-B and later Milag Nord, the staples were held in common and doled out by the kitchen to every member of the mess. Most of the time, the Dieppe POWs were given one parcel per two or four men, which provided needed nutrients but undercut the Red Cross's nutritional scheme. Each parcel provided a man with 2,070 calories per day, for seven days; this added to the German rations would have equalled sufficient calories to prevent the men from losing weight. However, to prevent Darch and his comrades from stockpiling canned goods that could be used while escaping, the Germans punctured the cans of Klim, Spam and bacon. The men would gorge themselves before the food turned rancid.[100]

19 JANUARY 1943, ZERBST, GERMANY

RCAF SERGEANT ANDREW CARSWELL BAILS OUT OF A BURNING BOMBER

"Your Lancaster bomber is a very good plan, *ja*? It is better than the B-17, *ja*?" asked Oberleutenant Schmidt. So as not to be tricked into divulging any information other than his name, rank and service number, Andrew Carswell, following his training, stayed silent.

A day earlier over Magdeburg, 100 miles southeast of Berlin, as the flames from his flak-damaged starboard engine burned toward the high-octane aviation fuel held in the wing, Carswell managed to level off his stricken plane. The fierce fire lit the fuselage enough so that he could see the maps and other papers being sucked out of it into the black night convulsed by exploding shells and the roar of the plane's three remaining Rolls-Royce Merlin engines. Within moments, the plane had dropped thousands of feet and all but Carswell and his navigator, John Galbraith, had jumped from the burning "kite."

Arguing that they could still make it home, Galbraith refused to jump. "Look at that fire, you fucking idiot!" screamed Carswell. "Get the hell out! The controls are shot and I can't hold it any longer."[101] Like most RCAF aircrew, Carswell had never practised a parachute drop. And, while he missed the river, until he punched the quick-release button, he suffered the indignity of dangling 20 feet above the ground after a tree snagged his chute. A few hours later, cold and wet from trudging through the snow, and shaken by the sure knowledge Galbraith was dead, Carswell knocked on a farmhouse door.

The old man who opened the door would have fired his rifle, Carswell believed, had the motherly-looking farm wife not intervened. Moments later, after sitting on a couch, he collapsed into unconsciousness. When he came to, he made it clear via the ten-year-old boy who was fascinated by his RCAF wings that he was from "Kanada." A few minutes later, the police arrived and whisked Carswell to a holding cell in Zerbst's town hall, where he was fed and asked about the relative merits of the American and British bombers.

20 JANUARY 1943, LOURDES, NOVA SCOTIA

RCAF Sergeant Ian MacDonald's Parents Read a Letter from London

It would take another fortnight for the MacDonalds to learn it, but in early January, their son had been to London. Because of the blackout, he hadn't seen much, but to his parents, who had never been past Halifax, just being at Waterloo Station, in Trafalgar Square and seeing the dome of St. Paul's underlined how far he'd travelled and how close he was to danger. For hundreds of thousands of Canadian parents, pride in their son's uniform was accompanied by fear, both for their safety and in the knowledge that the further they advanced into the war, the less they resembled the man who had left home.[102] That night when he wrote home, to show that he was still their Ian, MacDonald wasted little time before telling of going to Canada House, where he had glanced over the headlines of the *New Glasgow Evening News*.

On 20 January, a letter from Great-West Life Assurance, an insurance adjuster, informed Mr. MacDonald that Ian's life insurance policy was a month in arrears because, "for some reason or other," the papers that authorized the assignment of $4 per pay were "late coming through." It was a polite request that Mr. MacDonald bring the policy up to date.

27–31 JANUARY 1943, DULAG LUFT, FRANKFURT

Carswell Endures Several Rounds of Psych-Ops and Covers Up His Only Mistake

Since Carswell had been shot down only two days earlier and was a pilot, the intelligence machinery at Dulag Luft went to work right after he arrived there. The order to strip off his uniform had less to do with ensuring that he did not have access to escape equipment (the Germans did not yet know that he had a knife, saw and map hidden in his uniform) than with softening him up by removing the outward sign of his military status. Though it might be difficult for civilians to grasp the importance of a uniform, the intelligence agents knew that it was the outward sign of status and, for a serviceman, something approaching a legal document that brought Carswell under the Geneva Convention.

During the night, his small, bare cell was first so hot that he had to strip off his grey, shapeless clothes, thus infantilizing the Canadian pilot, and then so cold that he banged on the cell's steel door to implore the guard to turn the heat back on. Not until later the next day did he eat thin turnip soup and a small piece of close-to-inedible black bread. A day later, having seen only the guard who walked him to the toilet, he was happy when a guard threw his uniform, but not his flying boots, into his cell.

Knowing that the return of his uniform would make Carswell feel "like a human being again," the Luftwaffe moved its next piece on the chessboard in the person of a friendly-looking officer who, after opening the door to Carswell's cell, said "Good morning" and then asked, "Are you feeling better after your harrowing experience?" His friendly words and hearty handshake were designed to elide Carswell's three days in solitary, the dehumanizing effect of taking Carswell's clothes and the wretched food and return Carswell to the emotional trauma of the crash. The intelligence officer outranked Carswell but told him to sit down before asking, "Where do you live in Canada? . . . Vancouver? Toronto? Montreal?"[103]

The strain was intense. Before him sat an apparently friendly German speaking in unaccented English who had just asked a question of no obvious military import. The officer erred, however, by pausing long enough for Carswell to recall a British intelligence officer telling him that even harmless information could be "used to convince a prisoner that the captors already knew everything about him. . . . even the amounts and places of leave, all had their place in filling in the big picture for German intelligence." Fortified, Carswell demurred when the German asked, "Well, . . . what is your home address? I have spent some time in Canada myself. It is a beautiful country." When asked, "What possible difference could it make to anybody if you told us your home address?" Carswell admitted that he didn't know but that he was under orders to give nothing other than his name, rank and service number. The intelligence officer's bonhomie evaporated. "If you do not cooperate with us, you will be here for the rest of the war!"

The next day the officer was back, asking courteously if the Canadian would like a shave and a book to read. Carswell enjoyed the shave and wondered if he'd been given *A Tale of Two Cities* because of Mr. Manette's story of being a prisoner in the Bastille for 18 years. The following day, accompanied by another English-speaking officer, Carswell's interlocutor was back asking a series of seemingly innocuous questions about life in Canada. Again, Carswell refused to take the bait.

A day later, as promised, a man sporting several red crosses on his tunic and claiming to be Swiss official entered Carswell's cell, saying in a heavy German accent, "Ve are glad to see zat you are not voondet or anysink like zat!" What he didn't know was that airmen had been warned to expect fake Red Cross officials. Given the Canadian's previous refusal to say anything about his plane, the official must not have been surprised that Carswell did not fill out the form that asked for his address, type of aircraft, point of departure, squadron, bomb load and other sensitive information. Carswell stifled a laugh when the "Red Cross" official screamed, "You are a heartless brute!"—the same words the German official had used a day earlier.

The Canadian slipped only once during the pas de deux with the Luftwaffe. The day after his encounter with the "Red Cross" official, the two German officers returned and complained that Carswell had not been cooperative. Barely were the words "He's no Red Cross officer. . . . He's a phony!" out of his mouth when Carswell realized that he'd broken the rule about not getting drawn into a debate. "How do you know that?" they responded, and he realized he'd just given the officers an insight into what the Allies knew about Luftwaffe interrogation procedures.

Carswell moved quickly to cover his tracks. "He doesn't look like a Red Cross man . . . He looks like a German and he talks with a German accent!" The officer tut-tutted the poor, ignorant Canadian. "A lot of Swiss speak German." Their condescending acceptance of Carswell's response "Oh, . . . I thought they all spoke Swiss!" indicated that for all their training, the intelligence officers did not have a grasp of that Canadian speciality: dumb insolence.

On Carswell's fifth day in solitary, the Luftwaffe officer tried again, this time asking about navigator John Galbraith. Carswell, who figured that they found his name on his parachute pack, knew nothing of his whereabouts, of course, and threw the question back at them: "Okay, . . . where is he, then?" "We don't know. We're still looking for him. But we'll find him." The next day Carswell was released into the general camp population and a few days later transported first to Stalag Luft I and then, with several other POWs, including fellow RCAF Officer Bill Jackson, to Stalag VIII-B.

8 FEBRUARY 1943, ARBEITSKOMMANDO 1049, NIEDERORSCHEL, GERMANY

Letters from Home and Housekeeping

On 8 February, Jack Poolton received his first letter from home. "It didn't matter what the letter said," recalls Darch. "Any news or what today we would call gossip reached into us and made us feel warm." At this point in the war, it took between 12 and 16 weeks for a letter to get from Lamsdorf to Canada and for the return letter to arrive back at the POW camp. "That first letter that referred to a letter I wrote meant so much. I don't remember now what it was about. But I remember what it did. It told me that I was back in contact with my family, that even though I was stuck rotting in a POW camp in Germany, a part of me was back with the people I loved, that I was part of their everyday life and them, mine."[104]

Though they were warmed by greatcoats sent by the Red Cross and insulated from the cold ground and floors by wooden clogs that, for a few cigarettes, Remi Leroux made more comfortable with leggings made from greatcoat material, by the winter of 1942–43 the Dieppe survivors' clothes were wearing out. "I mended my own clothes, but some men didn't and daily wear meant that soon their clothes were getting pretty thin," says Darch. "Some other men were good with the needle, so for a few cigarettes they'd patch up the shirt or pants. Because no one had proper patches, we were soon a very motley bunch."

Keeping clean was a constant challenge. "Dignity demanded we shave and, rather than shave in cold water, after taking one or two mouthfuls of it to drink, we used the mint tea that was given to us in the morning to shave. They allowed us to shower every couple of months. We had three minutes of hot water and the rest was cold. The German soap wouldn't lather up, so we saved the soap from our Red Cross parcels and used it," explains Darch, chuckling at the memory of men smelling like Lux soap, which advertised itself as the choice of nine out of ten Hollywood starlets.

Poolton recalls a more ominous aspect of the showers. The

German guards in the shower room pointed toward their penises. Not knowing that circumcision was rather more common in Canada than Europe, "if they spotted one who had been circumcised, they would shout '*Juden*.'"

MID-FEBRUARY 1943, STALAG VIII-B, LAMSDORF, GERMANY

Carswell Meets an Old Friend

"Hey, Andy! What are you doing here?" The question seemed absurd. After all, Carswell had just arrived at the gate of Stalag VIII-B in the middle of Germany; who could know him here? At first he didn't see anyone familiar in the crowd of POWs; then he spotted a bearded man calling out "Jack Lyall" and "Malvern," the name of their Toronto high school. A few moments later while being marched through the Dieppe compound, during which Carswell saw his compatriots in chains, a Canadian officer walked up and started marching in step with Carswell. "Hi, Andy!" Now it was Carswell's turn to ask an absurd question. "What the hell are you doing here, George?" he asked George Barless, who had grown up one house away from Carswell's boyhood home at 26 Spadina Avenue.[105]

The sight of his countrymen in shackles shocked Carswell, as did the drabness of the barracks, the stench of the 40-holer and the bone-chilling temperatures that mocked the barracks' walls. An experienced Kriegie told him that sleeping in one's clothes did not keep one warmer during the night or in the morning. Hard experience had taught him it was better to lay the clothes on top of the thin blanket, thus providing a few more layers of covering and giving them a chance to dry out.

Within days, the crushing boredom set in. Carswell took some comfort in the outcome of the English lessons that a fellow Kriegie had given an Unteroffizier. At Appell one morning, the proud German officer announced to the recalcitrant airmen, "I know that you people think I know fuck nothing! But you are wrong! I know fuck all!"[106]

WINTER 1943, ARBEITSKOMMANDO 1049, NIEDERORSCHEL, GERMANY

Robert Prouse Wears a Grass Skirt in Play

In larger camps, the Kriegies had theatres and even repertoires. But even in small work camps like the one Robert Prouse shivered through during the winter, the men took pride in their theatrical skills. Whether the plays were by the Bard or others, they were a throwback to Elizabethan theatre, for young, slight men played the women's parts. In one particular play, Prouse was not only especially proud of working out the dance steps for the South Sea island "women" in grass skirts but of his own dancing and costume, made of shredded paper and a bra, this last producing a "a lot of good-natured 'cat-calls' from the audience, along with a few lewd suggestions."[107]

The catcalls were both good-natured fun and indicative of the kind of nervousness generated by dances, but not by boxing and hockey matches, French and German classes and orchestras like the one Father Barsalou formed. It was, recalled Canadian Private Geoffrey Ellwood, "one thing for guys to dance together because there's nobody else to dance with. But when you start dancing together and likin' it, and start snuggling up, it became very, very obvious" what was happening.[108] The flippant line "Home or homo by Christmas," which seemed at odds with the opprobrium attached to homosexuals back in Canada (not to mention the military regulations used to punish homosexual behaviour) even as it set up a hierarchy that clearly placed "straight" above homosexual sex and touched on the men's concern about both their sexuality and libidos.[109] It also underscores how starved the men were for physical affection.

Attitudes toward the homoerotic acts varied greatly.[110] Fisher, who found that the only examples of flagrant homosexuality occurred among medical personnel, believed that it was "abhorred by other prisoners."[111] Prouse, who records an incident where he shoved a man coming on to him against the wall, was even more disturbed by the possibility of where, "if the war went on endlessly," the human need for emotional support and physical affection would lead.[112] Ellwood took a more sanguine view: homosexual relationships were formed, "but nobody seemed to take it as serious, you know. They'd look at it and discuss it amongst ourselves, and that was it. It was accepted that some people are that way."[113]

MARCH 1943, STALAG VIII-B, LAMSDORF, GERMANY

Carswell Learns the Meaning of "Trouble and Strife"

The final decision for Carswell's plan to swap over with a British private so that he could try to escape with another British soldier lay not with the Escape Committee but with Carswell's barracks mates and muckers, for they would have to live and share meals with Dennis Reeves. Carswell's doppelgänger likely got on better with his new mates than Carswell did with John Donaldson, who disliked both Canadians and air force men with equal ardour.

Swapping over may have been easier than digging tunnels but it still required work. Reeves had the simpler job. Carswell had said nothing during his interrogation, was new to the camp and his letters home had been perfunctory, so the Germans knew little about him. Reeves, by contrast, was an open book thanks to the rifle butts and boots used on him when he was captured, as was Donaldson, just before Dunkirk three years earlier. Accordingly, Carswell had spent the early part of March learning the details of Reeves's life. Carswell's dress rehearsal occurred in the British Army compound. Since his accent would give him away, though he learned the ways of cockney rhyming slang, in which "trouble and strife" means "wife," he spoke as little as possible. What words that did pass his lips were affected Briticisms such as "blimey" and "foocking Jerries!"[114]

While Red Cross parcels never contained escape equipment, their contents still aided escapers. Carswell saved some chocolate bars, biscuits and cans of bully beef. His former barracks mates chipped in more chocolate and the all-important cigarettes. Some of this largesse never left the camp. To entice the guards into being less than thorough in their search of "Reeves," Carswell placed a cache of chocolate, cigarettes and soap on the top of his pack.

31 MARCH 1943, ON GERMAN TRAINS

RCAF Pilot Officer Kingsley Brown Learns the War News from a Talkative SS Soldier

"It's a scandal! They get all these poor Italians and Slovaks and Bulgarians in the country and let them wander around like lost sheep! . . . Here's two more. Look at them! Bulgarians. Steelworkers. And nobody had sense enough to tell them how to get to Strasbourg!"[115] The outburst by the elderly policeman in the Chemnitz train station told Kingsley Brown and his British escape partner, Gordon Brettell, that their cover was working.

The policeman's annoyance at the functionary who had sent the two tramp workers didn't stop him from helping them. When he saw that they were heading to Strasbourg via Nürnberg, he told them that they'd have to return to Leipzig and get a train from there, travelling to Nürnberg being impossible because the city had been heavily bombed. He then bought them tickets and told them to go have beer while they waited for the late-night train.

More than four decades later, Brown recalled the frisson of sitting in a train compartment with several German soldiers and a member of the SS. With millions of dragooned foreign workers in the Reich, the soldiers took no notice of two poorly dressed men but openly envied the uniform of the Hermann Göring Division. The SS's view of itself as the elite and the poster in the carriage that read "Beware the Third Person! The Enemy has Ears!" notwithstanding, the SS soldier let his comrades—and, unwittingly, two Allied officers—in on a little secret: his division was "being posted to the front to face the Anglo-Americans in Tunisia."

1 APRIL 1943, OUTSIDE A VILLAGE IN EASTERN GERMANY

Carswell and His Escape Partner Remind Some Kriegies of Their Duty

Neither Carswell nor Donaldson was impressed with the POWs they met at the brewery where they stopped for a night on the way to a work camp at a graphite mine. Nor were they impressed by the Kriegies they met at the mine. At the brewery, when Donaldson asked if anyone had tried to escape, as the window had only two bars and there was only one guard, he was stunned by the answer: "Don't be a bloody fool. . . . This is the best fucking job in Germany! Why would we want to ruin everything by some silly bugger trying to escape?" One of the men then turned on Carswell, accusing him of being a "fucking Yank or Canadian" and probably an air force swapover to boot.[116]

Donaldson defended Carswell, quickly adding that he had been shot down three months before, which lowered the temperature in the room. One soldier asked, "What's it like in England now, mate?" As they told him how they'd been half-starved and -frozen during the winter of 1940–41, Carswell understood why the fight had gone out of them, save for the times they urinated into the beer barrels destined for the SS.

The 15 POWs at the graphite mine had a tacit agreement with their guard, "Hermann the German." He'd go easy on them if they didn't try to escape (thus allowing him to spend time with his girlfriend). Donaldson angrily scotched their objections to their escape plans. "There is still a fucking war on. We are all British. The Jerries are the enemy, not us. It is our duty to try to escape, and it is your duty to try to help us. And remember one thing, this war will be over some day, and we are going to fucking well win it. After that, there'll be a fucking reckoning!"

2 APRIL 1943, PRISON, GROßHARTMANNSDORF, SAXONY, GERMANY

Brown's Impromptu Birthday Party

He was now 32 years and one day old, and the party the night before hadn't been half bad. Some New Yorkers, captured a few months earlier in Tunisia and then recaptured after escaping from a POW camp, attended, as did French POWs who brought cakes, cookies and strong Gauloises cigarettes; the jovial German guards brought extra-large canisters of steaming chicory "coffee." Still, as Kingsley Brown savoured the memory of the party, the question lingered: would he and Gordon Brettell have gotten farther had Sir Arthur Harris sent his bombers elsewhere a few nights earlier?

Had he, they would never have had to decamp to the air-raid shelter crammed with people who had nothing better to do but "notice the amateurish needlework that had transformed our bed blankets into civilian suits."[117] For a short time after the "All Clear"sounded, and while Brown and his partner enjoyed a beer, he thought they'd escaped—until two uniformed men stormed into the beer parlour and pointed directly at them.

Their only hope lay with their papers, which had passed muster with the old policeman, and Brown saying in heavily accented German that they were Bulgarian steelworkers. After seeing that their travel passes said they were going to Leipzig, the inspector left the room and made a phone call. When he returned, he said to the guards that they weren't Bulgarian but French, and again examined their papers. Brown tried to keep the story going, and the inspector played along for a moment, then told Brown that in Leipzig the steel company had only a sales office. Brown was crestfallen because the information for the papers came from the very database he himself had compiled. When the inspector dropped the word "Gestapo," the jig was up and they pulled out their dog tags. Fifteen days of solitary, what the Germans called "sharp arrest," followed when they were returned to Stalag Luft III.

14 APRIL 1943, ROME

RCAF Flight Lieutenant Vincent McAuley Meets a Very-Well-Dressed Soldier

Since enlisting in the RCAF on 26 June 1940 in Moncton, New Brunswick, Vincent McAuley had seen many colour of uniforms: the blue of the Commonwealth's air forces, the green of the US Army Air Forces and the GIs, and Canadian and British khaki. After being shot down on 11 December on his 45th mission after bombing Turin, Italy, he saw the green of the Italian soldiers and black of the Hugo Boss–designed uniforms of the Italian intelligence service. But neither he; his flight sergeant, Frederick Nightingale; nor British quartermaster sergeant William Cook, who had escaped with him from the Celio Military Hospital in Rome, had ever seen a uniform like this.

Before them stood a Catholic soldier belonging to the oldest standing army in the world, Pontificia Cohors Helvetica, the pope's Swiss Guard. He wore billowing britches with alternating wide red, orange and blue stripes that tapered to tights below the knee, the blue signalling the royal pretensions of the Medici family of Renaissance Florence. Where the airmen clipped on their parachutes, this soldier had buckled on armour, above which sat a white ruff collar, like those worn by Her Majesty and courtiers in the paintings of the only Queen

Elizabeth England had yet had. On his head sat a shiny morion helmet, like the ones worn by the Spanish conquistadors. He carried a sword and a halberd, a six-foot pole topped with a pike and axe blade designed in the 14th century to use against mounted knights.

After climbing the wall that surrounded the hospital, the escapers turned northwest and past the Colosseum, which glowed a ghostly white under the light of the quarter moon, before turning down the Via dei Fori Imperiali, which runs by the Roman Forum. Not far from the northeast corner of the forum, across the Piazza Venezia, stood the 230-foot-high and more than 400-foot-long monument to King Victor Emmanuel II. To avoid attracting attention from the guards around the monument, they likely turned left after the forum, which took them by the famous bronze statue of Marcus Aurelius and into the Jewish Ghetto before they crossed over the Ponte Sant'Angelo, at around 3:45 a.m.

Once across the Tiber, they avoided the quickest way to the Vatican, Via della Conciliazione, named for the Lateran Accords, which ensured the independence of the Holy See from Italy, the legal point upon which McAuley and his companions staked their freedom. The street ran straight from behind the Castel Sant'Angelo (Hadrian's Mausoleum) to the Piazza del Popolo where Gian Lorenzo Bernini's sweeping colonnades embrace St. Peter's Square (and, symbolically, the world). Even at that early hour, the street was too filled with people to be safe. Instead, the escapers trusted themselves to the ancient streets of the Borgo.

As McAuley and Nightingale followed at a safe distance, Cook asked a man in German to direct him to the Vatican. When, after following his directions, they remained within the cramped, narrow streets of the Borgo, unable to see even Michelangelo's famed dome, Cook asked a second man for help. Warily, he led Cook through the Porta Angelica on the eastern side of the colonnade and into St. Peter's Square itself. After the man vanished, Cook left the safety of the square and rejoined McAuley and Nightingale. Worried that the man who had guided him might have whispered a word or two to a *carabiniere*, Cook led his comrades into the square through another entrance. A few moments later they stood before the ornately dressed Swiss Guard, who mistook them for generals.

15 APRIL 1943, OVER PICARDY, FRANCE

MacDonald Joins the "Caterpiller Club"

The first whiff didn't quite register.

Then it strengthened to an undeniable smell of smoke. The instruments told Pilot Officer Lee Usher that the bomber's engines were operating normally, but standard operating procedure called for him to abort the mission. "We had just got turned round," recalls bomb aimer MacDonald, "when I realized that the smoke was coming from the elements that heated the bombs in the bomb bay. I told Usher that I'd forgotten I'd turned the heater on. Now that we knew where the burning smell came from, he decided to turn around to continue our mission despite the fact that we were no longer part of the bomber stream and would be flying alone."

As he neared the target, lying prone in the bomb aimer's glass-enclosed position in the plane's nose, lit up by searchlights, MacDonald thought, "I'm never going to live through this wall of flak and tracer bullets," which had already torn apart the plane's inner starboard engine. He fought to keep his eyes from being blinded by the searchlights and called "Right, Right, Steady, Steady, Left, Right" into the intercom to direct the plane over its target. In spite of his training, MacDonald found himself unable to keep looking through the bomb sight to watch the bombs fall.

Freed from the six tons of bombs, the damaged Halifax bomber leaped higher. That, combined with the extra speed Usher now had because the plane was lighter, allowed him to break out of the cone of light. "I wasn't a pilot, but I knew enough that Lee would have to feather the dead engine on the way back home. But we'd all seen much more heavily damaged planes land, so we thought we had a pretty good chance," says MacDonald.

A half hour later, Walter Reed, the plane's mid-upper gunner, called out that there was another Halifax not far below them. Harry Jay, the plane's rear gunner, leaned over his four .303 machine guns and saw to his horror not a Halifax but a Messerschmitt 110 night fighter shadowing them in what essentially was the gunner's blind spot. In an attempt to get Jay the angle he needed, Usher tried accelerating and decelerating. Desperate, Jay depressed his guns as far as he could and fired, only to see his tracers fall harmlessly behind the German plane.

The German pilot pulled back on his joystick and within seconds was flying more or less level with the Canadian bomber and firing. The stream of bullets caused, Jay later recalled, the senseless reflex of drawing his stomach in and "as far away as possible from the incoming shells that surely had no place else to go." Closer to the nose cone, MacDonald had the same reflex, cringing and pulling back from the starboard window as the bullets destroyed another engine. A moment later, through the intercom Jay called out, "I got 'im, I got 'im!"[118]

Even without its bombs and about half of its 7,500 tons of fuel already burned off, with two engines destroyed, the Halifax was an ungainly beast. But as long as Usher could maintain about 100 miles per hour, he could keep it in the air. Everything changed a half hour later, when another German plane fired and destroyed a third engine and set the plane on fire.

"I was in my position in the bomber's sight. I felt the thud of the bullets and immediately felt the plane begin a sort of wallow. Usher gave the order to bail out, and I reached for my parachute that was stored in the bin at my right elbow," recounts MacDonald. The bomb aimer's position may be the most exposed in the plane, but it was closest to the hatch, which MacDonald opened a moment after clipping on his parachute. Then, as he eased his feet into the slipstream beneath the plane, he realized he was about to break his neck because he was still wearing the leather flying helmet's connect to the intercom.

After pulling his feet back into the plane, MacDonald yanked off his helmet. In the moment before he jumped, the creaking of the fuselage and the roar of the functioning and stuttering engines merged with "a rushing sound that can only be compared to a waterfall."

As MacDonald fell at a rate of 36 feet per second (per second) and his plane, an ever-growing orange glow, flew on, he was enveloped in the most profound silence. After counting to seven and falling about 1,000 feet, he pulled the rip cord. "Suddenly I was floating," he says, "and to my horror, the German made one circle around me, and I thought he was going to fire. But for the grace of God it didn't happen."

15 APRIL 1943, BEAUMONT-EN-BEINE, FRANCE

MacDonald Is Fed and Given a Place to Sleep

"Confusion," recalls MacDonald, "stunned confusion that overrode everything, even what they tried to drill into our head in escape training back in England. I knew that as soon as I'd landed in the four inches of new grain, I had to uncouple my chute, bury it and get away because the German spotters would be watching for where I landed. But, for long moments, all I could hear was the gunfire that had doomed our plane, and hectic images of the bullets, the fire and rushing to the hatch crowded my mind until I sat down next to a tree and settled myself."

Once his training kicked in, MacDonald threw some leaves over his chute, then cut off the sergeant swipes and epaulets he'd worked so hard to earn before crawling under a bush. Later, he heard farmers in the field speaking French and wondered about his crewmates. Since in its last moments the plane was flying a tight circle, they must have landed nearby.

That night, the hungry and extremely thirsty evader realized that walking to Spain was impossible. Across an open field, near the village of Beaumont-en-Beine, MacDonald saw a light, a rare sight that could indicate that the building was military. "There were few street lamps back home, so I was used to walking only by the light of the night sky," says MacDonald. "But this night was dark, and I could not make out much about the building, which I approached from its rear, until I was very close. To satisfy myself that there weren't any troops about, I went around to the front—and relaxed a little when I saw a large opened gate." Then he looked up and saw through the lit window a woman and a little girl clinging to her nightgown. MacDonald summoned up his high school French for a strong whisper: "*Je suis Anglais*, and I am thirsty."

The light disappeared and, a moment later, another shone from what he correctly guessed was the kitchen. In traditional French peasant fashion, the woman who opened the door offered MacDonald a glass of wine and had trouble understanding not MacDonald's words—"*Pas d'vin, d'eau*"—but why he would want water. Nevertheless, Madame Dutilleul gave him a cup and pointed toward the pantry. A short time later, while he was eating toast and eggs and drinking a cup of coffee, the dog started barking. MacDonald's blood froze.

"She saw my fright and immediately said, '*Mon mari. Pas les Allemands*' [My husband. Not the Germans]. I had only a moment to wonder what this French farmer would say when he walked into his house in the middle of the night and found his wife feeding a downed Canadian airman. His eyes opened wide when he heard my story and said that I could sleep there that night."

18 APRIL 1943, IN THE SUDETEN MOUNTAINS, CZECHOSLOVAKIA

Carswell and Donaldson Pass as Good Germans

They were hiding in what "Down East" is called a two-holer, wearing the heavy coats, breathing the stench of shit and hoping that

Herman the German's replacement wouldn't feel nature's call. After hearing the guard hop on his bicycle to go see the Fräulein who had shared her favours with Hermann, Carswell and Donaldson slipped away from the *Arbeitskommando*.

By 3 a.m., they were well clear of the graphite mine. As the eastern sky lightened, they crawled under some bushes. Woken hours later by a barking dog, Carswell peered through the bushes and saw a lone farmer driving an ox forward, prompting the men to move to a nearby wood. As the hours passed and insects tormented them, they realized they had made a basic error: forgetting a filled water bottle. Even in the shade, thirst soon tormented them, as it would until well after dark, when they left the forest and found water. By midnight on the 18th, they were crossing a high ridge somewhere in the Sudetenland, heading west.

The Hollywood version of the Third Reich—that the Hitlerian state was a well-oiled machine—is overstated. At its height in 1944, the SS had some 32,000 agents, fewer than today's New York Police Department. Still, to lessen the chance of arousing suspicions, while still up on the ridge, they practised giving the Nazi salute and convincing renditions of "*Heil Hitler!*" Near a village, they saw two men approaching, and despite hearing his own heart pounding, Carswell was determined to act natural. The two POWs raised their arms in the fascist salute and shouted "*Heil Hitler!*" The startled farmhands quickly returned the salute.

22 APRIL 1943, THE SUDETENLAND, CZECHOSLOVAKIA

Carswell and Donaldson Get on the Wrong Train

A few more *Heil Hitler*'s greased their way across a bridge leading to a road that allowed Carswell and Donaldson to put 30 miles between them and the work camp. And while the bushes they crawled under near dawn a few days after they'd escaped provided a reasonable amount of cover from prying eyes, the copse of trees they were in now did little to protect them from the cold drizzle. The freight train struggling up a nearby hill offered both shelter from the elements and a more speedy way of heading southwest. Carswell, who, like many Canadian teens, had hopped freight trains for the fun of it, led the way—running in time with the train, then veering closer to it until he grasped the ladder between two cars. Donaldson tripped on his first try but then clambered aboard. As the train chugged through the night, they hid under the tarp covering a lumber car, enjoying the thought that they'd be near the Swiss border by evening.

Instead, as the sun set, they found themselves in a marshalling yard, which put them too close for comfort to the guards protecting the yard and also possibly in the crosshairs of Allied bombers. Their immediate concern, however, was the cold, which by midnight forced them to risk running to a hay wagon, where they hoped to cover themselves to keep warm. The hay, however, was frozen, and it took two hours to cut away enough to hide under the tightly tied tarp. Although warmed by their labours and now hidden, they continued suffering for having forgotten a water bottle. Eventually, sometime before dawn, they fell asleep.

Woken by the clanks and screeches of railcars being shunted about, the men felt their spirits rise when their car was attached to a train, only to plummet when the train started back in the direction from which they had come. Through the long day, as they snapped at each other or lapsed into angry silence, their tongues growing ever larger and their throats more scratchy, the train took them deeper into Germany. Late in the afternoon, the train stopped. As workmen unloaded a nearby car, they slipped off the train and hid under a nearby building that was raised on pylons.

A short time later, a workman walked under the building to urinate. As he did so, he looked up and saw Carswell and Donaldson and froze, then began to back his way out of the open basement. Donaldson called out softly to him in German, telling him that he and Carswell were escaped POWs. For a few moments it appeared that they'd been lucky and that the man wasn't a Sudeten German but a Czech. Then came the sound of running, blowing whistles and orders barked out in German.

16–20 APRIL 1943, PICARDY, FRANCE

Madame Zannie Takes MacDonald on an Important Bicycle Ride

Shortly after MacDonald woke up, a man arrived at the Dutilleuls' asking if he wanted to escape. "I was anxious as hell. Here I was, somewhere in France. I could have found a policeman, shown him my dog tags and surrendered. I was pretty sure I'd get the Geneva protections. But, strangely, doing so never crossed my mind. Here were strangers, men, a father and mother who were willing to risk everything for me, a stranger, who had [literally] dropped in from the sky," says MacDonald. He had been given civilian clothes that fit reasonably well and breakfast. Shortly after, a woman who he later learned was Madame Zannie arrived with two bicycles, and soon he was pedalling after her "at a respectable distance" to her wooden house, which doubled as a seed store. "No one came to the house and there was no telephone, so I assumed that the time Zannie arrived had all been arranged in advance," he says.

The next day, Zannie led him to Chauny, a small town nestled between the Oise River and the St. Quentin Canal. The low rolling hills covered in new shoots of grain and wildflowers reminded MacDonald of home. At a safe house, a Resistance leader unrolled a map and pointed to a location he wanted bombed. "He wanted me to take the coordinates in my pocket but, since I was already running a great risk by being out of uniform, I thought better of this because it would give the Germans another excuse to execute me for being a spy. Instead, I memorized the coordinates," says MacDonald.

That night, a bomber stream passing over Chauny was especially noticeable. "I was in the bedroom on the second floor of the stone house. I was used to saying grace at meals, but this wasn't done by these Resistance people. Before I climbed into bed, I took out my rosary and began praying, knowing that in just a few hours, when it was near 10 p.m. in New Glasgow, my parents and sister too would be on their knees praying for me. I hadn't been in bed long when I heard bombers. There were a lot of them and they were awfully low," says MacDonald.

About a quarter of an hour after the last of the bombers slipped deeper over *Festung Europa*, MacDonald heard a commotion downstairs. "Concerned that the Germans knew I was there, I quietly climbed out of bed, opened the door and went to the stairs. From the top of the stairs, I could see the front door, and through it I saw a number of bloodied men in RAF blue walk into the house. Just as I was about to say something, one of the French underground men who had brought the RAF men to the house shushed me and motioned me back to my room," says MacDonald. Whether the plane had malfunctioned or been shot down, in his mind's eye MacDonald saw the crew's terror-filled faces as their plane gyrated wildly in the sky and could almost hear the thuds of their bodies tossed against unyielding bulkheads. Knowing the fear that one might have only moments to live, he once again thanked the Lord that he had survived.

25 APRIL 1943, STALAG VIII-B, LAMSDORF, GERMANY

EASTER SUNDAY

The pain of Easter was both different from and the same as that of Christmas. The POWs were still separated from their families and had to make do with a meal prepared from supplies saved from Red Cross parcels.

The story of Jesus's arrest, trial, scourging, death on the Cross and Resurrection had special significance for the airmen who had escaped from their burning airborne trenches and for the soldiers who had been through the fires of Dieppe. Yet, Darch says, they felt an additional pain. The Canadian Corps went over the top on 9 April 1917 on their way to defeat the Germans on Vimy Ridge; nevertheless, for men like Darch, that great victory was more associated with Easter Monday than with the actual dates of the Battle of Arras. At Eastertide, therefore, the memory of the humiliation of the surrender on the beaches of Dieppe and the ongoing humiliation of being shackled, combined to deepen their feeling of having failed to live up to the standard set by their fathers.

The end of Easter vigil signifies the most joyous event in the Christian calendar, the Resurrection of Jesus Christ. As they did for Christmas, Darch and hundreds of his comrades, irrespective of their being Catholic or Protestant, went to hear Padre John Foote say mass. "It didn't matter to us who conducted the Easter service," explains Darch. "Two things were important. The first was that we were together saying prayers and celebrating the holiday. The second was that the service was one of the few times we knew that we were doing something in the same way we had done at home and that our families were doing that day."

Father Boulanger in Stalag XXI-A, in Schildberg, Poland, was perhaps the best equipped to celebrate Easter. Boulanger's congregants celebrated the Resurrection both in deed—the removal of the shroud that symbolized Christ's death from the Cross—and by chocolate and other sweets paid for with money donated by the children of the diocese of Grenoble.

LATE APRIL–MID-MAY 1943, FLAVY-LE-MARTEL, FRANCE

MacDonald Hides at Dr. Lupanov's

Two days after returning to Madame Zannie's house, the two were once again on bicycles and pedalling toward Flavy-le-Martel: "She led me to a fine two-story red-brick house that was much more substantial than her wooden house and even the one I grew up in in Nova Scotia. The house I had stopped at the night before had a gate, but it was an old one. This house was surrounded by a wrought-iron fence set into brick supports. Behind the house was a large backyard that was surrounded by a brick wall about seven feet high that afforded reasonably good protection, so I could go outside. Unlike both of the other houses I'd been in, this one had indoor plumbing."

MacDonald was welcomed by Dr. Lupanov, a Bulgarian who was also in hiding; his wife, Lucienne; and her brother Felix. They were friendly, gave MacDonald a room to sleep in and food but did not, to his surprise, ask any questions about Canada.

"The house fronted onto the town's main street, and I was told to be careful about showing myself there. About three days after I arrived, I was walking through the living room and stopped to look outside. The sound of a truck arriving made me more than a little apprehensive, but I continued to watch as the passenger door opened, and who should come out but 'Parky' our navigator," recalls MacDonald. For the next month and a half, MacDonald and Parkinson remained with the Lupanov family, sometimes taking bicycle rides to keep from getting cabin fever, and listening intently to Felix's stories of sabotage.

26 APRIL 1943, VATICAN CITY

McAuley's Audience with Pope Pius XII

Nothing in Royalton, New Brunswick, McAuley's hometown or in the cramped apartment buildings around Eglinton and Yonge, in Toronto, where he had lived before the war had prepared McAuley for the sweeping marble-floored hallways that led to the papal apartments. McAuley's trained engineer's eye could not have helped noting the foreshortening and other tricks of perspective in the 16th- and 17th-century frescoes adorning the walls.

As they would have for their king, George VI, all three knelt when they entered Pope Pius XII's study and saw the thin, bookish man sitting on the ornate chair, in front of which was a small stool for Catholics to kneel on when receiving the pope's blessing. Though controversy rages about Pius's actions (or inactions) vis-à-vis the Holocaust, there is no doubt about his commitment to protect Allied escapers who reached Vatican City; he refused an official request that the three escapers be turned over to the Italian police. Pius gave each escaper rosary beads and his benediction, and ended their meeting with the invocation "*Benedicat vos omnipotens Deus, Pater et Filius et Spiritus Sanctus*," some of which, thanks to his high school Latin, McAuley understood: "May almighty God bless you, the Father, the Son and the Holy Spirit."

26 APRIL 1943, LOURDES, NOVA SCOTIA

Mr. and Mrs. MacDonald Have a Moment of Hope

About the time the pope blessed a Protestant Canadian airman, Pius's co-religionists in Lourdes, Nova Scotia, were in church praying for their son, Ian. The blue aerogram that had arrived on the 24th seemed to have answered earlier prayers: it suggested that RCAF officials in London had made a ghastly mistake. For before them in Ian's flowing hand was his home address—and on the inside of the folded flimsy paper was his note written in the same, almost carefree tone they'd grown used to: "I just received your box of chocolates a couple of days ago. . . . Thanks a lot. They disappeared like wildfire."

Moments after reading Ian's words telling them that he'd written to Father Miller thanking him for the cigarettes (and pointing out that, since he didn't smoke, chocolate bars were preferable), the MacDonalds' elation dissolved. For while the Stellarton, Nova

Scotia, post office stamped the letter on 24 April, the squadron's stamp read 30 March. The date in Ian's hand inside the letter, 28-3-43 (28 March 1943), erased all doubt. Mr. and Mrs. MacDonald's boy had written the letter three weeks before he climbed into his Halifax on 14 April.

28 APRIL 1943, KASSEL, GERMANY

Prouse and His Escape Partners Do Some Sightseeing

Prouse, carrying papers saying he was a Czech labourer named Janek Mrachek, and two other Kriegies took advantage of the half-light to slip out of the line of POWs heading for a factory. They dropped into the ditch between the inner and outer fence, where they dug up escape gear that had been previously hidden. Behind the boilerhouse they tore off their uniforms and put on their washed-out red civilian clothes, dyed with a brew that the cauldron master convinced a guard was a soup made from rotten cabbage. As their comrades frustrated the morning Appell by moving about, they joined the column of civilian night workers leaving the camp. Prouse's heart sank as he neared the main gate: "Rat Face" was checking identity cards, and he knew Prouse's face well enough to see that it didn't quite match the one on his card. Prouse's "*Heil Hitler*," however, seemed to do the trick, as Rat Face broke off looking at him, allowing Prouse and the two other Kriegies to take a few more steps toward freedom.

Then came the sirens, and the three escapers pushed their way through the civilian workers in front of them before jumping a fence and running across a scrub field. Beyond it was a railway embankment, which the escapers climbed up. As they fought to catch their breath, 20 guards with police dogs approached, prompting Prouse and his comrades to slide down the other side of the embankment and run into a dense evergreen forest.

Since the dogs weren't bloodhounds and couldn't pick up the scent, the guards fired shots in the hope of flushing out the escapers. Over the course of his six long hours in hiding, Prouse, misremembering his high school Shakespeare, imagined, "a thousand deaths."[119] By mid-afternoon the searchers had given up, but the escapers didn't leave the wood until near 10 p.m., when they walked through an unusually cold late-April night to a freight yard, where they climbed onto a boxcar. Sometime before dawn they jumped from the moving train, and found a deserted shack in which they grabbed a few hours' sleep, then a shave.

This last was important, because Kassel, the town they walked to upon waking, was a good size and still undamaged, and its residents prided themselves on their propriety. The escapers' appearance and Kriegie Tom Glassey's German passed muster at the ticket counter and on the train to Warburg—and in the Warburg station's restaurant, where he ordered a round of beers. Before long, they were sleeping, their heads resting on the table.

When he awoke, Prouse didn't have time to worry about his bruised pride at having been put under by a single beer; of more concern were the German soldiers who had bedded down on the large round table. After slinking away to the toilets, where the escapers again shaved, Prouse nearly blew their cover by asking a station agent if the train pulling out of the station was going to Warburg. Prouse realized that in his poor German he'd asked if the train was going to the town he was already in. He ran to the train that was then boarding passengers for Arnsberg. A few moments later he spotted his companions, who had just boarded the train. Prouse sat next to a German soldier so enamoured with his own voice that, for the entire two-hour trip, he didn't notice that all the Canadian ever said was "*ja*" or "*nein.*"

When they climbed down from the train in Arnsberg, Prouse was so focused on looking out for police and soldiers that he didn't notice a woman. After knocking into him, the motherly-looking Frau whispered "*Aufpassen!*" (Watch out!), signalling that his disguise was anything but perfect. A short while later, after several worrisome looks from soldiers in the beer parlour, the escapers quietly got up and left. Years later, Prouse joked that when, once back on the street, they saw a troop of German soldiers walking toward them, and "cowardice being the better part of valour" they turned into a side street.

The side street ended at the foot of a hill, at the top of which they saw the ruins of the town's castle. An "apparition in the shape of a very old man seemed to emerge from the ground," Prouse recalled. The man, it turned out, was the caretaker of the castle, parts of which dated back 900 years. Napoleon had visited the castle during his bid to conquer Europe. The caretaker gave them something to eat and drink, and then a tour, never asking who they were, what they were doing there, "nor commenting on Tommy's quiet translations of the commentary."[120]

Chapter Seven

May–August 1943

The cords of death encompassed me;
the torrents of perdition assailed me;
the cords of Sheol entangled me;
the snares of death confronted me.

—Psalm 18:4–5

2 MAY 1943, STALAG VIII-B, LAMSDORF, GERMANY

Private John Grogan Gives a Grammar Lesson

For a moment, it looked as though the pretty Fräulein at the gate would put an end to his home run before it even began. "Prison life suits you. You look much better than your photo," she said, signalling some doubt that she believed she was talking to Frank Hickey, a British soldier captured at Dunkirk. John Grogan's compliment made her smile, and she waved him on.[121]

Grogan's next few minutes were an idyll. For the first time since being captured at Dieppe nine months earlier, the man who had grown up just east of Algonquin Park saw ahead of him not barbed wire and watchtowers but something soothing and familiar: tall pine trees. He tamped down the fear that swept over him when he realized his escape partner hadn't made it through the gate by concentrating on the wonder of "civilians moving about their ordinary tasks." It is a measure of how artificial life in a POW camp is that four decades later, Grogan remembered the details of an old man smoking a pipe and girls skipping rope.

The "strange feeling of freedom" extended even to his meeting with some Hitlerjugend who showed off their "*Sieg Heil*s" to the soldiers marching the POWs to the train station and the English they learned at school to the "*Engländer.*" "Who, whom . . . is going to win the war?" asked one brown-shirted teen, who was as surprised by Grogan correcting his shaky grasp of the distinction between the subjective and the objective case as Grogan's grade eight teacher back in Renfrew, Ontario, would have been pleased. "Who is correct, not whom." As for *who* was going to win the war, Grogan answered, "England."

3 MAY 1943, STALAG VI-G/Z, ARNOLDSWEILER, GERMANY

Robert Prouse Sees the Walking Dead

Czech workers, Robert Prouse and his escape partner later discovered, were barred from Munich, but it wasn't their cover story that aroused suspicions: it was the faded Red Cross on the bag holding their provisions. Later, the backwards swastika on their *Arbeitspass* gave the Gestapo a chuckle.

There was nothing funny about their body search, which included a painful examination of their penises, or about POW camp in Arnoldsweiler. The factory manager at Arbeitskommando 1049 violated Prouse's Geneva rights by making the NCO work, but during the long winter months he allowed the prisoners to mount plays, concerts and boxing matches. By contrast, the 13 days at Stalag VI-G/Z seemed something out of Dante's *Inferno.*

Shortly after arriving, Prouse was led to a shower room, where he saw a group of Russians, most just "naked human skeletons, so far gone that the force of the showers knocked them off their feet." A short while later, another POW stopped him from passing them some food, saying, "It's a waste . . . they're going to die soon anyway."[122] Starvation did not kill all at the same time. Each day, men with sunken cheeks and collapsed buttocks, their bodies, having burned off what fat they could find, cruelly mocked by their bloated bellies, carried dead comrades to ditches outside the camp, where the bodies decomposed in the open.

LATE SPRING 1943, STALAG LUFT III, SAGAN, POLAND

VERNON HOWLAND'S JOB

Although a year earlier Vernon Howland had helped dig a tunnel, at Stalag Luft III he wasn't assigned to work under RCAF Pilot Officer Wally Floody, who put what he learned working in the mines of Ontario to good use engineering the three most famous escape tunnels in history: "Tom," "Dick" and "Harry," all nearing the 60-foot mark and equipped with electricity and air-circulation systems. Each was shored up with slats taken from bunks and had rail systems to remove spoil. Nor was Howland one of the "penguins" who disposed of the earth, packed into eight-pound bags in each of their trouser legs.

Rather, as a member of the Communications Committee, at eleven o'clock each night, he was in Father Goudreau's room listening on the hidden radio to the BBC news, paper copies of which were distributed to the barracks in the morning. (Goudreau never asked what the news was and found out only when the news sheet was delivered to his barracks.) If the goons burst into the hut, Howland's job was to eat the message sheet, destroy the coils and hide other parts of the radio under the barracks' toilet before sitting on it, hoping that the delicacy of the situation would carry the moment.

6 MAY 1943, ARBEITSKOMMANDO E192, OELS, POLAND

GROGAN MEETS THE KRANKER

The "Kranker" was every bit an Allied soldier. Most of the time, all he needed to do was apply just enough force to dislocate a finger or shoulder and *voilà*, a Kriegie passed muster on the sick parade. (*Krank* is German for "sick.") RCAF pilot Ken Hyde recalled one time, however, when a Kranker's art stymied the Germans who found the body of an informer naked in the latrine with no signs of violence but quite dead.

In the moments between when Grogan realized he'd been surrounded and when the barracks leader, "Taffy," called out in his Welsh accent for the Kranker, Grogan fought to keep his story going. Fearing that he might be a German plant, but thinking that he might be a swapover from the RAF, Taffy asked, "What squadron do you belong to?" Grogan answered, "The Second Eleventh"—an Australian tank battalion. A rough voice called out, "What's your fucking game?" Grogan didn't answer, and his throat went dry when the Kranker arrived carrying two pieces of wood and an iron rod, asking if he should start with "two fingers." Seeing that he was unable to speak, Taffy gave Grogan some water, saying, "You are not an Australian, and you do not belong to the Second Eleventh battalion," adding that if Grogan's response wasn't acceptable, he'd be turned over to the Kranker.[123]

Not knowing how he'd substantiate his story, Grogan said, "I am a Canadian, taken prisoner at Dieppe. . . . I swapped over with Frank Hickey of the Second Eleventh Australian battalion to get to a work party." He was trying to escape, he continued. The words "Good old Canada" were music to Grogan's ears but cut no ice with Taffy, who called a soldier named Reggie over. Grogan answered his first question, "Who is Jiggs's wife?" without missing a beat. When he answered the second question equally quickly, the men who had been ready to kill him cheered. Later, Reggie told him that they were alarmed because no one in the barracks could place his accent. Grogan asked, "Did you ever visit the Ottawa Valley?"

Over the next few weeks, Grogan practised his German with the German and Polish workers with whom he unloaded bags of wheat. On the railway line that ran by the siding where they worked, trains passed that were made up of hundreds of cattle cars. Through the slats, Grogan could see teenaged girls, their hair shorn and with yellow Stars of David pinned over their breasts, staring through the barbed-wire covered openings. A guard told him that they were being moved to a "new modern camp, where they would be treated well," just outside the Polish village of Oświęcim, known in German as Auschwitz.

10 MAY 1943, BRNO, EASTERN CZECHOSLOVAKIA

Andrew Carswell and His Escape Partner Surprise Their Jailor with Their Exercise Regimen

The camaraderie of their first few nights in custody didn't last long. Their first jailor, a Czech, fed them well out of his own rations and, after John Donaldson asked whether his Blaupunkt radio could pick up England, listened with them to a BBC show, the English escaping the jailor, while Red Skelton's North American humour escaped Donaldson but not the Canadian, Andrew Carswell. Their second jailor, a German, was a "good-natured, heavy-set scoundrel," who at least shared the cigarettes he had confiscated from them, though he saw no need to augment their diet of turnip soup and hard black bread.[124]

After a few days of sharing a cell that was so small they had to take turns pacing it, and disagreeing about every subject they talked about, and despite the fleeting pleasures of seeing their jailor's buxom daughter, their nerves reached a breaking point. When Donaldson began his favourite rant—that RCAF sergeants merited less respect than a British Army private—Carswell said something insulting about Donaldson's parentage.

The British soldier stopped in his tracks, turned and punched Carswell. Thanks to his boxing training, Carswell recovered quickly and landed a blow on Donaldson's nose. As they rolled on the floor punching madly at each other, their stool and a bucket paid the ultimate price. When a guard rushed in yelling, "What's going on?" Donaldson replied, "We were just exercising . . . We do this to keep fit."

Their anger unspent, they refused to speak to each other for several days, until they realized the ridiculousness of preferring to speak only with their captors. The guard who took them back to Stalag VIII-B a few days later was surprised that they had taken express and freight trains instead of ordinary passenger trains, on which they could have blended in with workers.

25 MAY 1943, STALAG LUFT III, SAGAN, POLAND

Father Goudreau Is Given a Typewriter

Even Hermann Glemnitz, the guard nicknamed "Dimwit," knew something was up. So it is impossible to believe that Father Goudreau, notwithstanding his protestations to Father Ducharme about the monotony of the camp, knew nothing about the plan for some Kriegies to escape by walking out of the camp in faux German uniforms. Wally Floody definitely knew, and his time in captivity and his good German should have merited him a chance to escape, but the Escape Committee said he was more valuable directing the digging of the tunnels.

The German censor familiar with Goudreau's recent letters could be forgiven for thinking that the priest was something of an ingrate. A week earlier, he complained about the vulgarity of answering a friend's letter in the scant seven lines allotted to a card. Now he was writing a typewritten letter of several hundred words, and he could think of no better way to begin than by grousing about the mail delivery: Father Ducharme's December 1942 letter arrived at the same time as his February 1943 letter. By mid-1943, censors had read thousands of complaints about being "cooped up behind barbed wire." Few, however, were as eloquent as Goudreau's: "After three years of walking around like a bear in a barbed wire cage, your 'directives' are necessary for a compass that has gone crazy."

If noted at all, the sentence that ended a card the priest wrote a week later must have seemed just one more example of pious nonsense. But the elegant writer of French made sure that Rev. P.J. Forget would notice it. "When we cultivate flowers that are too beautiful, the divine gardener comes to pick them" is even more awkward in French than it is in English. Goudreau knew too that Forget would catch the echo of the final sentence of *Candide*, "Let us cultivate our garden," written by the arch-atheist Voltaire, and thus ponder Goudreau's garden just at the time it was one of the places Floody's men used to hide spoil from the tunnels.

29 MAY 1943, PARIS

Ian MacDonald in the City of Light

The beat-up tam-o'-shanter was dark brown and not tartan, so it could do duty as the ubiquitous French beret, which together with the dark shirt, worn trousers, old jacket and small suitcase constituted Ian MacDonald's disguise on the train trip from Sainte-Flavie to Paris. Six months earlier, Sydney Smith relied on Tante Dédée's wiles to protect him on the train to Bordeaux. If MacDonald and "Parky" Parkinson were stopped, their hopes lay with their forged documents, as both were well aware as they followed at some distance their helper, another young French woman risking her life for the Allies, onto the train to Paris.

"I'd been in Occupied France for a month and a half, and through Dr. Lupanov's window I'd seen many gendarmes, but it was only when we got off the train in Gare du Nord that I saw a German soldier in the flesh," recalls MacDonald. "Not just one but dozens, seemingly of every rank. Our instructions were to look at the crowd as though we were looking for familiar faces."

They did but with their hearts in their mouths. As the minutes passed, MacDonald worried that their contacts weren't there. His stomach tightened when a German soldier with a rifle slung over his shoulder started toward them.

Seventy years later, the scene still unrolls for MacDonald in slow motion. He was scanning the crowd. The soldier started toward them, looking as if he was going to ask a question. Not knowing any German and fearing that only a fool would miss the Nova Scotian accent behind his "*Je ne sais pas*," MacDonald took what he hoped looked like the most natural of steps backwards, thus putting him slightly out of the soldiers' line of march and making it more natural for the soldier to speak to the man behind MacDonald. To his surprise, it worked: the German soldier walked by and spoke to that man. MacDonald was still silently catching his breath when he noticed a couple discreetly signalling to him.

The street signs themselves signalled danger, for atop the French stood the street's name in German Gothic script. Still, MacDonald found being in Paris exhilarating as he and Parkinson followed Louis Vion and his wife down likely what is now rue de Dunkerque, across a wide boulevard and then onto the narrow, cobblestoned streets of Montmartre, to 7 rue Tardieu, a shabby five-story sandstone building with small shops on the first floor.

MacDonald marvelled at both the beauty of the Sacrè-Coeur Basilica, which rises over Montmartre like a Catholic Taj Mahal, and the bravery of the men and women who risked everything for young men so far from home. Had he known that the boxes behind the shop windows were empty and that, according to the collaborationist general René de Chambrun, the food situation in Paris had "reached its critical point" and on the black market potatoes went for six times their official price of 148 francs a kilogram, MacDonald would have been even more impressed with the personal sacrifice undertaken by the family that hid him and Parkinson.[125]

As had Smith, Parkinson and MacDonald posed as visitors coming to see the sights, which explained why they spent so little time in the apartment (thus limiting the chances neighbours might overhear an unguarded English word or two). On one of their walks, the Vions' daughter took them to a photographer's shop, where each was supplied with an identity card and a travel pass to the south. MacDonald became "Guy Labourer," a barber, and Parkinson a schoolteacher.

1 OR 2 JUNE 1943, PARIS

MacDonald's Train Is Cancelled

MacDonald, Parkinson and a Scotsman named David McKinnon, who had joined them earlier that morning, followed the Vions into Montparnasse train station, famed for the train that smashed through one of the station's walls in 1896. "The Germans in the station drove home the danger we were in," MacDonald recalls. "We were out of uniform, and we knew that if we were caught not only would it be terrible for the people trying to help us but we couldn't be sure that our dog tags would bring us under Geneva."

Despite being surrounded by enemy soldiers, MacDonald was not especially anxious. At one point, one of their guides discreetly signalled that the train had been cancelled. After bailing out of a burning bomber and being on the run for more than month, a cancelled train seemed small beer indeed. More important was making sure that they didn't lose sight of their guides, who led them northwest from the station to the Seine, across Pont de Grenelle, and to an apartment house overlooking the river in one of Paris's most exclusive areas, the 16th arrondissement. Out the fourth-floor window of the room he was given in this "swank apartment," MacDonald had a stunning view of the Seine, bisected by the narrow Île de Cygnes, the trees of which seemed like an Impressionist splash of light green against the shifting greys and dark greens of the river and the grey sandstone blocks of its bank.

What grabbed MacDonald's eye as he looked out from the apartment owned by the same Andrée de Jongh—Tante Dédée—who had helped Smith escape, however, was what he saw on the southern tip of the island: a one-quarter-sized replica of the Statue of Liberty.

SPRING 1943, BRESLAU, POLAND

Grogan Makes a Friend and Drinks a Beer

Frank Hickey's eye infection was real. And, as far as the guard named Ludwig knew, so too was the name of the POW he was escorting to an eye clinic in Breslau, Poland. Ludwig puffed himself up by calling Hickey—John Grogan—a *Schweinehund Engländer* and making him walk in the gutter.

In the waiting room of the eye clinic, a boy asked Grogan, "Are you a soldier?" A little girl asked her mother, "Is that the uniform of the Spanish Blue [Division]?" Ludwig replied, "He is an English Prisoner of War. I am his guard." The boy broke the hush that followed. "My name is Rudi. I like you." The other patients were taken aback when Grogan answered in German that he liked Rudi too.[126]

Do all POWs speak German, someone asked. "No, they don't," said Ludwig. "This one is a trouble-maker." An old man swiftly put Ludwig in his place. "Is one a trouble-maker because he speaks German? He looks no different from you except his uniform fits better." Grogan caused everyone, including Ludwig, to laugh by saying, "I'll bet you killed more of your men with your soup, than you did English with your rifle" after the man said that in the last war he'd been a cook and had shot "Englanders" while stirring his soup.

On a return trip to the clinic two weeks later, an old woman on the train did not realize Grogan was a POW and asked him to read a letter from her son, then fighting on the Eastern Front. The words "I will be home on leave soon and look forward to sleeping in my own room" made Grogan choke up and think of his own mother. After he told the woman that he was captured at Dieppe, she grasped his hand and, with tears in her eyes, wished him well.

5 JUNE 1943, PAU, FRANCE

MacDonald Crosses Himself

As their train neared the Restricted Zone, MacDonald knew that German soldiers would soon be examining their papers.

"We were living on the edge," says MacDonald. One slip in the printing, an untoward show of nerves or too-studied insouciance and they'd be unmasked. "The soldier who took my *carte d'identité* looked at it for what seemed a long time, then at me, then back at it. I waited for him to say something, hoping I'd be able to answer in passable French. Then he passed it back to me and moved on."

A short time before the train reached Pau, MacDonald, whose sandy hair was quite out of place in southern France, saw something familiar through the window. "I had a general idea of where we were but did not know the train's exact route. But I had no doubt that I was looking at the famous Grotte de Lourdes, which I recognized from pictures at school and the church in the Lourdes I'd grown up in," says MacDonald.

The woman at the small hotel about 25 miles from the Spanish border was friendly enough and fed them. A short time after the three escapers were back in their room, however, she knocked on their door. "She was very agitated and said that while we could spend the night, we had to leave early in the morning. We guessed from what she said that some of the staff were asking uncomfortable questions about us," says MacDonald.

Pau's old cobblestone streets provided enough sights so that evaders could wander for the day without drawing undue attention. With narrow windows, sharply angled roofs and support timbers standing out starkly from the white stucco, many of the two- and three-story houses recalled those from Shakespeare's time (and later Victorian versions) sprinkled across the towns and villages of England. Amid German soldiers also taking in the sights, MacDonald marvelled at the Château de Pau, the brick keep of which dated back seven centuries and where Henri IV was born—Henri IV being the king celebrated in MacDonald's Catholic school books for converting from Protestantism to Catholicism after uttering the famous line, "Paris is worth a mass."

As planned, late in the afternoon they started walking south from Pau on avenue Rauski, a road known to cycling enthusiasts because it leads the Tour de France into the Pyrenees. Shortly after turning on to a road going east, they stopped for a short rest. "It may not have been the best place to stop," says MacDonald, "because, soon after, a group of German soldiers came toward us and we thought we'd been discovered. But then I realized they were asking directions and were not asking for our papers." By saying nothing, they risked being taken for vagrants and being demanded to show their papers. "It looked better to simply say '*Je ne sais pas*' and hope for the best than to risk another examination of our papers." Used to such taciturn answers from the people whose country his army occupied, the soldier simply turned away. A short time later, a truck pulled up and the two Canadians and McKinnon climbed in for the ride to Oloron-Sainte-Marie, four miles from the Spanish border.

9 JUNE 1943, LIEBENAU, GERMANY

Prouse and Tommy Glidden Escape and Are Captured

The threat to shoot them if they were caught trying to escape couldn't be discounted, but that's the kind of things Kommandants said. But what rankled Prouse in the days before his and Tommy

Glidden's second escape attempt was the Kommandant's gall in presenting them with a bill for 140 reichsmarks for the uniforms lost during their first attempt a month earlier.

In the early hours of 9 June,[127] however, as they sweat bullets in a space they had prepared inside a pile of logs, they regretted not noticing the nearby pipes that fed hot water into the large vat that boiled the logs. Stripping off their uniforms brought some relief, albeit at the cost of an extremely itchy covering of fine sawdust.

A log that wouldn't budge momentarily held up their escape; when it did, the sound seemed to broadcast their plans. As a flashlight lit first this, then that part of the yard, the two escapers inched their way toward the barbed-wire fence. The fence snagged their clothing, and when they stepped off its final strand, it pinged loud enough to alert the guards to where they had just been. Nevertheless, the fence had become their ally, for to follow them, the Germans would have to run to the gate, giving the escapers a precious head start in reaching the rail yard two miles away. Reaching it safely, the two men snuck aboard a flat car loaded with tanks heading east toward Russia.

The next morning, a sign told them they were in Kassel. The reason the workers seemed interested in them when they climbed down from the boxcar became clear when they realized the workers were dragooned Serbs and Poles. A short time later, Prouse and Glidden found a beer parlour, and while the "guest workers" seemed to understand Prouse's request, they were too frightened to give the escapers civilian clothes.

Thinking that a home run was impossible dressed as British soldiers, they decided to give themselves up. Surprisingly, given the German officer corps' reputation for rectitude, several officers ignored their British battle dress and answered the Kriegies' "*Heil* Churchills" with the more orthodox reply. "How dumb can these guys be?" they wondered as they reconsidered their decision to surrender and walked through Kassel to a field, where they slept in some tall grass.[128]

Later that day, they climbed aboard a slow-moving freight train, taking shelter from the rain in its unmanned guard box. About an hour later, the train stopped and a civilian guard opened the door. He was as ignorant of Prouse's slang "Hi there, square head" as the Canadian was of his German. After recovering from a case of the giggles, Glidden told Prouse that in the series of *ja*s, he'd confirmed they were escaped prisoners. At the next stop, Liebenau, the village's police chief, wearing a spiked *Pickelhaube* dating from the last war, took them into custody.

9 JUNE 1943, PAU, FRANCE

MacDonald and Parkinson's Home Run Ends

They were alive. They were slapped and threatened by bayonets. They were disgusted and frightened by the blood-spattered cells they'd been shoved into. But they were alive.

Two days earlier, just as the eastern sky lightened, a small man in his late 40s carrying a rucksack filled with bread and cheese entered the barn and woke MacDonald, Parkinson and McKinnon. Soon the party was heading for the foothills of the Pyrenees. "From a distance, they looked like the hills back home. But soon it became a very sharp climb. Some of the points were almost vertical, and we had to pull ourselves up from tree to tree," recalls MacDonald.

"Sitting for a moment and having some water, and bread and cheese, we watched our guide look around. Then we got up and followed him a short distance. He stopped and went in a different direction. It slowly dawned on us that he was not sure of the way. But then he started again and we followed, believing we were heading into Spain."

The climb down was more difficult because of the need to find handholds. Partway down the mountain, the guide stopped and said he'd made a mistake, and they were not descending into

Spain but were still in France, not far from where they'd started out. MacDonald and the others struggled to control their emotions. "But we knew from our own experience on the mountain how disorienting it was," says MacDonald. "And, as we had since we'd been with the underground, we trusted the guide." He took them to a yellow stucco barn. There were no animals, though their smell was plainly evident. The guide promised to find another who knew the mountains better, and that he would have a farmer drop off food.

As the following day, 8 June, wore on, they began getting nervous. "What's taking him so long?" the evaders wondered. At one point, they ventured out beyond the trees that surrounded the barn and into a field. "Suddenly, we heard the sound of bloodhounds. We ran across the field and into a stream, which we ran through for about 150 feet, and then crossed into a small wood," says MacDonald. A few minutes later, MacDonald saw three German soldiers, each holding tightly to a leashed bloodhound, which had lost their scent in the water of the stream. The Germans searched for about an hour. "We waited in the wood until nightfall and then made our way back to the barn," adds MacDonald.

Early the next morning, a truck drove up. "The driver told us that he was going to drive us to another spot where it would be easier to climb into the mountains." With freedom beckoning, they clambered into the truck. At a bend in the road that ran between a swift-flowing river and a cliff, the truck slowed. "Then," recalls MacDonald, "three German soldiers with rifles stepped out from behind a clump of trees ahead of us, and I said to Parky, 'Well, that's the end of the road for us.'"

The soldiers spoke neither English nor French, and none of the Allied servicemen spoke German, but the rifles trained on them spoke clearly as they climbed out of the truck with their hands up and then lay prone on the ground. "When Germans started treating the driver rather amicably, we realized we'd been betrayed," recalls MacDonald.

When bailing out of a burning plane, survival depends on immediate actions and the immutable laws of physics and chemistry. Now, however, MacDonald and the others were subject to the whims of the enemy pointing rifles at the backs of their heads. Their identity disks were sewn into their pants, but they were enemy servicemen in civilian clothes hundreds of miles from where they'd been shot down, which meant they had information about the Resistance that the Germans wanted.

Given the silent testimony of blood splattering his cell, MacDonald expected the worst when he was interrogated in Gestapo headquarters in Pau. Asked who had helped him, MacDonald demurred, giving only his name, rank and service number as stamped into his indentity disks, which he handed over to the German, who ordered him to empty his pockets. Upon seeing MacDonald's rosary, the Gestapo officer insulted it. After parachuting from his bomber, MacDonald had checked to make sure that the rosary he'd been given years ago was still with him, and in the barn he'd used it to pray each night. Without thinking, MacDonald clenched fists, ready to defend the physical manifestation of his faith. The Gestapo officer noticed and slapped MacDonald hard across the face.

As he turned back to look the Gestapo officer in the eye, MacDonald's legs tightened in preparation for a lunge forward; seeing this, the soldier who had been behind the officer stepped forward, bayonet at the ready. "Even when I saw the flash of the bayonet I was almost beyond caring. It took every ounce of willpower I had not to move, as I realized he'd run me through before I could reach the arrogant German. I forced myself to unclench my fists and resumed a regular standing position," recounts MacDonald. Having got nowhere with the angry Canadian, the Gestapo officer ordered him back to his cell, where he spent two nights before he, Parkinson and McKinnon were transferred to a jail in Bordeaux.

MID-JUNE 1943, STALAG LUFT III, SAGAN, POLAND

RCAF Flight Lieutenant Ted Kipp Helps Set Up Foodacco

The German guards, who served a state that knew its last free election more than a decade earlier, must have looked on with wry amusement at the spirited debate over Foodacco that took place during that exceptionally hot June. Foodacco was a trading company that bought and sold Red Cross supplies such as canned fruit, salmon and condensed milk, as well as soap. Unlike the bazaars in other camps, Foodacco was centrally organized, using cigarettes or chocolate to purchase items that it then sold at a profit. Day in, day out, Foodacco could "make a profit of ten or twenty cigarettes on the sale of condensed milk," which Ted Kipp, an RCAF officer from Winnipeg, and his RAF pilot business partner then used to purchase other items to sell before "paying" themselves.[129]

Men who were willing to spend their cigarettes were able to "keep themselves in comparative luxury."[130] To do so, Brown wasn't above doing another officer's laundry: a shirt brought in ten fags, while a pair of socks netted him five.

Prices rose and fell, though not always according to the law of supply and demand. The price of soap, say, did not necessarily fall even after a shipment of Red Cross parcels arrived and supply went up. For those same parcels brought thousands of cigarettes into the camp, in effect increasing the money supply, thus creating inflation.[131] Accordingly, prices for desired goods could remain high even when there was no shortage of the item, which enriched Foodacco because it made a greater profit that could then be used to buy other items that could be stored until the shortages began.

Critics argued that the POWs were all servicemen and were owed support more or less equally. This principle lay behind the decision in some camps to pool all officers' pay and to use it to purchase what amenities the Germans from time to time allowed.

The vigorous campaign played out even on the latrine's walls. As expected, the capitalist side won. However, Wing Commander

Harry Day, the camp's Senior British Officer, overruled the plebiscite and decreed that Foodacco was part of "the war economy," and thus, while it could continue to operate, its profits had to be given to the camp kitchen.[132]

The debate about Foodacco may have been the noisiest but it was not the only one that added to the June heat. The other was occasioned by the news from a suborned guard that the Americans were going to be moved to a new compound. Since they had provided much of the muscle that dug the tunnels, the Escape Committee felt they were owed a decent chance to escape, but none of the tunnels was yet beyond the fence. The committee easily agreed to close two and concentrate on "Tom." What caused all the heat was the suggestion to angle the tunnel upward to obviate the need for a full exit shaft. In the end, this idea was turned down.

20–21 JUNE 1943, MILAG UND MARLAG NORD, NEAR BREMEN, GERMANY

The Fathers and Brothers Write Different Types of Letters Home

As did the other POWs, the fathers and brothers wrote home to family and friends, at times keeping up a brave, even playful, front, others showing the strains of imprisonment. In early January, Father Desnoyers mocked himself for being kitted out in a military uniform and told his parents that he "cheated," making the bag filled with his Christmas presents and their wrappings serve double duty as his pillow. The following day, he wrote his sister a very different letter. After telling her that the Germans were now doubling the missionaries' allotment of letters and postcards, he paints her a picture of his daily life living with at least 10 other fathers and brothers in a small room. At any one moment, one was doing his laundry while another "hums or sings loudly. Half are smoking. . . . some read, some draw, play cards or sew. . . . on several clotheslines are spread our rags, men clog the shelves overloaded with bags stuffed with clothes, hats, pictures, books, boxes."

Brother Cournoyer's 20 June letter tells the dean of the Oblate College in Richelieu, Quebec, that Father Barsalou and Brother Georges-Aimé Lavallée were in the hospital and that Father Pâquet had been suffering from kidney pain and rheumatism, ailments Pâquet skips over in his extant letters.

Father Barsalou's 15 June letter to his sister-in-law, Jacqueline, unites his priestly vocation and his personal sorrow for his brother Jean-Paul's sudden departure for "our heavenly home." He admits to coping with his pain by throwing himself "at the feet of our Lord to beg him to have mercy on you, his dear wife." He tells her that if she submits to the will of God, she will find both courage and consolation. He hopes that she will draw comfort from knowing that his prayers and those of "my whole parish" (words indicating that, at least momentarily, the good father had slipped the surly bonds of wire and imagined himself once again in a proper church) are with her.

LATE JUNE 1943, FRESNES PRISON, PARIS

MacDonald Finds a Way to Trip Up the Gestapo

The view out their window on the fourth floor of the notorious Fresnes Prison was filled with promise. Millions of tan stalks heavy with wheat waved in the gentle breeze. Off in the distant green fields, lowing cattle fattened themselves. But German requisitions meant that almost none of this food reached the capital a few miles away.

Built as a showcase in the late 1800s, Fresnes held political prisoners, captured secret agents and Allied airmen shot down over France. Despite producing their identity disks, because they were captured in civilian clothes, MacDonald and Parkinson were told by the Gestapo told that they could be treated as spies. "And," one

German told MacDonald coldly, "as you know, in all countries, spies are shot."

Likely because the Germans knew they were airmen and thus actually came under the jurisdiction of Göring's Luftwaffe, the Canadians were not tortured or roughed up, though the terror of what the Gestapo did to civilian prisoners at 11 rue des Saussaies was ever-present. In the corridors and in the exercise yard of Fresnes Prison, these "poor men showed me broken limbs, bruised flesh and the slashes in their skin left by whippings with electrical wire," recalls MacDonald.

MacDonald knew he was to give only his name, rank and service number. However, he figured, holding fast to Geneva risked the Gestapo upping the ante. "The greatest danger was getting tripped up. No matter what tactic they used, as long as I said I did not know anyone's name, I could keep that story going." Descriptions were, however, more difficult, until MacDonald and Parkinson decided that MacDonald would use his parents as models to describe his helpers, while Parkinson would use his mother, which meant that the Gestapo was building up a dossier about three middle-aged Canadians.

EARLY JULY 1943, FRESNES PRISON, PARIS

MacDonald Receives News of the War

The meagre rations at Fresnes were not supplemented by Red Cross parcels. As the weeks wore on, MacDonald and Parkinson tightened their belts and, as Kriegies across Europe did, recalled favourite foods and meals. As long, hungry days passed, punctuated only by another questioning session or the few minutes allowed in the 10-by-20-foot exercise yard, MacDonald found himself fighting an indoor version of barbed-wire psychosis, the first symptom of which was the feeling that he was weakening during the interrogations. "We had some French books that I could read a little but nothing else to do. With time on our hands and the sure knowledge of what the Gestapo was willing to do, it was difficult to keep all sorts of terrible scenarios from passing through your mind," MacDonald says. The men's spirits were strengthened by the news, brought by other POWs who were thrown into their cell, of Russian advances in the east and, especially, of the invasion of Sicily. "We didn't know the numbers of Canadians involved, but we knew they were now fighting Germans in Europe, and that meant the world to us," he recalls.

29 JULY 1943, OVER THE TYRRHENIAN SEA

RCAF Flight Lieutenant Stewart Cowan Is Shot Down

Seconds after seeing a smudge on the horizon, the telltale sign of an Italian destroyer flotilla, Stewart Cowan ordered his flight of fighter bombers to go in for the kill. Within moments, the Italian anti-aircraft gunners created what amounted to a minefield in the sky. Above the sound of the plane's engines and exploding shells, Cowan called out to his navigator, Tony Crawford, "My God, Tony! We're sitting ducks in the sky!" Cowan's training held as he pitched his Beaufort diver bomber toward the destroyer and saw his stream of 20-mm cannon shells put one of the destroyer's gun crews *hors de combat* just before bullets turned his windscreen black.[133]

Then Cowan felt his doughty plane start to shake, the effect of a piece of flak cutting through the starboard engine's propeller. Moments later, with the port engine aflame, Cowan prepared to ditch in the Tyrrhenian Sea off Italy's western coast. The two Canadians scrambled out of the hatch and onto the starboard wing, at the end of which a dinghy, which had automatically inflated when the wing touched the water, awaited them. As the plane began to sink, they couldn't find the knife to cut the cord attaching the dinghy to the wing. Anxious moments passed before the cord suddenly broke.

2 AUGUST 1943, STALAG X-B, SANDBASTEL, GERMANY

Brother Antoine Lavallée Is Amazed at the Power of a Bombing Raid

For days they had heard long bomber streams sawing through the night toward Hamburg 40 miles away and seen the sky glow an otherworldly pink from the incendiary and other bombs that rained down on the great port city in the air-raid campaign that the Sacred Heart Brother would have considered aptly named: Operation Gomorrah.

Nature's fury—jagged flashes of light and great peals of thunder—merged with the man-made explosions that convulsed the night of 2 August. At about 11 p.m., a bomb, likely dropped from a plane in its death throes, fell a scant 3,000 yards away. The explosion lit the sky while the blast wave "shook the barracks so strongly that pictures," but not the Cross to which Brother Antoine Lavallée had devoted his life, "fell off the walls."

13 AUGUST 1943, POW CAMP, NEAR THE VATICAN

Cowan Momentarily Forgets the Science of Bombing

When he'd been shot down, everything had happened so quickly that Cowan did not know fear. There had been a moment of frisson seven hours later when the flying boat coming to pluck him and Crawford from the Tyrrhenian Sea turned out to be an Italian Red Cross plane. But the crew had been friendly, as had the commander of the base near Naples and the guards, who provided a large spaghetti dinner and led them to a bomb shelter during a bombing raid that night. The sight of German soldiers taking up defensive positions in Italy—Mussolini having fallen—was not comforting, and hearing a German crow about persuading British Sikh POWs to wave the Geneva prohibition against handling ammunition by withholding water from them (when the temperature routinely climbed above 110°F), sickened Cowan, but he was in Italian hands. The worst that could be said for the POW camp that he and Crawford stayed in for eight days was that the sight of birds enjoying the hot, sunny days and heavy grapes growing nearby made the solitary days even harder.

In the early afternoon of 13 August, after having been transferred back to Rome, Cowan stood on a balcony of a building serving as a POW camp, overlooking the Vatican a mere 300—unbridgeable—yards away, listening to an American officer. An air-raid siren cut off the impromptu lecture about how, during the 1527 Sack of Rome, Pope Clement VII escaped with his life by running through the fortified corridor connecting the Vatican and the Castel Sant'Angelo. True to form, the Romans in the streets below ignored the siren until they heard the sound of the bombers.

The shock of seeing the plane open its bomb bay doors as it flew directly overhead toward the great dome designed by Michelangelo, and then over St. Peter's Square as the space filled with thousands of panicked men, women and children, made Cowan forget the science of bombing. He turned to prayer, something he didn't do when he was shot down. Had the moment not been so charged, he would have known that, since the Marauder bombers were 4,000 feet high, the bombs released over St. Peter's would not explode in the Vatican but, because of inertia, about a mile away.

Moments after the roar and shock wave generated by the explosions washed over them, the American officer pointed to the black smoke rising above the dust as evidence that the bombers had hit an oil tank car, and added that the rail yard had likely been wrecked. During the London Blitz, Cowan had "stepped over mangled bodies and tried to get help for the wounded," and had not flinched at firing his cannon at men on a destroyer.[134] Yet when he looked at the smoke-stained sky over the Eternal City, his eyes filled with tears.

19 AUGUST 1943, STALAG VIII-B, LAMSDORF, GERMANY

STAN DARCH REMEMBERS THE HORRORS OF DIEPPE

Chewed up by machine guns or blown apart by mortar bombs, the Canadian soldiers at Dieppe had been dead for a year. Some of the scars of battle, such as the burned-out landing craft and tanks, remained on the beaches. The wind, rain and remorseless scrubbing action of the sea had long since worn away the copper-red stains of Canadian blood and the bits of flesh smeared on the beaches of France.

The more than 1,500 survivors of Dieppe remembered, however—mostly in private. "I don't remember talking with anyone," says Stan Darch. "Perhaps I didn't have to. We all knew what each of us had in our mind. I thought of everything, the hours leading up to the landing, the explosions before we went ashore, the confusion on the beaches." Men, some friends, all comrades, remained frozen in his mind in the positions in which rigor mortis had taken hold one year earlier.

24 AUGUST 1943, MANDØ ISLAND, DENMARK

RCAF SQUADRON LEADER ROY MCLERNON AND SERGEANT ROBERT BROOKS'S BOMBER IS SHOT DOWN

RCAF bomb aimer Sergeant Jim Plenderleith dropped thousands of aluminum strips through his Halifax bomber's flare chute as the plane approached Mandø Island, off the west coast of Denmark. For more than a month, Bomber Command's planes had been dropping "Window," which disrupted the German radar by bouncing the radio waves back to the receiver in a random fashion, making it all but impossible to vector the night fighters. Some 14,000 feet above Mandø, however, the glittering pieces of aluminum had no effect on a lone wolf, Leutnant Kurt Böttinger; a burst from his machine gun set one of the bomber's two starboard engines on fire at 2:30 a.m.

Before RCAF pilot Roy McLernon could pitch his plane into a corkscrew dive, Böttinger's guns set his wing on fire. As fire burned toward the fuselage and the plane filled with smoke, Sergeant Robert Brooks in the Perspex dome above the plane's midsection opened fire with his twin Bofors. But he could not depress them enough to hit the German plane.

With the fuselage already afire, Plenderleith crawled toward the escape hatch in the plane's nose and jumped, followed by the crew's British flight engineer and then the plane's navigator, RCAF Sergeant Randolph Welters. Brooks should have jumped from the rear escape hatch but fire blocked his passage, forcing him to crawl 70 feet through thickening smoke to the front of the plane. As soon as McLernon saw Brooks, his face burned and eyebrows singed, he stepped aside so Brooks could bail out before him.

A moment after the slipstream opened Brooks's chute, the Halifax began a near vertical dive. Then an exploding fuel cell threw McLernon against a bulkhead with such force that he thought the plane had crashed. Fortunately, McLernon quickly realized that the Halifax was still airborne and jumped out into the Danish night.

25 AUGUST 1943, STALAG XVIII-A, WOLFSBERG, AUSTRIA

Father Paul Juneau's Theological Innovation

After more than two years in prison camps, for *les religieux*, much remained the same. In July, writing for an illiterate French-Canadian soldier named Charles to his fiancée, Fernande, Father Juneau carefully couched the news that Charles was in the hospital, having hit his head against the wall in a football game, between mention of Charles's great joy at receiving pictures of Fernande and of his fervent desire to learn more about "our beautiful religion." "No doubt you have remained faithful to the dream of one day joining your destiny with his, if it be God's will" was balm for the young Montrealer.

Yet much had changed. Earlier in the month, Father Larivière had written to Father Antoni Toupin that the entire structure of the Oblate order and, indeed, the Catholic Church, which places priests and brothers under the authority of an ecclesiastical superior such as the Provincial in Ottawa, had become "rather theoretical." The POW camps may not have been the wilds of North America during the time of the Jesuit Relations (1610–1636) but, since they could not communicate with their Oblate superiors or the Vatican, Larivière wrote something that would have been unthinkable a mere two years earlier: "In practice, I am my own superior general, as I am my own bishop, though I take into account the opinion (and possible direction) that comes from three continents with whom I have a relationship."

An even more striking example of how the war had affected the Oblates is what Father Juneau told his brother on 25 August 1943. The holding of Pentecost mass (13 June) on a "basket-ball pitch" had no theological import. That on Pentecost and again on the Feast of Corpus Christi (27 June) he conducted mass on an altar that was "placed so that the celebrant was facing the congregation" was little short of revolutionary, for priests did not start saying mass in this fashion till after Vatican II in the early 1960s.[135]

26 AUGUST 1943, MANDØ ISLAND, DENMARK

McLernon Escapes to the Mainland while the Resistance Hides Brooks

From his position in the middle of the haystack he'd crawled into, McLernon couldn't quite tell what language the men a few yards away were speaking. If they were Danes, they would likely help him. The machine gun in the lookout post he saw on the beach may have been unmanned, but it indicated that German troops were not far away. Pressed by thirst and hunger after almost 30 hours on the ground, McLernon made the decision to reveal himself.

The men near the haystack were indeed Danes, who not only gave McLernon much-needed food and drink but also trousers and a sweater to put on over his RCAF tunic. He also needed shoes because the vacuum effect of the slipstream had burst the zippers on his fur-lined boots and ripped them off his feet. Thinking that even disguised as a workman McLernon would arouse the suspicions of the Germans patrolling the causeway connecting Mandø Island to the mainland, Søren Christensen, one of the Danes, sent a coded message to Knud "Skipper" Hansen that, were it to be intercepted by the Germans, would hardly have raised an alarm: "An object looking like a mine was drifting toward the North."[136] By the evening of the 26th, McLernon, who had travelled from Mandø secreted under a tarp in the engine compartment of Hansen's fishing skiff, had been seen by a doctor, given a complete set of civilian clothes and was now being grilled by the chief Special Operatives Executive operative in the area.

Meanwhile, driven by thirst and hunger, on 26 August Brooks revealed himself to Herluf and Holger Anderson, who gave him milk and loaded him into their horse-drawn cart for the trip to Mandø village. The Andersons may have been in their teens, but they knew their business. To ensure that soldiers who might be walking to or from their barracks in the north end of the village couldn't see Brooks as they took him to Hans Rasmussen's house, they had him sit with his back to the village. With Germans nearby, Rasmussen judged keeping Brooks in the village too dangerous. To make him look like one more labourer, Rasmussen gave him a change of clothes, a cap and, to complete the disguise, a rake before putting him on a bicycle, with directions to hide in a concrete drain near an old dike.

LATE AUGUST 1943, CAMPO CONCENTRAMENTO PRIGIONIERI DI GUERRA NO. 21, CHIETI, ITALY

Cowan Pines for His Sweetheart Back in Toronto

Keeping his spirits up at the POW camp 125 miles northeast of Rome to which he'd been moved proved difficult. First, there was the Senior British Officer, who, to Cowan's dismay—and to stop the Canadian from freelancing an escape—ordered him to surrender his compass. Then there was his hair, tufts of which remained in his comb, causing him to fear that he'd be bald at age 23. The street scenes—mothers and children, families, even an assignation in the shrubbery right outside the Vatican that he'd witnessed from the balcony in Rome the day after the bombing—were recent enough to remind him just how unnatural the all-male environment of the POW camps was, and what it was like to hold your sweetheart in your arms and feel her "warm kisses and the sound of her voice."[137] Then another POW's "Dear John" letter put him ill at ease about his own sweetheart, who was in Toronto training to be a nurse.

Cowan attributed his loss of hair to his mental state, whereas it was probably caused by the meagre rations, which also caused him to lose weight. As in the German camps, the POWs did not receive the planned allotment of Red Cross parcels, which meant they lacked nutrients and fats. The importance of tasty food to mental stability can be seen in the credit Cowan gives to his navigator Tony Crawford's cooking—a plate of fried pasta and raisin pancakes or the sort of twice-baked biscuit Admiral Nelson's men ate, soaked in condensed milk and then fried—for being his "salvation."

But food could do nothing to alleviate his concern about his elderly parents. Did they know he was alive? Were they? "Am I," he wondered through the lonely nights in pungent rooms where the stillness was punctuated by snoring officers, "destined to be part of the dust of Italy?"

Chapter Eight

September–December 1943

The first angel sounded, and there followed hail and fire mingled with blood, and they were cast upon the earth: the third part of the trees was burnt up, and all green grass was burnt up.

—Revelation 8:7

8 SEPTEMBER 1943, STALAG LUFT III, SAGAN, POLAND

"Tom" Is Found

Oberfeldwebel Hermann Glemnitz may have been rather dim, but he was dogged. And on 8 September, he was lucky. His hunch that something was up in Hut 128 seemed wrongheaded until, as he was leaving, a ferret dropped a tool that chipped off a piece of the thin cement camouflaging the trapdoor leading to "Tom."

The disappointment of the men who had dug out more than 25 tons of earth was partly ameliorated when the explosion meant to destroy the 260-foot-long tunnel blew their hut from its foundations. Glemnitz may have "doubted that there would be another tunnel because all available wood [bed slats] had been used up," but he was wrong.[138] The digging of "Harry" and "Dick" continued apace, as did work in the workshops. In an attempt to lessen the chance of an escaper being taken for a spy, engraved into the the bottom of the compasses they made were the words "Made in Stalag Luft III—Pat Pend."

9 SEPTEMBER 1943, CAMPO DI CONCENTRAMENTO PER PRIGIONIERI DI GUERRA NO. 21, CHIETI, ITALY

Stewart Cowan Is Ordered Not to Escape

Upon hearing that Mussolini's successor planned to surrender to the Allies, the Italian guards vanished. Then, after a night of eating as much Red Cross chocolate as they could, failing to make a quick batch of homebrew and singing ribald songs, the POWs found themselves on morning parade listening to Colonel Marshall, the camp's Senior British Officer: "Every POW will remain in the camp. Anyone disobeying these orders is subject to court martial at a later date! You will be kept informed of any changes in my directive."[139]

No one was happy with this order, though given the fluidity of the situation in the countryside, it had merit. What dismayed Stewart Cowan and the other men were armed NCOs now standing guard in the watchtowers and the implication that they'd shoot anyone attempting to escape.

12 SEPTEMBER 1943, NEAR VESTER VEDSTED, EASTERN DENMARK

After Walking Across a Mud Flats, Robert Brooks Is Betrayed

Skipper Hansen was willing to move Robert Brooks, whose presence had become an open secret to everyone except, somehow, the Germans who regularly walked by the farm where the Canadian had been taken after heavy rains began flooding the drainage ditch he was hiding in. However, on 28 August, Germany's erstwhile Aryan allies in the Danish government stopped cooperating with Berlin, prompting a series of surprisingly mild reactions, one of which was the mandatory searching of boats plying the Danish coast.

In an attempt to get Brooks off the island, after dark on the night on 11 September, a night of exceptionally low tide, the village postman led him two-thirds of the way across the muddy flats of the Wadden Sea. To avoid minefields, Brooks followed a small brook inland. Near midnight, knowing how much the Danes had done for him, he approached a farmhouse to ask for help.

The farmer welcomed him. Only when the police arrived about a half hour later did Brooks realize that after three weeks on the run he'd been betrayed. Since he was in civilian clothes, Brooks was handed over to the SS. The officer who interrogated him was less interested in the RCAF-issue identity disks than with how Brooks came to be clean-shaven, presumably so the SS could unravel the Resistance circuit that had helped him. Thus the officer's dismay at learning that a guard had lent Brooks a razor.

By the time Brooks arrived at Stalag IV-B, near Zeithain, in Lower Saxony, Roy McLernon was in Frederikshavn, on the east coast of Denmark, where he met Verner Jensen, who arranged for his passage to freedom in Sweden.[140]

EARLY SEPTEMBER 1943, HAINA, GERMANY

ROBERT PROUSE SEES EVIDENCE OF THE HOLOCAUST

His first visit to the eye hospital in Haina was less painful, if no more successful, than his visit to the village doctor in Arnstadt had been a few weeks earlier. *Herr Doktor* treated Robert Prouse's intense back pain by having two other POWs hold him upright while he smashed his educated fist on Prouse's head, saying, "No blood, no swelling, back to work!"[141] Prouse's barracks mates were more understanding, covering his work shifts and surreptitiously moving him from bed to bed during the day so what was likely a herniated disk could heal. The eye doctor in Haina, at least, gave Prouse some drops.

On his second visit to the hospital, a doctor found a scratch on his eye. Despite being assured that he'd be able to leave the hospital as soon as the freezing came out of his eye, when it did, the doctors decided to keep Prouse; in total, he spent ten days in the hospital. There, night brought not the relief of sleep, during which a few more hours of incarceration slipped by, but rather the sickening sound of screams coming from the neighbouring "experimental hospital housing political prisoners," most of whom, he'd been told, were Jewish.

His improved sight only heightened the horror. One morning, disbelieving that he'd actually seen a truck being piled high with dead bodies, Prouse closed his eyes. When he opened them, he saw still another load of naked bodies being hauled into the truck. The macabre scene elicited emotions beyond what even the terrible fighting and doleful sights on the beaches of Dieppe did. That early morning, horror "mingled with a touch of fear at the closeness of death."

23 SEPTEMBER 1943, CAMPO DI CONCENTRAMENTO PER PRIGIONIERI DI GUERRA NO. 78, SULMONA, ITALY

Cowan Is Taken Prisoner by the Germans

The Liberator bombers flying low over the prison camp were taken to mean that allied troops were close indeed. Then, as Cowan and the others stood at ease during an unexpected parade on the 20th, came the devastating news: the Germans were moving fast to consolidate their hold on Italy and were going to take possession of the camp the next day. Their arrival within an hour rendered the rescission of the No Escape order moot.

Two days later, Cowan and the others were loaded at bayonet point into trucks that took them to Sulmona, 80 miles east of Rome. The conditions were wretched, with the thousands of bedbugs providing the only diversion: checking for new bite patterns every morning.

28 SEPTEMBER 1943, STALAG LUFT III, SAGAN, POLAND

Father Goudreau Keeps an Open Mind

Trying to help Father Goudreau bear his load, in either his April or July 1943 letter, both of which arrived in Sagan in late September, Father Ducharme recalled the regimen they willingly accepted as scholasticates and as Oblate missionaries: pre-dawn prayers, hours of contemplation and being apart from society and submission. Goudreau reacted strongly, noting the difference between the "overflowing life of the scholastics" and the "strange kind of winter sleep" of being a POW.

Goudreau knew enough about the Basutos to know that the women would be wearing only shifts. Still, during a recent heat wave, he found the POWs' "biblical nudity" shocking. But thundering against it in his homily would cause his parishioners to go "cross-eyed" and earn him the reputation of being "narrow-minded." Equally significant, it would put a distance between him and the men, who would stop coming to his courses in ethics, French and Latin, important for camp morale by giving some meaning to the time behind the barbed wire.

LATE SEPTEMBER TO 8 OCTOBER 1943, VILLALAGO, 80 MILES EAST OF ROME, ITALY

Cowan and George Escape and Are Surprised by Who Helps Them

It had been a close call but not because of the Shoot to Kill order. Rather, just before Cowan and his escape partner, a British soldier named George, were to jump from the top of a railcar carrying them to Germany, the train entered a tunnel. When they did jump, rifle shots into the darkness told them that at least one guard had seen something. Slowed by the knee Cowan twisted upon landing, they found a pile of hay into which they burrowed to hide and sleep.

In the morning, to make better time going south toward the Allied lines and knowing that since the Italian Army had disintegrated the countryside was filled with men making their way home, the two POWs risked using the roads. A couple of well-placed "*Buona sera*s" bought the goodwill they needed from men obviously happy to be out of the war. Late on 1 October, they took shelter in a cave George had found some distance up a rise. The brisk air and early October snowfall they awoke to reminded Cowan of home.

Sometime after noon, just moments after the men heard the sound of breaking twigs, a boy about 12 years old, who they soon learned was named Egidio Gatta, spotted them as he stepped in front of the cave. George's "*Canadese, Canadese*" meant nothing to the boy balanced between fear and wonder; "*Inglese, Inglese*," by contrast, caused him to break out "into a friendly smile."[142] George soon learned that not only did an American woman and her daughters live in the boy's village but, even more importantly, no Germans had come looking for escapees.

Their woollen Red Cross blankets hardly kept out the cold on the wet night of 4 October. And, during the day, the sight of Germans looking over the countryside scouting for food and wine was worrisome, but since Egidio told them that there was no path running from the road to the rise, they felt safe. Near dusk, Egidio appeared carrying fresh bread and wonderfully runny goat's milk cheese.

The next day, even before she said "I'm Elda DiIanni" in an unmistakable New England accent, Cowan was smitten with the beautiful black-haired girl who flouted the warning that "anyone hiding POWs would be shot on the spot." The girl from Massachusetts told them that she, her sister and mother had been vacationing in their ancestral village when Italy declared war on the United States. Elda also told them that before coming to meet them, she had spoken to the village's mayor, both because she needed help finding a family to take them in and to preserve her honour—and their lives. Airmen like Cowan may have gone into battle on the wings of cutting-edge technology, but in remote European villages, people lived and died by harsh, though clear, codes: "In Villalago, a girl was expected to be a virgin for her marriage and anyone violating a young girl's virginity deserved to be shot, or killed in some other ignominious manner."

Egidio returned the following day with more food and a note saying that the next day a man would come with him to lead the men to a safe house belonging to Signora Iafolla. Elda quickly explained that Iafolla was risking her life and that of her two daughters to help the Canadian and his escape partner, George, because they regularly received letters from Iafolla's son-in-law telling how well he was being treated in a POW camp in Alberta. Grateful to be able to offer their host something special, Cowan passed Elda a tin with a Red Cross sticker on it, and soon they were "sipping hot cocoa and conversing about far away Canada."

12 OCTOBER 1943, POW CAMP, LANGENSALZA, NEAR ERFURT, GERMANY

Prouse Misses Out on Being Included in a Prisoner-of-War Exchange

A month earlier, his scratched eye would have resulted in Prouse being one of the 66 Canadians being repatriated after being declared Definitely Unfit for Service.[143] By contrast, recovering resulted in his being one of hundreds of Kriegies herded into boxcars for transport to a makeshift camp at Langensalza.

The overcrowded camp was as far from the rules laid down by Geneva as was the transport, which was so overloaded that the men stood shoulder to shoulder on powered lime on the cars' floors, their shuffling feet stirring it into a choking, eye-burning cloud. A hole with two long boards across it served as a latrine. Worse than the physical discomfort was the humiliation that came with trying to defecate while sitting on boards that were open to all sides, the natural function made all the more difficult by the poor diet that tended to constipate. Men who had to answer nature's call weren't shy about yelling for those who were struggling to hurry up.

13 OCTOBER 1943, BARANELLO, ITALY

Corporal George Reid, Motorcycle Dispatch Rider, Is Captured

"He hadn't been dead too long because he didn't smell too bad," recalled George Reid, the motorcycle dispatch rider who, like Reid and the other man in his patrol, wore the flash of the Seaforth Highlanders of Canada.[144] As Sergeant McKee removed the dead rider's .38, the gentleness of his doing so serving as a battlefield elegy, Reid, wracked by malaria-induced chills, hoped that the extra gun wouldn't be needed on this, his last patrol before ten days' rest. Charged with bringing back a German for interrogation, the Canadians found instead an Italian family that provided an excellent pot of spaghetti and word that the Germans had withdrawn across the narrow Biferno River, which Reid and McKee soon found themselves wading across.

The family in the farmhouse on the top of a hill told them the disquieting news that Germans were heading for Baranello, where the Seaforth's "D" Company was supposed to be. Fed by the absence of even a single Canadian patrol challenging them on the road to Baranello and whiffs of Turkish tobacco smoke from German cigarettes, Reid and McKee's concern heightened. The men inside what appeared to be a police station told them that the Canadians had taken cover when the Germans shelled the town. As if on cue, someone knocked on the door and said in an unmistakable English accent, "We are pulling out of the town. Come out or be left behind." After opening the door a few inches,

Reid found himself "looking down the barrels of automatic pistols and a Schmeisser machine gun," unable to pull back because of the Italians pushing him out the door.

Determined to protect McKee, Reid stayed silent when asked where his companion was, which prompted the German to ignore Geneva's prohibition on slapping prisoners. After the answer that he'd been looking for some wine brought still more blows, Reid tried saying he'd been looking for a "girl." A moment later, he caught a break when someone, likely McKee, threw a number of small hand grenades into the street; their explosions caught the German by surprise and gave the Canadian just enough time to demonstrate why in Vancouver he'd earned the nickname "Speed Reid."

It's doubtful that Reid's brigadier, Bert Hoffmeister, ever said that "Germans are lousy shots." Yet, as he ran from two machine gunners, the flash of their traces showing that they were firing on fixed lines, and struggled to keep his balance in his hobnailed boots as they hit the cobblestones, it served Reid to think he had. He surely thought the Germans searching for him were a less than skillful group when, from his hiding place, 19 men rushed by him. Reid's hope of playing possum ended when a sergeant saw him and kicked him in the ribs. Reid's jump caused the German to say, in that surprisingly sportsmanlike tone that men who have just faced each other in battle sometimes use, "*Ach, nicht kaputt. Komm. Komm raus!*

MID-OCTOBER 1943, FRESNES PRISON, PARIS

Ian MacDonald Thinks about the Last Rites

It seemed too much like a movie.

The guard ordering Ian MacDonald to take his few personal belongings, the walk down the white-and-black tiled corridor to the stairs that he'd taken before but which this time ended not at the door to the exercise yard but at another cell. After seeing its bloodless walls and bed with clean sheets, MacDonald asked why he'd been moved. "This is the cell that is kept for those who are condemned to die," he answered.

MacDonald found it difficult to square this nicer cell with the prospect of being hanged or shot in the morning. "I spent the night with rosary beads praying and thinking about what this would do to my dear mother and father, and brothers and sisters. And of dying without being given the last rites."

As the door opened, MacDonald readied himself for the inevitable. Instead, he was told, "We're going to take you now into Germany."

19 OCTOBER 1943, DULAG LUFT, FRANKFURT

MacDonald's First Letters Home

"After the weeks I'd spent in the Gestapo's hands, and the night in the cell when I thought I'd die in the morning, arriving in a real POW camp was a relief. I wouldn't, of course, have my liberty, and I was still subject to German military law, but signing papers, being photographed and, especially, being given prisoner identity disks with POW number 3038 all meant that now I was a regular POW and therefore came under Geneva," says MacDonald.

The *Postkarte* and blue aerogram sheet on which he wrote home a letter a few hours after being assigned to his barracks arrived on 10 and 15 January 1944 respectively. Both were censored, though it is not possible to determine if the words etched out by acid were removed by German censor *Geprüft* no. 37 or by British censor D.B. 643. In the postcard, the interrupted sentence reads:

> *I was 2 months trying to escape, caught & held prisoner—— Paris for four months.*

In the aerogram it is:

I managed to escape as far as the Spanish border but was betrayed and sent to a prison in Paris for four months (7 June–Oct. 17)———.

MacDonald confirms that what alarmed the censor were the words "Fresnes Prison." Censors on both sides would have wanted to keep secret that RCAF personnel were being held in civilian prisons and thus in the Gestapo's hands. Neither censor noticed that in the letter MacDonald signalled this by writing that he'd "just received the privileges of a prisoner of war today so now I am doing quite nicely."

MacDonald's youngest brother, Leo, confirms that the family parsed the tone and even the handwriting, which was strong and regular and therefore supported the somewhat awkward sentence "I'm feeling fine & entirely unwounded" that appeared in the middle of the postcard's message. The request in the letter for "a couple of shirts, a sweater and belt" was more important than it might seem on the surface of it. It indicated that, while MacDonald was physically well, he lacked basic material possessions. As well, it gave Mrs. MacDonald something to do—shopping for his clothes—that linked her in an immediate way to her son's welfare.

The latter part of the letter was equally important. After asking for updates on the family, he inquired as to whether his parents had received the $240 he had asked J.C. MacDonald (no relation) in England "to look after" for him. Although the money no doubt helped the MacDonald family's stretched finances, MacDonald's question was even more significant as an indicator of his emotional state. It told his family that, despite all he'd been through, he continued to value his role in their welfare.

LATE OCTOBER 1943, ON THE ROAD SOUTH FROM VILLALAGO, ITALY

COWAN HEARS HIS FATHER'S VOICE

Two papers figured prominently in the hours before Cowan and George headed south toward the Allied lines in the company of eight former Italian soldiers making their way home. The first, placed in the pocket of Cowan's jacket, now buried to keep the Germans from finding it, read: "The occupants of this house have given me food and shelter for a period of two weeks, during which time I was recovering from an injury" and asked the Allied soldiers to show "reciprocal consideration."[145] The second was a card with the picture of St. Domenico Abate, who died in 1031, the patron saint of Villalago, that Signora Iafolla pressed into Cowan's hand just before he walked out of her house and endangered the entire village. Had the Germans discovered either paper, reprisals would have followed

The homeward-bound Italians provided some cover, though not enough to obscure the four or five inches the six-foot-tall Canadians had over them, as well as useful information—for example, the spotter plane that alarmed the Canadians was likely searching for cattle or sheep the locals hid up in the mountains. But the Italians' loud arguing and expressive hand motions that Cowan feared would draw attention to them during their discussion on whether to cross the bare Piano della Cinquemiglia (a five-mile-wide, 4,000-foot-high plain in central Italy) during the day or at night, alarmed Cowan; the opening up of a previously unseen anti-aircraft battery on a Spitfire settled the question in favour of those advocating for a night crossing. Then there was the fact that their leader prepared two fewer corn shucks (which they were to hold so that they might look like peasant farmers) than necessary, with the result that a German patrol noticed George and Cowan and shot at them as they crossed a road. Luckily, in the gathering dusk, the Germans missed the zigzagging airmen. Thus Cowan's relief when one morning they woke up to find that the Italians had pushed on without him and George.

* * *

After about a week of avoiding increasingly thick German patrols and memorizing landmarks near where anti-aircraft guns were located so that Allied forces could later bomb them, Cowan and George divided their last square of Red Cross chocolate. "Scarcely willing to swallow, I let it melt slowly on my tongue and savoured the last taste before allowing it to trickle into my starving stomach," recalled Cowan. For days they'd travelled at night and avoided villagers and farmers; now, however, they had no choice but to risk revealing themselves. What struck Cowan about the family standing in their farmyard was their lack of "surprise or alarm" when the two shaved but filthy escapers stepped out of the wood. George explained that they were *Canadese* and asked for food. The farmer gave them bread and cheese but was too frightened to let them stay.

Like almost every other Canadian POW, Cowan was not a career soldier. He had stepped onto the stage of history yet remained at heart a civilian, willing if necessary to sacrifice himself to defeat the enemies of his way of life, though when sleeping on the cold, damp Italian ground more likely to dream of being in his sweetheart's arms than of performing heroic deeds in battle. The ache he felt for her became all the more painful near noon on the next to last day of October when, shortly after the sun began to warm the air, he saw a young couple lingering by the well near a picturesque cottage.

George timorously approached them, but before he had uttered three Italian words, the young man interrupted, "So you are from England, British 8th Army, I reckon?" Nonplussed, George could only answer "Yes," with Cowan quickly adding, "I'm a Canadian, RCAF pilot." If anything, the young couple was in even greater danger than the escapers because the young woman was the daughter of Carlo Bergamini, the Italian admiral who was killed by a German air attack as he sought to surrender the Italian fleet to the Allies; the young man was a Vatican lawyer. He told Cowan that the Canadians had driven the Germans out of Campobasso, some 50 miles to the south, and were now somewhere north of that town.

The next day, Cowan and George learned that the Canadians weren't as far north as the Sangro River, but the Germans were. Risking being declared a spy, Cowan made pinpricks on his map to mark the anchor of the *Gustav Line*. Built by Organisation Todt, this German defensive line cut across the peninsula anchored in the west by the mouth of the Sangro River, which on the night of 31 October, Cowan and George waded across, each holding their clothes above their heads, after they crawled away from a sentry who gave himself away by lighting a cigarette in the moonless night.

As he dressed, Cowan inexplicably heard in his head his father intoning the familiar line of the 23rd Psalm; the words "Yea, though I walk through the valley of the shadow of death" never seeming more real to this son of the manse. After the war, Cowan learned that at about the same time as he heard his father's voice, his father, the pastor of a Methodist church in Manitoba, was, as he was every day, on his knees in his study reciting the psalm "for the boys who went to war."

EARLY NOVEMBER 1943, LOURDES, NOVA SCOTIA

MacDonald Knows He Cannot Write about What He'd Seen

If the person who stamped *Geprüft* 83 at Stalag Luft III, where the airmen's mail was censored, had a sense of humour, the censor likely cracked a smile upon reading MacDonald's 23 October postcard, on which he wrote that he was "on the permanent staff here [at the Dulag Luft] for a while." In fact, what Ian was telling his parents, who wouldn't receive the card until the following April, was that he had joined the sickbay staff at Dulag Luft.

Even after seeing at Fresnes Prison how the Gestapo could break a body, MacDonald was astonished at the injuries he saw and about which, of course, he could not write. "It's the burns that stand out," he says. "Even though these poor men had already been in hospital for some time, the burns and scars were heartbreaking. In their disfigured faces, many stretched and frozen by scar tissue, the absence of eyebrows and lashes made them seem almost alien."

10 NOVEMBER 1943, NEAR CAMPOBASSO, ITALY

Cowan and George Meet a Freelancer for the Canadian Army

At first, George was delighted to meet the two British 8th Army sergeants who had teamed up with several Italians heading for their homes further south. The soldier named "Red" convinced the Italians to allow Cowan and George to join them for the night. Neither their shared nationality nor the fact that the three were all captured at El Alamein was enough to make the two sergeants share their food with George, let alone Cowan. After finishing the little food they had, Cowan and George ate potatoes found in a field and roasted over an open fire. Cowan knew that the code that bound escapers together pertained only to men who had escaped together, so it wasn't this that made him wary of the desire of Red and the other sergeant for Cowan and George to join them to reach Allied lines.

Rather, in addition to feeling that four men who didn't look Italian were more conspicuous than two who didn't, he was unimpressed with the Tommies' vigour. Before asking to join him and George, they had decided to wait for the Allied line to come to them. When Cowan asked what Red and the other soldier would add, George answered, "Not a Tinker's damn."[146] And in the predawn darkness, Cowan and George slipped silently out of the camp.

Wracked by diarrhea, the acidic remains of which he cleaned as best he could with some of the thousands of surrender leaflets littering the ground, Cowan, who was also infested with fleas, leaned heavily on George and was thankful for his comrade's willingness to share his water bottle after Cowan emptied his in an effort to ward off dehydration. Toward dusk, they spotted a group of Italians and wondered if they were the same group that had left Villalago with them. Driven by the need to refill their water bottles, George called out, "*Inglese . . . Canadese*," and for the second time in a week was nonplussed by the response: "I am Giovanni; I am working with the Canadians at Campobasso."

Had they known that the Germans were offering 1,800 lire for each downed airman (when the average factory worker earned 29 lire per day), the escapers would have been more reticent about trusting this man who said he'd been tasked with picking up escaped POWs and directing them to Canadian lines. But neither was in much shape to refuse Giovanni's offer to lead them to a safe house. Fortunately, the offer turned out to be genuine, and the farmer and his wife at the house gave them hot soup, bread and clean hay to sleep on, in a loft.

The next morning they listened intently as Giovanni gave them directions that would take them around villages and German positions; since his directions were based on landmarks, they would have to travel during the day. After arranging for them to spend another night resting, Giovanni asked them for a favour. Cowan readied to write out a paper attesting to the help he'd given them. Instead, the Italian asked that they shave with the razor and basin of water the family had offered to provide. Their gaunt faces and bony cheeks revealed by their razor strokes didn't surprise them. But neither man was prepared for the pallid skin he saw reflected back in the mirror, nor the deep shadows under his eyes.

Even though he'd washed the sores on his feet and covered the hole in the sole of his shoe with leather the farmer gave him, Cowan found walking agonizing. Only the promise that each step brought them closer to Canadian lines sustained him through the morning, during which they saw Germans destroy a bridge and even found themselves walking along a road following a German officer. Near midday, Cowan spotted a small white cigarette box on the ground. He didn't care that it was empty; what mattered were the words "Sweet Caporal," which told him a Canadian had been there. As dusk fell and Cowan's strength ebbed, George started to lead him to a stand of trees a few hundred yards away, where they could shelter for the night.

They had taken only a few steps toward the trees before a voice called out, "Halt!" Recognizing the Canadian accent behind the words "Who are you guys?" Cowan answered "Canadian pilot—British officer." After confirming their identities with a few random questions, the Canadian sergeant called to his commander some miles back in Campobasso. The officer who agreed to send a Jeep for them was named Captain Farley Mowat.[147]

12–13 NOVEMBER 1943, STALAG III-A, LUCKENWALD, GERMANY

Reid Turns Down a German Offer

The two weeks in the hospital during which he slept between clean, white sheets recovering from malaria was now a memory all but obscured by the more recent experience of freezing in a cattle car filled with dysentery-ridden POWs going through the Brenner Pass into captivity in Germany.

At Stalag III-A, the intelligence officer who came into Reid's small concrete cell provided the opportunity for Reid to crack a smile when he asked about a new Canadian tank. "How much do German generals tell their privates?" answered Reid. Even more amusing was what the German said after he explained that he spoke English so well because he'd lived in Canada before the war: "Win or lose, I'll go back to Toronto. I have a corner lot there, and I'm going to build a gas station on it."[148]

His bonhomie evaporated, however, when he threatened to have Reid shot if he didn't start giving straight answers, and when he tried to entrap Reid by leaving his Luger on the table well within Reid's reach. Bizarrely, the would-be entrepreneur's friendliness returned when he offered Reid the opportunity to join in the Reich's fight against the Russians after having two weeks of leave with good food and all the girls he might want.

16 NOVEMBER 1943, PARIS

Lucien Dumais and Raymond Labrosse Return to France as MI9 Agents

Raymond Labrosse's first words after stepping onto French soil as "Marcel Desjardins" were "*Laissez ça tranquille!*" which warded off an overeager MI9 operative who had bent down to pick up the suitcase carrying the nascent *Shelburn Line*'s link to London.[149] Like "Lucien Desbiens," the erstwhile mortician from Amiens, Desjardins, whose documents attested to his career as an electronics salesman, had been to France before. The first time was as a student before the war, the second time as "Paul," a radioman and then co-organizer of *Oaktree*, an escape line affiliated with the same *Pat Line* that spirited Lucien Dumais out of France not long before it was betrayed by Roger (Leneveu) Le Légionnaire. Because of this, the Gestapo had at least one picture of Labrosse and some information about "Paul," who, after *Oaktree* was broken, narrowly avoided being captured in Paris before leading 27 "parcels" through France to Spain.

The Germans also had Dumais's picture and name, though they were in the Wehrmacht's Dieppe files. After returning to England from Dieppe, Dumais served a four-month stint in North Africa as an observer with the British Army before being recruited by MI9. Upon accepting the mission to return to France and establish the *Shelburn Line*, Dumais's name joined Labrosse's on the "Q-List," servants of His Majesty the King about whom no information was available.

The former Fusiliers Mont-Royal sergeant major outranked the Ottawa-born Labrosse and would lead their mission, but in the month they had to get to know each other, Dumais had a lot of catching up to do. First, he needed to learn how to fold, then use, a parachute. And each man had to learn his new identity so that it fit like the old suit of clothes he wore when, after what would be three aborted flights, their Lysander touched down in a small field outside Paris on 16 November 1943.

23 NOVEMBER 1943, BERLIN

Father Desnoyers Survives a Major Bombing Raid

The science of bombing was not taught at the Oblate colleges. Yet after years of newspaper reports of bombing raids pummelling German cities, Father Bernard Desnoyers's beloved scholasticates likely knew more about what awaited him as he set out from Milag und Marlag Nord with a guard to replace Father Charbonneau (who had been in Poland for 14 months) than did Desnoyers himself. His guard would have told him that the trip would be long because Berlin had been paralyzed by a heavy bombing a few nights earlier. On the 20th, both English and French papers carried Associate Press news that "A record force of nearly 1,000 RAF and RCAF bombers ravaged Berlin and Ludwigshaven [*sic*] with 2,500 tons of bombs," causing fires that raged for more than 12 hours. Despite wartime information-misdirection, the reporter was close to the mark; the actual number of bombers was 835 and he had intuited that "an all-out campaign to obliterate Berlin and smash Germany's war sinews" had begun.

As Desnoyers's train neared Berlin at 7:30 p.m. on 22 November, the clouds glowed from the thousands of searchlights that combed the night sky looking for the bomber. The staccato bursts of thousands of anti-aircraft guns and resulting flak in the 40-mile-wide arc around the city washed over Desnoyers's train as it arrived in the station. Moments after climbing down to the platform, his guard hustled him into the crowd, making for the station's bomb shelter. Meanwhile, bomb aimers in 750 planes, including those belonging to three Canadian squadrons—428, 429 and 434—counted down the seconds before releasing their payloads.

Earlier in the war, Desnoyers had been shocked by the power of one bomb exploding several hundred yards away. Now he found himself in a shelter filled with frightened men and women in a city that, in just over 20 minutes, 2,500 tons of high-explosive and incendiary bombs rained down upon. The well-designed shelters offered adequate protection against all but a direct hit, though nothing lessened the terror that began with the roar of the first explosions. Desnoyers emerged into a Berlin that was utterly changed. Some 1,750 people were dead or dying; 7,000 had been injured. Close to 200,000 were homeless, including those who had lived in a six-story building across from the station that, like the far end of the station, "burned like a torch."[150] Such famous areas as the Tiergarten, the fashionable Unter den Linden, the diplomatic quarter and important buildings including the Ministry for Weapons and Munitions and the Waffen-SS's administrative building were smouldering rubble made darkly visible by the light from thousands of fires reflected down from the clouds. As they made their way through the shattered streets, the priest and millions of Berliners—who, despite a dozen years of Nazi rule, were in the main Lutherans—could not help thinking of the end time foretold in Revelation.

Told that the station in the eastern part of the city, where they were to board a train to Breslau, Poland, had been destroyed, Desnoyers's guard decided they should spend the night at a public shelter, which was packed with hundreds of men, women and children, now refugees in their own city. Through the night, the cries of terrified people and the sounds of crumbling buildings filled the air.

The next morning, Desnoyers and his guard walked through the city. The devastation was so great that even Nazi Propaganda

Minister Goebbels said, "Hell itself seems to have broken loose over us."[151] They passed knots of dazed people, many muffled in scarves and covered in grey dust from the collapsed masonry, standing among the ruins in the ravaged cityscape. As they made their way five miles outside the city to a working train station, here and there they saw amid the rubble a facade, its empty windows suggestive of a vulture and its blackened stone recalling the blasted remnants of trees in that place called No Man's Land.

LATE NOVEMBER 1943, PARIS

Dumais Sets Up the *Shelburn Line*

After the exchange of passwords established their identities, Dumais and Christine got down to business. Dumais promised to pay the 40,000-franc debt she had run up working for MI9, and she put him in contact with Suzanne, who agreed that Dumais and Labrosse, who used still another set of names with her, could stay at her apartment. Two weeks later, when Dumais and Labrosse returned from a trip to Normandy (from where Labrosse had been able to contact London and inform MI9 that his radio could not pick up London from Paris), the two Canadians were stunned to discover a note (written in French) on the floor of Christine's apartment:

> *Christine and Suzanne have been arrested; you'd better get out fast.*
> —*A friend*[152]

Dumais's belief that Christine and Suzanne wouldn't talk was well-founded. While neither Canadian's training included briefings on what MI9 knew about the extent to which the Gestapo was willing to go to break *les femmes de la Résistance*, he knew of London's deep respect for these women's moral fibre.[153] Still, his instructions were to assume that they would talk and thus he was to chart a path away from them and their contacts.

Warily, they approached Paul Campinchi, whom Labrosse knew from his days with *Oaktree* and, just as warily, he again threw in his lot with MI9, connecting Dumais and Labrosse to a woman named Guette. One can only guess how the vivacious 50-year-old woman, for whom events were "either sublime or tragic," reacted when she heard that on the train from Normandy the two Canadians had entered a compartment filled with Wehrmacht officers and, after checking their papers, a military policeman had berated them for going into the wrong car.[154] Dumais understood her heightened emotion, for after the gendarme left the car, the only soldier in the car who spoke French told the two "Frenchmen" that he hated army life. All the while, despite its absence, Dumais could feel the weight of his rifle in his hands and "imagine ramming it into his belly."

The fate of *Oaktree*, Christine and Suzanne's arrest, his MI9 training and his worries over the French penchant for "careless talk" led Dumais to insist on ten security rules for the *Shelburn Line*. To ensure against the entire network being rolled up, agents were to keep their addresses secret even from one another, and "evacuees [were] to be passed along the line without their guides meeting one another." To guard against being infiltrated by fake evacuees, each one was to be interrogated as soon as possible after making contact with the escape line, which cast Dumais as the quizmaster asking RAF officers about cricket, and RCAF and USAAF officers about baseball.

Following his first rule, Dumais did not know where Labrosse rented a room. Nor did he know where he stored their radio equipment. The shortage of apartments forced Dumais to take a room in a hotel owned by one of Guette's friends, which meant that were the police to stumble on the trail, they would have little difficulty connecting some of *Shelburn*'s dots. Dumais risked providing another dot when, contrary to his orders to behave like a monk, he took Guette's friend, Marcelle, back to his hotel, where they became real-life lovers in a dangerous time.

EARLY DECEMBER 1943, BRITTANY

Dumais's Cover Story Leads Him to Become Queasy

The Gestapo had recently broken both *Jade-Fitzroy* and *Jade-Amicol* escape lines, and Dumais's handlers in London had reservations about Campinchi. Dumais had his own doubts, but about Campinchi's decision to bring the "parcels" to Paris, where it was more expensive to hide and feed them, rather than about his trustworthiness. And although the first meeting he had with Henri Le Blais—a contact he'd been put in touch with by Dr. Le Blach (whom Labrosse knew), in the small village of Plouézec, on the Breton coast—went well, the next day Dumais was dismayed to find that Le Blais had ignored the order to keep *Shelburn* a secret; his brother and sister-in-law, he protested to Dumais, were trustworthy.

Duly chastened, Le Blais drove Dumais around (running his car part of the time on alcohol from a secreted tank), looking for the place London had indicated they could exfiltrate the evaders. Though Dumais's (Desbiens's) identity card said he was a mortician, Le Blais introduced him as a doctor, which resulted in several tense moments when, while visiting a farm, word came that a woman on another nearby farm was about to give birth and no one could find Le Blach. Keeping his cover meant attending the birth, even though the art of midwifery was not covered in his MI9 training. Le Blach's timely arrival spared Dumais from having to play the part of *monsieur le docteur*, though to keep his cover, he had to assist, finding to his surprise that watching a baby being born made him feel more queasy than watching men die at Dieppe.

DECEMBER 1943, STALAG VIII-B, LAMSDORF, GERMANY

Kingsley Brown Has Trouble Proving He's Kingsley Brown

The last thing the swapovers wanted to hear was their real names being called over the camp's loudspeakers, as Kingsley Brown's and British Army Lieutenant Joe Ricks's were four days after they arrived at Stalag VIII-B. Brown's Canadian accent could easily have been hidden among Darch and the other Dieppe veterans and Ricks's English among the other 45,000 Kriegies; indeed, several men already were being hidden. And that, the camp's Man of Confidence told them, was the rub. If they hid them and the Germans started a major search, they might find a young POW who sabotaged a power plant's turbine, and "if they find him, they'll hang him."[155]

The last thing the swapovers who had just turned themselves over to the Kommandant's office wanted to be told is "You don't fool me. You're not Brown and Ricks"—and to stop wasting his time. Even after he finally arrested them a day later, the Kommandant said he didn't believe they were Brown and Ricks: "They are still in the camp. But we'll find them, we'll find them."

Equally curious was the camp's cooler. The food and amenities at Stalag Luft III were better than at Stalag VIII-B, but the cooler at Göring's "guest house for Allied officer air crew," Brown knew from experience, was rather austere, quite unlike the one to which Brown and Ricks were consigned. Brown recalled it having "the disorderly charm of a stevedores' poker club," complete with late-night bull sessions with German guards anxious to share Red Cross cigarettes.

MID-DECEMBER 1943, STALAG III-A, LUCKENWALD, GERMANY

Reid Cites the "King's Regulations, Canada"

The Senior British Officer was an officious bastard.

Overlooking the evidence, including how Reid's uniform hung

off his sickly thin body following a two-week bout of malaria and ignoring the obvious fact that the Germans had not provided him with water to wash, as soon as he saw Reid, he upbraided him—for not having shaved. Unimpressed with British authority (and aware that the officer had surrendered his men in Greece without a fight), Reid answered that while fighting the enemy and scouting in the front, he didn't carry his razor. The brigadier ordered him to borrow one. "Under K.R.Can., I can't do that," said the Canadian, which flummoxed the brigadier.

"Under what?"

"King's Regulations, Canada," said Reid, earning himself a loud dressing down and the threat to be placed on report once they were registered in a POW camp.[156] The brigadier, however, was harmless, unlike the German guards who a few weeks earlier had beat Reid unconscious after they saw him watching them through a window beat an old man and young woman unconscious, then turn a hose on them and leave them on the cold November pavement to die. The beating violated Geneva, as did the blacking out of Reid's cell, the removal of his cot and the denial of medical care when his malaria returned. As his temperature spiked dangerously high, the Germans provided him with a soup can's amount of food and water per day. On the cold concrete floor in a darkened room, Reid lay curled up in his thin blanket, "shaking, freezing but sweating," while waiting to die.

MID-DECEMBER 1943, STALAG VIII-B, LAMSDORF, GERMANY

Brown Tries His Hand at the Bar

After about a week of being men with no names, Brown suggested to an intelligence officer that perhaps he might check their fingerprints. Two days later, Brown and Ricks found themselves before a court martial charged with *Namentausch*, name exchanging.

The trial was allowed by Geneva and, given everything Brown and Ricks had done to prove who they were, they had no defence. However, Brown, who had covered many trials for the *Toronto Star* and had no high opinion of the officer corps at the Stalag, shocked the court by asserting, "You have no jurisdiction, *mein Herr.*" The adjutant could only ask, "Why?" Neither he nor the Kommandant could answer Brown's argument. "We are air force personnel. We are under the personal protection of Reichsmarschall Hermann Göring. The Wehrmacht has no jurisdiction to try us."[157] This generated a request for clarification from Berlin and another few days for Brown and Ricks to enjoy chess, poker and philosophical discussions enveloped in blue cigarette smoke.

That Berlin sided with the Kommandant was hardly a surprise; Brown had always known his point was as irrelevant as it was elegant. Thus, the guilty verdict, and the pro forma 15-day sentence in the cooler. Brown remained quick on his feet, however. For when the Kommandant added that they were going to serve their sentence in Stalag Luft III, Brown objected: "But *mein Herr*, we have already served eleven days of solitary here." No doubt anxious to avoid another appeal to Berlin, the Kommandant shrugged his shoulders and told his adjutant, "Give them a receipt for eleven days."

24 DECEMBER 1943, PLOUHA, BRITTANY

DUMAIS HAS TO HIDE 15 ESCAPERS AND EVADERS TILL THE NEW YEAR

At 6 p.m. on 15 December in François Le Cornec's house, the man who had agreed to be the beachmaster at Bonaparte Beach turned his old radio to the BBC. At the end of the broadcast *Les Français parlent aux Français*, the announcer said, "*Yvonne pense souvent à l'heureuse occasion*," confirming what Dumais and Le Cornec already suspected: because of the storm churning through the Channel, the Royal Navy's pickup of the 15 "parcels" now in Brittany had been postponed 24 hours.[158]

Yvonne was still thinking of happy occasions the next night. And the next, and the one after that. Hopes rose when the sky lightened and fell when it darkened. Worries about keeping the men making home runs hidden from the prying eyes of the villagers of Plouha competed with personal discomfort generated by the fleas that infested the beds Dumais and Labrosse slept on at Le Cornec's house. Day and night, the strong wind that blew the damp Breton cold under the door and through gaps in the window sashes was more than a match for Le Cornec's small supply of firewood. As Christmas neared, Dumais wished for a break in the weather and "some good flea powder!" The lump of coal, which, it is said, Santa Claus leaves for naughty British children, would have been much more welcome than the message on Christmas Eve that the pickup operation had been postponed until the end of January. In the interim, Dumais and Labrosse returned to Paris, while Le Cornec hid the evaders on farms, where they posed as mute labourers.

24 DECEMBER 1943, STALAG LUFT III, SAGAN, POLAND

John Grogan's Surprise Christmas Present

Three weeks earlier, an Australian POW arrived at Arbeitskommando E192 with a bundle of letters for John Grogan and some bad news. The real Frank Hickey was suffering from tuberculosis and was slated to be repatriated to Canada as "John Grogan." Grogan had less trouble convincing the authorities that he was a swapover than did Kingsley Brown. Before being returned to Stalag VIII-B, however, he was transferred to Stalag Luft III for a punishment stint, which is why on Christmas Eve he was not far from Brown, who was serving out the last few days of his sentence in the camp's cooler.

For reasons that are unclear, Grogan was put in a hut where, ironically, he became ill and developed jaundice. His second Christmas in Germany was lightened only slightly by the loudspeakers, which broadcast a German band playing "O Come, All Ye Faithful" and a song the German guards could sing, albeit with different words from those Grogan learned in his youth: "Stille Nacht"—"Silent Night." Brown too heard the songs, as he remembered how on Christmas Eve the year before a truck had arrived in the camp compound with several kegs of beer sent with his "best wishes" from Reichsmarschall Hermann Göring.[159]

25 DECEMBER 1943, DULAG LUFT, FRANKFURT

CHRISTMAS DAY

Despite the requirement laid down by Article 16 of the Geneva Convention, the Germans made no provisions for religious services at Dulag Luft. Ian MacDonald recalls, "In a very private way, I made sure to say my prayers. I thought of and, of course, prayed for my family back home. Even in the drab surrounding of the Dulag, I remembered what it was that was so important to me back home about Christmas—and that was the reason for the day, the birth of the Christ Child."

The fresh snow of Christmas morning only heightened Brown's forlorn feeling. Not only was he a prisoner far from home but also he was not allowed to partake in any of the Christmas masses read by Father Goudreau. Nor could he join in the conviviality of the barracks, which in some included full-dress dinners with table service and ornate menus. The dinner at Stalag Luft III promised Hors d'Ouevres Royaux, Potage Klim de Tomates, Viande d'Invasion Imagineé with Pomme de Terres Smashed à la Timoshenko (Timoshenko was a Soviet general), plum pudding and a number of other courses.

Since he hadn't indicated he needed to go to the latrine and he'd already been given his breakfast of black bread, margarine and fake jam, Brown did not know why his guard was opening the door to the cell. His cellmate, Joe, stood closer to it, so he saw the guard put his finger to his lips, wink and motion them out of the cell. Brown followed, taking care to keep quiet and wondering why the guards, who were all NCOs, were lounging about with conspiratorial looks on their faces. Then he heard the familiar deep, sonorous chimes of Big Ben and the words "This is London calling . . .," followed by King George VI's studied voice coming over a radio as he read his Christmas message, a "gift of a half-dozen German soldiers to two other soldiers wearing a different uniform."[160]

Chapter Nine

January–March 1944

Look! Through the port comes the moonshine astray!
It tips the guard's cutlass and silvers this nook;
but 'twill die in the dawning of Billy's last day.

—Benjamin Britten, *Billy Budd*

MID-JANUARY 1944, PARIS

Lucien Dumais Breaks Off with Marcelle

Notwithstanding the enticing birthmark just below Marcelle's hip, Lucien Dumais was having second thoughts about his liaison with her. Though she was a prostitute, morality was not the issue. His fiduciary responsibility for the tens of thousands of francs entrusted to him by MI9 and the security of his mission was. Knowing of his access to seemingly limitless funds, she pressured him to buy her more and more clothes, which risked drawing unwanted attention.

Cutting Marcelle off, however, risked her ire and the possibility that she would whisper Desbiens's name and address into the ear of an official and collect a handsome reward. Dumais did not know whether Marcelle thought he was simply a sugar daddy or a British agent. But he knew it was the latter when she immediately answered "*Non*" when he asked her to live with him. In the hall-of-mirrors world Dumais lived in, the very fact that she knew that he was a British agent provided some protection, for she would then know also that he had powerful, if distant, friends. When he moved from Guette's a few days later, he did not tell Guette where he would be living.

MID-JANUARY 1944, STALAG LUFT III, SAGAN, POLAND

RCAF Flight Lieutenant Wally Floody Solves Two Tunnelling Problems

Wally Floody was pleased with "Harry." Closed since the decision to concentrate on "Tom," Harry needed only a few days' work before men who had signed up to fight from the sky resumed moiling toward freedom.

More perplexing was what to do about the yellow spoil that couldn't be disposed of on the snow. After much discussion, Roger Bushell, who headed the Escape Committee, decided to risk hiding the spoil under the theatre—since it was built with Red Cross tools and its productions used Red Cross supplies, many thought it had what amounted to parole tool status.[161] Bushell knew also that if the Germans discovered the spoil stored in the theatre's basement, things could become difficult for Father Goudreau, for that's where his chapel was, though perhaps the chapel's very presence would dissuade the Germans from searching there.

Another problem was that the Canadian digger Scruffy Weir, who had been sent to Stalag Luft III after recovering from his burns, the sight of which had so shaken Brian Hodgkinson, dug too far to the right, while fellow Canadian Hank Birkland dug too far to the left. To keep Harry true, Floody hit on the idea of scheduling one to dig immediately after the other.

28 JANUARY 1944, BONAPARTE BEACH, BRITTANY

Dumais Sends His First Shipment of "Parcels" to Britain

The BBC announcer was no longer concerned about Yvonne's happiness. Instead, he said "*Bonjour tout le monde à la Maison d'Alphonse*," prompting Le Cornec to open a bottle with which he, Dumais and Labrosse toasted what they hoped would be "a busy season." A few hours later, the Allied airmen who had been hiding in nearby farmhouses arrived at Jean Gicguels' stone cottage, not far from Geulit Cove. There, at what became known as La Maison d'Alphonse, they met what appeared as just another Frenchman doing his bit to redeem the honour of the country that had collapsed before Hitler in May 1940. Command came easily to the diminutive Canadian, who shocked the escapers by addressing them without the trace of an accent. "Well, fellows," said Dumais, "this is the last lap of a long journey. It is the last, but the most dangerous one. We are about a mile from the Channel; if everything goes well, you'll be aboard a British warship in two hours and in England by nine o'clock in the morning."[162]

There was no moon that night, so each escaper had to hold the coattail of the one in front of him. The first man in the column held on to 18-year-old Marie-Thérèse Le Calvez's coattail. Dumais forbade them from smoking or talking, and enjoined from coughing. "When you reach the coast, you'll have to go down a steep [150-foot] cliff. Lie on your backs and slide down. When you get to the bottom, you'll be told where to sit," Dumais told them, skipping over the fact that a few hundred yards on either side of the cliff sat German listening posts.

28 JANUARY 1944, DULAG LUFT, FRANKFURT

Ian MacDonald Aches for Mail

As Father Desnoyers would write later in the year, to glean every scintilla of life from the paper that came from beyond the wire, Kriegies "read, reread and reread letters." Words were a balm for the soul, whether from a distant wife, parent or priest who knew you so well that he could say mass in your cadence. The healing quality of letters was so profound that many men let others read their letters so they too could hear voices from far beyond the barbed wire. Yet the happiness Ian MacDonald felt for one Canadian who received a letter turned to gnawing emptiness when he discovered that the letter was postmarked some five weeks *after* MacDonald estimated his own parents had been given his address.

When he wrote home later that day, instead of dwelling on his disappointment, which would only distress his parents, MacDonald sought to give them a glimpse of his life, affecting a worldly nonchalance about bombing raids: "Life is still much the same as ever, our boys in England supply excitement for us but it's rather annoying when you have to get out of the bed in the early hrs. of the morn."

30 JANUARY 1944, PARIS

Dumais Finds an Unlikely Ally in the Montmartre Métro Station

Compared with the heart-stopping moments Dumais endured at the checkpoint in the Métro following his return to Paris, the exfiltration of 17 "parcels" from *Festung Europa* was routine. The inky darkness and sound of the surf hid the men as they slid down the cliff to the beach where the Royal Navy was scheduled to pick them up. It had taken only 12 minutes to unload six crates filled with weapons, ammunition, chocolate, a wireless and four million francs, and then escort the evaders into the boats.

The Montmartre Métro station, by contrast, swarmed with Gestapo and gendarmes, who were checking every suitcase. When he realized that instead of working in pairs the German and French officials were at different tables, Dumais headed for one manned by a young gendarme and tried to disarm him by joking that his suitcase contained grenades and machine guns. The time he took looking for the suitcase's key gave Dumais the opportunity to say, "If you look in those cases, you're a dead man . . . I'm not alone and others have your number." The threat was believable because the Resistance had recently killed a number of zealous gendarmes, but it left the Frenchman unmoved, as did Dumais's next words: "All right then, you're either with me or against me."[163]

As Dumais felt his heart beat wildly, the gendarme responded calmly, "The inspectors are watching, so you'd better open them. We're searching for food" before making a show of lifting a few shirts out of the suitcase. The young policeman kept his composure when he saw the stacks of francs and Dumais told him, "It's Resistance money."

31 JANUARY 1944, MILAG UND MARLAG NORD, NEAR BREMEN, GERMANY

Father Robert Barsalou Jokes

While the winter had not been cold and there hadn't been much snow, Father Robert Barsalou wrote his family in mid-January that there had been "much darkness" due not so much to the early sunset but, rather, to the 4 p.m. "*obscuration*," a word he assumed they would know from the Blitz. "In Canada, you have no experience of the 'blackout,' and I do not wish you to."[164]

The POWs were supposed to write in pencil, but on 31 January, Barsalou was allowed to use a pen. That he found this mundane joy "interesting" says volumes about the boredom of camp life. Equally telling is the exuberance with which "*l'enfant missionnaire*" lists who he sees in the two pictures he had just received: father, mother, brothers, sisters, sisters-in-law, nieces, nephews and "new additions." The only rank vacant in "*Le Régiment* Barsalou" (the use of "*Régiment*" being another sign of the years he'd spent with the military) was "brothers-in-law." Their absence explains his plan to create "Sister-in-law's Day," which he knew would make his family chuckle and that showing that, after years in a POW camp, he still had his sense of humour.

26 FEBRUARY 1944, BRITTANY

DUMAIS SHOWS HE MEANS BUSINESS

Twice in the past few weeks, Dumais had reached for his gun. The first time, he handed it to an American with orders to keep watch on a certain "Olafson," whose weak command of English didn't jibe with his story of having had radio training in the United States, and his ignorance about the plane in which he claimed to have parachuted out of prompting a message to London. In the end, Dumais couldn't carry out MI9's order to "Get rid of him" because Olafson had escaped, though without enough information for the Germans to roll up Dumais's escape line.

The second time, the gun stayed in Dumais's hand, pointed at the chest of a man who'd been one of the senior members of *Oaktree*, the escape line that both Labrosse and Campinchi had worked for. In deference to them (and against his better judgment), Dumais had agreed to allow this man to join the second exfiltration from Bonaparte Beach: Operation Bonaparte II. But not only had the man Dumais called a lunatic, incredibly (given Dumais's insistence on security), attended a loud farewell party organized by Campinchi, but the "lunatic" came south from Paris with a former helper whom he promised would also be exfiltrated. Worse, on the train they spoke English and smoked English cigarettes. Once in Brittany, the "lunatic" attended still another farewell party, at which, gun in hand, Dumais took him into custody. Dumais refused to allow the second man to join Bonaparte II and made clear what would happen to him if he returned to Brittany. The Canadian MI9 agent was equally blunt with London; if they sent the "lunatic" back to France, Dumais would "shoot him on sight."[165]

Bonaparte II went off without a hitch, though Dumais was disappointed that his first Canadian "parcel" was arrested in Saint-Brieuc. "By way of compensation," he wrote years later, "a British fighter pilot shot down near Boulogne was picked up by a post van, taken to Saint-Brieuc, joined Bonaparte and was back in England five days after he had left!"

27 FEBRUARY 1944, STALAG II-D, STARGARD, NEAR STETTIN, GERMANY

Sergeant Major Liscomb Stands Up to a New Kommandant

They knew Stalag VIII-B was getting crowded. Still, the orders to board a train for another POW camp came as a surprise. "It was a strange feeling leaving the camp," recalls Stan Darch. "Of course, we didn't like it, but we knew it and we knew the guards and their routines. We knew that 'Spitfire' was a son of a bitch, and we knew which guards were gullible enough to supply us with what we wanted." The going price for a radio tube was a reasonable 1,200 cigarettes. On their march to the train station, the 1,400 Canadians could not help but notice the black muzzles of the automatic weapons pointed at them.

They'd heard and seen the fleets of bombers overhead, and new arrivals had brought news of the victory in North Africa, the defeat of Italy and the Russians' advances in the east. The train trip was, however, the Canadians' first opportunity in a year and a half to judge the progress of the war themselves. "We were struck by the civilians that we saw. When they saw us, they did not appear too happy," says Darch. The winter snows had covered the fields but could not hide the terrible toll the bombers had taken on houses, factories, roads and railways.

When they arrived at the POW camp near Stargard, the Kommandant asked if anyone could speak German. A man named Schillenberg of the South Saskatchewans said he did. "Later," recalls Darch, "he told us that the Kommandant said to him, 'That's a German name. Why are you in the Canadian Army?' and he answered, 'I made my bread and butter in Canada. That's why!'"

The men expected the usual statements about not trying to escape. Instead, Schillenberg told them that, according to the Kommandant, they'd all volunteered to work for Germany and as a result would be eligible for extra rations. As soon as the fetid men who had not yet been fed heard this, they started cursing. After a few moments, Sergeant Major Liscomb of the Essex Scottish stepped forward and the catcalls stopped, and the nonplussed Kommandant must have assumed that the natural order of command had re-established itself. Through Schillenberg, Liscomb told the Kommandant that he and the other NCOs would, quite simply, not be going out to work.

"Are you refusing to work as ordered?"

Liscomb answered, "No. We are not refusing. We [wish] to speak to the Swedish Red Cross representative before we go."

The Kommandant stood his ground. "You have until tomorrow to make up your minds or you will be shipped to Poland."

"Then you had better arrange for the train, sir. We could do with a ride anyway."[166] Then he turned his back on the Kommandant and returned to his place in the ranks. In the tense moments that followed, Liscomb wondered if his stand would cost him his life. It didn't, but the Kommandant cut off Red Cross parcels and ordered a reduction in German rations. Not only did both actions violate Geneva but they degraded the men by underscoring their powerlessness. Were it not for the Canadians' stock of cigarettes, which they bartered for food with other POWs, Darch and his comrades would have suffered severe malnutrition.

4 MARCH 1944, STALAG XVIII-A, WOLFSBERG, AUSTRIA

Father Juneau Has Doubts

As the third anniversary of their capture neared, *les religieux*'s moods diverged. A month earlier, Father Larivière had written of the men of "doubtful or no baptism" among whom he'd been cast and seen religious ignorance, disinterest and, in some cases, something approaching "paganism." Father Pierre-Paul Pellerin agreed: "In my two years of imprisonment here, I have not found a single Christian heart. I assure you, the mold is not easy to cast."

Writing from Austria on 3 March, Father Juneau told his brother, Romeo, that he regretted that "the whole country admires" him (presumably he means the people of Saint-Paulin de Maskinongé, who had read the letters that his family had published in the local paper) because as time went on he felt "less and less up to the task." In a letter written a few weeks later to his father, Juneau returns to this theme: "The priest in a camp does not have the right to be sad or morose. It is his duty to spread joy from the moment he enters a room. . . . and repeat: 'Everything is O.K. All for the best! Carry on, my boys! It won't be long! Have a smoke, a Canadian "fag." Nothing but the best!'" The emptiness of these stock phrases is all the more evident because he wrote them in English.

15 MARCH 1944, BRITTANY

Dumais Runs the "Cross-Channel Ferry Service"

The decoder in London must have thought Labrosse had made a mistake when he called for pickups on the nights of 15, 19 and 23 March. With Paris convulsed by the discovery of dozens of dismembered and charred bodies in a house in the 16th arrondissement, it was a good time to move the 75 "parcels" stashed around the city. The discovery that the coast was under an alert prompted Dumais to send Labrosse back to Paris to cancel the pickup on 19 March. Despite the alert, on 15 March, the escape party reached the beach without incident. A moment after hearing over the walkie-talkie that the Royal Navy was a mere four miles away, an explosion rent the night. "We'll have to pull out for the time being," the British sailor said, "but we'll be back."[167] After several nervous hours marked off more by the growing numbness in the arm that held the walkie-talkie to his ear than the watch on his wrist, through the static Dumais heard the code word.

The delay meant that when the boats approached the beach, dawn was close. The naval ratings and Dumais's men quickly emptied the boats of supplies and loaded the "parcels." As dawn broke, the ringmaster of what one wag dubbed the "Cross-Channel Ferry Service" could still make out the redoubtable boats, but the German gunners, mercifully, had not seen them.

17–18 MARCH 1944, REMERANGLES, FRANCE

RCAF Pilot Officer Ken Woodhouse Is Shot Down and Taken to Paris

Ken Woodhouse could not see the man asking, "*Avez-vous vu un parachutiste?*" But his German-accented French told him how close he was to being captured. The interval between hearing the Frenchman answer "*Oui*" and "over there, over there"— was just long enough for the RCAF pilot to wonder if he'd blundered by climbing into the coffin-like box on the back of a truck that drove up to him just moments after he bailed out of his Spitfire (on his 65th mission) 60 miles north of Paris.[168]

Maurice Rendu did not speak English, but his meaning was perfectly clear when, a few minutes after he had warded the German off and after a few more minutes' drive, he stopped, let Woodhouse out of the box and motioned for him to crawl into a haystack and remain quiet. After Rendu drove off, Woodhouse filed the "Made in Canada" label off his nail clippers, cut the pilot wings off his shirt and cut down his flying boots before taping his dog tags to his ankle.

By dusk the 22-year-old had been moved to the house belonging to Rendu's father, Wilfred, who warmly if embarrassingly welcomed him by exclaiming, "*Mon Dieu, il est un enfant!*" (My God, he's just a child!). Soon, however, "two rough-looking men dressed in typical French farm clothing" stood by ominously as Maurice peppered him with questions that Woodhouse guessed were meant to determine that he was, indeed, an Allied pilot but which he could not answer because of his inability to speak French. As his fear built, one of the two men broke into a smile and said in unmistakable American English, "Hi Mac. Welcome to France."

Before dawn on the 18th, Woodhouse and the two American airmen were in a truck that picked up three more men before stopping at a door set curiously in the wall of a brick building. The door led to a loading chute; from the white powder on the floor, the Canadian from Prince Albert, Saskatchewan, knew they were walking into a flour mill. A second door led them into the living room of a house, where still another evader waited for them. A few hours later, the men were on a truck on their way to see a forger who was readying their identity cards. In the front seat was a gendarme who had thrown his lot in with the Resistance. There were some moments of tension when they came across German troops marching a work detail of British POWs. But, seeing the gendarme, the Germans waved the truck on and the tension lessened, though Woodhouse's pity for his captured allies did not.

The instructions on how to behave on the train were detailed. No talking, showing that they knew each other or acting like tourists. Smoking had to be done in the French way; that is, by leaving the cigarette in the mouth. Even picking up their tickets was choreographed. Each evader had to pass through a crowded area, in the middle of which someone would slip the ticket into his hand.

Shortly before arriving at Gare du Nord, the two Resistance men shepherding Woodhouse and the American airmen to Paris asked to see their identity cards. The evaders were stunned when their "helpers" ripped up the cards and threw out the pieces, explaining that "the cards were incorrect and it was better to have none at all." If they were captured, they could now at least pretend to be escaping unaided.

Several pairs of eyes were watching them once they arrived in Paris. Some belonged to the Gestapo. Others were unseen friends who, as the evaders circled the block outside the station, watched to see if they were being followed. Woodhouse was quite unprepared for the helper who picked them up in front of a bakery.

Instead of another brawny male, a "little old lady appeared from somewhere, . . . [she] strutted along without a care in the world, stopped to buy some bread whilc we waited outside, and eventually delivered us to an apartment—and then disappeared, we never saw her again."

23–24 MARCH 1944, PLOUHA, BRITTANY

Woodhouse and Two Other RCAF Officers Escape from Bonaparte Beach

Between Genevieve Schneegan and Olympe Vasseur, at whose apartment he stayed in Montmartre, and Marie-Thérèse Le Calvez, who, when they arrived in Saint-Brieuc, led Woodhouse and eight other men, including two other Canadians, to a farmer's shack fitted out with rough-hewn beds, Woodhouse had been in the hands of three helpers. Monsieur and Madame Maurice Cavalier hid Woodhouse and arranged for new identity cards from a forger whose palette consisted of papers, inks, examples of signatures of mayors of hundreds of villages, German officials and numerous rubber stamps.

Mirielle Catherine Herveic led Woodhouse, RCAF officers Russel Barnlund and Ken Lussier, and the six other evaders onto the train from Paris to Saint-Brieuc—and, to ensure that they had their reserved compartment to themselves, threw a proper Parisian fit that cleared the compartment of the squatters. Save for the moment when the American Bob Sweatt unthinkingly lit a German soldier's cigarette with a Ronson lighter, the trip from Saint-Brieuc to Guingamp was uneventful: because Guingamp was inside the 15-mile Restricted Zone, the evaders expected heavy security. Woodhouse and Sweatt were taken to safe house; in addition to sheltering evaders, Monsieur and Madame Laurent stored arms, ammunition, explosives and radios.

The next evening, Francis Kerambum, whose day job hauling supplies for the Germans provided both cover and much-needed petrol, drove Woodhouse, Sweatt and several other evaders to their meeting place with Le Calvez. To the men's surprise, she immediately led them "through fields, along hedgerows, past some darkened houses and then, in a final fifty yard dash," first to a barn and finally to the shelter.[169]

The following day, she brought food and, after 26 of the Allied servicemen had assembled, under the cover of darkness Le Calvez and another guide led them toward La Maison d'Alphonse. Woodhouse experienced some anxious moments, first in the minefield and then while moving along a sunken road when a German patrol unexpectedly appeared above them, which prompted Le Calvez to order the men to scatter. But he was amazed at her grasp of the topography when, in total darkness and after reassembling the group, she led them on a 200-foot course through rough cliffs down to Bonaparte Beach. There, Lucien Dumais handed Woodhouse and another man each a thermos flask filled with brandy—and copies of his action report telling them that if they were intercepted at sea, they "were to throw them overboard and let them sink." Neither Dumais nor Woodhouse ever realized that they were countrymen. After long minutes of waiting, Woodhouse realized that the little surfboat that would ferry them to the PT-like fast boat was near when, through the sound of the waves lapping the Breton shore, they heard the swishing of muffled oars and then the soft voice of their guardian angel whispering last instructions to the men. The first group silently climbed onto the boat as soon as the crates of weapons and money were unloaded.[170]

As he waited anxiously below deck for the second group of men, including Barnlund, to be taken off the beach, Woodhouse marvelled at the sailors who rowed through the minefield in the dark.

24–25 MARCH 1944, STALAG LUFT III, SAGAN, POLAND

THE GREAT ESCAPE

Had Hermann Glemnitz not sensed something big was coming, Wally Floody would have been among the first to climb out of "Harry." In late February, however, Glemnitz shipped him, Kingsley Brown and 17 other men to a satellite camp. Therefore, the first man to climb out of the tunnel onto the snow-covered ground was RAF Flying Officer Johnny Bull, who had been shot down just over four years earlier.

Hollywood's *The Great Escape* takes more than a few liberties with the facts, but it gets right that, instead of making a run for it, Bull immediately climbed back into the shaft and told Roger Bushell that Harry had emerged from the ground 25 feet short of the wood that was to give the escapers cover, a mere 25 yards from a goon box and inside the perimeter walked by the guards.[171] With more than 100 men in the tunnel behind them or in Hut 104 ready to climb into it, the decision on whether to go ahead with the break had to be made quickly and turned on the fact that their travel passes and other papers were stamped 25 March 1944. To lessen the chance of the escapers being spotted as they climbed from the 336-foot-long tunnel, a controller who, like the controllers in the tunnel, signalled via a rope when it was safe to move forward, stood behind a fence that hid him from the nearby perimeter guards.

By the time Tommy Thompson climbed out into the pre-dawn darkness and dashed to the pine trees half a football field's distance away, six other Canadians had already begun their home runs. One, RCAF Flight Lieutenant William Cameron, immediately preceded Thompson and was his escape partner. Neither they nor the 46 men between them and the group ahead would have got anywhere had RCAF Spitfire pilot Hank Birkland, who was serving as a stationer in the tunnel, not jumped into action when he saw the tunnel collapse around RAF Squadron Leader Thomas G. Kirby-Green, on the trolley being hauled forward. It took Birkland, working in total darkness, about an hour to dig out Kirby-Green and clear and reshore Harry. Dozens of men, including at least four RCAF officers, owed their chance at freedom to another Canadian Flight Lieutenant, George McGill, who upon reaching the wood served as a controller, signalling when the sentry had passed the escape point. Sometime before he was replaced at 4 a.m., McGill froze when one of the sentries stepped into the gap of trees beyond which he was secreted. The sentry unbuttoned his pants and relieved himself before continuing his post.

Thompson and Cameron stepped into the chilled early morning air near 5 a.m., not knowing that the strengthening light of dawn had prompted the decision to halt the escape stream at number 87. As Thompson and Cameron cleared the wood, back at the shaft, Ottawa-born and -bred RAF Pilot Officer Keith Ogilvie climbed out of the tunnel. A moment later, he and several other escapers took to their heels as a guard who had just noticed several escapers lying face down in the slush as they awaited the rope-borne signal fired his rifle; thanks to another escaper who jumped up and yelled "*Nicht schießen!*"—Don't shoot!—the guard shot wildly.[172]

As other guards came running and the alarm went out to the surrounding area and, ultimately, the entire Reich, the escapers tried to put as much distance as they could between themselves and the camp. Even before Birkland climbed out of the tunnel, Flight Lieutenant Gordon A. Kidder and his escape partner, Kirby-Green, had reached the Sagan train station, having walked by the town's great fountain. In the cavernous station, Kirby-Green's broken Spanish (and weak German) aroused a woman's suspicions but was enough to convince the policeman she called over that they were indeed Spanish workers. At 1 a.m. they boarded a train for Breslau.

James Wernham and the other 11 men in his escape group had a longer walk and wait. Knowing that the sudden arrival at the Sagan train station of a number of dishevelled men speaking poor German would trigger an alarm, Polish-born flight lieutenant Jerzy Mondschein led the group toward another station southeast of the camp. The ticket agent's consternation when Mondschein asked for a dozen tickets to Boberröhrsdorf (then in Germany but now in present-day southeast Poland) caused a few anxious moments for the escapers, who studiedly looked nonchalant. By the time they boarded their train at 6 a.m., a machine-gun-equipped squad had descended on Hut 104 and the guards were pulling the rest of the would-be escapers from Harry.

The men arrested in the tunnel and in Hut 104 expected the harangue from the Kommandant, who, after all, would have to explain to Berlin how the Kriegies had dug yet another tunnel through which more than 80 men had escaped. Thanks to a few unsupervised moments in the Kommandant's office that, a few days earlier, allowed a POW to rifle through the open safe, the Escape Committee knew the gist of the 4 March *Aktion Kugel,* Hitler's Bullet Decree stating that escaped POWs were to be turned over to the Gestapo.[173] From suborned guards, the POWs also knew that this did not apply to British and American POWs. Thus, even after the arrests began, the Kriegies were not overly alarmed; according to RAF Flight Lieutenant Tim Walenn, "The Germans would never be so unsporting as to shoot prisoners in cold blood."[174]

A year earlier, Walenn would have been correct. But March 1944 was not March 1943. Since then, Italy had dropped out of the war, the Germans had been driven from North Africa and the Russians had pushed the Nazis out of the eastern Ukraine and Belarus (Belorussia). During the last week of February, American, British and Canadian bombers flew almost 7,000 sorties, bombing more than dozens of cities and factory complexes. Berlin was bombed four days in March, the bombing on the night of the 24th explaining Generaloberst Wilhelm Keitel's bad mood at a mid-morning meeting on the 25th. Keitel, who commanded the Wehrmacht, had not planned to bring up the escape. However, Hitler's satraps constantly angled to wound one another in order to seize more power for themselves. Accordingly, near the end of the meeting, Gestapo chief Heinrich Himmler raised what he called, with devastating understatement, "*Ein kleiner Punkt*," that there had been "another escape from the prisoner-of-war camp at Sagan." The "small point" quickly grew in importance: first to the fact that "upward of 70 air force officers" had escaped and then to the prediction that "we will have to mobilize 70,000 auxiliaries to deal with the matter."[175]

Hitler exploded in anger. "These officers are an enormous danger. You don't realize that in view of the six million foreign people who are prisoners and workers in Germany, they are the leaders who could organize an uprising!" After catching his breath, the Führer continued in a way most congenial to the SS chief, whose secret police had long clashed with Abwehr, the army's intelligence service. "The escaped air officers are to be turned over to Himmler."

Knowing that the Bullet Decree exempted British and American POWs, Keitel tried to object, which only fanned the flames of the dictator's ire. "They are all to be shot! All of them—they will not trouble us again!" Himmler, who had overseen the killing of millions in the east and in concentration camps, was not the slightest bit averse to shedding innocent blood but quickly moved to modify Hitler's position. His stated argument, that shooting all of the escapers "would do harm to our relations with the neutral countries" is hard to credit; what exactly would Spain, Sweden or Hungary do about a few more executions? Rather, it seems as if he raised the point merely to give Hitler the opportunity to continue venting his spleen. "More than half then!" Knowing well Hitler's lack of interest in the mechanics of his own orders, Himmler seized the moment: "Perhaps fifty would be a suitable number," he said. When the Nazi leader did not object, Himmler added, "Very well, I shall contact my deputy [Ernst] Kaltenbrunner and have him draft an order."[176]

26 MARCH 1944, NEAR SAGAN, POLAND

CAMERON'S HALLUCINATIONS CUT SHORT HIS GROUP'S HOME RUN

As Kidder and Kirby-Green boarded a train for Breslau, where they changed trains for Czechoslovakia—their goal being to reach Yugoslavia—and Wernham's party of 12 travelled toward the town of Hirschberg, Cameron and Thompson began walking through the forest. At one point, they saw that they were being followed, but when the followers did not start shooting or come running, they realized that the two men were also escapers: RAF Flight Lieutenants Brian Evans and Chaz Hall. Near 4 a.m. on the 26th, the four cold and wet men took shelter in a barn's hayloft. When Cameron started shaking and talking to himself, the others realized he was hallucinating.

Cameron's crisis forced the men's gut-wrenching decision to turn themselves in. Given the number of troops and police searching for them and how close they were to Sagan, the escapers were surprised that they could not find anyone to whom they could surrender. In the end, they left the door to the barn open so that the farmer would find Cameron, and slipped away.

Late in the day, while trying to find a freight train to hop, Thompson, Evans and Hall were arrested outside a nearby village. When the Home Guard brought the three to an inn to await transfer to the prison in Sagan, Keith Ogilvie, who had been arrested by a pistol-wielding civilian, was already there. The Canadian made no sign of knowing them, and they did not acknowledge him. Thompson, who yearned to escape because he did not feel that he had pulled his "weight in this war, getting bounced in the first week," tried arguing that he was a French worker making his way home; his Penetanguishene, Ontario, French made for a less than convincing performance.[177]

Cruelly, given the frigid winters he had faced walking to school in Spearhill, Manitoba, Birkland was undone by the cold and waist-deep snow he and two other men waded through that afternoon of the 26th. Like Cameron, he became delirious and started talking to himself. Whatever hope he and the others may have had about the farm family that lived in the house they made their way to evaporated when the door they knocked upon opened to reveal four German soldiers.

29 MARCH 1944, GÖRLITZ, GERMANY

Tommy Thompson Drops Hermann Göring's Name

The Canadians and 13 other escapees caught near Stalag Luft III spent a day in Sagan's prison before being transferred to the prison in Görlitz 50 miles southwest of Sagan. Meanwhile, the dragnet captured more escapees, including Pat Langford and George Wiley, and the Gestapo readied to carry out Himmler's orders. Kaltenbrunner sent a teletype to every Gestapo district office in Germany, which, after taking the opportunity to rub Keitel's face in it for a larger audience, relayed the order that 50 of the escapers or almost 60 per cent of them were to be executed instead of being returned to prisoner-of-war camps.

Surprisingly, only two escapers, Kidder and Kirby-Green, captured as they neared Austria, were tortured before being killed. Germany was in violation of Geneva by holding captured POWs in the civilian prison in Görlitz, but what bothered the men more was the boredom. Hall gave the others in his cell, including Ogilvie, a few laughs by writing on the wall the famed line spoken by gladiators to the Caesars before the games began: "*Morituri te salutamus*"—We who are about to die salute you. Nor did every interrogation seem all that threatening. RAF Flight Lieutenant T.R. Nelson recalled being held in a room that could have been the setting for a bad film, complete with a bright light shining on him and the strong smell of Gauloises cigarettes—though there were some tense moments and the mention of a concentration camp after his interrogator jumped to the erroneous conclusion that Nelson was Jewish because his mother's name was Rebecca. Others, however, returned to their cells with more troubling stories. Wiley was told that he would not survive to see his parents.

Thompson responded, "I don't care who you are. I'm still protected by the Geneva Convention" after his interrogator told him, "You are not in the hands of military authorities. . . . Anything might happen to you without that [Geneva] protection—you might never go back to the camp." The Gestapo agent's chuckle prompted Thompson to play his best card. "Well I don't think that Göring would be very happy if anything happened to me. We met once, you know, back in 1939."[178]

Göring was no longer the force he had been in September 1939. The populace now openly ridiculed his Luftwaffe for its inability to prevent Allied bombing raids. Furthermore, the agent knew that, since the Gestapo had been tasked with dealing with the escapers, his boss, Himmler, was in ascendance over Göring. Thus, the German's apparent dismissal of Thompson's claim to be under the Reichsmarschall's personal protection: "Be that as it may, you are in civilian clothes—you are probably a spy."

Yet Göring was still head of the Luftwaffe, minister president of Prussia and an intimate of Hitler and hence not a man to cross lightly. Since the Gestapo knew who Thompson was, the female typist's search of Thompson's clothing to see if it was air force issue was hardly necessary. This *pièce de théâtre* concluded with the words "You are fortunate—you have escaped in a soldier's uniform; therefore you will be tried before a military court. The others will not be so lucky." Ogilvie's interrogation ended the same way Thompson's did. Before leaving the office, Ogilvie saw on the Gestapo agent's desk a paper on which 20 names were typed. Ogilvie assumed the list was the names of those in the first group of men to arrive at Görlitz Prison.

1. Pilot Officer "Tommy" Thompson (*second from right*) and Squadron Leader Phillip Murray with German Officers.

COURTESY OF JESSY BEAUCHAMP

2. The SS *Zam Zam* sinking after the Germans blew open her hull on the morning of 18 April 1941.

DR. ULRICH MOHR, COURTESY OF CAROLYN GOSSAGE

3. The men's hold aboard the *Dresden*, where the Oblates and Sacred Heart Brothers spent five difficult weeks.

DR. ULRICH MOHR, COURTESY OF CAROLYN GOSSAGE

4. Father Robert Barsalou saying Mass under a tarp on the deck of the *Dresden.*

COURTESY OF THE OBLATES OF MARY IMMACULATE, CANADA

5. Stalag VIII-B (Sandbostel), where *les religieux* were held before being transferred to Milag und Marlag Nord.

COURTESY OF THE OBLATES OF MARY IMMACULATE, CANADA

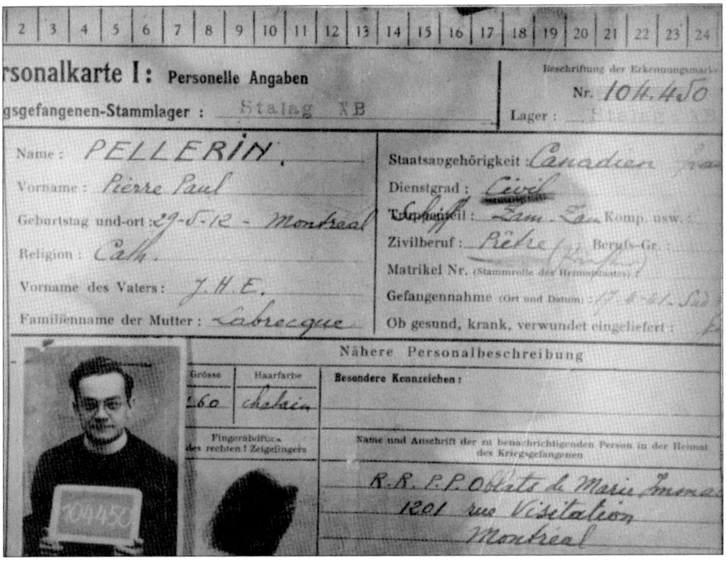
2 3 4 5 6 7 8 9 10 11 12 13 14 15 16 17 18 19 20 21 22 23 24

rsonalkarte I: Personelle Angaben
gsgefangenen-Stammlager : Stalag XB

Beschriftung der Erkennungsmarke
Nr. 104.450
Lager :

Name : PELLERIN.
Vorname : Pierre Paul
Geburtstag und-ort : 29-5-12 - Montreal
Religion : Cath.
Vorname des Vaters : J.H.E.
Familienname der Mutter : Labrecque

Staatsangehörigkeit : Canadien
Dienstgrad : Civil
Truppenteil : Zam Zam Komp. usw. :
Zivilberuf : Prêtre Berufs-Gr. :
Matrikel Nr. (Stammrolle des Heimatstaates) :
Gefangennahme (Ort und Datum) : 17-4-41
Ob gesund, krank, verwundet eingeliefert :

Nähere Personalbeschreibung

Grösse	Haarfarbe	Besondere Kennzeichen :
160	chatain	

Fingerabdruck des rechten ! Zeigefingers

Name und Anschrift der zu benachrichtigenden Person in der Heimat des Kriegsgefangenen

R.R. P.P. Oblats de Marie Immac
1201 rue Visitation
Montréal

6. Father Pierre-Paul Pellerin's *Personalkarte*, issued at Stalag X-B. The card was kept in Stalag's record office.

COURTESY OF THE OBLATES OF MARY IMMACULATE, CANADA

7. Sergeant Major Lucien Dumais, Fusiliers de Montreal.

8. Canadian POWs being marched through Dieppe.

COURTESY OF LIBRARY AND ARCHIVES CANADA, PA 20058

9. Father Philippe Goudreau at Stalag Luft III. He used this typewriter to write letters to his family and to Oblates in Canada. To protect Goudreau, the men who took part in the Great Escape did not use the typewriter to forge documents.

COURTESY OF THE OBLATES OF MARY IMMACULATE, CANADA

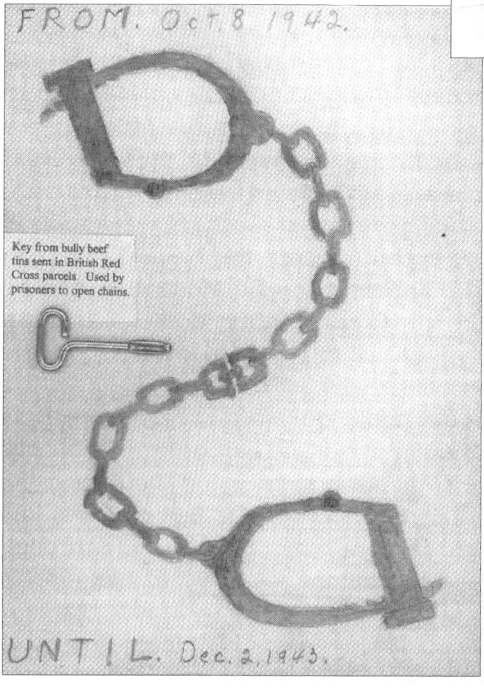

10. An example of the type of handcuffs used to shackle Privates Stan Darch, Robert Prouse and the other Dieppe POWs.

COURTESY OF ROBERT PROUSE

11. Ian MacDonald (*far left*) with Madam Zinne (*next to MacDonald*) and her family. Because he was out of uniform, MacDonald was no longer clearly protected by the Geneva Convention.

COURTESY OF IAN MACDONALD

12. Ian MacDonald's home in Lourdes, Nova Scotia, with his sister Rita outside.

COURTESY OF IAN MACDONALD

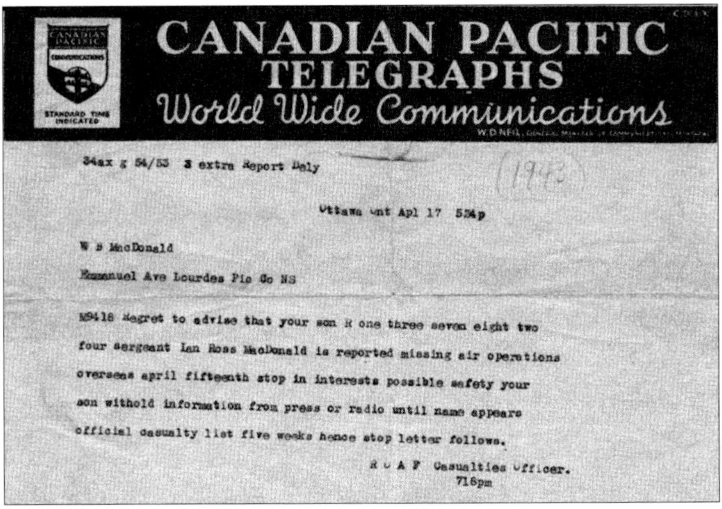

CANADIAN PACIFIC
TELEGRAPHS
World Wide Communications

34ax g 54/53 3 extra Report Dely

Ottawa Ont Apl 17 534p

W S MacDonald

Emmanuel Ave Lourdes Pic Co NS

M9418 Regret to advise that your son R one three seven eight two four sergeant Ian Ross MacDonald is reported missing air operations overseas april fifteenth stop in interests possible safety your son withold information from press or radio until name appears official casualty list five weeks hence stop letter follows.

R C A F Casualties Officer.
716pm

13. The telegram Miss Mable MacLean delivered to her neighbours Mr. and Mrs. William MacDonald, saying that their son Ian was missing after a raid on Stuttgart on 15 April 1943.

COURTESY OF IAN MACDONALD

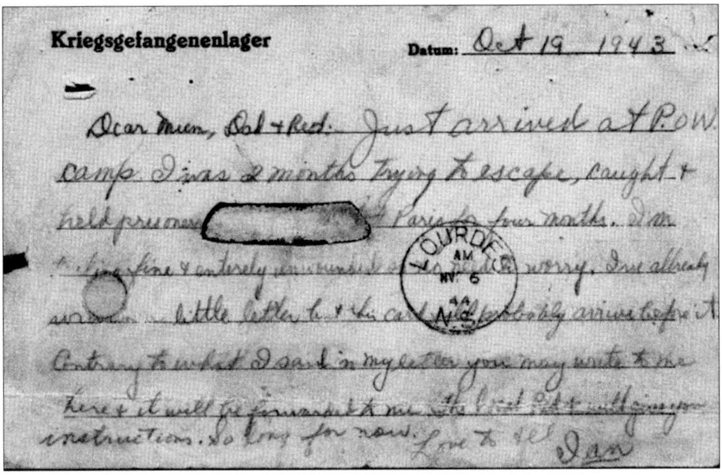

Kriegsgefangenenlager Datum: Oct 19 1943

Dear Mum, Dad + Red. Just arrived at P.O.W. camp. I was 2 months trying to escape, caught + held prisoner [redacted] Paris for four months. I'm feeling fine & entirely uninjured so don't worry. I've already written little letter but this card will probably arrive before it. Contrary to what I said in my letter you may write to me here & it will be forwarded to me. The last letter will give you instructions. So long for now. Love to all Ian

14. The first postcard Ian MacDonald sent to his parents after arriving in Dulag Luft, Frankfurt. The words "Fresnes Prison" were deleted by either a German or a Canadian censor.

COURTESY OF IAN MACDONALD

15. Ian MacDonald (*far right*) in Dulag Luft, Frankfurt.

COURTESY OF IAN MACDONALD

16. Stella Maris, the chapel the fathers and brothers built at Milag Nord.

COURTESY OF THE OBLATES OF MARY IMMACULATE, CANADA

17. Father Philippe Goudreau's chapel in the basement of the theatre at Stalag Luft III.

COURTESY OF THE OBLATES OF MARY IMMACULATE, CANADA

18. Father Herménégilde Charbonneau saying Mass at the chapel in Blechhammer.

COURTESY OF THE OBLATES OF MARY IMMACULATE, CANADA

To all Prisoners of War!

The escape from prison camps is no longer a sport!

Germany has always kept to the Hague Convention and only punished recaptured prisoners of war with minor disciplinary punishment.

Germany will still maintain these principles of international law.

But England has besides fighting at the front in an honest manner instituted an illegal warfare in non combat zones in the form of gangster commandos, terror bandits and sabotage troops even up to the frontiers of Germany.

They say in a captured secret and confidential English military pamphlet,

THE HANDBOOK OF MODERN IRREGULAR WARFARE:

". . . the days when we could practise the rules of sportsmanship are over. For the time being, every soldier must be a potential gangster and must be prepared to adopt their methods whenever necessary."

"The sphere of operations should always include the enemy's own country, any occupied territory, and in certain circumstances, such neutral countries as he is using as a source of supply."

England has with these instructions opened up a non military form of gangster war!

Germany is determined to safeguard her homeland, and especially her war industry and provisional centres for the fighting fronts. Therefore it has become necessary to create strictly forbidden zones, called death zones, in which all unauthorised trespassers will be immediately shot on sight.

Escaping prisoners of war, entering such death zones, will certainly lose their lives. They are therefore in constant danger of being mistaken for enemy agents or sabotage groups.

Urgent warning is given against making future escapes!

In plain English: Stay in the camp where you will be safe! Breaking out of it is now a damned dangerous act.

The chances of preserving your life are almost nil!

All police and military guards have been given the most strict orders to shoot on sight all suspected persons.

Escaping from prison camps has ceased to be a sport!

19. A poster put up after the Great Escape, warning POWs that escaping from camps should not be considered a sport.

COURTESY OF ROBERT PROUSE

20. The contents of a Canadian Red Cross food parcel. Note the can of Klim (*milk* spelled backwards), a dried milk powder. Klim cans were used for making blowers and digging tunnels.

COURTESY OF THE OBLATES OF MARY IMMACULATE, CANADA

21. A Christmas card produced at Milag und Marlag Nord. To arrive in time, cards had to be sent by late August.

COURTESY OF THE OBLATES OF MARY IMMACULATE, CANADA

22. Robert Prouse's sketch of the "cooler," where he was imprisoned in Mulhausen in 1944.

COURTESY OF ROBERT PROUSE

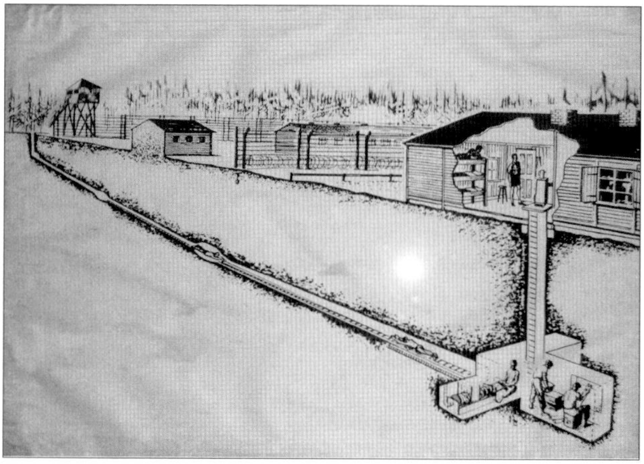

23. A drawing of the path of the tunnel nicknamed "Harry" at Stalag Luft III.

NATHAN M. GREENFIELD, WITH THANKS TO THE POW CAMPS MUSEUM STALAG LUFT III

24. Yellow spoil from tunnels dug at Stalag Luft III. The "penguins" hid soil in bags in their pants and released it by pulling on a drawstring.

NATHAN M. GREENFIELD, WITH THANKS TO THE POW CAMPS MUSEUM STALAG LUFT III

25. The entrance to "Harry," the tunnel through which Tommy Thompson and others made the Great Escape from Stalag Luft III, was underneath a stove such as this.

NATHAN M. GREENFIELD, WITH THANKS TO THE POW CAMPS MUSEUM STALAG LUFT III

26. The remains of the theatre that housed Father Philippe Goudreau's chapel. The entrance to the tunnel called "George" was just behind the chapel.

NATHAN M. GREENFIELD, WITH THANKS TO THE POW CAMPS MUSEUM STALAG LUFT III

27. The original monument to the 50 Allied Airmen executed for their role in the Great Escape was built by the Kriegies in the German military cemetery in Sagan. After the war, the bodies of Canadian and other Commonwealth airmen were exhumed and reburied in a Commonwealth cemetery in Posen, Poland.

NATHAN M. GREENFIELD

28. Norman Reid survived after being shot down on both his twenty-eighth and forty-first bombing runs.
COURTESY OF NORMAN REID

29. The four Chetniks to whom Reid entrusted himself after parachuting into Yugoslavia. Presumably none of these four, who took Norman Reid to safety, knew that two weeks earlier Winston Churchill had shifted his support from their leader, the Draža Mihailović, to Josip Broz Tito's Communist partisans.
COURTESY OF NORMAN REID

30. The avenue at Buchenwald Concentration Camp that ran by the hut where the Canadians lived.
NATHAN M. GREENFIELD

31. Romeo Sabourin, killed in Buchenwald along with fellow Canadians Frank Pickersgill, Ken Macalister and ten other SOE agents.

32. The staircase of the *Zellenbau*, which housed Buchenwald's crematorium, leads to the basement where Romeo Sabourin, Frank Pickersgill, Ken Macalister and ten other SOE agents were strung up with piano wire.

NATHAN M. GREENFIELD

33. The *Leichenkeller*, the room where thirteen SOE agents, including Canadians Romeo Sabourin, Frank Pickersgill and Ken Macalister, died. Note the meat hooks from which they were hung by piano wire.

NATHAN M. GREENFIELD

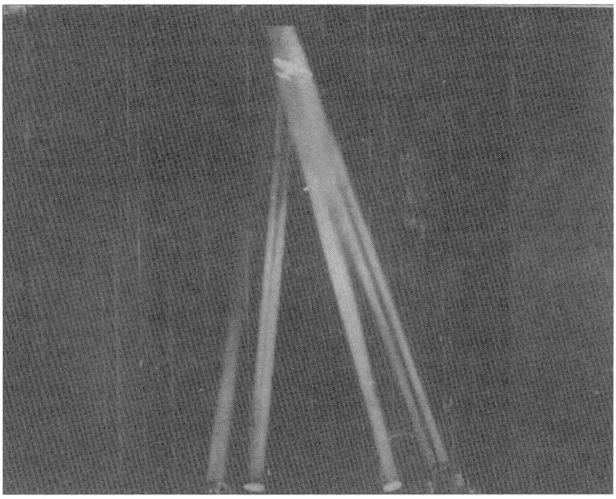

34. Every airman dreaded the possibility of being caught in the cone of German searchlights. Here, a British bomber is coned near Milag und Marlag Nord. Note the plane at the apex of the triangle formed by the search-lights.

COURTESY OF THE OBLATES OF MARY IMMACULATE, CANADA

35. Bomb damage at the camp at Wolfsberg, Austria, where Father Paul Juneau was held captive for 1,330 days.

COURTESY OF THE OBLATES OF MARY IMMACULATE, CANADA

36. A cardboard suitcase given to Father Raoul Bergeron by the French Oblates. He used it to carry the materials needed for saying Mass.

COURTESY OF THE OBLATES OF MARY IMMACULATE, CANADA

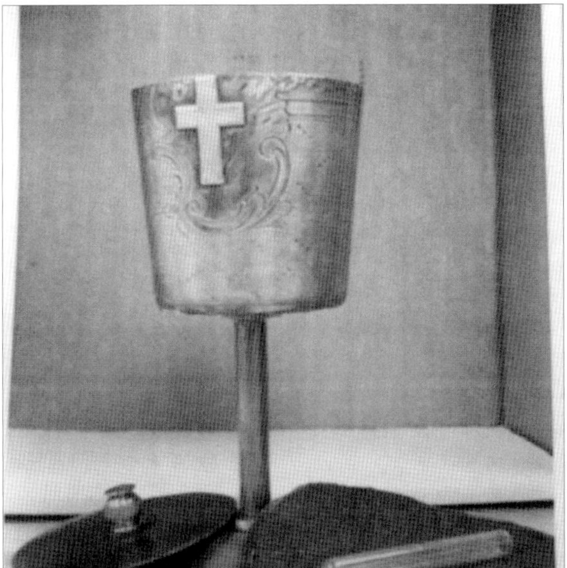

37. During Mass, the fathers used this pipette to place four drops of wine into this chalice made from Klim cans.

COURTESY OF THE OBLATES OF MARY IMMACULATE, CANADA

38. Father Charbonneau (*in foreground*) in the trench where he slept during the last days at Milag und Marlag Nord.
COURTESY OF THE OBLATES OF MARY IMMACULATE, CANADA

39. RCAF Squadron Leader "Teddy" Blenkinsop (*left*) and 20-year-old resistance fighter Hilaire Gemoets, three days after Blenkinsop was shot down during a bombing run.
LEA GEMOETS, COURTESY OF GRUB STREET PUBLISHING, LONDON, UK

40. Grave of "Teddy" Blenkinsop, the only uniformed Canadian to die in a concentration camp.
PETER CELIS, COURTESY OF GRUB STREET PUBLISHING, LONDON, UK

31 MARCH 1944

FOUR CANADIANS ARE KILLED IN THE GROUP OF GREAT ESCAPE EXECUTIONS

"You lucky bastards. It's back to Sagan for you," Ogilvie recalled another POW at Görlitz calling out in the early morning darkness as ten of their handcuffed comrades, including Canadians Birkland, McGill and Langford, strode the same path through the prison that a day earlier Wiley and five other men had taken. Ogilvie asked RAF Flight Lieutenant Albert Hake where they were going. "No idea. I imagine we've got another round of questioning ahead of us."[179]

Wiley's group was chosen by SS-Gruppenführer Artur Nebe, who headed the Kriminalpolizei and who, despite having commanded Einsatzgruppe B, which was responsible for murdering tens of thousands in Poland in 1941, found selecting from among the names disquieting. Looking at one group of cards, he brusquely said to his clerk, "See whether they have wives and children." But orders were orders, and after some shuffling of cards from one pile to another, he passed a pile of 50 cards to his clerk, who arranged to have the names telegraphed to the appropriate offices.

By the close of day on 31 March, German firing squads fired 16 times, killing four Canadian and 12 other Allied airmen.

Chapter Ten

April–May 1944

Down on the vale of death, with dismal cries,
The fated victims shuddering cast their eyes
In wild despair; while yet another stroke
With strong convulsion rends the solid oak:
Ah, Heaven!—behold her crashing rib divide!
She loosens, parts, and spreads in ruin o'er the tide.

—William Falconer, *The Shipwreck*

6 APRIL 1944, STALAG LUFT III, SAGAN, POLAND

Father Goudreau's Personal Reason to Pray for the Souls of the Executed Great Escapers

In the days following the escape, Father Goudreau's Roman collar did not exempt him from the extra hours standing on Appell as the Kriegies were counted, recounted and counted again. Anxiety for those still on the run and the captured (none of whom had yet been returned to the general camp population) combined with the heightened religious emotion of the last days of Lent in his prayers for the men, some having taken communion from his own hand.

Only those members of the Escape Committee who had not shimmied their way through the narrow tunnel knew that, as he knelt in his chapel and prayed for the 86 men, the priest from the tiny village of Saint-Pierre-Baptiste de Mégantic, Quebec, had a very personal reason to thank Jesus. To better their chances of blending in with workers and farmers, escapers wore the best approximations of civilian clothes they could tailor. Alone among the thousands of men in the compound, Goudreau wore civilian clothes; indeed, the camp's thespians often borrowed his slacks and shoes so that the guards attending the performances would not see their tailoring skills or that the leg portion of their flying boots had been cut away, leaving a fair approximation of civilian shoes. For that reason and because of the length of time Goudreau had been a

POW, he was offered the chance to escape. As Father Larivière had three years earlier when the Polish underground arranged for him to escape, Goudreau turned down the offer because it would have meant abandoning his flock in the camp. Like Father Boulanger, who in late 1943 had been offered the chance to be repatriated, Larivière and Goudreau (and *les autres religieux*) were now called to be not only witnesses for Christ in the fallen world but *témoins de l'histoire.*

Goudreau's prayers on the evening of 6 April, the third to last day of Lent, were different. Now, he prayed for the souls of 41 as yet unidentified men whom the camp's new Kommandant, Oberstleutnant Erich Cordes, told the Senior British Officer, RAF Group Captain Herbert Massey, "were shot while resisting arrest or in their endeavors to escape again after having been rearrested."[180]

9 APRIL 1944, EASTER SUNDAY, POSEN, POLAND

Father Larivière Says Nothing about Surviving a Bombing Raid

Two weeks earlier, Father Desnoyers wrote Father Cyr Roy, "It seems as you talked too much: ten lines [of your letter] were blacked out and are illegible." Now it was Father Larivière's turn to wonder what Father Antoni Toupin had said in the nine lines the Germans removed from his 3 January letter. As Toupin accepted the admonition to remain "*en garde!*" he welcomed the news that on Easter Sunday Larivière presided over three masses and, knowing of Larivière's love of music, that two were sung.

Larivière could not spell out the implications of the decision that, come the end of the war, the Oblates and Sacred Heart Brothers would be repatriated as "interned Canadian civilians and not military chaplains of British troops." His years' long effort to have the priests and brothers brevetted into the Royal Navy had failed, and thus in order to buy supplies needed to conduct mass, the Oblates would remain dependent on both German goodwill to pay them a stipend and on their fellow prisoners, who gave them a portion of their pay.

Used to Larivière's formal tone, Toupin would have been struck by the emotion and psychological insight in the last part of the letter: "My flock are almost all old prisoners (i.e. soon four years). The *duratio dura* (!) [hard times] of their captivity, the longer it is, becomes all that much harder on the nervous system. It's not an additive factor but, rather, is multiplied by the length. It's time for it to end, otherwise, neuroses will multiply." Larivière was unable, of course, to tell his friend in Ottawa that these anguished words stemmed not from an outbreak of barbed-wire psychosis but from the terrifying experience on the Easter Sunday that had just passed.

Despite what he wrote, Larivière did not conduct three Easter masses, presumably dissembling because the censors knew he had previously written of such plans. As he and his guard were making their way through the picturesque streets of the city to the work commando site ten miles from Posen, where Larivière was to say the third mass, the steady drone of aircraft engines triggered the wail of air-raid sirens. When Larivière turned to join the throng heading for an air-raid shelter, his guard pulled his gun to stop the priest. [Larivière later learned that the guard had lost his family when a bomb hit a shelter and that he had spent four days living in rubble.] The guard led the priest to the Posen-East train station, a mile away. A second wave of American bombers heading for the Telefunken and Focke-Wulf factories, near the city's beautiful medieval core, passed overhead, their bomb bay doors open.[181] The two men scarcely had time to take shelter at the foot of one of the station's concrete walls before the roar of the blast wave washed over them and the earth began trembling. When they looked up, they saw grey plumes of smoke and pulverized stone and brick rise up into the sky above the town square.

15 APRIL 1944, STALAG LUFT III, SAGAN, POLAND

Tommy Thompson Wonders, "Did One of These Men Die in My Place?"

The sullen mood that had fallen over Stalag Luft III after the Kriegies learned that 41 men had been executed dissipated slightly around midday on the 15th when some of the captured escapers returned to the compound. For Father Goudreau, who reckoned time by both the Julian and ecclesiastical calendars, their return seemed the fulfillment of the previous day's offertory prayer that recalled the Israelites' deliverance from bondage in Egypt.

Whatever joy the POWs felt drained away a short time before dusk when a Kriegie stopped to read a notice pinned to the bulletin board. Too many men gathered round after he called out that it was a list of names for them all to see it, so he read it out. The names of Canadians George McGill, Pat Langford, Hank Birkland and George Wiley were among them. Dead too was Roger Bushell. "That's not forty-one—it's forty-seven!" called a man who counted what amounted to a dirge.[182]

More than a month later, while the Kriegies were building a memorial for the murdered men, which still stands in the German military cemetery, another paper was posted in the compound bearing another three names of men executed by the Gestapo. According to Tommy Thompson's grandson, Jesse Beauchamp, for the rest of his life, Thompson was haunted by the fact that to execute 50 men, another man died in his stead.

LATE APRIL 1944, THE *ARBEITSKOMMANDO* AT EIKHAMMER, NEAR OPPELN, POLAND

Andrew Carswell and Mac Escape

Andrew Carswell was at it again under his old identity as Private Dennis Reeves; as his new partner, Mac, was Private Joe Parsons.

Once they had escaped from the *Arbeitskommando* at Eikhammer, each "became" a Czech electrician, with papers authorizing them to report to the work bureau in the port city of Stettin, from where they hoped to board a freighter bound for Sweden. The German guard at the farmhouse near Eikhammer where they were billeted accepted their papers. By contrast, the British corporal who served as the interpreter at the *Arbeitskommando* and to whom Carson introduced himself as a veteran of Dunkirk was less accepting. "Captured at Dunkirk, my fucking arse! . . . You're a fucking Yank, me lad. What are ye doing in that British uniform?"[183]

Catching the Irish lilt in the officer's voice, Carson responded in kind. "Well, actually, I'm not a 'fucking Yank,' if you must know, I'm a 'fucking Canydian,' and we're both swapovers from the RAF. We're hoping that you'll help us escape." As they had been a year earlier, these last words were met with stony silence, which prompted Carswell to remind the British soldiers that it was their duty to escape. Like the Kriegies at the brewery and graphite mine, these men had every reason not to rock the boat; their wood-cutting quota was set so low that each day's work was finished before lunch. Carswell's argument, backed up by Mac's (and his British accent), won the day, though the British corporal made it clear that their escape would have to be managed so that the Germans would not take it out on the men who remained in the *Arbeitskommando*.

29 APRIL 1944, 4:33 A.M., OFF THE COAST OF FRANCE

HMCS *ATHABASKAN* IS SUNK

As did the men behind the guns on a thousand other ships and boats, those aboard HMCS *Athabaskan* and HMCS *Haida* called it "fucking around off the coast of France." They were referring to part of the preparation for the long-awaited assault on *Festung Europa*. Just after 3 a.m. on 29 April, the two Tribal-class destroyers were ordered to leave the motor patrol boats laying mines that they had been keeping watch on, in order to intercept two German destroyers. At 3:49 a.m., *Athabaskan*'s radar picked up the two German ships and a moment later *Haida*'s gunners opened fire, while *Athabaskan*'s forward gun fired star shell that dissolved the dark night under a garish light of burning phosphorous, revealing the German ships. "Enemy Shipping Ahead. Stand By," called out one of *Athabaskan*'s officers. As Captain John Stubbs's gunners awaited the order to fire, the helmsmen aboard both ships steered toward *T24* and *T27*, a manoeuvre designed to put them between the German torpedoes they assumed were racing toward them at some 20 knots.

Athabaskan's leading writer, Stuart Kettles, recalled the moment the torpedo exploded as a kaleidoscope of a muffled roar, a dull red flash and then the dropping away of the 377-foot-long ship from beneath his feet, an after-effect of the blast wave that lifted the 2,500-ton ship partway out of the water. The blast destroyed *Athabaskan*'s aft port quarter, killing almost every man there and causing heavy bunker oil to flow into the sea. As *Haida*, still firing on one of the destroyers, made smoke to cover her stricken sister and Able Seaman Harry Liznick reached the Oerlikon guns amidships, Kettles heard Stubbs call out, "Stand by to abandon ship. BUT DON'T ABANDON YET!" Liznick must not have heard Stubbs's order, for when the aft fuel bunkers exploded a few minutes later, he was still at the gun.

The blast blew Liznick against a bulkhead, stunning him, and sent sheets of flame more than 40 feet high. "Boiling hot oil, red-hot pieces of [metal turned into] shrapnel, flying timbers and anything that had been torn lose by the explosion filled the air," recalled Kettles, who had crouched on the open deck and covered the back of his neck with his arm. As shells in the magazine began exploding, Harry Hurwitz, Liznick, Kettles and more than 120 other ratings and officers shed their steel helmets and joined the "Paratroop Battalion." The light from their burning ship showed clearly the oil-covered water and, worse, the absence of even one of *Athabaskan*'s lifeboats or Carley floats, all of which had been destroyed by the explosions.

29 APRIL 1944, ON A GERMAN DESTROYER

STUART KETTLES SURVIVES *ATHABASKAN*'S SINKING OFF THE COAST OF FRANCE

For a moment, Stuart Kettles thought Able Seaman Lester McKeeman, who was wiping heavy bunker oil from Kettles's mouth, nose and ears, was joking when he said, "On a German destroyer. They picked us up about nine o'clock this morning." Soon, however, McKeeman had rubbed enough oil from Kettles's eyes so that he could see the German eagle on the uniforms of ratings with Sten guns and rifles at the ready.

Kettles couldn't remember how he ended up aboard a German destroyer. He recalled jumping, the drop to the sea and, after bobbing back to the surface, "wiping the oil out of my eyes, and spitting the English Channel back where it belonged." He remembered the slow rollers that threw George Parson onto his face and his own attempts to wrap his legs around Parson so that he could hold him in place long enough to turn on Parson's life jacket's light. He also remembered the transformation of a "ghost like form" into *Haida*, his swim toward her, the sailor yelling to swim toward her fo'c'sle, which didn't register for a few vital moments. By the time Kettles began swimming toward *Haida*'s bow, the false dawn of nautical twilight made it too dangerous for the ship to remain stationary to pick up survivors. To signal to the men in the water that he was about to leave, Captain Harry De Wolf ordered his engine room to briefly engage the ship's screws in reverse. The wash generated by the ten-foot, six-inch screws pushed Kettles a half mile away.

In the minutes that followed, despite there being 84 other men in the same waters, Kettles found himself alone. Soon his legs and arms grew numb in the cold water near where Admiral Nelson destroyed Napoleon's fleet at the Battle of Trafalgar. The slow-rolling waves of the ebb tide were even more dangerous, for they rocked Kettles like a baby in a cradle. "It wasn't long before this motion made me very sleepy," he recalled, and with no one to speak to, Kettles knew he could not stay awake much longer. He likely saved his life by pulling up the headrest of his life jacket just before losing consciousness.

Not far away, Harry Liznick and a number of other men who had made their way to a Carley float thrown into the water from *Haida* were taken aboard a German ship. Liznick was tormented both by the large blisters caused by splotches of burning oil that fell on his face and arms, and the memory of Lieutenant Clark, who died of exposure as they swam toward a float. Led at gunpoint into a hold, Liznick saw some of his shipmates trying to shower off the thick oil. Just when he'd given up doing so because the hot water had run out, a German sailor came into the hold and motioned for Liznick and another man to follow him back onto deck, where the German naval rating pointed to the body of Able Seaman Charles Pothier, who had just died of exposure. The naked and oily men were ordered to move the body out of the way.

A short time later, the Germans gave Liznick and each of his comrades a blanket and a cup with which to scoop out a measure of warm gruel.

EARLY MAY 1944, BREST, FRANCE

RCN Able Seaman Harry Hurwitz Drops the "Z" from His Name

Since fishing him from the sea, the Germans had been softening up Harry Hurwitz. The psych-ops had started even before they were landed in Brest, France, when the German sailors pointed to and praised the fortifications of the Atlantic Wall. Once ashore, the Germans divided the RCN men into two groups and then put them into small single-man cells in austere barracks. The monotonous food, which was never quite enough to fill their stomachs, and the foul ersatz tea were calibrated to weaken the Canadians' resolve. The Germans' most important psychological tools, however, were the denial of cigarettes (which the men got around by rolling mattress straw in old paper and smoking it) and the Sten gun–enforced ban on speaking to each other.

"*Du bist ein* Yid?"

As the black-uniformed Gestapo officer looked down intently at him, Hurwitz fought to keep a poker face. "No, I'm not Jewish," he said, wondering if his attempt to hide his origin—by dropping the *z* from his name when he was first interrogated—had failed. The German, speaking English with only the slightest of accents, then asked where Hurwitz's parents came from. Hurwitz knew that Geneva required he give only his name, rank and service number. But the Gestapo officer's question prompted the 21-year-old, who knew that before the war his parents had lost contact with family in Germany, to try to hide his Jewishness. "My mother's family is from Lithuania, but both she and my father were born in London."

The Gestapo officer leaned over and with a thin, unnerving smile repeated, "*Du bist ein* Yid!" Hurwitz tried again to argue but was waved off with "You're Jewish and from Montreal."

Seeing no way out and knowing that his life now depended on an officer in one of the most Nazified services of the Third Reich honouring Germany's signature on the Geneva Convention, Hurwitz asked, "How do you know?"

The officer smiled and said, "Before the war, I worked at the General Electric plant on 1st Avenue and LaSalle Street in Saint-Henri in Montreal [a Jewish neighbourhood], and I used to see you walk past the plant on your way to and from school." As the officer spoke, Hurwitz's hands grew clammy and his stomach tightened in panic. Would the thin metal of the identity disks around his neck protect him from Germany's rage against the Jews, he wondered. Choosing to ignore the Reich's regulation, which violated Geneva, that Jewish prisoners of war were to be segregated from other POWs, the Gestapo officer said, "Your secret is safe with me."[184]

4 MAY 1944, OTTAWA

THE DIRECTOR OF MILITARY INTELLIGENCE'S REPORT ON POWS

Canadian officials in Ottawa knew that the Germans were not complying with Geneva's requirement to provide the same rations to POWs as to garrisoned troops. Citing the amount of food contained in the Red Cross parcels, at Oflag VII-B, in Eichstätt, Bavaria, the Kommandant cut the POWs' rations by 30 per cent. A month later, on the same page as the banner headlines announcing the invasion of Normandy, the *Globe and Mail* reported the docking of the SS *Gripsholm*, carrying several hundred repatriated wounded and sick POWs, 36 of whom were Canadian and from whom Ottawa learned how POWs supplemented their meagre rations. A guard in the guard tower would lower a basket with a chicken, eggs and bread, and haul it back up with cigarettes, cocoa and a couple of chocolate bars. Information also came from letters, including one by MacDonald written from a POW camp in Heydekrug, Lithuania; in it he wrote: "The boys were catching sparrows and eating them. They say sparrow stew tastes very good."

Nevertheless, Ottawa knew, morale remained high. So did the Canadians' allegiance to their Allied comrades. When camp officials at both Stalag Luft III and Oflag VII-B, responding to reports by repatriated Germans of how well they had been treated in Canada, offered the Canadian officers special preferences, such as an extra letter home a month or more parole walks, the "Canadian Club" refused them unless they were extended to all British officers.

5 MAY 1944, STALAG LUFT VI, HEYDEKRUG, LITHUANIA

Ian MacDonald's Letter Home

The drought was almost over; in two days, Ian MacDonald would receive two letters from his parents. Some weeks earlier, frantic over the possibility that, since he had not heard from them, they had not received any of his letters or postcards, MacDonald wrote a short note on a Red Cross form reserved for POWs who had not received mail for three months.

He also wrote a regular aerogram, the bulk of which explains the instructions he had given the Air Ministry vis-à-vis his pay and insurance. In the 15 months since he last heard from them, MacDonald had grown more concerned about his family's finances and instructed the Air Ministry to send his parents the maximum amount possible. Sensitive to the implication that his proud father was unable to provide for his wife and three children still at home, MacDonald wrote, "Use whatever you need regardless of how much it is."

Knowing that the German censors would not allow him to explain why he was now in a POW camp in Lithuania, MacDonald did not bother trying to find a way to slip past the censors the fact that he had been moved from Dulag Luft because bombing raids had devastated the area.

7 MAY 1944, FILIŞIA, SOUTHWEST ROMANIA

RCAF Warrant Officer Norman Reid Touches the Lips of a Dead Friend

The pre-flight ritual prior to his 41st, and what was to be his final, mission over Occupied Europe did not include urinating on their Wellington bomber's tail wheel. "As romantic as this image is," says Norman Reid, who in 1944 was an RCAF navigator, "our engineering officer made it damned clear that peeing on the wheels was dumb because the uric acid ate into the wheels' bearings' housing and the synthetic rubber tires, thus increasing the chances of an accident on takeoff or landing." Preparation at the aerodrome in Foggia, Italy, included careful study of the location of the 300-foot-long, double-span steel bridge over the Jiu River near Filişia, and the optimal altitude for dropping the 4,000-pound armoured "cookie bomb." As well, since they were going to be flying close to Yugoslavia, which the Germans did not fully control and thus was a better place to bail out, if necessary, than over Occupied Romania, Reid's crew was briefed on the complicated politics of the kingdom established after the First World War; although they did not know it, just weeks earlier, Churchill had shifted his support from the monarchist general, Draža Mihailovic, to the Communist leader of the partisans, Tito.

"We were the only plane on this mission, and the hope was that the Germans might take us for a photographic mission and not send up any interceptors," recalls Reid, who when the bridge did not come into view as expected did some quick calculations, which revealed that a wind shift had pushed them off course and they would have to circle back some 50 miles to the town of Turnu Severin (present-day Drobeta-Turnu Severin), Reid's navigation point, and then fly east again. After locating the bridge, Tom Bradshaw pitched his plane toward it, though they were not yet closing in for the kill. Destroying a bridge cannot be done by flying over it perpendicularly because the bridge's span would flash too quickly under the bomb sight. Instead, a plane must track along the bridge. "To ensure this, our captain steered a dummy run over the bridge at 1,500 feet," explains Reid. "We'd been told that the bridge was undefended; still, even though I'd been on 40 other missions and shot at many times, and shot down once, in the minutes between the dive, the run and when we began to climb again, I had to remember to take a breath."

After circling around, the plane flew between 100 and 150 feet above the train tracks leading to the bridge. Seconds from it, a flak train's 20-mm rapid-fire guns opened up. "Even above the noise of the four Bristol Hercules engines," recalls Reid, "I could hear the explosions of the shells that formed flashes in the darkness around us. Almost at the same time, the plane began to shake, and I heard our bomb aimer, Ibar 'Mac' McKenna, yell through my headset in a pained voice that said he'd been hit and that he'd released the bomb. Relieved of 4,000 pounds, the plane lurched up about 100 feet and out of the line of fire." The plume of fuel streaming from its starboard tank turned to fire that trailed hundreds of feet behind the plane. The two-ton armour-piercing bomb severely damaged the bridge, which trains had used in carrying important petrochemical products to Germany.

The 20-mm shells badly damaged the plane's engines. A starboard one was losing power, while a port engine, its constant-speed unit damaged, raced, causing the plane to veer to starboard. "We didn't have a co-pilot on this trip," recounts Reid. "So, as Bradshaw struggled to control the plane, I jumped into the co-pilot's seat; it took both of our strength to right the rudder and ailerons." Reid's precise words, reflecting a lifetime as an engineer, hardly convey the scene. As they fought to control the plane, he was breathing through a mask, the plane that was elegant in flight was shuddering and the steady throb of its engines had been replaced by the roar of the out-of-control port engine.

A few moments later, the wireless operator made his way back into the cockpit. "Mac's had it," he said. Reid, who had flown with Mac more than 30 times, told Bradshaw that he had to check for himself and unbuckled his belt while the pilot continued to battle for control of the stricken plane. As the burning aircraft slipped over the Yugoslav border, "I managed to snake my hand under Mac's flying tunic, which was covered by his Mae West and parachute harness, and felt no signs of his heart beating or breathing," says Reid. "Then I ripped off his mask and put my lips to his in the hopes of detecting any sign of breathing. I did not and went back to the cockpit and told Bradshaw that, indeed, Mac was dead."

SPRING 1944, MILAG UND MARLAG NORD, NEAR BREMEN, GERMANY

An Arrogant German Bends His Knee

Alerted that the Germans were going to search his chapel for a radio, Father Pâquet was already there when a guard named Shöfe, backed by five other guards with bayonet-tipped rifles, arrived. After Shöfe said that he was sure Pâquet would not object to the search, the priest appealed to Shöfe's sense of honour, insisting that the search be conducted with dignity.

When Shöfe approached the table on which bread and wine became the body and blood of Christ, Pâquet politely asked the German to go no further. With a sneer, Shöfe said, "I trust you, Father, but wouldn't that sacred table be a perfect place in which to hide a radio?" After the "arrogant Nazi" dismissed Pâquet's plea for the sanctity of the altar, the priest played his last card.[185]

"Okay. But, I have to open the tabernacle myself and since you are here in a Catholic church, you have to conform to our ways: you will have to be on your knees before the Blessed Sacrament." Then, as the Germans stood watching, the Oblate lit two candles, put on his surplice, opened the tabernacle and genuflected, leaving enough room for Shöfe to shine his flashlight in for a moment. Then, to Pâquet's surprise, the fanatical Gestapo officer was on his knees before the altar.

Though Pâquet was not hiding a radio (it was in Charles Fisher's sick bay), the Kommandant was right to suspect that, despite their holy orders, the Oblates were not above being involved with smuggling and hiding radios. As noted earlier, Father Goudreau hid a radio in his room, and Father Charbonneau helped a British Kriegie smuggle radio tubes into camp in a cast after he feigned a broken leg on a work commando site.

8 MAY 1944, NEAR ŽAGUBICA, EASTERN SERBIA, YUGOSLAVIA

Reid Wonders, "How the Hell Did Mrs. Reid's Boy Get into This Mess?"

They were not in uniform, but the bandoliers of ammunition slung over their shoulders, the automatic weapons they carried and the lack of coal shovel helmets told Reid they were Resistance fighters. Still, the 20-year-old from Edmonton watched and waited. He had been alone since parachuting out of his burning Wellington bomber—and experiencing, for a few seconds, the inertia-generated sensation of not so much falling as moving forward in tandem with the aircraft, surrounded by the din of the plane's engines. Given that his landing was so hard it knocked the wind out him, it was a good thing that he had pulled the rip cord after counting to five, rather than waiting until ten.

"How the hell did Mrs. Reid's boy get into this mess?" he thought as he unclipped his parachute so he could bury it. "It's difficult to compress silk, and the hole I'd dug wasn't deep enough. So I threw dirt and leaves and twigs on it," recounts Reid. He then took stock of what was in his escape kit. A six-inch square of chocolate, some malted milk tablets, a tablet to purify water, two Benzedrine tablets, a hacksaw and 48 American dollars would not go far.

When the four men he took to be Chetniks (Yugoslav partisans) neared his hiding place, he stood up and, despite the pain of a rapidly swelling sprained right ankle, jumped up and down with his hands raised. "They noticed me and soon I was looking down the wrong end of their automatic rifles," says Reid, who hoped that "they did not shoot first and ask questions later." Asking and answering questions, however, was all but impossible, since the men did not speak English and Reid did not speak Serbian. Worse, although he'd managed to make his story of being shot down understood, he knew that they were skeptical, since the Germans attempted to infiltrate underground Resistance units; skeptical, that is, until he took them to see his ill-buried parachute.

The Chetniks then led him to a peasant's hut. A few hours later, another peasant brought them honey, feta-like cheese and unleavened corn bread. When, upon deciding it was time to move on, they saw that Reid's ankle was too swollen for him to walk, they put him in a cart filled with maize and being pulled by two oxen directed by an elderly Serbian woman dressed in warm peasant clothing, a scarf wound round her head; to hide and keep him warm in the high altitude, the Chetniks covered him with the maize stalks. Reid spent his first full night in Yugoslavia in a hut "made of a pile of stones that were held together with some kind of mortar on top of which was a roof, with a hole in the middle for smoke, made of woven twigs."

MID-MAY 1944, BREST, FRANCE

LIZNICK KNOWS MORE ABOUT GERMANY THAN HIS INQUISITOR COULD GUESS

During his interrogation, the Germans provided some unintended entertainment. The 70-year-old interrogator feigned believing that "AB" (standing for "able seaman," Liznick's rank) signified "AA" (anti-aircraft gunner) and that Liznick had fired on the Germans who had abandoned the torpedo boat that HMCS *Haida* shot up. After Liznick set him straight, the interrogator changed tack and said that he thought the Allies would win the war. He seized on Liznick's quick agreement to ask, "Why, did you see something?" Liznick was not, of course, going to say anything about the buildup of Allied forces he'd seen in England, so he took shelter in the anodyne comment: "No, I just feel it. We know it in our hearts."[186]

The 19-year-old Kriegie may have been raised in the postage stamp–sized village of Iroquois Falls, Ontario, but he knew more about German history than his interrogator guessed. Liznick's parents had lived through the German occupation of the Ukraine during the First World War and had watched Hitler's rise to power with dismay. Liznick had to stifle a laugh when the Gestapo officer told him the Jews caused the war because they were trying to corner German women.

LATE MAY 1944, PEISKRETSCHAM, SILESIA, POLAND

Jack Poolton Becomes a Saboteur

The argument the POWs raised against unloading tanks damaged on the Russian Front from a train was as much about what the Geneva Convention meant by "war work" as it was about giving a short and thin Kriegie time to crawl into a tank and steal a headset that was later used as part of a radio set. Equally frustrating for the guards was the day Jack Poolton broke three shovels—and, since every member of the work party admitted to being the miscreant, the guards had to forgo punishing anyone, lest the bomb-damaged rails remain unrepaired.

Emboldened, Poolton and a British soldier risked death a few days later when they removed the rubber seals between air-brake hoses, which rendered the train's brakes useless. Other times they removed the packing that lubricated the axles of the freight cars——some loaded with Hungarian Jews being transported to Auschwitz—and replaced them with crushed stone.[187]

29 MAY 1944, MILAG UND MARLAG NORD, NEAR BREMEN, GERMANY

Father Pâquet's Pentecost Is Interrupted by a Bombing

While *les religieux* were proud of Stella Maris, the small wooden chapel at Milag und Marlag Nord, it took only a glance upward to see the rough wooden beams and thin ceiling of a German POW barracks. The floor on which they knelt, too, told the truth of where they were, for it was not marble but unvarnished wood, recalling the room in which the Pentecost occurred 50 days after the Resurrection more than it did the marble or closely fitted and highly polished wood of the churches that generations of the faithful had built in Quebec. From a distance, the chalice on the left side of the altar, itself a rough-hewn table covered with a white tablecloth, was similar to the simple silver ones used in churches like those in Saint-Ludger de Beauce, the village where Father Gérard Boulanger had grown up, or Missisquoi, Quebec, where Father Bernard Desnoyers had first learned the catechism. Up close, the chalice's lustre was less intense and the hammer marks became visible, as did the blobs of solder that cemented the reshaped Klim can to the stem and the stem to the stand.

In the middle of the Pentecost service, Luke's 2,000-year-old words never seemed more appropriate. For just as Father Pâquet finished reading "And suddenly from the heaven there came a sound like the rush of a violent wind, and it filled the entire house where they were sitting," hundreds of anti-aircraft guns opened up on the hundreds of American bombers flying near the camp. The explosions drowned out Pâquet as he started to read from the Acts of the Apostles: "Divided tongues, as of fire, appeared, among them, and a tongue rested on each of them. . . . [as they] began to speak in other languages" (2:2–4).

The guns being situated so close to Milag Nord—the reverberations of the exploding propellant and the shells above shaking the barracks so severely that Pâquet broke out into a sweat—was in violation of the Geneva Convention. Fear, and faith in what lay beyond the Pentecost ceremony, ensured that no matter how frightening the explosions, no one left the chapel.

Chapter Eleven

June–July 1944

Murder in the murderer is no such ruinous thought as poets and romancers will have it; it does not unsettle him, or fright him from his ordinary notice of trifles.

—Ralph Waldo Emerson

EARLY JUNE 1944, ON A TRAIN TO STETTIN, GERMANY

Andrew Carswell Tries to Ignore Mac's Message

The tapping on his boot wasn't random, nor did it transmit the kind of intelligence officers had in mind when they told downed airmen to use Morse code to communicate with each other when in public. Andrew Carswell didn't need Mac's message, "Did you ever see such a gorgeous ass?" or the sequences of taps to tell him that the buxom girl whose body swayed with the movement of the train, had lovely -. .- . . .. Because of the crowding of their train compartment, her boot-clad legs straddled his as she held onto an overhead strap, which put her "tits" all but in Carswell's face.[188]

Fearing that if they made eye contact the beauty would read his mind, Carswell resolutely kept from doing so, concentrating instead on their escape, the planning for which had begun weeks earlier. First, they had to reverse the 76 bolts on the door that locked them into the cellblock, a feat accomplished over a number of nights while the guard was distracted by a friendly chat or hot cocoa, a rare commodity in Germany at that point in the war. The songs the other Kriegies belted out to cover the sound of removing the door the night Carswell and Mac escaped were so loud that the guard threatened that if they didn't shut up, he'd shoot someone. The two hours it took "Paddy" to file down the duplicate key until it opened the stubborn second door passed to the tattoo of the guard's snoring, which also hid the clamber of Mac and Carswell climbing the fence.

At four o'clock in the morning, their "Ile 'eetlah" fooled a man on the bicycle. Mac's weak German garnered them the two tickets for Breslau and the ticket agent's contemptuous look. To add to their posed status as uncouth foreign workers, they puffed away on cigarette butts and sat while old ladies stood. At Breslau, they nearly gave themselves away by heading for the exit marked "*Soldaten.*" On Track 9 in Frankfurt, they could hear their heartbeats as they waited amid German soldiers.

In Küstrin, after a trainman upbraided them for giving him the wrong fare, they decided it tempted fate to wait six hours in the station for the 4:30 a.m. train. The remains of the haystack just outside town that they'd burrowed into still clung to them, making them look even more like tramps, when they boarded the train for Stettin a few stops before the girl who fired the Kriegies' imagination climbed aboard.

2 JUNE 1944, STALAG LUFT VI, HEYDEKRUG, LITHUANIA

Ian MacDonald Knows More than He Can Ask

The vagaries of the POW postal system that Ian MacDonald catalogued—his parents' first letter of 12 January arriving almost a month after their third and fourth, and his 12 January letter not being postmarked by the military authorities for almost two weeks—bewildered even as it entertained his family. They were less happy to read that he had taken up the "vice" of smoking. "The Red Cross supplied us with 50 cigarettes a week. And one of my friends suggested I start smoking them as a way to pass the time. They sure helped do so," recalls MacDonald.

MacDonald knew his parents would have to search through his old letters to find the addresses of Mrs. Parkinson in Toronto and

John Courtney's family in Liverpool, and that having lived for so long without word of Ian's fate, the MacDonalds would feel for the Courtneys. "We enquired again sometime in February, I believe, about John Courtney's fate, but the Germans have no record of him at all," MacDonald wrote. He also knew that they'd long ponder his next sentence: "There's a lot of questions I'd like to ask but just can't."

In fact, MacDonald knew a great deal. At Dulag Luft, he had asked a superior officer to make an official inquiry. When the German replied that they had no record of him, MacDonald wasn't completely surprised. "I knew from the Resistance that Courtney left the plane alive," he says. "But he landed in a canal, became tangled in his parachute and drowned. What I didn't know is what became of his body. Together with the German's answer, I surmised that the Resistance secretly buried it." MacDonald kept his counsel, for to ask specifically about Courtney's body risked endangering the people who had helped him.

5 JUNE 1944, BLECHHAMMER, POLAND

Father Desnoyers Worries about the Strain of Long-Term Captivity

It wasn't every day that an Oblate priest admitted to being perplexed by a statement from the bishops. Father Desnoyers's confusion was not, however, the first sign of a crisis in faith. Rather, Father Ferragne realized as he continued reading Desnoyers's letter written in April, the POW's confusion stemmed from the fact that he did not know that in February the Quebec bishops had called for special prayers for *les religieux*.

The rest of the letter, by contrast, was alarming, made even more so by the onrush of events that began a few hours after Desnoyers deposited the letter in the camp's mailbox. Since 6

June, Canadians had been caught up in the drama, first of D-Day, when 160,000 Allied troops stormed ashore at five Normandy beaches, including almost 21,500 Canadians at Juno Beach; the bloody fight for Caen, which cost almost 1,200 casualties; the daring escape of the Germans at the Falaise Pocket; the breakout from Normandy by US General Omar Bradley's Fifth Army; and the race toward Paris. What, if anything, the imprisoned priest knew of these events and how this knowledge affected the psychological picture Desnoyers sketched, Ferragne could not know. Instead, though the reality in the camp 5,000 miles away may have completely changed, words on the flimsy paper before him created—as all letters do—what might be thought of as the "epistolary present tense" (wherein the past is present for the reader)—and that present was deeply troubling.

Desnoyers's observation that captivity "produces a curious psychological effect among most of us. In the absence of other elements, accidental details of life [in the camps] are often blown out of proportion" signalled that the camp's psychology had moved beyond the strains that Ferragne might guess at. That on particularly rainy days they had to treat certain Kriegies with "*extrême délicatesse*" spoke for itself.

6 JUNE 1944, NORMANDY

D-Day

By nightfall, several hundred Canadians lay dead on Juno Beach, but the 3rd Canadian Infantry Division had made a lodgement in France. Sergeant C.B. Morris of the North Nova Scotia Highlanders and his men were in a field about three miles from Saint-Aubin-sur-Mer. True, the Canadians had not reached their first day's objective, Caen (and wouldn't for weeks), but neither had the British at Gold or Sword Beaches, or the Americans at Utah and Omaha.

Indeed, the forward elements of the Canadian force were deeper into France than those of any other division that attacked Hitler's vaunted Western Wall that famous day.

None of the POWs knew these details, of course. But across the length and breadth of Hitler's empire, hundreds of thousands of POWs knew that the long-awaited Second Front had finally been opened. At Heydekrug, in Lithuania, Andrew Cox (who had arrived there a few months earlier) and MacDonald learned about it when it was broadcast over the camp's loudspeaker: "There has been an attempted landing on the Cherbourg Peninsula. And it has been repulsed." MacDonald, who had been bashing the circuit recalls laughing at the idea that the Germans would throw the Allies back into the sea. Near Stargard, Germany, Jacques Nadeau, who, as his landing craft approached Dieppe almost two years earlier had seen two dozen of his Fusiliers Mont-Royal comrades blown apart when a mortar bomb exploded in their landing craft, heard about the landing in Normandy from a radio that belonged to German civilians working on the farm.

In Yugoslavia, where he was one of many supplying prison labour, Norman Reid heard about the invasion while listening to the Chetniks' radio. Though they didn't speak English like MI9 and SOE agents scattered throughout Europe, the Chetniks tuned to the BBC to hear coded messages. Reid's joy at learning of the invasion competed with his worry about his parents; he knew that they would have received word that his plane was missing and wouldn't be able to stop worrying that he had died before this, his 21st birthday.

From the quantity and type of stores being landed with each Bonaparte and the increased bombing of rail yards, Lucien Dumais had guessed the invasion was near. Yet excitement shot through him when, at 11 a.m., he heard the radio announcer state: "Early this morning the Allies landed in Normandy."[189] Stuart Kettles and the other survivors of HMCS *Athabaskan* were still in solitary confinement and didn't learn of the invasion for 11 days.

Carswell and Mac did not hear about the invasion until they were returned to Stalag VIII-B almost a month later. After arriving in Stettin on D-Day, they survived Carswell's dropping of his POW identity disk right in front of two German guards—who missed the glint of metal because they were frogmarching two British POWs. Mac and Carswell were less lucky a few hours later when a local policeman enforced the laws against foreign workers being away from work during work hours. Their admission at the police station that they were "English prisoners of war" caused one officer to pull his gun and another to call the Gestapo.

The two SS men who burst into the room looked and acted as if sent from central casting, brandishing Lugers, with one yelling, "Move it! Fast, you English pig-dogs!" as they pushed Mac and Carswell down the hall into a black Mercedes.[190] The men in the building, which, to Carswell, was reminiscent of the buildings on Toronto's University Avenue, sported Schmeisser machine pistols. Carswell's offer of a Sweet Caporal cigarette to the Charlie Chaplin lookalike brought another round of "*Schweinehund Engländer*," which didn't violate Geneva, and a blow to the side of his head, knocking him down, which did. Both Carswell and Mac had given the police their POW identity disks. After an interrogation, during which the interpreter's poor English was exceeded only by their poor German, the two were marched down a hallway. When they didn't move fast enough, each was kicked so hard he landed face first on the floor.

Worse was to follow: being left to shiver while naked and being crammed with 18 other men into a 10-by-20-foot cell lit by one dim bulb. "The idea of dying scared the hell out of me," recalled Carswell, "but what really frightened me was the idea of dying under someone else's name. If I died, I wanted at least my parents, friends, and relatives to know what had happened to me."

6 JUNE 1944, 10:30 A.M. TO DUSK, NORMANDY

Canadian Sergeant C.B. Morris Sees the Hitlerjugend Murder Other Canadians

"Live fire" exercises barely approximate battle. Still, the pre-invasion training gave Morris and his men some idea of what they'd face when they waded through the Normandy surf, as they did at 10:30 a.m. on 6 June under the protective fire of three Royal Navy cruisers and fighter bombers rocketing and strafing German positions. However much Private Lorne Browne and his comrades in the North Nova's 7 Platoon cursed the planners of training exercises, those exercises did teach them how to avoid shrapnel and the deadly splintered remains of trees blown apart, like those in the orchard they'd just run into on the outskirts of the village of Authie. Those exercises also taught them to use their Browning automatics, which took a toll on Oberstleutnant Karl-Heinz Milius's 3rd Battalion, which was part of the 25th SS-Panzergrenadier Regiment Hitlerjugend. No training regimen could have ensured that all of the men who, near 2 p.m., ran back through the narrow streets of Authie would zig, zag or hit the dirt in time to avoid the vectors of death created by German guns in a village the North Novas thought they'd cleared a few hours earlier. Yet like Captain Frederick Fraser and the tank officer whom Morris saw being blown up while trying to get their tank out of the orchard, his comrades who died on Authie's dusty streets died soldiers' deaths.

Even before seeing the stylized lightning bolts of the SS on their shoulders—or that some of soldiers to whom he and his comrades were surrendering were too young to shave—Morris realized that these Germans were nothing like regular soldiers, whom he expected to conduct themselves like battlefield bookkeepers, interested only in names, ranks and service numbers. Instead, the Hitlerjugend "behaved like a crazy bunch of fiends," wounding several Canadians in the legs with gratuitous automatic weapons' fire. In shock from being hit in the face and arm, another North Nova,

Corporal W.L. MacKay, who had already seen a victory-drunk teen shove Browne to the ground, step on his head and repeatedly bayonet him, witnessed killing after killing—none of which could be attributed to the blood-dimmed tide of battle.[191]

In an alley off Authie's main street, MacKay saw Privates John Murray, Anthony Julian, James Webster and five other Canadian POWs sitting on the street being ordered to take off their steel helmets, and watched helplessly as an SS man shot each in the head. Then, in an act that hearkened back to the barbarity Sophocles decried in *Antigone* more than two millennia earlier, the killers dragged two of the bodies into the middle of the street, where they revelled in the sight of a tank running over them. What remained of them "could be collected in a shovel," recalled Authie resident Constance Raymond Guilbert, who a few minutes earlier had seen another SS trooper use his rifle butt to bash in Private William Nichol's skull as he tried to surrender.[192] Other SS soldiers took a Canadian corpse, propped it against a wall, placed an old hat on its shattered head and shoved a cigarette into its mouth.

Private John Metcalfe, another North Nova, paid for being unable to pull the small metal box containing his emergency chocolate out of his tunic fast enough with four bullets in his abdomen, minutes of agony and then three shots to his head. If Lance Corporal Joseph Arsenault thought that answering an SS commander's question in his Summerside, PEI, French might soften the German's demeanour, he was mistaken; the SS officer killed Arsenault with one pistol shot to his neck. Private Jeffrey Hargreaves was murdered because with a wounded leg he had trouble keeping up with the POWs being marched from the village of Buron, while a blast from a machine pistol killed one POW and mortally wounded another some distance up the column.

The six Canadians an SS officer shoved into Madame Godet's house knew that its thin roof and stone walls wouldn't provide much protection if one of the heavy shells British warships were firing at the defences of nearby Caen fell short, but at least it would protect them from shrapnel, like that which wounded another North Nova's leg so badly he fell out of the line of march. Nothing could protect them from the SS officer who shot each of King George's Canadian soldiers in the head. Not far away, the SS man who pushed Louis Alaperrin, a brave Normandian, away from the wounded North Nova was no less imbued with his Führer's cause; he fired two shots that destroyed the Canadian's head. About the same time, an SS NCO in nearby Authie ignored the Red Cross brassard on the arm of a Canadian who was tending to still another North Nova and shot the medic dead. The SS reinforcements rushing to the front barely broke step when they met up with the column of Canadian POWs being marched toward Caen but slowed down long enough to shoot nine men in cold blood.

As they neared the outskirts of Caen toward dusk, the injured Private J. MacDonald, in a horse cart being pulled by other exhausted and battle-shocked men, was at the end of the line of men who had been told, "For you, the war is over." Since the road was wide, at first MacDonald thought nothing of the oncoming truck. But as it neared, the driver swerved and drove into the column of defeated men, killing privates Douglas Tobin and Roderick McCrae outright and wounding two other Canadians before swerving back to the other side of the road.

This time, the Germans did not leave the dead on the road. Instead, they ordered Morris and a few other men to carry the bodies behind a schoolhouse. Oddly, given the sheer bravado of these and other killings, the guard tried to cover up the driver's crime by marking the graves with the killed soldiers' steel helmets, the way battle deaths are marked. As well, reported Lance Sergeant Stanley Dutka, "the officers in the [captured] group were forced to sign a paper saying that the men died of wounds."

The burst of gunfire that killed Lance Corporal J.H. Greenwood and wounded Lieutenant W.F. Grainger, after they and Captain Walter Brown of the Sherbrooke Fusiliers raised their hands in surrender when their Jeep was spotted by a German patrol, left Brown untouched. The young SS trooper who thrust his bayonet into Brown's body could not have missed seeing the Anglican padre's clerical collar.

7 JUNE 1944, D-DAY +1 NIGHT, NORMANDY

Murders in the Abbey

During the day, the German commander on the scene in the Caen sector watched as his troops contained the Canadians around Authie and Buron. But under the cover of darkness, enraged that he hadn't driven the Canadian "small fry" back into the sea, SS-Brigadeführer Kurt Meyer lashed out at the impudent invaders. Near 8 p.m., he ordered the bulk of the Canadian prisoners to be marched to Bretteville-sur-Odon, a village about a mile away, while a group of randomly selected POWs were marched from his headquarters at L'Abbaye d'Ardenne to an adjacent château. According to historian Howard Margolian, there, six Canadians were first slapped and then killed "by crushing blows to the head" when they refused to indicate the location of their battalion's headquarters.[193] Another five Canadians were soon executed with a single shot each to the head.

By mid-morning the next day, 8 June, when seven Canadians were brought before him, Meyer's exasperation burst forth: "In the future, no more prisoners are to be taken." This became a key piece of evidence in Meyer's war crimes trial.[194] According to SS-Private Jan Jesionek, after the first man was killed by a machine pistol shot to the head, in their remaining moments alive, each man saw the pile of Canadian corpses and the spreading pool of blood. These seven deaths brought the total of Canadians executed in cold blood since the Canadians had touched down on Juno Beach to 55. Over the next 24 hours, another 25 would be murdered, some with a shot to the head, some by machine guns.

11 JUNE 1944, NORMANDY

Six Canadian Tank Troopers Are Shot Dead

As Dumais and Raymond Labrosse made their way to Chartres, where they would spend the night in a safe house keeping mum while their hostess, a talkative woman from Quebec, expounded on the glories of Canada, still more of their countrymen breathed their last breath, most having seen the faces of their murderers.

Six were tank troopers. The first to die was Lee Peston, who was shot in the back by the SS men who had taken him and two of his comrades prisoner near the hamlet of Le Mesnil-Patry. Four other tank troopers were executed by an SS soldier named Mischke in a field covered with clover. The NCO escorting four other tank troopers yelled "Run, run" before pulling the trigger on his machine pistol.[195] At least one of the stream of bullets ripped through Trooper Lawrence Sutton's head; others mortally wounded Trooper John Dumont, who groaned in agony for several minutes before dying.

While the deaths of sappers John Ionel and George Benner were recorded in the Royal Canadian Engineers' war diary and Rifleman Allan Owens's in the war diary of the Winnipeg Rifles, they died together. A few minutes after a military policeman ripped off their identity disks, a burst of machine pistol fire tore through their backs and pushed their dying bodies into a bomb crater a couple of hundred yards from the grey stone farmhouse that housed SS-Brigadeführer Wilhelm Mohnke's headquarters. As Mohnke looked on to make sure they were dead, more bullets were fired at their bleeding, broken bodies. In total, Mohnke's men were responsible for 41 murders; neither he nor any of his men were tried for their war crimes.

Just as four days earlier the Red Cross brassard didn't protect the Canadian medic tending to a wounded North Nova, the Red Cross flag flying from Dr. Shütt's first-aid station on 11 June did not protect Major J. Forbes of the Queen's Own Rifles, nor did the proximity of the first-aid station to SS-Obersturmbannführer

Bernhard Siebken's headquarters, just steps away. Sometime after nightfall, Forbes and tank troopers Arnold Bowes and Glibert Scriven were taken from the German first-aid station and killed. In total, in the ten days starting with D-Day, 156 Canadians were murdered in cold blood.

MID-JUNE 1944, 30 MILES NORTHWEST OF ŽAGUBICA, EASTERN SERBIA, YUGOSLAVIA

Norman Reid Convinces the Chetniks That the American Airmen Need a Doctor

Their uniforms told him that they were Americans, perhaps some of the very men who dangled from the parachutes Norman Reid had seen blossom beneath planes with smoking engines. Or were they from planes whose absence was marked by the holes in the ragged bomber stream making its way home? Wherever they were from, upon hearing one singing a song he couldn't understand, Reid was amazed at the speed with which the Yank in the yard they were approaching had picked up Serbo-Croatian. "It was a real treat to be able to speak English. But imagine my surprise when I was told that the song he was singing wasn't Serbian but, rather, top of the *Hit Parade*. The words I couldn't make out were, '*Mairz doats* [Mares eat oats] and does eat oats and little lambs eat ivy.'"

Not every American was in shape to sing. Four had broken legs. Reid's St. John Ambulance training could have dealt with three, but Lieutenant Estop had a compound fracture that was already showing signs of gangrene. Using hand signs, Reid explained to the Chetniks that Estop needed medical help. "At first they shrugged their shoulders and then made clear the difficulty of getting a doctor. I don't know exactly what convinced them, but something did, and soon they sent for a doctor," says Reid.

While they waited, peasants dressed in baggy woollen pants and tops, and many with goatskin hats three inches tall arrived carrying cheese, sheep's milk and unleavened bread. To Reid's delight, he saw someone light a fire, set up two forked sticks and begin cooking a freshly slaughtered lamb. "I never smelled anything so good in my life," he recalls. "When it was finished, we sat around a great wooden table and ate chunks of meat off the bone."

Sometime later, the doctor arrived; he, like Reid, spoke some French. Slivovitz—plum brandy—was all they had to help numb the men's pain, and it didn't do much. "Their screams were awful, but I simply had to hold on, stretching each man's leg, until the doctor managed to get the splints into place and then bind them with twine."

17 JUNE 1944, STALAG LUFT VI, HEYDEKRUG, LITHUANIA

MacDonald Hopes the Rumour of a Priest Coming Soon Is True

It is a measure of how the military situation had changed that on D-Day plus 11, when the Americans were still slogging through the Normandy *bocage* and the Canadians were stymied outside Caen, the censor let pass the sentence "News of the invasion has cheered us up quite a bit." But this was not, MacDonald knew, what would most interest his parents, who hardly needed to be told what effect news of the invasion would have had on their son. Nor were they overly interested in the weather, which, of course, had long passed by the time they would be reading about it. What would really matter to them, especially after his recent admission of having taken up smoking, was that he maintained his faith. They hoped that a padre had, in fact, arrived at MacDonald's camp. But they took solace in the fact that even without one, MacDonald, who had been an altar boy, continued to say a "service of Rosary and Prayers."

MID-JUNE 1944, A GESTAPO PRISON, STETTIN, GERMANY

Carswell Hears Even Worse Torture

The intense beatings had stopped. Yet whenever Mac and Carswell were marched from one part of the prison to another, if they didn't move fast enough, guards kicked them and hit them with their rifle butts. Even given their diet of one bowl of thin soup and a piece of sour black bread a day, they were made to stand throughout the day, except when they were taken out for "exercise." In the yard, an SS guard with a long leather stick ensured that the malnourished men ran around a track and performed long stretches of calisthenics. The tormentors amused themselves by making the soldiers crawl—so often that Carswell's knees were raw and bruised.

The screams of male and female prisoners being tortured were, if anything, even harder to bear.

18 JUNE 1944, STALAG XXI-D, POSEN, POLAND

Father Louis Larivière Finds That War Leads to Questions about Catholic Doctrine

Given the substance of the letter to Father Ducharme, it's likely that the German censor had an easier time with the Latin close "*Tibi in Sapientia!*" (Onwards to wisdom!) than with Father Larivière's complex theological arguments. We can be certain of two things, however; the censor did not enforce the rule that POWs were to write in English or French only and, probably because Larivière hid it in Latin, missed the Oblate's riff on the title of the collection of Churchill's speeches (that men captured after 1943 would have known), "Onwards to Victory!"

Larivière's concerns grew directly out of his wartime experience tending to huge flocks and flocks in widely separate camps. For years he had exempted himself from the rule of Eucharist

Fasting for practical reasons. Now, the priest raised in the village of Saint-Zacharie de Beauce, Quebec, went further and told his brother in Christ that the rule made sense only if transubstantiation *was* the miraculous conversion of the Host and wine into the body and blood of Christ and not symbolic, as believed by the Protestants whom Larivière had come to know well for the first time in his life.

After years of close contact with men who were so different from the devout rural Catholics he grew up with, the Oblate asked in his letter if the mass itself "could be generalized for the workers." The question, let alone the answer, placed him some distance from the Quebec Church's embrace of corporatism, which saw workers as a subservient group in society, and especially from Abbé Lionel Groulx, who called for *les Canadiens français* to return to the land where they would be insulated from industrialism, Anglo-Saxon individualism and socialism in equal measure.

Earlier in the war, Larivière's letters emphasized the uniqueness of the priesthood. Pushed by the strain of having to travel hundreds of miles to and from different camps without priests (and his recent extensive reading of European history, including, it would seem for the first time, of the Reformation), Larivière asks whether "sacerdotal power" (the ability to give communion and give absolution) should be given to deacons, the minor orders and even "the laity," who were the "faithful living in the world."[196] Such questions display an openness of mind that is inverse to the reality of his imprisonment.

MID-JUNE 1944, SERBIA, YUGOSLAVIA

Reid Meets General Draža Mihailović

Reid understood the reasoning, but the Chetniks' decision to divide the group of evaders into smaller groups so that the Germans could not recapture all at once disturbed him. He knew he'd been well-treated and that Draža Mihailović's men had done what they could for them. Still, he couldn't shake the doubt left by the RAF intelligence officers who advised seeking out Tito's forces. The safety Reid had felt when with the Americans (whose intelligence officers had told the evaders that the Chetniks would cut off their ears) vanished when he once again found himself the lone Westerner with five or so Chetniks, moving in a generally northwest direction.

"I knew showing that I was nervous would only arouse their suspicions, so I tried to remain indifferent," remembers Reid. "I was able to compare the silk map from my escape kit with the terrain I was moving through and knew generally where I was. Each day, we met peasants who supplied us with unleavened bread, cheese and sometimes beans and occasionally hard-boiled eggs." Though an Albertan who had ridden working farm horses, Reid had little experience on a saddled horse.

The same could not be said of the group that Reid saw riding toward him and the others when one day they had stopped in a village for food. "Though they wore British battle dress, they were a ramshackle lot, but they rode like experts. Then the peasants called out '*checha*,' which I later learned means 'uncle' in Serbian."

This bearded man who resembled a university professor spoke some English, but Reid found it easier to converse with Mihailović in French. "He seemed to recognize my uniform, and we exchanged a few words. But what stands out was the obvious esteem with which the peasants and his men held him," says Reid. "Later I learned about his military prowess and expert knowledge of Yugoslavia's forbidding topography. But there, in the lightly wooded area where peasant huts were scattered, what I saw was an almost medieval fiduciary relationship between him and these people who revered him."

28 JUNE 1944, MILAG UND MARLAG NORD, NEAR BREMEN, GERMANY

Father Charbonneau Considers the "School of Darwin"

Father Desnoyers's letter showed none of the joy that coursed through Father Pellerin's a week earlier, only part of which was due to Pellerin's receipt just prior to his birthday of a parcel that included clerical robes that fit him perfectly. Feeding Pellerin's mood was the "joyous news on the breeze bringing us hope that we might soon find liberty," a manifestation of the post–D-Day optimism.

The military situation, about which they had only the haziest idea, was not what weighed on Desnoyers, nor on Father Charbonneau. Neither regretted doing missionary work in the POW camps, yet after three years, they found the numbers of their flocks and their apostolic influence disappointing. In a time and place when it could be expected that men would turn to religion for hope and support, Charbonneau estimated that only 5 per cent of Catholics came to mass of their own volition and that 90 per cent of Catholics were hostile to their faith. The Catholics were so poorly educated that, like the polite Anglicans Charbonneau lived with, they embraced the "school of Darwin." According to Desnoyers, this "pseudo-scientific materialism" did more than simply draw a false division between science and religion; it determined on which side of the divide each man stood. Compared with the Basutos, who were hungry for the Word, even the Catholic Kriegies were practically atheists all but indifferent to the religion of their forefathers.

Charbonneau was not wrong to summarize the difference between the curates and the other POWs with the term "Darwinism," though the divide actually had less to do with different views on evolution (which had been rejected by Pope Leo XIII in 1880) than it did with differences between fathers' and brothers' education and view of agency in the world and that of the other POWs.[197] Having passed through the *collège classique* system in Quebec, taking bachelor's and then master's degrees, the brothers and fathers not only were the best-educated prisoners (they were fluent in Latin and read Greek) but they also had areas of specialization—for example, theology, holy scripture and canon law—that were nothing like what even other university-educated prisoners studied: accounting, engineering, law.

The gap yawned even wider between *les religieux* and the thousands of tradesmen. Moreover, despite superficial similarities between the monastic life and that of the sailors at the camp—such as the regulation of the day by bells—the seamen were concerned with load balancing, pipe fitting, navigation and engineering. The green dots on the radar officer's cathode ray tube could peer almost into the future, while an asdic (sonar) operator listened for pings that revealed the deadly U-boats in the deep. Even as religious a man as MacDonald, who wrote home telling of his great joy that he'd gone to his first full mass since being shot down and asking for a missal, saw himself as active in the world in a practical way different from *les religieux*, for his tool was the bomb sight.

LATE JUNE 1944, ON A TRAIN TO STALAG VIII-B, LAMSDORF, GERMANY

Carswell and Mac Are Recognized as POWs Again

After weeks of mistreatment and hearing the screams of other prisoners being beaten senseless, Carswell and Mac found themselves being hustled down a windowless hallway by an SS man with a machine gun at the ready, and thinking, "Please, God, don't let it end here!"[198] The moment of greatest terror—rounding a corner—ended not with the rattle of the machine gun but with the sight of a short, fat, ordinary German soldier leaning on his rifle, waiting to pick up his charges.

LATE JUNE 1944, RAVNA GORA, SERBIA, YUGOSLAVIA

Reid Narrowly Avoids Being Captured

After weeks of walking through the rugged mountains of southwest Serbia, bathing in streams and experiencing the extreme temperature changes of day and night, Reid had a new appreciation of the poor bloody infantry's lot in life. One day, as the Chetnik-led party approached a town, he got to put into practice some of what his father had learned as an infantryman in the First World War: "One of the Chetniks went ahead until he saw a light in the window, and then we advanced that far. Then, in a repeated leapfrog-like manner, we came to the centre of the small town.

"It had been a hard day, and when the sun went down the temperature dropped quickly, so the chairs, hot food and especially the slivovitz [at the restaurant we stopped at] were welcome," says Reid, his voice quickening as he recalls the almost theatrical moment when, after hearing some commotion outside, the fat restaurant owner came rushing into the backroom and spoke to Reid and his comrades in an excited yet low voice. "I didn't understand a word he said. But from his face and hand motions, even before I saw the others jump to their feet I knew we were going to have to make a run for it."

Reid and the Chetniks slipped out the back door before the Germans came in the front, but the Germans too could read the restaurateur's face. By the time the Germans had run back to their trucks, started the engines and turned on the headlights, Reid and the Chetniks were on their stomachs, each crawling through a different row in a maize field. "I hadn't got very far into my row when, thanks to the headlights and inspection light, I saw a German soldier in the next row." As his heart pounded so hard that he could hear his blood flow, Reid doubted that the thin stalks of the animal feed corn would keep him hidden. But the stalks produced just enough shadow for the German to pass him by. "A few moments later, he turned around, and we could hear the others walking back toward the restaurant. I guess they were more interested in getting some food and a good drink than in searching for us," says Reid, who followed the Chetniks to the northeast corner of the field, where they climbed aboard a wood-burning truck, something the Canadian airman had not known existed.

EARLY JULY 1944, RENNES, FRANCE

Lance Sergeant Stan Dutka Is Interrogated

Stan Dutka was one of a group of 15 North Novas to surrender to Oberstleutnant Karl-Heinz Milius's teenaged thugs. He saw the bodies of the eight Canadians shot in Authie, the remnants of the body the tank ran over, the two men murdered by the truck driver and the murdered body of Tom Davidson, whom he'd grown up with and worked with in a mine in Stellarton, Nova Scotia. The Germans' handling of the POWs they captured and let live in Normandy was eerily similar to how they treated the survivors of Dieppe. Rooms so full of men—in one more than 40, like Dutka, wounded when an American pilot unable to distinguish between a column of POWs and German troops swooped down in a strafing run—that they could not sit or lie down. No matter what Geneva said, hour followed hour without food or, more importantly, water appearing, until 7 June turned to the 8th and then the 9th.

Two Canadians died on the six-day march from Caen to the hospital at Rennes, during which the Wehrmacht refused to supply bandages and medical aid, though French civilians did what they could. After spending ten days in the hospital, which was so denuded of supplies that the French medical personnel believed the soldiers would be better off in German hands, Dutka and several other men were turned over to the Germans, who promptly crammed as many as they could into a truck bound for a POW camp. Once there, when asked how many troops had landed,

Dutka answered, "Fifteen million," adding helpfully that for every man there was also one tank.

EARLY JULY 1944, RAVNA GORA, SERBIA, YUGOSLAVIA

Reid and Some Americans Try to Make a Home Run on Their Own

They'd been travelling for about three days, since the pre-dawn darkness when they'd crept silently away from the Chetniks, who had been leading Reid and a few downed American flyers further and further from the part of western Yugoslavia controlled by Tito. "We were a pretty sorry-looking lot," recalls Reid, whose RCAF battle dress was dirty and torn, "which was good, since it allowed us to make it look like we were peasants tilling the land when German patrols came by." Difficult as these moments were for his American friends, they were even more nail-biting for Reid: he realized after they'd struck out on their own that the cord around his neck had broken and he'd lost his identity disks. "Without the flashes on my uniform or my identity disks, the Germans would have been able to ignore my claims to falling under the Geneva Convention and turn me over to the SS instead of sending me to a regular POW camp," he says.

Reid had used some of the money in his escape kit to buy bread, cheese and Turkish delight, so it wasn't hunger that prompted the evaders to approach a peasant wearing homespun clothes. "Rather," says Reid, "we realized that while we had no trouble determining which way was west, the rugged land made actually going west extremely difficult and we would need help." The peasant was friendly but to Reid's dismay led them back to Ravna Gora, from where they had just come. Fortunately, none of the Chetniks he turned them over to realized that Reid or the other men had slipped away from another group of Chetniks and, rather, simply assumed that they too were recently downed airmen.

21 JULY 1944, STALAG XX-A, TORUŃ, POLAND

MacDonald Explains "Uncle Joe's" Role in How He Came to Be at a New Camp

Neither Ian MacDonald nor Andrew Cox knew the name of the Russian offensive, Operation Bagration, or the numbers involved, which would have shocked them: more than 1 million Russian troops; 24,000 artillery pieces and mortars and more than 4,080 tanks and 6,334 aircraft, divided into a number of armies attacking across a front that ranged from the Baltic to the Black Sea. By early July, however, they could hear the guns of the 3rd Belorussian Front, which their families back home in Canada knew from the newspaper headlines had already pushed the Germans back 300 miles, and from Smolensk and Minsk. The Soviet advance was so quick that MacDonald, Cox and the other POWs were moved from Heydekrug in Lithuania first to Toruń, in north-central Poland, and a few weeks later to Stalag XI-B, near Fallingbostel, in Lower Saxony, with the result that the postcard MacDonald wrote on 21 July does not have a censor's stamp.[199]

MacDonald chose his words carefully, including "As you can see, we've changed camps for military reasons," which likely would have passed muster with his usual censor, *Geprüft* 3, as would rote lines about hoping that the war would end soon. MacDonald was uncharacteristically daring, however, when he explained in a parenthetical comment what the military reason was: "old Joe was getting too close"—"old Joe" being a reference to "Uncle Joe Stalin."

LATE JULY 1944, RAVNA GORA, SERBIA, YUGOSLAVIA

Reid Has a Strange Conversation with General Mihailović

"It was obvious that all of this had to do with someone important," says Reid, referring to the long table laid with plates and fine cutlery that had been set up in the field by a small house not far from

Ravna Gora. "Eating is an extremely important communal activity for the Serbs, so I wasn't surprised that I was invited to this picnic, though I was embarrassed by the ragged flea- and lice-infested remains of my uniform, especially when a Chetnik officer directed me toward one of the two vacant seats at the middle of the table."

A short time later, to Reid's great surprise, General Mihailović strode up to the table and sat down next to him. In more than passable English, he started discussing Canadian constitutional arrangements, of all things. "I was astonished that he knew the difference between the governor-general and the lieutenant-governors. The discussion was surreal. In front of me were people who lived by a blood code and who fought their war on horseback. And there I was, an airman from half a world away, discussing the reserve power of the British and Canadian monarchies," says Reid.

After they'd finished eating, the general asked Reid if he would stand at the end of the table so that, as an honoured guest, he could take the salute of the Chetnik platoons. Having had three shots of slivovitz, Reid was a little concerned about how steady his hand would be while saluting. He needn't have been, though diplomacy demanded that Reid not let on that he realized that, just as Confederate General Magruder had famously done in 1861, Mihailović made his force look larger than it was by having the men march by Reid several times. Before Mihailović rode off with his detachment, he signed and gave the Canadian a 500-dinar note, on which he had also written in Serbian: "May Godspeed find you safely home." Reid still has it.

LATE JULY 1944, STALAG LUFT IX-C, MÜHLHAUSEN, GERMANY

Robert Prouse Is in "the Cooler"

Amid hope and rumours generated by D-Day, the fact that he was due a 21-day stint in the cooler for having escaped slipped Robert Prouse's but not his Kommandant's mind. When it came time to serve his spell, he was better prepared for the sensory deprivation of sour, sawdust-filled black bread and water than he had been during his previous spell in the cooler; as long as his eyes were closed, a few grains of salt allowed Prouse to imagine that the tasteless, cold black bread was a pork chop or a piece of steak.

Each day, having awoken with sore hips from sleeping on bare boards and a stiff neck (his neck having been propped up on a couple of paperbacks, the stories of which were interrupted by missing pages), Prouse kept his mind busy by planning more and more audacious escapes, composing doggerel and computing how many minutes and seconds remained to his punishment. Although well aware that if he lost, his time in the cooler would be extended, Prouse couldn't help enjoying the game of cat and mouse he played with the guard known as "Plank-face," who never did catch Prouse smoking his contraband cigarettes.[200]

Chapter Twelve

August–September 1944

We brought nothing into this world, and it is certain we carry nothing out. The Lord gave, and the Lord hath taken away; blessed be the name of the Lord.

—The Book of Common Prayer
(Order at the Burial of the Dead)

EARLY AUGUST 1944, NEAR PRANJANE, YUGOSLAVIA

Norman Reid Radios for Help

USAAF Lieutenant Tom Oliver's plan to radio the Allies in Italy to tell them that there were some 150 downed American, British and Canadian airmen around Pranjane, Yugoslavia, faced at least two obstacles. First, they lacked a challenge letter—a password—that would indicate the message was truly from downed Allied airmen and not the baiting of a trap. Second, to give their location and status, the message might be long enough to give the Germans time to home in on it, thus revealing the location of the Chetniks' encampment. Despite these misgivings, Norman Reid agreed with Oliver, who had been an evader one day longer than he had, that the Chetniks weren't in any hurry to deliver them to the Allies. To their surprise, the Chetniks provided a radio operator.

In the absence of a codebook, the message had to be sent "in clear," that is, in plain English. "The messages had to be short but had to contain enough air force jargon to pass muster," explains Reid. "Because the rescue planes would have to land and take off on grass, and because they would have to pick up so many men, many of them wounded, the rescue could be affected only by DC-3 Dakotas, which every flyer called 'workhorses.' Accordingly, one message was 'Shoot a workhorse to us. TKO' (Thomas K. Oliver)," Reid recalls. Another used the American nickname for pilots and their penchant for nose art: "Driver of Fighting Mudcat down in Yugo, need help." A third relied on slang: "Situation SNAFU, 150 GIs down, wounded sick. TKO."

6 AUGUST 1944, STALAG XX-A, TORUŃ, POLAND

Ian MacDonald Takes Communion

Thanks to the maps published in the newspapers showing the relentless push west by the Red Army, MacDonald's parents were not at all surprised to learn in January 1945 that the previous August MacDonald had been evacuated from Stalag Luft VI in Lithuania, or that he expected "another move in a couple of days' time for the same reason." What they didn't know, of course, was where he was that January or how he—one of millions of POWs, survivors of concentration camps, terrified civilians and *Soldaten* belonging to broken regiments—were faring on the icy roads of Germany.

MacDonald knew that his parents could answer how his brothers Alexander and Leo were "making out in the Senior Service" in only the most general way.[201] Both were serving in the Royal Canadian Navy, Leo as a radar operator in the north of Scotland and Alexander as HMCS *Ottawa*'s anti-submarine officer. After two years of writing to her prisoner-of-war son, Mary MacDonald didn't need to refer to the Red Cross's *Revised Regulations Governing Communication with Prisoners of War in Enemy, Enemy Occupied or Neutral Countries* to know that she couldn't even allude to the secret message in Sandor's 15 May letter: "Oh yes, I ran into your cousin Sandor over here. He's still in the Merchant Marine and expects to be running out of the South of England for a while." After some confusion, compounded by the fact that William Alexander MacDonald—but always called "Alexander" or just "Sandor" by his family—signed the letter "Willie," the

MacDonalds realized that he was speaking about himself and that the invasion of France was imminent.

EARLY AUGUST 1944, RAVNA GORA, SERBIA, YUGOSLAVIA

Reid Learns Help Is on the Way

Reid's doubts about whether the Chetniks' radio operator was playing straight evaporated when the man handed him a paper reading "HELP WILL ARRIVE" and asking for their location. "Using the Chetniks' maps, determining our longitude and latitude was easy," says Reid, who later learned that the message was actually received—and disbelieved—by his own 205 (Heavy Bomber) Group. "What was difficult was figuring out how to send the coordinates without alerting the Germans. Oliver hit on the idea of using one of his men's service numbers, to which we added the longitude and latitude and then the instruction to subtract Staff Sergeant Sullivan's numbers."

The Germans may not have broken their code, but when a spotter plane appeared overhead, Reid feared that their directional-finding teams were on to them. The anxiety caused by a lone spotter plane was nothing compared with the frisson that followed the appearance of three Junker JU-52s, which could drop parachute troops. After a few circles, they flew on, likely to the Luftwaffe base a scant seven miles away.

10 AUGUST 1944, FRESNES PRISON, PARIS

RCAF Flying Officer John Harvie Is Betrayed

The German occupation of Paris meant that RCAF navigator John Harvie saw nothing of the traditional pageantry associated with Bastille Day, 14 July, as he sat in the back of a large black car that drove him through the streets of Paris. Though somewhat discomforted by being alone (he'd volunteered to be the first from the four evaders he was with to be moved to another safe house), he took heart from the fact that since being shot down on 5 July northwest of Chartres the men and women he'd relied on for help had embodied the French Revolution's motto, *Liberté, egalité, fraternité.*

The car passed the swastika flag–draped Arc de Triomphe, and as Harvie saw soldiers at the ready lining one side of rue des Saussaies, his worry increased, only to ease when the car made a ninety-degree turn and drove through an archway and thus, he thought, away from the Germans. A moment later, the driver slammed on the brakes, and he and the other man in the front seat leaped out of the car, then swung around, revolvers drawn, yelling, "Hands up!"[202] The entire incident seemed so much like a B movie that it took Harvie a moment to realize that he'd been delivered to Gestapo headquarters at 11 rue des Saussaies.

The interrogator's language skills far exceeded his concern with Harvie's rights as a prisoner of war. The mere mention of the Canadian's Geneva protections brought a slap to the face, despite the fact that he'd handed over his identity disks.

Mercifully, the threat "It does not matter anyway, you will all be shot within the week" was not carried out.[203] Instead, Harvie was taken to Fresnes Prison, which already held a number of RCAF men, including Edward Carter-Edwards (shot down a month earlier) and scores of other Allied flyers; by mid-August, 168 Allied airmen, including 25 other Canadians, were held there.

Deprived of reading material and kept in isolation, Harvie occupied his mind with creating puzzles, whistling the tunes of popular songs, reciting poems learned at school and passages from the Bible, doing Latin translations of texts remembered from high school and debating with himself whether he should become a doctor, lawyer or engineer. The gnawing hunger nearly broke him.

In early August, Harvie heard the sound of explosions that, he reasoned, came from long-range Allied guns. To him they beat a tattoo that he hoped heralded his release. Harvie knew nothing of Hitler's order to destroy Paris, but the 21-year-old was enough of a military man to guess that the warlord who'd ordered the Blitz would not hesitate at ordering the destruction of the City of Light. Fearing that the retreating Germans would bundle their prisoners onto a train and take them to the Reich, on 10 August, Harvie scratched out this message:

F/O John D. Harvie
J 27573
RCAF
Prisoner here
July 14/44–Aug 10/44
God Save the King!
Long Live the Allies!
Oh to be in Canada![204]

10 AUGUST 1944, RAVNA GORA, SERBIA, YUGOSLAVIA

Reid Is Rescued

For three nights, as he heard the American planes circling overhead, obviously searching for the landing field Reid and Oliver had prepared and marked with a fire in the shape of an "X," Reid kept thinking, "Here's your chance to get out of this place—a few thousand feet up in the air is your way home, and they can't find you!" Then, on the fourth night, instead of the sound of planes coming in for a landing, Reid and Oliver heard a great crash, followed by chickens squawking. They ran toward the chicken coop and found three Americans, OSS Captain George Musulin and two others, radio operators, carrying C-rations and radio gear. "I was, of course, overjoyed to see them. Since the DC-3s that would take us out would not be arriving for another day, I can honestly say that in those hours, the C-rations—or to be more precise, the powdered coffee in them—meant even more. After months of drinking ersatz coffee, powdered coffee tasted like ambrosia, and so did the thick piece of fruitcake." Musulin paid the woman who owned the shed he had destroyed on landing 15,000 dinars, or $10.

At dawn on the 10th, six DC-3s, flying more in a gaggle than in formation, appeared overhead. The planes were accompanied by a squadron of P-51 Mustangs. "I could tell from their markings that this was not just any squadron. The pilots sent to protect us were the Tuskegee Airmen, the only squadron manned by black Americans." Once all the planes had landed, the Tuskegee Airmen took the occasion to shoot up the nearby Luftwaffe base.

Before boarding a plane, Reid gave his boots to a Chetnik and his Smith and Wesson pistol to another, who gave him two kisses, one on each cheek—the second one being a sign of how well they'd come to know each other. "It was a tight fit. The DC-3s were designed to hold about 18 people, but each had to take about 25, many of whom were wounded. The takeoff, during which we brushed the trees, was only the beginning of a white-knuckle flight, during which we were protected by the Tuskegee Airmen flying in formation on either side of us," recalls Reid.

14 AUGUST 1944, NEAR LANGEAIS, FRANCE

Stan Dutka Survives Strafing and Escapes

In the scant seconds the pilots had to decide whether to fire their guns, they looked for a large red cross on the train in a siding near Langeais, France. Instead, they saw men trying to camouflage the train, marking it as a "target of opportunity" for the Allied pilots who now commanded the air. The strafing scattered the Germans and allowed some nearby French women to rush to the train and open its doors.

By the time Stan Dutka jumped from the train, the Germans had returned and were shooting at the prisoners. Instead of running, Dutka stopped to help the wounded, whose numbers soon grew when the planes strafed again. Then the Germans began shooting at some of the women who had helped the POWs.

Covered in other men's blood, Dutka pretended to be injured and limped to where a guard had gathered some wounded men. The guard told him that the train also contained about a hundred Luftwaffe officers, arrested after a bomb failed to explode in an attempt to kill Hitler a month earlier, which was the first the POW had heard of Claus von Stauffenberg's plot.

Thinking that Dutka was lame, neither this guard nor the others took much notice when he moved closer to the nearby wood. There he waited until, shrouded by darkness, he was able to slip into the wood and begin running. Before long, he came across two civilians, who took him to a house, where he ate, washed, and was given civilian clothes before being taken to a second house. There he was hidden just over a week, until 14 August, when he was driven to the nearby town of Angers, which had been liberated by General George Patton's army two days earlier.

14–15 AUGUST 1944, ON A TRAIN OUTSIDE PARIS

Harvie, RCAF Sergeant Edward Carter-Edwards and the Other Allied Airmen Almost Choke to Death

John Harvie was right.

Even as the sounds of battle closed in on Paris, Harvie's SS captors loaded him, Edward Carter-Edwards and the other Allied airmen (and, to Carter-Edwards's horror, the couple that had guided him to Paris) first into trucks and then into boxcars, 90 to a car built to hold 40. The heat of August combined with the fetid smell of unwashed men, vomit, urine and the remains of dysentery attacks that dripped down the legs of embarrassed men to create a nauseous miasma that not even those near the openings between the slats could fully escape.

Not long after it wheezed out of Paris and into a tunnel, the prisoners felt the train jerk to a stop. Their first worry, that the SS would massacre them if the Resistance had blown up the tracks, was quickly replaced with the fear of suffocation as thick black smoke began seeping into the boxcar. Carter-Edwards remembers wondering as the blackening air burned his eyes and throat, and as he heard the choking and coughing around him, if this breath would be his last. As men breathed carbon dioxide and even more deadly carbon monoxide, some began to hallucinate. American pilot Roy Allen, who had been breathing through a sweat-soaked piece of cloth, was aware enough to feel the train backing up. By the time Harvie and Carter-Edwards's car was opened, Allen and the men in his car were already on a field, gasping in smoke-free air.

A short time later, the SS troops divided the men. One group was hostages. The men in the other, larger group, some of whom were forced to carry German equipment, were marched down a dusty country road. When they neared the far end of the tunnel, they saw that the track had indeed been blown up, thus preventing the train from reaching the bridge that spanned the Marne, the river at which the French had stopped the German advance on Paris in September 1914.

At one point on the three-mile forced march, a few prisoners broke file to go to a well near the side of the road. A few hand pumps brought forth a welcome flow of cool water and threats by the guards that they'd shoot the men if they didn't get back in line. Some of the people in the hamlets they passed bravely gave the "V" sign made famous by Churchill and threw them potatoes, tomatoes and small loaves of bread. A few even "darted out from their doorways, carrying cups of water or cider, even wine."[205] Despite his weakened state, Harvie considered charging down the slope and into the river but then realized that the Germans could toss hand grenades into the water.

The POWs expected that once they were in the town they'd be taken to a prison and so were surprised when they were led across another bridge and to a waiting train. Before forcing the prisoners onto it, the SS guards allowed Red Cross workers to give them rough brown bread, sweetened with "jam" that left a decidedly chemical taste. While this group of POWs ate, the second group of prisoners arrived.

16–17 AUGUST 1944, ON A TRAIN IN FRANCE

HARVIE LEARNS TO HATE THE GERMANS

This cattle car was somewhat less crowded than the previous one, and it had a barrel for use as a latrine. But what heartened Harvie and the other men most was that, just before leaving the car, the French workman who had been covering the ventilation cuts with barbed wire dropped to his knee and with his hammer pried up a floorboard. Escaping was not, however, simply a question of waiting until the train was underway and then dropping to freedom, for a barbed-wire broom had been attached to the rear of the train. To survive, an escaper would have to roll over the rail and between the wheels of the moving train.

A total of five men, including RCAF pilot Joel Stevenson, escaped before the Germans realized what was happening and started searching the underside of the cars.[206] As three men stood on the plank to hold it in place while the guards prodded beneath the car, Harvie thought the prisoners had caught a break when the train inched forward, which he took as the signal for the guards to climb aboard. He knew they hadn't when he heard a burst of gunfire and the train stopped. A few moments later, the guards stormed into the car and nailed shut the escape hatch.

As mile after mile of France slipped away beneath them, the earlier threat that they'd be shot began to seem less ominous. Then, shortly after dawn, the train stopped and the door to Harvie's car was opened, revealing a row of young SS troopers pointing machine guns at the other prisoners. Some of the SS men entered the car, screaming, "*Raus, ihr Schweine.*"[207] When the "pigs" refused to move, a few of the heavily armed troopers started shoving POWs toward the door; others pulled whomever they could reach to the ground. Soon some 50 men, including Harvie, were standing in a field in the middle of France and ordered to strip. "The bastards," Harvie feared, "are going to shoot us naked so that our clothing can be recovered . . . without bullet holes and blood stains!"[208]

The SS's plan proved more benign. Stripping the POWs naked ensured that they would not try to escape from the train. A few hours later, the train stopped again. The men who had dived for the floor upon hearing a submachine-gun blast had just climbed to their feet when the Germans opened the car's door and demanded to know who had been looking out the vent. For a long moment, no one moved. Then a young prisoner came forward. The SS men ignored the cries of the other POWs that the boy needed medical attention for the hand just hit by bullets fired to enforce the order against looking out the vent. Instead, Himmler's men grabbed the boy and pulled him to the ground.

He was so terrified that he couldn't answer when the Germans demanded to know if he was French. The shout of "*Engländer?*" shook him enough to answer "*Français. Je suis Français.*"[209] An SS officer gestured for the naked young Frenchman to start down the slope just beyond the tracks; then the officer fired his rifle and the Frenchman's body fell down the slope. The helpless airmen watched as the SS officer walked up to the body, put his Luger to the back of the neck and fired.

"This was the first time I had ever felt hatred towards anyone," wrote Harvie. "I had often seen photographs and read about wartime atrocities, but they had always been too distant and impersonal to be true. After what had just happened, I felt sick because I realized for the first time that man can be worse than any wild animal."[210]

19 AUGUST 1944, STALAG II-D, STARGARD, NEAR SETTIN, GERMANY

Sapper Russ Burrows Remembers the Cauldron of Dieppe

The memory of the battle. The rattle of machine-gun fire. The body's recall of the concussive force of an artillery shell or mortar bomb that blew up just far enough away not to kill you. The sight of men with whom you'd trained, showered and got drunk now sprawled on the ground, some with barely a puncture wound, others armless, legless, headless, was never more than a nightmare or, indeed, a quiet moment away. The daily parsing of inadequate rations and husbanding of Red Cross cheese, butter, raisins, chocolate and cigarettes underlined the difference between their lives now and when they stepped onto the stage of history at Dieppe.

Hugh Smith had been dead these two years, yet when Russ Burrows closed his eyes, the dreariness of camp life receded behind memories of gambling with his fellow sapper, who won at cards and dice. Smith won so often that, long before they had gone into battle, the sapper from Oshawa, Ontario, mocked his friend from Windsor, his imprecations signalling their closeness. "You're lucky at gambling. Someday we'll find out, you son of a bitch, if you're lucky in battle."

They had been on the beach for less than half an hour. Exploding mortar bombs, the slicing sound of a machine gun and screams of another injured or dying man providing the metronomic beat by which the minutes ticked by. They were halfway up the beach when Smith asked for a light. Burrows struggled to get his Ronson out of his pocket, still wet from the surf they'd waded through, then tossed it his friend, who tossed it back to him a moment later.

"As I pushed the lighter back in my pocket, I noticed Hughie's head fall back. I shimmied over to him and saw that a sniper, who must have seen the small flame of the lighter, put a bullet right through my friend's head," says Burrows. "Even though getting up and running made me a bigger target, I figured I'd be safer on the lee side of the seawall."

Word that two French escapers had made successful home runs was welcomed by Burrows and his countrymen, as was the nearby raid by heavy bombers, for it showed that after two years, history had almost caught up with them. As they recalled their agony on the beaches of Dieppe and their pain over the past two years, the Canadians could do little more than chuckle when they read the opening sentence of a leaflet their German captors distributed: "As a result of repeated applications from British subjects from all parts of the world, wishing to take part in the common European struggle against Bolshevism, authorization has recently been given for the creation of a British volunteer unit." However much men like Burrows and Prouse may have been impressed by the author's grasp of English, they could not help but note how the proposed unit's very name, "British Free Corps," was just a little too close to the armed right-wing Freikorps that had tried to overthrow the fledgling Weimar Republic in the early 1920s and which served as the training ground for the Nazi Party's own armed wing, the SD. Even more outrageous was the insinuation that, by taking the King's schilling, they were serving the "interests of Jewry and international finance."[211]

20 AUGUST 1944, BUCHENWALD CONCENTRATION CAMP, WEIMAR, GERMANY

Harvie and the Allied Airmen Pass through the Gates of Hell

They knew they weren't at Dulag Luft because that was in Frankfurt am Main and the sign on the far end of the railway siding read "Weimar." While they wondered about the squat buildings on either side of the siding, which they later learned were armaments factories, they had no doubt as to the purpose of the submachine gun–toting SS troops who lined the way to what was obviously the prison camp's main gate. As the airmen climbed down from the train, the stale smell of smoke coming from the tattered clothes that had been returned to them gave way to "air so filled with the stench of burnt death" that Carter-Edwards and others disbelieved their own senses.

Moments later, the airmen saw their first evidence that Buchenwald, which took its name from the beech-tree woods that surround it, was no ordinary prison camp. Barely had they spotted the gallows that rose above the electrified barbed-wire fence when they saw hundreds of spectral forms of men and women, with gaunt faces and impossibly thin arms, their heads shaved bare, and each with a yellow, red, purple, black, brown, green, or pink triangle pinned to the striped "pyjamas" that hung off their bodies. As the men were marched through the gate, set incongruously in a faux rustic wooden structure that recalled a Teutonic hunting lodge, topped by a clock tower, a few of them saw that a short distance beyond the gate and set strategically behind a screen of trees was a small *Zoologischer Garten*, where guards could rest peacefully and watch animals frolic.

21 AUGUST 1944, BUCHENWALD CONCENTRATION CAMP, WEIMAR, GERMANY

Three Canadian Secret Agents Are also in Buchenwald

Harvie, Carter-Edwards and the other 24 RCAF officers were not the only Canadians in this patch of hell. Two days earlier, a train carrying 37 Special Operations Executive (SOE) agents, including three Canadians and a number of French Resistance agents, arrived at Buchenwald. Though the airmen had never met the SOE agents, they'd heard their screams as they were tortured in Fresnes Prison.

Romeo Sabourin, who in 1940 lied about his age to join the Fusiliers Mont-Royal and later joined the SOE, had been in the Gestapo's hands since shortly after he was inserted into France in early 1944. Frank Pickersgill and Kenneth Macalister (before joining SOE, Pickersgill had been a civilian; Macalister had been an officer in the Intelligence Corps) were picked up by the Gestapo within hours of their landing in France on 19 June 1943; their radio and codes allowed a faux "Pickersgill" to "play the radio game," calling in drops of arms, supplies and, sadly, more SOE agents, who were scooped up.[212]

Over the next year, Pickersgill and Macalister were transferred between several prisons, where they were repeatedly tortured. Knowing that Pickersgill's brother, Jack, was Prime Minister Mackenzie King's principal secretary, the Gestapo tried to suborn him. At Fresnes Prison, Pickersgill attacked a guard with a bottle and jumped through a second-story window. He was shot, recaptured and tortured.

On 8 August 1944, the SOE agents and Resistance men were bundled into a stifling train compartment. The following night, a strafing run damaged the train. The guards manning the trucks sent to pick them up kicked, punched and beat the prisoners with their rifle butts before taking them to a concentration camp near Saarbrücken. Five days later, they were again pushed and prodded into a cattle car. When, that afternoon, they were transferred to a passenger carriage, prisoner solidarity soon broke down. After a

Resistance fighter picked the lock to his handcuffs and opened several others, the SOE agents and some of the other Resistance fighters argued that, if the opportunity arose, they should kill the German guards and try to escape. Others believed the German promise that "their destination was a special camp for officers where they would enjoy concerts, a cinema and theatre, a well-stocked library, and perhaps even the company of women."[213]

22 AUGUST 1944, BUCHENWALD CONCENTRATION CAMP, WEIMAR, GERMANY

Learning the Ways of Buchenwald

In the first light of day, as the picturesque farms and villages, and, even more hopefully, a church spire shimmered into view, Harvie could almost forget the first hours he spent in Buchenwald. For hours they stood—without food or water—on the *Appellplatz*, then led into a building where their heads, faces and crotches were shaved before being swabbed with a burning disinfectant, after which they were issued shapeless, worn civilian clothes. Nothing could weaken the memory of the sleepless night he spent without even the barest of blankets on a patch of ground littered with sharp pieces of coal. In that same place in 1939, hundreds of Polish prisoners had died from exposure.

The light of dawn, however, revealed the horrors of the night: six bodies were carried from the barracks area. "If this many died on a summer night," Harvie recalled thinking, "how many might die in the cold of winter?"[214] The answer was tens of thousands, an untold number shivering into death as cold winds bled away the last bit of heat from their emaciated bodies as they stood on the *Appellplatz* clad only in thin pajamas.

Harvie wondered where the huge cemetery was that would be needed to bury the dead and how the record-keeping system that notified next of kin was organized. "Was any kind of a service said for them to mark their passing in this place, far from their homes and loved ones?" he wondered. Later, after learning that the oily smoke and white ash rising from the smokestack above a squat brown building few hundred yards to the right of the main gate were the remains of Jews, Roma, Russians, homosexuals, Jehovah's Witnesses, political prisoners and others who, according to the Nazis' twisted lights, received their due, as proclaimed by the words cut into the camp's steel gate—*Jedem das Seine*—this last question must have seemed impossibly naive.

The SS's power went beyond its monopoly on the use of force, the naked display of which included beating prisoners senseless, making Jewish prisoners sing anti-Semitic songs and rubbing their faces in excrement. The same guards who forced elderly men to climb trees and then shook them so violently that the old men fell and broke their necks controlled how long the airmen would suffer on the old coal dump. The guards fed their snarling dogs meat, milk, cereal, potatoes, eggs and claret, while issuing a scant seven ounces of poor-grade boiled horsemeat per prisoner per week. They dined on "steaks of heroic size," washed down with real coffee and wines and brandy stolen from occupied countries or bought at ruinous exchange rates, while giving inmates rotten potatoes, or "liver sausage" that contained ground fish bones.[215] Rations were so insufficient that a few months after the Canadians arrived at Buchenwald, the Organisation Todt complained that chronic starvation made it difficult to form an efficient slave labour workforce from the Buchenwald inmates.

The men who had broken the spirits and bodies of hundreds of thousands understood the importance of soldierly comportment and used it to ill effect. In the latrine, men had to crouch over an open cesspool, balanced on a rail that was never cleaned; all knew that those who had fallen in had drowned with gulps of this seething mass in their mouths. The same SS that spent more than 250,000 reichsmarks building Kommandant Karl-Otto Koch's wife, Ilse ("The Bitch of Buchenwald"), a 30,000-square-foot riding hall with mirrored walls did not provide either toilet paper or water to wash with after using the *Abort*.

23 AUGUST 1944, BUCHENWALD CONCENTRATION CAMP, WEIMAR, GERMANY

Harvie Seeks Medical Aid from a Russian "Medic"

Exhaustion from nights spent trying to sleep on the rocky ground, the dehydrating effects of dysentery, hunger, and scenes and stories of horror tore at Harvie's morale. So too did the infected flea and lice bites on the bottom of his bare feet, which Harvie feared would lead to sepsis. (Perhaps in a backhand compliment for the airmen's penchant for escaping, the SS did not issue them even the rudimentary wooden clogs given to other prisoners.) Harvie never considered going to the infirmary, where, he had been warned, patients were used for research that ended with another body being carried across the compound to the building above which, several times a week, a flame roared.

Worried that the infections would grow worse, Harvie took his chances with a "medic" in the Russian compound. The Russian did not speak English, but upon seeing the pustules understood the situation and pricked them open with an unsterilized needle so he could squeeze out the yellow liquid filled with dead white blood cells. The Russian then swabbed the affected areas with a purple disinfectant and wrapped them in a crepe paper–like bandage.

24 AUGUST 1944, BUCHENWALD CONCENTRATION CAMP, WEIMAR, GERMANY

The Bombing of Buchenwald

Carter-Edwards calls it the "best damned pinpoint bombing I've ever seen," but every Allied airman knew that, despite its impressive name, strategic bombing was anything but an exact science. Even after Pathfinder aircraft started marking targets with flares, "creep back" meant that most of the bombers dropped their loads miles short of their intended targets; indeed, only one in five bombs fell within five miles of its intended target. Thus, near noon, the turn from elation, which the men felt when they first saw the two box formations of American B-17s, to horror, when unseen anti-aircraft guns hit their marks and planes began breaking apart, to sheer terror, when more than 50 bombers broke away from the main stream and headed directly toward the concentration camp. Even as he cursed the Americans for flying so high they couldn't see him, Harvie wanted to jump up, wave his arms and scream, "No! No! No! Can't you see that we are fellow airmen! Stay away you fools, you'll kill us by mistake!"[216]

Buchenwald had no bomb shelters, so there was nowhere to run. Instead, tens of thousands of prisoners threw themselves on the ground and did their best to shield their heads from the falling flak. In spite of his rising panic, Harvie calculated when and where the bombs would have to be released for them to hit the camp. He knew he was right when he saw the flare dropped by the first bomber as it passed over the Deutsche Ausrüstungswerke, which manufactured ammunition, and Gustloff-Werke factory, which in addition to other armaments made components of V1 and V2 rockets. Then came the black specks, moving so fast that they didn't seem to grow much larger before he heard the express train–like sound wave their fall generated. Before it had fully ended, the sound wave caused by the explosion of 150 tons of high-explosive and incendiary bombs washed over him, and the ground heaved.

Barely had the earth stopped trembling when Harvie saw about 70 B-17s bank 90 degrees and streak toward the camp. Through the "agonies of fear and despair," he correctly calculated that they'd drop their bombs somewhat closer to where he and the other Allied airmen were lying on the ground, their mouths open to prevent the tremendous forces generated by detonation of some 500 bombs from bursting their eardrums. By the time the force of the explosions had died away and Harvie looked up, the stream of Flying Fortresses had already turned westward for home.

Thick black smoke rose above the blasted remnants of the factories and lighter, thinner smoke billowed forth from the SS compound and from parts of the prisoner compound. Save for some superficial flash burns, the airmen were unhurt, but hundreds of other prisoners closer to the targets had been torn apart or burned by the incendiary bombs; when a proper Appell was conducted, it became clear that hundreds of prisoners had been killed, and some bodies had simply ceased to exist. The rumour that the Kommandant and his family were killed was quickly dispelled. On 27 August, the SS reported to Berlin that 80 SS men had been killed, 65 were missing and presumed dead, 238 had been wounded and 24 wives and children of SS men had been killed; as well, 316 prisoners were killed and 1,462 wounded. One famous casualty in the camp was the Goethe Eiche, a several-hundred-year-old oak tree that Johann Wolfgang von Goethe, author of *Faust,* Germany's greatest poem, rested under during his many visits to the area.

When Harvie realized the scope of the damage and that fire raged in the SS compound, he expected the SS to massacre what the Germans called Luftgangsters. So he was not surprised when, within minutes, the Kapo arrived with a number of SS officers, Schmeisser machine guns at the ready and swinging bullwhips and clubs, and calling for the Americans and the English to move.

Harvie's infected feet saved him from being herded toward the burning armaments plants. Other prisoners, including the American Roy Allen, were forced to fight the fires irrespective of the fact that they were barefoot and lacked hoses or buckets for water. Carter-Edwards was tasked with removing people from the rubble, which cut and burned his bare feet. As Allen and others were sent into the burning factories to try to salvage equipment, other prisoners were forced to carry food and clothing from a warehouse. Yet another prisoner had to defuse an unexploded incendiary bomb.

Having seen the SS's casual brutality, the Allied airmen who picked up bodies outside a V2 factory were not surprised to find those people had been shot in the back. Nothing, however, prepared Harvie and the others for the story some told of finding in the rubble a "museum," prepared for Ilse Koch, in which shrunken heads, and lampshades and book covers made from tattooed human skin, were proudly displayed.

25 AUGUST 1944, LES HOGUES, NORMANDY

RCAF Squadron Leader James Griffin Young Is Murdered

Within hours of General Charles de Gaulle's speech from the Paris Hôtel de Ville's balcony in which he claimed that Paris had liberated herself, one hundred miles to the northeast in Les Hogues, an SS NCO walked toward five Allied prisoners of war in an improvised POW compound calling out, "Where are the Canadians?" His special interest in the Dominion's soldiers likely stemmed from the fact that, as a member of the 2nd Company of the Leibstandarte Adolf Hitler, he had been engaged with the Canadian Army almost nonstop since D-Day.

The NCO ordered the POWs to get up and push a vehicle. Since they did not understand German, they did not move, nor did they respond when he repeated the order in French. The enraged and apparently drunk NCO stormed off, only to return a few moments later with two other soldiers and Obersturmführer Güteman. By then, even though four of the POWs had stood up, Güteman went up to the man who was still sitting, James Young, who had been shot down earlier in the day, pulled him to his feet and began punching him in the face, causing his nose to bleed.

In the meantime, perhaps having realized what their captors wanted, one of the Allied soldiers started walking toward the gate. He was shot in the back. Seeing this, another prisoner started running toward a hillock beyond the gate. He too was shot in the back. A third prisoner managed to get through the gate before he was felled by a rifle shot. The NCO then went up to Young, screaming at him and shaking him by the collar, while another SS man slunk behind Young. Following a signal from Güteman, this second SS man fired directly into Young's back. The fifth prisoner was shot as he tried to crawl away.

According to a certain Stabsgefreiter named Maier, who defected to the Allies on 27 August, Güteman ordered that the two POWs who had not been killed outright be given the *coup de grâce*. Young was "finished off" with a shot to his chest. In an attempt to cover up this war crime, Güteman ordered that the men be buried nearby and prepared a report saying that the Canadian and others had been "shot while trying to escape," which he ordered Maier to sign.

30 AUGUST 1944, STALAG XX-A, TORUŃ, POLAND

Ian MacDonald Finds It Harder to Remain Optimistic Despite the Good War News

From the camp's jungle telegraph, Ian MacDonald knew that in just the past week, Romania had switched sides, that Paris, Toulon and Marseilles had been liberated and that the Red Army was at the gates of Warsaw. But, for the dutiful son, who had drawn so much strength from his family's letters, and who continued to be concerned about the finances back in Lourdes, Nova Scotia, and about his brother on HMCS *Ottawa*, the months without letters weighed heavily on him.

The reason he had not received any parcels recently was purely administrative; his parents had the wrong POW number. But that didn't make the lack of word from them any less painful for MacDonald. With the end of the war almost in sight, perversely, instead of each passing day being felt as one day closer to the end of his indeterminate sentence, it seemed as if each further day of imprisonment bore the weight of every other day he had been locked away—and that the days to come would bear an even heavier burden. In a letter home, after listing two upcoming birthdays that he hoped to make it back for, he mentioned his father's, which was in late December, and then wrote, as if to buck himself up, "I prefer to be optimistic."

4 SEPTEMBER 1944, MILAG UND MARLAG NORD, NEAR BREMEN, GERMANY

George Shaker Begins a Diary

The first few entries in George Shaker's "wartime log," a slightly larger than 8½-by-11-inch diary bound in dark beige canvas and supplied by the Canadian YMCA, seem oddly like filler. However, the detailed lists of Canadian, British, New Zealand, American and Argentinian Red Cross parcels underline how important they were to their survival. When the Detaining Power bothered to respond to complaints about the adulterated black bread and weak soup provided, the Germans pointed to the calories and nutrients contained in a one-pound tin of Maple Leaf butter (Canadian), a 12-ounce tin of fish or bacon (British), a one-pound tin of cheese (New Zealand), half a pound of chocolate (American) or a one-pound tin of Irish stew (Argentinian) as making up the difference. These supplies helped keep Shaker from falling below 100 pounds, two-thirds of what he weighed when captured in early 1941, and they made all the difference for Paul Gallant and the Canadian officers and ratings in Marlag Nord, on the other side of the camp's wire, after 4 September when, because the RCN men refused a work order, they were put on half rations.

On 4 September, the men from the *A.D. Huff* had no choice but to follow a work order. Had they not, their meagre possessions and, more importantly, their stock of Red Cross food would have been contaminated by the gas used to fumigate the barracks. The gas was so poisonous that they had to spend the night on the floor of another building, which, they regretted on that surprisingly cold September night, did not have a stove.

Shaker's diary entries make no reference to religion. Its importance to him, however, is evident from the sketch of Stella Maris on page 9. To the right and left of the Cross that rises from the altar are the signatures of the eight priests and brothers who had been imprisoned at Milag und Marlag Nord since 1941.

5 SEPTEMBER 1944, MILAG UND MARLAG NORD, NEAR BREMEN, GERMANY

Les Religieux Are Allowed a Religious Retreat

In German, the word could be translated as *Rückzug*, which describes what their armies were doing on both the Eastern and Western Fronts.

For the Oblates, *une retraite* had a very different meaning. In the letter published in *L'Apostolat* in December 1944, Brother Roland Cournoyer credits the "sweetness of Providence" for the extraordinary privilege that the Kommandant of Milag und Marlag Nord bestowed on the Oblates. Perhaps in recognition for their work (and perhaps also in an attempt to curry favour) the Nazi officers agreed to allow Cournoyer, Brother Parent and Fathers Pâquet, Barsalou and Charbonneau to join Father Bergeron in a religious retreat. According to Father André Dubois, who knew *les religieux*, "in the situation they were in, separated from their superiors and often from each other, this opportunity for spiritual renewal was extremely important. At the retreat, in addition to celebrating mass together, they would have spent time in silent meditation and prayer."

Their meals too were likely also religious events, for instead of eating to the buzz of barracks talk, there would have been either silence or the stately words of a devotional reading. "By pulling back from their day-to-day life in the camps and concentrating on these observances, despite their great distance from Canada, the fathers and brothers were renewing their ties to their community," says Dubois.

EARLY SEPTEMBER 1944, BUCHENWALD CONCENTRATION CAMP, WEIMAR, GERMANY

Harvie and Most of the Other Allied Airmen Are Sent to Block 58

After weeks sleeping on the ground without any cover during unseasonably cool and wet nights, Harvie, who had turned 21 on 3 September, and most of the other airmen were shepherded into Block 58; one who wasn't was Carter-Edwards, already so sick with pneumonia, pleurisy and grippe that he had no choice but to risk going to the infirmary. The large, windowless, wooden, barn-like structure would have beggared all description. Six hundred men were crammed into a space designed for a third of that. The smell was overwhelming. There was no place to wash; in any event, the bombing raid had destroyed the camp's water-pumping system.

At Fresnes Prison, each man had had a narrow bunk. In Buchenwald, the blocks were filled with row upon row of wooden shelves fouled with men's waste; the shelves lacked paillasses and were so narrow that the men had to sleep on their sides. Rather than breathe into each other's faces, and to provide a modicum of privacy, they lay "on the same side at the same time." Changing sides required not only everyone's agreement but also a volunteer to act as "the unlocking key" by working his way out and climbing to the floor so that the other men could turn over, and then shimmying his way back in.[217]

In September 1944, Buchenwald, designed for some 20,000 prisoners, held upward of 84,000 men, women and children, the largest single group being Russians but also including thousands of Roma, French, Poles, Slovenes, Jehovah's Witnesses, Jews, the Allied airmen and SOE agents. The desperate thousands were housed in the same appalling conditions the Allied airmen now lived in and were fed the same inadequate food—and had been for years; ironically, the SOE prisoners were fed marginally better rations. The hours on the *Appellplatz* were an especial torment for these desperately weak men, many of whom collapsed, some in death, while their tormentors tallied up the numbers. Other numbers were tallied up too: those who died working in the quarry; in the infirmary; of having committed suicide by throwing themselves on the electrified fence; of "natural causes"; or by execution in a room with a floor painted red so that the accumulation of blood would not discomfit SS men assigned there, and which was conveniently placed beneath the crematorium. On Sundays, the ropes of the gallows in the centre of the *Appellplatz* rarely hung limply.

The politics of Buchenwald was entirely different from the politics of the POW camps, where military order existed under the Senior British Officer or senior Allied officer and the camp's Man of Confidence, who served as the liaison with the German authorities. As at other concentration camps, huts were ruled by Kapos appointed by the SS. He ensured that the inmates appeared on the *Appellplatz* and were assigned work details, which included picking up the daily dead and small food ration. The Kapo of Block 58 had a private room with a single bed, bedding, a writing table and books and magazines he could read while sitting on a real chair, beside which stood an electric lamp. Whatever injustice the airmen may felt about the Kapo's perks, the most important one being that he did not have to eat the swill they did. What mattered more was that he was considered a good Kapo, because he didn't beat or otherwise mistreat either the airmen or the hundreds of Roma under his charge.

Fear and degradation suffused the camp. The broad avenues between the rows of barracks were designed not so the inmates could march eight abreast comfortably, though they could, but so SS machine guns could sweep the lane clear. In the Russian compound, which the Germans patrolled heavily, the SS beat starving POWs with clubs, rifle butts, bullwhips and the sharp end of their jackboots; earlier in the war, to drown out the sound of shooting of 10,000, Himmler's men forced others to sing loudly, though presumably not the "Buchenwald Song" or the more famous "Peat Bog Soldiers," with its haunting lyrics: "Up and down the guards are pacing, / No one, no one can get through. / Flight would mean a sure death facing, / Guns and barbed wire greet our view. / We are the peat bog soldiers, / We're marching with our spades to the bog."[218]

EARLY SEPTEMBER 1944, AN *ARBEITSKOMMANDO* OF STALAG XI-B, FALLINGBOSTEL, GERMANY

George Reid Works Underground

George Reid knew, thanks to a family story from what he'd grown up calling the Great War, that the elevator was taking him and 20 other Canadian POWs into a salt mine, where they joined Russian murderers, other criminals and women as slave labourers. The mine, however, was not destined to produce salt. Rather, it had been hollowed out to house one of the armament or aircraft factories that Armaments Minister Albert Speer had ordered to be built in such mines so that they were safe from Allied bombers. Although conditions were marginally better than those endured by the Canadians who laboured in the coal mines in Japan, the weakened men did most of the work with shovels and 16-pound sledgehammers.

By September 1944, control of POW labour had passed into Himmler's hands and the institutionally ruthless Speer organized the labour; thus, this *Arbeitskommando* bore no resemblance to the brewery and graphite mine Andrew Carswell passed through. For 12 hours a day, six days a week, Reid and the other slave labourers worked filling huge mine cars, with top openings of six by six feet—260 cars per day for each work gang, no matter whether there were 5 or 20 men in the gang. The Germans never provided enough food: only a bowl of soup and a piece of bread each day, its thinning from one and a quarter inches to near one-half inch being a measure of the shrinking Reich. The water ration was so small that torturous thirst caused by the salt dust often caused the slave labourers to faint.

10 SEPTEMBER 1944, BUCHENWALD CONCENTRATION CAMP, WEIMAR, GERMANY[219]

Execution of Frank Pickersgill, Kenneth Macalister, Romeo Sabourin and 13 Other SOE Agents

The sentence of "*Tod*" did not surprise Pickersgill, Macalister, Sabourin or the other 13 SOE agents who, after hearing it, were quickly marched to the *Zellenbau*, a whitewashed one-story building that, on either side of a centre aisle, had cells no larger than small horse stalls. Toward the front of the cellblock were larger rooms, one an office, another a torture chamber equipped with whips, cudgels, chains and electrical equipment that could be attached to the testicles. Each man was savagely beaten, and forced to stand at attention with their faces against the open peepholes in the heavy steel doors for hours on end.

Near 5 p.m. on 10 September, they were forced to drag their bruised and battered bodies across the camp. A hundred or so yards after they passed the main gate, they made a slight left turn and entered a fenced-in area in the middle of which sat a low building with a gabled roof that vaguely resembled a smokehouse. They walked around the building to a narrow flight of concrete stairs leading to the basement, to a room they may never have heard the name of but of which, after they'd finished limping down the steps and their eyes had adjusted to the dim light of one or two bare bulbs, they could have no doubt about its purpose. Lining the walls of the *Leichenkeller* (corpse cellar) about eight feet from the floor and each separated by about four feet were dozens of large meat hooks.

SS-Scharführer Walter Warnsädt was anxious to squeeze the last quantum of suffering he could from these broken men. Instead of tying their hands behind their back with their wrists crossed, they were tied with the arms parallel, which has the effect of slowly dislocating shoulders, the pain being only increased by the deep breaths taken by the petrified men watching their comrades die.

By design, despite their last request, they did not die cleanly and honourably. Instead, Warnsädt's men slipped nooses made of thick piano wire around each man's neck and, after throwing the other end of the wire over a meat hook, hauled the man up to its level before tying off the wire. This was not hanging but the medieval practice of death by suspension, an agonizingly slow death by strangulation as the wire slowly crushed the carotid artery and jugular vein. It was death extended by the involuntary jerks of the body, for each, momentarily, relieved the pressure on the artery and vein, thus allowing blood to once again flow and the brain to revive—only to again feel the pain of the noose—and the mind to clear enough to register the terror of suffocation. It was the destruction of the men's bodies in the most intimate form.

As they slowly strangled and jerked, in Warnsädt's men's eyes, the SOE agents would have turned into mere simulacrums of men, into something akin to puppets with faces blue not from paint but from cyanosis. Long before they died, their bodies would have begun to stink from the involuntarily voiding of urine and feces, which were easily washed down the oversized drain in the middle of the *Leichenkeller.* The desecrated bodies were loaded into the electric lift that brought them upstairs, where, as tens of thousands had been (and thousands more would be), they were placed on a metal platen that slid into the coke-fired ovens adapted for the SS by a well-known bread-oven manufacturer that still has its factory in nearby Erfurt.[220]

24 SEPTEMBER 1944, STALAG VII-B, MEMMINGEN, GERMANY

Father Boulanger's *Cri de Cœur*

Father Boulanger's letter to Father Eugene Marcotte on 24 September shows that he would have benefited greatly from joining the retreat earlier in the month, for his *cri de cœur* comes close to tipping over into bitterness: "Canadians," by which he meant French Canadians, "don't care about religion!" How could this be, given their sufferings on the beaches of Dieppe? Even the English Catholics (most of whom were of Irish background) were less foul-mouthed than the Fusiliers Mont-Royal, a reference to the fact French-Canadian swear words are liturgical, *hostie* taking the place of "fuck" and *tabernac* for "shit."

Boulanger's observation that "war is not a school for virtue" is hardly original. The additional observation that, for young men, "neither is two or three years of inaction" points to a problem with morale that became more pronounced the closer the end of the war appeared. Just a week earlier from the relatively salubrious confines of his POW camp in Austria, Father Juneau wrote, "This long captivity is dangerous! It is here that man reveals his true self. Life in the barracks is sometimes at an extremely low level—but the priest must be the counterweight."

28 SEPTEMBER 1944, MILAG UND MARLAG NORD, NEAR BREMEN, GERMANY

Father Barsalou Hides a Forbidden Message in a Discussion about Tomatoes

The failure at Arnhem, immortalized in the phrase "A bridge too far," and stiffening of resistance on the Eastern Front meant that the predictions made after the Allies secured Normandy that the war would be over by Christmas had turned to dust. There were scattered cases of the Germans surrendering, but most *Soldaten* fought on.[221] Though the Nazi high command knew that Speer's armaments production miracle had passed its apogee and, even more ominously, that the Reich's supply of gasoline and aviation fuel had dropped to critical levels, the state's organs remained as radical as ever. After severely torturing 60-year-old Joseph Müller, on 11 September the regime beheaded the teacher, who had told a joke in which a mortally wounded Luftwaffe officer asked to place a picture of Hitler on his left and one of Göring on his right so that "now I can die like Jesus."[222]

The day-to-day business of the POW camps did, however, continue. On 28 September, the guards at Milag Nord spent part of their day searching for alcohol stills and tunnels. A few earned themselves commendations for finding a complete crystal radio and parts of another, both likely being plants.

The censors too remained active, deleting 12 lines (or almost half) of a letter written by Father Robert Barsalou's father. Aware that any obvious mention of the deletions would itself be censored, Barsalou deftly places the words "12 *lignes censurées*" after a long—and triumphal—statement about how his 12 tomato plants have produced 400 tomatoes, albeit ones smaller than those in Canada, and before what the censor no doubt viewed as a routine statement about placing oneself in the hands of divine Providence.

Chapter Thirteen

October–December 1944

We have to fight this battle not only with guns in daylight, but alone in the night, communing with our souls, strengthening our faith that in common men everywhere there is a spring of innocent aspiration and good will that cannot be sealed.

—Joseph Priestly

EARLY OCTOBER 1944, BUCHENWALD CONCENTRATION CAMP, WEIMAR, GERMANY

EDWARD CARTER-EDWARDS SURVIVES IN THE INFIRMARY

The memories are indistinct, which makes them so different from what Edward Carter-Edwards remembers of the last moments aboard his plane: the explosion of the shell, the burning port wing and his crawl to the escape hatch in the Halifax Mk III's nose cone. His memories of being in the infirmary are of voices too far away to hear, hazy faces and hands that he knows helped but that he could never shake—memories so different from those of landing and of running down the moonlit path and of taking the right at the fork in the road, or of the British woman (herself trapped in Occupied France) who brought him food while he hid in a barn for a week.[223] He can remember the second safe house, where a Resistance leader said he'd be shot if he couldn't prove he was a downed Canadian airman, and, some weeks later, the moment of betrayal when he and three other Allied airmen were pulled from a car in Paris and beaten by jackbooted Gestapo agents. The memories of Fresnes Prison, where he had so little food he passed blood, where fleas and lice infested his clothes, and the sounds of other prisoners being beaten and shot there are also clear. He sees the bed changes in the night in Buchenwald's infirmary, the *Doktor* barking out orders that barely registered in his feverish brain, as through a glass darkly.

Few who entered Buchenwald's infirmary lived. The guttural order that hovers still in Carter-Edwards's consciousness came from the *Doktor*, who followed the principle laid down by the camp's first Kommandant, Karl-Otto Koch: "There are no sick men in my camp. They are either well or dead!"[224] The word *Krematorium* that the *Doktor* pronounced on his daily rounds meant "kill this one"—usually with an injection of carbolic acid, followed by a fiery end.

Carter-Edwards survived for two reasons. First, at night the orderlies "submerged" the Canadian delirious with fever; that is, they moved him from bed to bed so that the *Doktor* would not recall him from the day before and order his death. The orderlies, who belonged to the Communist underground, took this risk because they saw Carter-Edwards and the other Allied airmen as military leaders for their planned uprising. The second reason he survived was that one night he heard a voice that he not only understood but for some reason trusted, telling him to stand. When he did, Professor Alfred Balachowsky, whose work at the Pasteur Institute interested the SS enough to ignore the fact that he was Jewish and to assign him the laboratories at Buchenwald, stuck a large needle in Carter-Edwards's back and into his infected lung. As he pulled back on the syringe's plunger, he drew into the needle many cc's worth of infected fluid, saving Carter-Edwards's life.

3 OCTOBER 1944, MILAG UND MARLAG NORD, NEAR BREMEN, GERMANY

George Shaker Learns the Details of D-Day

It was, all in all, a good day.

Toward evening, a lecture by a Royal Marines commando captured in Normandy thrilled George Shaker and the other men from the *A.D. Huff*. Lieutenant Hart whet their appetite with stories of training in Scotland. Then he told of D-Day—of tens of thousands of men marching into hundreds of ships, of hundreds of planes towing gliders, of the parachutists, of the huge naval guns and of the landings on the beaches the Kriegies now learned were named Gold, Juno, Sword, Omaha and Utah. He told them of his dash across the beach, of capturing two villages and of being captured in a third. Not even hearing of the men who died terrible deaths dampened their mood. For Hart's words fleshed out the BBC reports and what the flights of hundreds of Allied planes above heralded.

And that morning, Shaker and some of his shipmates received personal parcels. The cold and rainy weather that had set in early (and which would soon both bog down the Western Allies and slow the Russian juggernaut) made the warm clothes all the more welcome. The thousands of cigarettes, sent in packages of 500 from the T. Eaton and Hudson's Bay companies, too cheered the men, even as their arrival triggered one of the inexorable laws of economics. On the black market, the price of 100 cigarettes fell by more than half, to between 30 and 35 reichsmarks.

5 OCTOBER 1944, BUCHENWALD CONCENTRATION CAMP, WEIMAR, GERMANY

John Harvie Watches in Horror as Military Discipline Frays

The morale and nutritional boost provided by the arrival of some 2,000 Danish policemen could not have come at a better time. For weeks the Allied airmen had subsisted on tasteless, dry sawdust-enhanced *Brot*, made somewhat more palatable by rubbing garlic on it, and an intermittent ration of "sausage" paste that even dogs ran from. Near starvation had caused ribs to appear and bodies to retreat further into the amorphous clothes that provided no protection against the cold winds blowing through the wide avenues of Buchenwald. Military discipline, which Squadron Leader Phil Lamason (the Senior British Officer in the camp) moved on their first day in Buchenwald to enforce, produced, the airmen believed, a pool of mental strength necessary for them to survive. On 5 October, the bonds of discipline frayed when, after the midday soup did not even approach sating his hunger, a flyer "broke ranks and ran to the food tubs which were about to be carted back to the kitchen."[225]

All knew the hopelessness of finding anything in a tub, for as disgusting as the slop was, the men who ladled it out made sure nothing went to waste, any amount that wasn't divided by the ladle's own justice being distributed by way of a lottery. The flyer's hunger they knew too. More frighteningly, each step he took toward the food tubs measured the distance each of them was from violating his own oath, the man's footsteps marking the path from being "an officer and gentleman" to the final collapse into the Hobbesian world, where those whose strength was not completed wasted stole food from the weak.

Divided among the more than 80,000 souls in Buchenwald, the Danes' food could have supplied only a few calories or grams of fat or protein per person. Although committed to a concentration camp, the Danish police thought of themselves as prisoners of war and so gravitated toward the Allied airmen, with whom they generously shared their food. Even this largesse would not last long, but for a few days, John Harvie and the other Allied airmen tasted sweetness or the unctuousness of fat, which lifted spirits and, if not filling bellies, held off the inner beast for a while.

15 OCTOBER 1944, MILAG UND MARLAG NORD, NEAR BREMEN, GERMANY

Shaker's Diary Records the Quickening Tempo of the War

Shaker's diary records the ferrets' discovery of the tunnel that had been in use for two months and the stately progress of fleets of bombers, the dull thud of their bombs exploding somewhere near

Bremen providing the bass line. The war news seemingly spills forth so fast that on 8 October, Shaker resorts to bullet points:

- *American 1st army made small breakthrough around Achen*
- *Canadians have a hard struggle in Holland*
- *Russians staring heavy offensives and wiping up back territory*
- *Landing on Greece progressing favourably*
- *Largest air-raid over Germany yesterday*

A day later, his diary tells of the capture in Holland of four Canadian soldiers, who arrived at the POW camp ragged and torn, and in need of medical attention. He knew of the impending liberation of Budapest by the Red Army. Shaker errs by thinking the glowing night sky meant that the important naval base at Wilhelmshaven had been bombed; the 1,000-plane RAF raid was, in fact, against Brunswick and caused a firestorm that killed hundreds and destroyed much of the city.

MID-OCTOBER 1944, *ARBEITSKOMMANDO* OF STALAG XI-B, FALLINGBOSTEL, GERMANY

George Reid Is Beaten

The foreman at the *Arbeitskommando* did nothing when, on his first day in the salt mine, George Reid insulted the Reich by saying, "Ah, in Canada *nicht Schaufel* [not shovels]. All is machine."[226] The German got his revenge a few days later when, after accusing Reid of spitting at him, he beat the Canadian. The trigger for two further beatings, one with a pick handle, was the foreman's frustration at not being able to finger who was sabotaging the mine's electrical system; Reid, as it happens, was not responsible.

After an altercation with another guard, Reid served an official sentence that, like the beatings, violated Geneva. He was locked for an entire shift in a room that was so filled with salt dust that the Germans did not let prisoners work in it for more than two hours at a time. After ten hours, his "throat felt like someone had run a wire brush down it" and he coughed up blood.[227] The salt burned his eyes, making them so sore that opening or closing them was a struggle, while the jagged edges of the miniscule shards of salt crystal ripped open the lining of his nose, which bled copiously.

16 OCTOBER 1944, BUCHENWALD CONCENTRATION CAMP, WEIMAR, GERMANY

Carter-Edwards Owes His Life to a Brave Dutchman

In the quarry, men whose skeletons were barely covered by paper-thin skin chipped out stones using picks and sledgehammers. There, bored guards took aim at prisoners covered in sweat and dust, or soaked by the rain, and then shot them for target practice. Today, second growth hides the scars in the earth carved by thousands of men, many of whom died, their bodies dragged back to the main camp, where they escaped the torment set in the pleasant hills of Thuringia the only way possible: "up the smokestack." It is to this *Steinbruch*, or literally, "place of stone breaking," that Carter-Edwards was ordered on the morning he was released from the infirmary.

The walk from the *Appellplatz* to the quarry took Carter-Edwards's work commando past the gallows, past where three of his fellow Canadians had breathed their last, and through the SS compound, where Carter-Edwards saw the SS bandshell and a building that held the SS *Kasino*. But none of this registered in his befogged brain, which managed, still, to direct one foot in front of the other.

"My only clear memory is of that brave Dutchman, Kurt Baars, who must have been the foreman. When I reached the quarry, he took me aside and said that I was clearly too sick to work there and that he was going to put my name on the list as having died. 'You're going to go back to the infirmary. How you survive [there] is up to you, but this is all I can do to save your life,' he said," recalls Carter-Edwards in a tone of reverence for Baars's risk.

16 OCTOBER 1944, STALAG XX-A, TORUŃ, POLAND

IAN MACDONALD IMAGINES HIS MOTHER IN THE KITCHEN

At least his mail, though not the packages his mother carefully packed for him, had started arriving again, so Ian MacDonald knew that, three months earlier, his parents had been well. The letters did strange things to time. No matter when the letter was written, POWs tended to read them as if they had been written just a few days earlier, and they had the effect of transporting the POWs back to Canada in an almost "cinematic" way. He "saw" his house and yard in the spring, when the trees were leafing and the flowers, coming up. He was as if at home watching the garden come to life, and his mother at the stove, an apron over her housedress, making apple preserves to use in pies.

The card written on 16 October arrived in Lourdes, Nova Scotia, on 21 December, while the letter he wrote at the beginning of October arrived on Christmas Eve. Though the letter dealt with what could appear as a serious topic—forced inoculations—MacDonald adopts a jocular tone, saying, "We'll probably be riddled with needles when we get back." The card doesn't mention the inoculations, but its banter reflects better than did the letter's assurance that his arm "wasn't too sore" that he had suffered no ill effects from the inoculations.

On Christmas Eve, as the MacDonald family knelt to pray at midnight mass, they could not help but think about how, at the beginning of October, Ian was already thinking about their reception of his letter at Christmastime, and that on that holy night MacDonald's overriding emotion was his desire for freedom.

21 OCTOBER 1944, BUCHENWALD CONCENTRATION CAMP, WEIMAR, GERMANY

Thanks to Reichsmarhsall Hermann Göring, Harvie and 156 Allied Airmen Leave Buchenwald

The Allied airmen's hopes rose when they heard that officials from Berlin would be coming to Buchenwald to investigate what even Kommandant Hermann Pister admitted was the mistaken commitment of the Allied airmen to the concentration camp. To help the officials establish that they were indeed airmen—and hence came under Geneva—Squadron Leader Phil Lamason ordered the airmen to go beyond giving only their name, rank and service number to also say when they were shot down and what squadron they belonged to; they were still, however, to refuse to answer any question that would tip off the Germans about the Resistance.

On 21 October, the airmen's fading hope turned to anxiety when they were ordered to assemble at the *Effektenkammer*, the storage building where the SOE agents had been ordered to surrender their personal effects before being marched to the *Leichenkeller* to be murdered. The airmen knew that their identity cards were stamped with the acronym DIKAL (*Darf in kein anderes Lager)*, which meant "Not to be transferred to another camp," and that Berlin had authorized kangaroo courts to try to execute what Goebbles called Luftgangsters or *Terrorfliegers*.

Instead, they found themselves in the final moments of a bureaucratic affair that began when a Russian prisoner who worked at a nearby airbase gave a note Lamason had written to a Luftwaffe officer telling of the airmen's plight. Sometime later, two Luftwaffe officers, including Luftwaffe ace (58 victories) Hannes Trautloft came to Buchenwald, ostensibly to inspect the damage caused by the Allied bombings. In reality, however, he came to meet with Lamason to determine whether he and the other "airmen" were in fact airmen and not spies. Trautloft's report, which told of the imprisonment of the Allied airmen, landed on Hermann Göring's desk. The Reichsmarshall demanded that his officials get the airmen out of Heinrich Himmler's bureaucratic empire and transferred to his.

Inside the *Effektenkammer*, the vaunted German bureaucracy returned to each airman the shabby clothing he'd worn when hustled out of Fresnes Prison, clothing that provided scant protection against the October cold. For the men who had been captured wearing their cut-down flying boots, the fleece lining provided the first soft and warm sensation they had experienced in months. Then the SS cross-checked numbers with identities, and the Luftwaffe officers checked each name against the nominal role authorized by Berlin. Finally, as the rain fell, the SS, unwilling to miss a chance to impress Göring's men, provided a row of black-uniformed, machine-gun-toting troops who marched the 156 Allied airmen to the gate that when closed left behind 12 men, including Carter-Edwards and his fellow Canadian, Harry Bastable, and the American Roy Allen in the infirmary.

22 OCTOBER 1944, SAINT-JEAN-SUR-RICHELIEU, QUEBEC

Jacqueline Writes to Her Fiancé, Jacques Nadeau

The unseasonably warm weather that graced the small town along Quebec's Richelieu River only intensified her loneliness. But in a mirror image of the tens of thousands of letters POWs wrote that strove to maintain their position within their families, Jacqueline's letter shows that, despite his absence, Jacques Nadeau remained present. "Where is a small prisoner who awaits his hour of deliverance?"[227]—which in her native French is less a question about location than about time—she writes and then assures him, "*Oui,*

Jacques, elle sonnera bientôt cette heure" (Yes, Jacques, the bell will soon toll that hour). Her prayers at morning mass asked that her fiancé come home safely.

Aware that he would not be reading her words for months, Jacqueline continues, "When you receive this letter, the winter's coat of snow will probably cover the ground. It might even be 1945." These sentences do more than tritely take into account the time lag between when the letter was written and when it would be read. By sketching Nadeau's world as it exists when he reads the letter, Jacqueline placed herself in his time frame. Though the snow would not fall for months, she was writing about the scene as the snow crunched beneath his feet at Appell the morning the letter arrived at Stalag II-D, in Pomerania. By extending the period before Nadeau received the letter into 1945, Jacqueline was being realistic; by late October, no one believed that the war would end before 1945. Rather, Jacqueline brackets time and space so that even though they are separated, in the way that matters to Nadeau, she is with him in his present.

LATE OCTOBER 1944, STALAG LUFT III, SAGAN, POLAND

Harvie Has Trouble Adjusting to a POW Camp

Later they would learn about the 50 men murdered after the Great Escape. Later still, some of the men of the self-styled Konzentrationslager Buchenwald (Buchenwald Concentration Camp) club would come to feel that the Kriegies they met at Stalag Luft III, who had electric lights, regular if meagre food, and amenities such as toothpaste and single bunks, lacked, as RAF Squadron Leader Stanley Booker said (somewhat unkindly), "the soul, the magic of real companionship and dependence on each other."[228]

But in the hours after leaving Buchenwald, while in boxcars loaded with only 25 men, a pot of ersatz coffee warming on a small coke stove, Harvie and the others could not believe their good fortune. Over the course of the three-day trip they ate bread, margarine and sausage, and, once each day, real soup prepared by a field kitchen. The guards were still armed, but they were old enough to be the airmen's fathers and were shocked at what they heard about the men's treatment in Buchenwald.

As they walked the two miles from the siding to the POW camp, instead of the foul smell of death, their noses were filled with the scent of pine. Instead of the dance of death by human skeletons behind electrified barbed wire, they saw men in uniforms playing football, and RAF and Luftwaffe officers on the sidelines watching the game. Instead of being ordered to strip to be sheared like sheep, Harvie and the others were led to a shower room, where "they were able to luxuriate without harassment, in the delightful warm water, with smooth Red Cross toilet soap, and . . . dry themselves, not on rags as [at] their last shower in Buchenwald, but on fresh white towels also supplied by the Red Cross." Instead of stained rags or worn clothing stolen from those burned in the ovens, they were given uniforms, two sets of clean underwear, socks and two shirts. Instead of being led to a rock-strewn field or desperately overcrowded barracks, they were led to a barracks with pictures of loved ones pinned to the walls; with cubby holes for personal possessions; with bunks, one for each man; and with tables complete with plates, knives and forks. Even a gramophone played music.

The same latrine and "Smelly Nelly" that had so distressed Father Goudreau years earlier delighted Harvie. Later Harvie would learn that hunger stalked Stalag Luft III. Given their wretched condition, it was unlikely that any of the new arrivals was a German plant, but with a new tunnel begun, the Escape Committee took no chances. After the execution of the 50 escapers, the Kriegies feared that as the Reich crumbled, Hitler would order the execution of all Allied POWs. Therefore, instead of leading out of the camp, "George" led toward the German guards' compound, where if necessary the POWs would seize weapons and fight their way toward whichever Allied army was closest. Unlike when the Germans discovered "Tom," the discovery of this tunnel would endanger Father Goudreau; he could hardly have claimed ignorance of the escape tunnel that began immediately behind his chapel.

Harvie was interrogated a few hours after he attended his first church service since the one at which his squadron asked for God's help on D-Day. The following Monday, after having been initiated into the mysteries of circuit bashing, Harvie was given his first high-protein Red Cross parcel. Later that day, he received his full security clearance, which meant that, though no longer a bombardier and still so weak that he could barely make one circuit, he was again a man at war.

LATE OCTOBER 1944, VICTORIA, BRITISH COLUMBIA

Hubert and Winsome Blenkinsop Learn Something about What Happened to Their Son

Although written by a lowly British signals corps driver named Ernest Betts, the letter was like manna from heaven. One day, Betts had stopped at a country house near Webbekom, Belgium, to barter for some eggs. Welcomed into the Pypens' house, he saw a photo of what he took to be an RAF officer. When he asked who he was, the family told him that they had hidden RCAF Squadron Leader Edward Blenkinsop in the weeks leading up to 11 August. Betts's letter showed that Hubert and Winsome's son had survived the crash of his Lancaster bomber, and he had known kindness. Not only this, but he "was not hurt much," wrote Betts. His abbreviated story of Blenkinsop trying to teach the Pypens' three daughters English sounded so much like their Teddy. The Pypens, who "thought the world of him," were, Betts told the parents in Victoria, "very lucky not to have been shot for hiding him."[229]

Betts probably knew more than he wrote. No censor would

have allowed the words through telling of Blenkinsop being blown out of his Lancaster bomber and landing so hard he dislocated his shoulder and was knocked out. Likewise, Betts could not write what he knew of Blenkinsop's move from safe house to safe house, or that for a few weeks he had lived in a vermin-infested hovel. And delicacy might have kept the Pypens from telling Betts that, the morning after Blenkinsop arrived, Mrs. Pypen found him in tears from the incessant itching, the shame of wearing lousy rags and the fear that he might infect the children of his benefactors. According to Paula Pypen, who was then 18 years old and smitten with the airman, her mother did more than just wash the Canadian evader again and disinfect the bedding; she cared for him as she would have her son, who would have been the same age had he not died when he was little. Betts likely also knew of Blenkinsop's plan of waiting for the advancing Allied armies to reach him. But in early August, following the murder of a prominent local collaborator, the SS moved to settle accounts with the Resistance. Blenkinsop was arrested with the Pypens' son, Jos, and another man as they ran from the Pypen farm moments after word arrived that the SS had started mass arrests in the village.

St. Gilles Prison, where Blenkinsop was taken after being arrested, already held some 50 Allied airmen. Ironically, the prison named for the patron saint of fear of night was a Bruxellois version of Fresnes, another island of torment shrouded by what the Gestapo itself called *Nacht und Nebel*—Night and Fog. In addition to the beatings, isolation and putrid food, the Germans staged mock executions, which Blenkinsop knew about because other officers tapped out word of these horrors in Morse code on the prison's pipes.

Word that Blenkinsop had been seen alive in Belgium heartened the pilot's family in Victoria, who paid special attention to the news stories that told of the Canadian Army's advance toward Belgium. They had no way of knowing, however, that on 30 August, German guards evacuated St. Gilles Prison.

Even as 40,000 German soldiers fled Holland and Belgium, the SS made plain its demands: each prisoner was to prepare two parcels; one with toiletries and some food to be taken with them, and another with valuables that would be sent on later. Shoved into trucks and then cattle cars, the prisoners were in various states of shock and panic. The moment of elation vanished quickly when the train stopped almost as soon as it started. For instead of the doors being slid open by Allied troops, whose guns could be heard in the distance, or by Resistance workers, the train sat under a baking sun for hours.

As was true of so many other trains filled with civilian men, women and children—and POWs—there was not enough room for everyone to lie down. Nor, of course, was there adequate food or water. As October passed into November, the train crossed into Germany. Just after midnight on 3 November, it reached a suburb of Hamburg. Then, Blenkinsop and 52 other Allied airmen and more than 300 Belgian prisoners disappeared into the Neuengamme Concentration Camp.

9 NOVEMBER 1944, AT A TRAIN STATION ON THE WAY TO STALAG LUFT III

Carter-Edwards Is Amazed That German Soldiers Protect Him

The stamp on his POW record is clear. Carter-Edwards was transferred to Stalag Luft III on 9 November 1944. The words spoken by a Luftwaffe officer are, however, less distinct. All that mattered was that after 101 days, Carter-Edwards was about to leave Buchenwald.

"I don't remember gathering up anything or even how we arrived at the train," says Carter-Edwards. "Harry Bastable who, like Carter-Edwards, had been shot down on 8 June 1944], who had also been in the infirmary when the rest of the boys left, told me we left the camp together. The only part of the trip to Stalag Luft III I remember is when, at one of the stops, the guards wanted to get something to eat, so they led us out of the train car and into the station. It didn't take long for the people in the station to realize we were airmen—*Terrorflieger*—and they soon started threatening us. The guards pointed their rifles at the crowd and, to protect us, led us back to the train."

MID-NOVEMBER 1944, STALAG LUFT III, SAGAN, POLAND

HARVIE FINDS THAT A CHURCH SERVICE MAKES HIM HOMESICK

Since arriving at Stalag Luft III, Harvie had been initiated into the mysteries of tin smithing, tunnel engineering and how ferrets searched for tunnels; how a well-timed cup of real coffee, piece of chocolate or cigarette could suborn a guard; and, amazingly enough, ballroom dancing. When he first saw the paper on the bulletin board offering dancing lessons, he thought it was "a subtle British joke" but soon found that the men viewed these classes as seriously as they did those in accounting or the common law, or the lecture by the Kriegie who once raced at Monte Carlo.[230] The presence of three of his barracks mates in the class did not lessen his nervousness when he went to his first lesson. The instructor drew on a blackboard, mapping out foot movements with the precision of a navigator.

Harvie was surprised by his reaction to dancing with the male instructor, who took the female part. It took only moments, but the drab barracks in the middle of Silesia in a camp that held 40,000 dissolved as he fantasized about asking a girl at the Ritz-Carleton in Montreal to dance and surprising her with his footwork. In his daydream, Harvie held the girl in his arms as he "effortlessly led her through the most intricate steps and routines. . . . We would retire to the candlelit table in the corner where, holding hands, she would easily persuade me to talk about my heroic wartime adventures." When the reverie ended, he saw another POW "with a faraway look on his face humming to himself while taking odd little steps and turns" and knew that, for at least a few moments, he too was dancing with his girl.

Five weeks earlier, just after arriving at the POW camp, had Harvie talked to Father Goudreau after Sunday services, he likely would have agreed with the priest's complaint that the men were not devout enough. Now, the Canadian pilot had stopped going to Padre Douglas Thompson's services, though not because he had suffered a crisis of faith. Rather, he found that, far from linking him to the Divine or to his family back home, the hymns and music he had learned as a child made him unbearably homesick.

20 NOVEMBER 1944, DEUTSCHE WERFT SHIPYARDS, NEAR HAMBURG

Blenkinsop Is a Slave Labourer

The letter from Squadron Leader W.R. Gunn shattered the hopes the Blenkinsops had carefully built on corpsman Betts's letter. True, Blenkinsop had survived the crash of his plane, but he was now under a death sentence for having been caught out of uniform. Hoping that a statement from Sir Anthony Eden might save their son, the Blenkinsops wrote to him; their decision to work through the British foreign secretary showing just how underdeveloped Canada's machinery for dealing with its POWs was.

Unlike Reid, who was given every Sunday off and laboured in the dry salt mine, during the coldest and wettest winter in generations, Blenkinsop slaved away outside at the Deutsche Werft shipyards near Hamburg, wearing only a paper tunic and wooden sandals. Day after day without any breaks, Blenkinsop's day started in the middle of the night. At noon, he and the other slave labourers were given their one meal: 200 grams of sour black bread, 10 grams of margarine and the ubiquitous watery soup. By late November, the Canadian, who shivered through the night on a paillasse while sharing a thin blanket with a prisoner named François Fernand, had fallen desperately ill.

4 DECEMBER 1944, MILAG UND MARLAG NORD, NEAR BREMEN, GERMANY

Les Religieux Hear the Promise of Repatriation

Many POWs report that even as conditions in the camps became harsher because Allied bombing prevented the transportation of coal from the Ruhr Valley, guards became friendlier and some Kommandants relaxed a few rules. Earlier in the war, when each was serving in adjoining parts of Milag und Marlag Nord, the SS had prevented Fathers Barsalou and Bergeron from meeting for sacramental purposes. Now, however, for the second time in just a few months, some of *les religieux* were attending a religious retreat.

Just after finishing the mass, Father Pâquet announced, "The [Swiss] ambassador delegate is in the camp in order to tell you some very happy news." Later, toward the end of the retreat banquet, which consisted of chickens and duck, Pâquet rose and, with a glass of wine in his hand, said, "Those passengers who remain of the *Zamzam* will be repatriated. All that we lack is a boat, and we expect one at the beginning of January." Several of the priests and brothers wept openly. Brother Georges-Aimée Lavallée was not at all surprised that after 66 days of rain, that afternoon the sun shone brightly.

MID-DECEMBER 1944, STALAG LUFT IX-C, MÜHLHAUSEN, GERMANY

Robert Prouse Digs Up Tree Stumps for Firewood

The order to draw their Red Cross parcels was not accompanied by the usual excitement. For according to the Kommandant, these would be their last because of the ceaseless bombing of depots and trains. Combined with the earlier cut-off of coal-dust briquettes, this foretold a sorry Christmas and a cold and hungry winter.

The deep cold soon forced the Germans to agree to allow the POWs to forage for wood to heat their barracks; to heat their own barracks, the Germans imposed a 10 per cent "tax" on them. For the first few trips, the Kriegies had use of an old, sway-backed horse, but it soon died, leaving the weakened men to drag the wood back to camp. Though the POWs could have overpowered the guards "with the Allied advance and constant bombing, plus the increasing itchiness of the Jerrys' gun fingers," recalls Prouse, there was no point in doing so.[231] Further, had they made a break for freedom, the Kommandant would have cancelled all future foraging parties, and those left behind would have remained desperately cold.

The foragers used some of their dwindling supply of Canadian cigarettes to bribe guards, who not only allowed the POWs to remain unguarded in a room in the guest house where they ate lunch but also bought them good stout German beer. Several hundred miles away, at a POW camp near Schivelbein, Poland, not far from the frigid Baltic Sea, Stan Darch paid a teamster a pack of cigarettes to bring his wife a ball of yarn that came from worn-out socks to knit the POW a pair of gloves. For her troubles, Darch paid her with a bar of Camay soap.

18 DECEMBER 1944, STALAG XVIII-A, WOLFSBERG, AUSTRIA

FATHER JUNEAU SURVIVES A BOMBING RAID

The POW knew that while the fleets that sailed across the Reich's skies, some with more than 1,000 planes, heralded their freedom, they did not come without danger. Near noon on 18 December, six American planes mistakenly dropped their payload on Father Juneau's camp, in Austria.

The blasts threw men some distance away to the ground and killed 48 men, including two doctors in the small hospital, which was all but obliterated. Others, including Joseph Charles Hobling, the Anglican chaplain with whom Juneau shared a room, died in their barracks. Juneau would have died with him, but just as he reached the door to their room, he heard a voice saying not to enter it and he remained in the corridor. Thanks to "God's mercy," he told his parents in a letter written three days later, "I was not even wounded." Providence did not, however, save a French priest.

When the smoke cleared, Juneau saw that the tabernacle had been smashed. Some consecrated Hosts—which Juneau knew were the very body of Christ—lay on the floor among the wreckage, while others lay among the broken plaster, smashed into shards.

24 DECEMBER 1944, MILAG UND MARLAG NORD, NEAR BREMEN, GERMANY

CHRISTMAS EVE

The men at Stalag Luft III knew that there'd be no repetition of 1943's Rabelaisian celebration during which both the Kriegies and goons got so drunk on rotgut whisky that some of the former climbed the inner barbed-wire fence before collapsing in the area between it and the second fence (the Christmas spirit explaining why the guards didn't open fire), and several of the latter ended up sleeping off their drunk under the POWs' bunks. "How could the drab life of a prisoner of war," Harvie wondered, "[have] room for such frivolous things" as Christmas decorations; the answer lay in the chapel.[232] Harvie found there light glinting off the decorations and the chalice, and the white linen napkin in which Father Goudreau held it in the joint service with the Methodist Chaplain, Douglas Thompson. Whether they intensified homesickness, as they did for Harvie, or spun mystic chords linking POWs closer to their families, the carols unleashed a flood of memories, as did the tinned turkey, cranberry sauce and plum pudding in the special Red Cross parcels distributed on Christmas Eve.

At Milag Nord, where the light covering of snow added to the festive atmosphere created by the garland strung around Brother Antoine Lavallée's barracks and the chapel, midnight mass in Stella Maris began at 11 p.m. By contrast, the Kommandant at Stalag VIII-B ordered that the mass be conducted earlier, which is why the chapel was full at 7:30 p.m. when the air-raid siren began to wail, just as Father Desnoyers was preparing the offering and the choir sang "Adeste Fideles." A moment later, the camp lights went out and, as the choir continued singing, a few men rose and put up the blackout curtains. With only enough light for the congregants to see Desnoyers's white chasuble and the shimmering of the chalice, the choir intoned the "Sanctus." The siren's wail had been long forgotten, but the chapel remained in shimmering darkness as the choir sang "Agnus Dei" in celebration of the birth of the Lamb of God.

Near 3 a.m. on Christmas Day, as POWs across Europe lay either sleeping or remembering Christmases past, in one small corner of Westertimke, a subcamp of Milag und Marlag Nord, something akin to the Christmas truce of 1914 occurred. Six days earlier, Father Bergeron had agreed to conduct a second, clandestine midnight mass for 32 guards. The mass was unlike any other Bergeron had ever conducted. At no point were all his congregants present; rather, there was "a continuous coming and going of armed soldiers, of clanking genuflexions, of entrances and exits."[233] Since some soldiers could not be there for the blessing of the Eucharist, to ensure that the mass "counted," Bergeron prepared Hosts for the sentries to take when they arrived—no matter where he was in the service. To lessen the chance that their officers would notice that the sentries had abandoned their posts, for which they would have faced the death penalty, prisoners took their places as the first light of dawn broke on the faux guards' homeland across the sea.

27 DECEMBER 1944, STALAG LUFT III, SAGAN, POLAND

Harvie Wonders about His Family

This being his third Christmas away from home, Stan Darch, who was on a work party on a farm, knew that the buildup to Christmas would lead to a letdown. "It's most memorable for the booze we made from prunes and raisins from the Red Cross parcels. There were 20 of us and there was no ceremony, but we enjoyed the booze we made. And then when alone, of course, I thought of my family," he recalls.

Harvie lay awake on Christmas night wondering if his family even knew he was alive—and if Jean and Bert were married, and Bert already flying with Bomber Command. He picked up his pen and, after writing another letter home and a postcard to friends in Scotland, took out a slip of paper that he had found in the pocket of the flight jacket he'd been given upon arriving at Stalag Luft III. On the paper was a female's name and address, which he assumed came from a girl working in the Birmingham factory that made RAF flight jackets. Perhaps she collected letters from airmen posted to exotic locales. In any case, here he was, a young man forced to cool his heels in a German POW camp, with an address of a girl whose hands had actually touched the jacket that now kept him warm. Later he wrote that he "had fun" writing a postcard to her and imagining her surprise when she heard from a prisoner of war.[234]

28 DECEMBER 1944, VANCOUVER

Mrs. E.M. Callaghan Receives a Curious Letter

The letter that arrived at 1368 West 8th Avenue in Vancouver troubled Derek M. Warner's mother enough to bring it to the attention of Canadian Army officials with whom she worked.

Her son had an expert knowledge of the Vancouver area coastline, yet he had written, "Do you think you could try and get me thru the right connections at your work some D.N.D. 1/25,000 maps. Particularly of the Vancouver area. I would like to get some as they would be very handy for making pleasure trips. I have been doing some work on my Spanish of late and a lot is coming back." From this illogical request, together with other letters to his wife and grandmother telling them not to bother writing because they would soon be seeing him, Canadian intelligence officers determined that he was sending a message through them to MI9: that the soldier captured in Holland on 13 October was busy planning an escape.

31 DECEMBER 1944, MILAG UND MARLAG NORD, NEAR BREMEN, GERMANY

Stuart Kettles Sees Airmen Die Terrible Deaths

Thirteen hours before the turning of the year, on Brother Antoine Lavallée's 1,354th day of captivity, Kettles and the other POWs at Milag und Marlag Nord watched the sky in awe and horror. As much as they were awed by hundreds of bombers attacking targets in and around Hamburg, and by the huge clouds of black smoke that billowed into the sky, presumably from burning oil tanks, they were horrified by the human cost they saw when planes broke apart.

Lavallée wrote of "white parachutes balancing for what seemed long periods in the clear blue sky." Kettles was stunned by the sight of one parachutist turning from a white blossom into a fireball that fell to earth. Then he saw two of a group of four burn. Elsewhere in the sky, nine men jumped from one plane, and one man's chute did not open. It was, he later wrote, "a hard thing to watch him come down, his arms and legs dangling in all directions." He saw the man slam into the ground and his lifeless body then bounce almost 20 feet in the air.

Chapter Fourteen

January–March 1945

The times are nightfall, look, their light grows less;
The times are winter, watch, a world undone:
They waste, they wither worse; they as they run
Or bring more or more blazon man's distress.

—Gerard Manley Hopkins,
"The Times Are Nightfall"

5 JANUARY 1945, STALAG LUFT III, SAGAN, POLAND

John Harvie Worries about What Imprisonment Will Have Done to His Male Prowess

Even for someone raised in the Laurentian Mountains north of Montreal, the cold and snow were remarkable. The footsteps of tens of thousands of men were not enough to tamp down the continuous snow that fell on the *Appellplatz*. Still, had he not twisted his right knee by slipping on a patch of ice, John Harvie would have been out bashing the circuit, readying himself for the long walk to freedom. Another cut in their bread ration increased the siren call of their Red Cross parcels, but the Kriegies resisted dipping into the stock they knew they'd need soon. Yet even as the excitement built after BBC reported the start of the Russian winter offensive and someone quickly figured out that, at the rate they were advancing, the Reds would reach Stalag Luft III by the end of the month, the daily rhythms of the camp continued.

Of equal concern to the men was a debate sparked by the repatriation of a Royal Navy Fleet Air Arm flight lieutenant, whose claim of mental illness from "self-abuse" was accepted by Red Cross medical officials. Though steeped in Victorian values, thanks to the spread of Freudianism, and devotees of pictures of Hollywood starlets like the buxom Rita Hayworth, the Kriegies had a much more public consciousness of sexuality than did prisoners taken in the First World War. Military leaders did not, of course, encourage masturbation, but they took a less jaundiced view of young men than did religious leaders, who decried the sin of onanism, and doctors, who linked it to mental illness. On a ship steaming toward Dieppe, for example, Lieutenant Colonel Cecil Merritt roused the men of the South Saskatchewan Regiment from their hammocks with the words "Hands off your cocks, pull on your socks!"[235] The Kriegies discussed in worried tones what their long years away from women would do to their male prowess.

14 JANUARY 1945, MILAG UND MARLAG NORD, NEAR BREMEN, GERMANY

Les Religieux Discover They Are Not Being Repatriated

The announcement over the tinny loudspeaker that 45 American civilians were to be repatriated raised the Oblates' and Christian brothers' hopes. Word that 86 sick men would also be repatriated brought their emotions to a fever pitch. When the expected third announcement did not come, *les religieux* realized that, despite what the Swiss delegate promised in December, their prayers to be delivered from the sombre life of the prisoner of war had not yet been answered. Though happy for their American friends, they were pained by the realization that it was God's will that they not awake from their four-year-long nightmare.

18–19 JANUARY 1945, SUDETEN MOUNTAINS, CZECHOSLOVAKIA

John Grogan Is Freezing and Hungry on the Roads of Germany

The order to evacuate the camp came earlier in the morning than the usual guttural "*Raus*," but it was not a surprise. For several nights running, John Grogan and the other men (including about 12 who had been prisoners since being captured at Dieppe) at a farm labour camp had seen the flashes of Russian guns not 30 miles away. Before leaving the camp on the morning of 18 January, each man was given as many Red Cross parcels as he could carry.

The sky was clear and the weather a dry cold of -25°C, which made snow crunch and skin burn. Still, despite their shivers, Grogan was in good humour, knowing that whatever the guards said about the evacuation being necessary to save the POWs from falling into the hands of the Bolsheviks, his freedom beckoned ever closer.[236] His mood darkened considerably when the sun began to set and he saw armed guards wearing warm boots and greatcoats prod more than a hundred ill-clad emaciated men and women (almost certainly from one of the many subcamps connected to nearby Auschwitz), each with a yellow Star of David pinned to their clothing, down a snow-choked road. Grogan had no way of knowing that on a nearby road RCAF Flying Officer John Patterson, who had been a prisoner at an *Arbeitskommando* connected to Auschwitz, was falling so ill from pleurisy, tuberculosis and a foot infection that the German doctors placed him in the hospital.

A few hours later, the POWs reached another *Arbeitskommando*, where they hoped they would spend the night, for the temperature had fallen another seven degrees. But they were soon ordered back onto the road. As ice formed on the POWs' eyebrows and around their mouths, and the wind whipped away what warmth their bodies produced, Grogan saw guards burning documents and wondered what crimes they sought to hide.

The next day, the swirling snow seemingly summoned ghosts of the Royal Regiment: Joe Coffey, Ernie Good and Grogan's childhood friend, Earl Ricard, who drew their last breaths on the beaches of Dieppe. Cursing the heatless burning of his feet and face, Grogan remembered how during route marches in England their sergeants had bucked up the men out of fatigue with a word or two.

The Catholic from the Ottawa Valley, who drew strength from the Scapular of the Sacred Heart that hung around his neck, grieved for his dead and suffering comrades—and for "old men and children, potato bags covering their heads and shoulders to ward off the bitter cold, eye holes cut in them like Halloween masks.[237]

21–23 JANUARY 1945, ON A ROAD IN UPPER SILESIA, POLAND

ANDREW CARSWELL FINDS SHAME FEELS WORSE THAN FREEZING COLD

The Canadians, including Andrew Carswell, Father Louis Larivière and Father Desnoyers (who had recently been transferred to Stalag VIII-B), knew the hardships they and the thousand other men being evacuated from the POW camp in Lamsdorf were about to face on the snowy roads on a -17°C night. Still, as much as he was a prisoner of war who guarded the justice in the cutting of the hard black German bread and learned to parse out his Red Cross parcel, Desnoyers was first and foremost a priest. While around the camp, men packed the contents of hastily distributed Red Cross parcels into rucksacks, backpacks and, in a few cases, bags on makeshift sleds, Desnoyers gave his attention to a German guard who came with tears in his eyes asking for a benediction before leading the POWs on what the guard knew would be a terrible march and for which no provisions had been made.

Whatever joy the marchers felt at leaving the barbed wire behind them was tempered by the howling winds and the knowledge that, although the guards' rifles were not tipped by cold steel, they were loaded. Carswell's worldly possessions—a blanket, some extra clothing and a Canadian Red Cross parcel—were in an RAF kit bag slung over his back. Seeking to conserve every calorie their bodies had as they marched through ten inches of snow, the men hunched over and shoved their hands hard into their pockets. The ten minutes every hour given over to rest may have been necessary to conserve strength on this first night of their march to Görlitz, 60 miles to the northeast. Yet as the Canadians knew well, standing in the snow wasted scarce body heat, so they stamped their feet. Late that night, the crooked line of humanity stopped at a barn, where soon more than 1,000 men collapsed into sleep on damp, foul-smelling straw crawling with vermin.

A decade older than most of the Kriegies, Desnoyers found it difficult to start moving in the 3 a.m. chill. Red Cross parcels provided nourishment, but the absence of anything hot, even the reviled ersatz coffee, meant the men remained cold. Later, under bright sunlight, they passed frozen farms. Unfolding across the bleak landscape were scenes akin to those they'd seen on newsreels of the fall of France five years earlier: groups of refugees, their clothing torn and tattered, pushing baby carriages or carts loaded with whatever remained of their lives, their situation made all the worse by snowdrift-blocked roads, howling winds and sub-zero temperatures.

Carswell never knew who the female prisoners shivering on the ice and snow on the side of the road were. Perhaps because of the watch kept by the warmly dressed and well-fed guards, perhaps because the prisoners—just a handful of the thousands of men and women around them who were the detritus of a war that was on its way to claiming 40 million lives, including 25 million civilians—had fallen so deep into hunger or into a cold-induced stupor, they looked at Carswell's column but, he felt, did not see them. None made eye contact. Then one woman, whom Carswell guessed to be about his age, looked expressionless at him. Their eyes met for an instant and he thought, "She must have been very beautiful at one time." Then they both glanced away, and the man who had bailed out of a burning plane and endured years in captivity felt shame for not being able to do something for this woman on a frozen stretch of road in the middle of Europe. In the days to come, as dysentery set in and men soiled themselves, shame was an emotion that none could afford to feel.[238]

23 JANUARY 1945, NEUENGAMME CONCENTRATION CAMP, NEAR HAMBURG

TEDDY BLENKINSOP DOES NOT DIE ALONE

The letter arrived in June 1945 and confirmed what Edward Blenkinsop's parents already knew: their son was dead.

There were some things to hold on to. He had not been tortured to death. He had not died alone; François Fernand and a few others were with him. As tuberculosis ravaged Blenkinsop's lungs, his fellow POWs tried to find him wholesome food. Neither at Neuengamme nor at the Deutsche Werft shipyards could the vital calories and nutrients be found. Nor could medicine be found in a camp where the bodies of more than 50,000 men, women and children were reduced to ash in ovens.[239]

By the time Fernand wrote to his friend's parents, the horrors of Auschwitz, Bergen-Belsen, Buchenwald and Treblinka had been splashed across the pages of Canada's newspapers and seen in newsreels. From these images, Blenkinsop's parents in Victoria had some idea of the wretched conditions their son lived through during his last days: the overcrowded barracks; the bare wooden shelves that served as bunks; and the raw, barren landscape. They'd seen pictures of desiccated humanity—bone-thin men and women with sunken eyes and shaved heads. They'd read of slave labour camps. Little would have distinguished the bodies shown in the newsreels from the body, wasted to 100 or fewer pounds, they never did see and which during the last week of January wheezed toward death.

Blenkinsop's body was treated no differently from any of the other millions killed by Germany's willing executioners. It was burned. Hidden in the camp and later found and given to Mrs. Pypen were his escape compass and signet ring. Wanting to keep something of Teddy's, the woman who had washed the Canadian's lousy body kept the compass but arranged to have the ring sent to the mother who grieved for the only uniformed Canadian serviceman to die in a concentration camp.

27 JANUARY 1945, ON A FARM IN POMERANIA, GERMANY

Jacques Nadeau and Other Canadian POWs Are Saved by the Word "*Amerikanski*"

With the Russian troops so close, Jacques Nadeau and a number of other Canadians on a farm in far eastern Germany saw the Germans round up old men and adolescents, give them an hour's training with a rifle and then march them off to the front; by March, more than 60,000 16- and 17-year-olds were in the German army. On the 26th, the Germans ordered the Kriegies out into the frigid Pomeranian air for a march to the west, which gave Nadeau and the other Canadians the opportunity to hide. Shortly after the column departed and as Nadeau began to worry about how Stalin's troops would treat them, the guards, having come up two POWs short in a count, returned and found the would-be escapers.

A few moments after Nadeau was locked into a room on the second floor, artillery began pummelling the stone building. As he hugged the floor, Nadeau wondered if the Russians would take the same slow, leap-frogging approach his unit would have made toward the house. Even once the explosions and machine gunning stopped, fearful of being shot by a sniper, Nadeau remained beneath the window. When he heard French prisoners call out to the Russians, he shouted through the shattered window for someone to come open the door.

The Russians looked warily at the soldiers in unfamiliar uniforms who walked from the blasted château with their hands clearly visible. Knowing that hundreds of thousands of Ukrainians had either joined or been pressed into the Wehrmacht, the Russians' suspicions were scarcely allayed when two soldiers belonging to the South Saskatchewan Regiment spoke to them in Ukrainian. Seeing that "*Kanadesky*" meant nothing to the Russians, Nadeau suggested using the term "North Americans." Upon hearing this, the Russians' attitude changed; yelling "*Amerikanski! Amerikanski!*" they kissed them on their cheeks and even their mouths.[240]

28 JANUARY 1945, NEAR SAGAN, POLAND

THE HUNGER MARCH FROM STALAG LUFT III BEGINS

After marching through a blinding snowstorm, Father Goudreau was thankful for the Luftwaffe officer who ordered him to spend the night after the evacuation from Stalag Luft III in a farmhouse not far from the village of Priebus. The warmth of the house dried his boots, greatcoat and clothes, and a hot dinner that filled his stomach formed his present, but two other realities unspooled in his mind.

The first began with the hastily organized evacuation of the camp, with men carrying full rucksacks and pulling jury-rigged sleds made from doors, the boom of Russian guns a mere 16 miles away taking on the roll of a bell chiming midnight. Ten thousand men felt first the cold of a sub-zero night on their faces and hands. Then it seeped into their greatcoats, overcoming the heat generated by the effort of pushing through deep snow as that same effort produced sweat that dampened their clothes and conducted heat away from them. Here and there the debris of war poked through the snow, showing where the lives of men, women and children had been leached from isolated villages. As they struggled through the snow, the men whose boots had cracked felt the stabbing pain of cold. They soon found their packs too heavy and began dropping what was no longer essential—pots, carvings made in prison, a copy of the New Testament, a volume of the poet John Keats's essays and, more surprisingly, blankets. The sun that lit the day did nothing to melt the thickening rime that surrounded their faces. The hunks of black bread they'd been given, which disintegrated to granular bits and pieces as it was pulled from pockets or sacks, did little to fill their stomachs.

Goudreau also thought of the men much less fortunate than he, of the thousands who would grab what sleep they could on the frozen bare ground of barns. The corner of the barn in which Kingsley Brown spent the night had been designated as a urinal—and, in the middle of the night, one unfortunate man close to it called out, "Jesus Christ, old boy, that was my face!"[241]

John Harvie was luckier; the Germans herded his group into a church, which, though unheated, soon began to warm from the body heat of the several hundred men. Each claimed what spot they could—under a pew, in the aisle, choir stall, pulpit or organ stall or, as two Canadians did, on the communion table itself. Some who did not collapse into a stupor found the strength to open a tin of cold bully beef or to eat a few dried prunes; the men from RCAF Flight Lieutenant Robert Buckham's barracks ate better, having taken a page from Canada's voyageur past and prepared something close to pemmican. Had he known of it, Goudreau would have approved of Harvie's inner debate about what constituted sacrilege when the pilot saw the two men lying on the communion table, and the radio that had been set up at an electrical outlet in a corner of the pulpit so that they could listen to the BBC. The priest would also have approved of Harvie's theological reasoning, "Churches were supposed to offer comfort and shelter to the needy. Surely we were in desperate need!"[242]

LATE JANUARY 1945, ON THE ROADS OF CZECHOSLOVAKIA

Jack Poolton Steals Food to Survive

Priestly delicacy no doubt led Fathers Desnoyers and Larivière to write only of the atrocious suffering of men from frozen feet and skin. Carswell was less reticent. On the seventh night of the march, his group was herded into sheep pens. "Sheep shit," he later wrote, "smells worse than cow shit. And the smell of sheep shit mixed with the human variety is indeed a very disgusting smell."[243]

The Kriegies' vale of frozen tears turned tragic when the biting cold vanished during the day and the roads turned into quagmires. The muddy water soaked the men, who, when the temperatures plummeted at night, became even colder and more susceptible to diseases such as pneumonia and pleurisy, which quickly killed those already weakened by dehydration and malnutrition. To supplement the meagre bread ration, delivered only every fourth or fifth day, Jack Poolton snuck into root cellars and stole life-preserving potatoes. Later, driven by hunger, he "stole a bucket of swill that was being prepared for pigs."[244]

29 JANUARY 1945, ON THE ROADS OF EASTERN GERMANY

Some Kriegies from Stalag Luft III Find Warmth in an Abandoned Factory

Harvie and the other men were thankful that instead of ordering them onto the road immediately, the Germans allowed them enough time to eat breakfast. Thus, though once again cold, Harvie felt relatively good. However, walking through the icy purgatory of eastern Germany soon sapped their spirits. Perhaps because the men had had a relatively warm night and started the day hopeful, when their morale began to fall, it fell quickly. The signs of depression—listless steps, silence and vacant stares—so alarmed Padre Douglas Thompson that he took the bottle of communion wine Harvie had been carrying in his pack and "moved up and down the line offering a sip to anyone who seemed to be in trouble."[245]

Harvie, Scruffy Weir, Father Goudreau and the other Kriegies, their fingers benumbed and their ears and cheeks windburned and frostbitten, trudged on. The still traumatized Carter-Edwards recalls, albeit hazily, the second night of their frozen odyssey, when they stopped at a warm factory. Left to their own devices by the German guards who stood outside, the Kriegies quickly found that the glass factory's furnaces were still hot, which allowed them to cook their food and make tea and coffee. The discovery of hot water in the boilers prompted them to strip and wash themselves and their clothes, which were then dried by putting them near the hot furnaces. The luxuriousness of sleeping in clean, dry clothes in a warm room, even if on a hard concrete floor, was something Carswell and Fathers Desnoyers and Larivière could only dream about.[246]

EARLY FEBRUARY 1945, SUDETEN MOUNTAINS, CZECHOSLOVAKIA

Grogan Mourns a Dead Civilian

Russian guns were close enough to blow up the bridge Grogan and the other Dieppe survivors had just crossed. Close enough so that among the mass of humanity streaming east were German soldiers, the wounds of some wrapped in paper bandages long since stained brown. Close enough so that, of the column of women they passed, none dared pause to try to scratch out a grave in the frozen earth for the dead babies they carried. Lying unburied but partially covered by the unrelenting snow were soldiers and civilians killed by American bullets "by light of day, Canadian and British by night, and Russian fighter planes at any time."[247]

Although most of Germany's transportation infrastructure had been destroyed, the railway line from Spremberg in the southeastern part of the country to Tarmstedt in the northwest still ran, albeit fitfully. It took the Kriegies from Stalag Luft III three days (2–5 February) to travel the 300 miles to Tarmstedt, from where they were marched first to Westertimke and then to Milag und Marlag Nord. While there was no snow, they had to endure a five-hour wait in the rain as small groups were admitted into the camp and processed. Father Goudreau was sent to a subcamp at Tarmstedt two miles away, where he met Father Raoul Bergeron. Even in the barracks the men could not shake the chill, for the wet wood shavings the Germans provided produced little heat. The arrival of the RAF and RCAF officers necessitated the transfer of the merchant marine prisoners, including the survivors of *A.D. Huff* and several naval prisoners, including the survivors of HMCS *Athabaskan*, to a nearby subcamp.

In eastern Germany above the Sudeten Mountains, chilled, weary legs provided the only means of transportation, which meant that no additional food reached the men in Grogan's column, who had long since exhausted their Red Cross parcels. Each day the men marched some 30 miles in sub-zero temperatures through the petrified wastes of Germany, and spent nights in frigid barns. Every third day, the German guards handed out a piece of hard black bread and a small amount of cheese and unidentifiable canned meat. The frozen sugar beets Grogan and the others ate to supplement this meagre diet provided belly-filling bulk but hardly paid back the calories needed to dig them out of the cold, hard ground.

The German killing machine continued to spit out death. The dead from Grogan's column awaited the next snowfall for their shroud. In words that belie his grade nine education, Grogan recalled another dead man: "We passed a huge wooden crucifix at a wayside shrine; an old Jew had chosen this spot to stop and rest. His body now lay in the snow beneath the cross, a gaping bayonet wound in his chest. The threshing of his feet in his death struggle had sent his wooden shoes and the cloths that had been wrapped about his feet some distance away. His white bare feet stuck up out of the snow, and his glassy eyes were fixed on the wooden image of the crucified Jew on the cross."

7 FEBRUARY 1945, STALAG VIII-A, GÖRLITZ, GERMANY

Poolton's Sufferings on the Road Pale in Comparison to What He Sees at Stalag VIII-A

Neither Father Desnoyers nor Father Larivière wrote about their forced march to Görlitz. Even for men who had known the cold of both rural Quebec and Ottawa winters, when the temperature can fall to where centigrade and Fahrenheit are the same, -40°, the words of Matthew 24:20 were never far from their minds: "Pray that your flight may not be in the winter." It's unknown whether either was aware enough to notice that as the 3,000 marchers neared Görlitz their condition so shocked villagers that, despite all the propaganda (and contrary to the urgings of the Nazis herding the POWs along), they stood and watched the "cortège" with tears in their eyes.

The sights in Görlitz recalled the Dark Ages. A member of Jack Poolton's Royal Regiment was "confined in a wire cage."[248] And the Germans had made the imprecation *Schweinehund* (pig dog) real, as some prisoners were in a sty standing up to their knees in mud.

EARLY FEBRUARY 1945, NEAR GOTHA, GERMANY

Robert Prouse Trades on the Black Market and Tastes Wild Meat

The German was nervous. Trading on the black market risked death. Still, the lure of cocoa was too great. So as planned, when he saw Robert Prouse's foraging party, the German quickly walked past it. A mile down the road, Prouse followed him into the wood, where they exchanged a tin of cocoa for two loaves of bread, which Prouse stuffed into his tunic. A guard had noticed Prouse's absence but bought the story that he "had to take a crap" once Prouse handed him a cigarette.[249]

Prouse and his buddies ate well that night. On the way back to the camp, he picked up a large Belgian hare that had been killed by a truck. After cutting off the hare's head, the cook threw the carcass into a pot and boiled it with potatoes. Removing the fur required repeated effort but was worth it, for the excellent "soup that had grease bubbles with the distinct taste of meat" was something that had not passed their lips in months.

16 FEBRUARY 1945, STALAG LUFT III, SAGAN, POLAND

Father Gérard Boulanger Is Liberated by the Russians and Begins His Trip Home via Odessa

Had Marshal Zhukov's long-range forces not destroyed the railway line linking the POW camp near Tost, in the southeast corner of Poland, then Father Gérard Boulanger and several hundred other POWs would not have found themselves tramping through the same cold and snow that had tormented the POWs who marched away from Stalag Luft III. The men in Boulanger's column fought not only for purchase on the icy roads but also to tamp down the fear generated by the "orchestra of cannons," the most ominous notes being the screaming sounds of the Katyusha rockets, the so-called Stalin's organ. The Russians kept the approaches to the bridge under such heavy fire that, despite the Germans guards' desperate desire to put the river between themselves and what they considered to be the barbarian hordes, their will failed them and they led the shivering men to a nearby POW camp at Cosel.

A few days later, the Germans found an old steam engine and some cattle cars. Since crossing the Oder was impossible, the train chugged its way northeast. Boulanger later described the trip in cattle cars as torture. Because of the open spaces between the slats, frigid air and snow poured in. It does not appear that the men were fed any hot food or given anything hot to drink. On 3 February, the train stopped a few miles outside Sagan, and Boulanger marched with the other men to Stalag Luft III, unbeknownst to him, to the same compound where Father Goudreau and the other Canadians had been held.

Thirteen days later, the German guards fled and the Red Army took possession of the camp, making Boulanger the first of the Zamzamers to be liberated.

LATE FEBRUARY 1945, ON A ROAD NEAR WEIMAR, GERMANY

Father Desnoyers Sees a Senior British Officer Face Down the March Führer

Görlitz itself was now a memory; so too was the companionship of Father Larivière—he had been ordered to remain behind to work in the camp's hospital when, just a few days after arriving in Görlitz, the 4,000 POWs from Lamsdorf, including Desnoyers, were once again struggling—at gunpoint—through the numbing cold and snowdrifts in a march toward Weimar, 175 miles further east. If lucky, they slept in drafty barns, perhaps with a little straw to throw under or over them to keep in some body heat. Father Desnoyers could not miss the irony. He had devoted his life to preaching the word of the babe born in a manger, and now he had sought what shelter the barns of Saxony and Thuringia could give.

Later the priest discovered that words could not describe the horrors of the march. Men desperate for the warmth of food starved. Dysentery took some, despair others. None could be buried in the frozen earth of Germany. Despite the snow, water was scarce, and the Canadians knew the dangers of taking a mouthful of snow, which sucked out more heat from the body than what it returned in water. The priest's heart ached when he heard that during a thaw, a soldier was so driven by thirst that, despite the protests of his comrades, he put his head down and drank dirty stagnant water saying, "I would like better to die having had a drink than die thirsty."[250]

Day after day, step by step, under unforgiving skies and cruel winds, they shuffled across that tormented land. Men who in the camps had striven to keep themselves mentally fit became little more than automatons, somehow putting one numbed foot in front of the other. Hunger that did not kill drove men into snow-covered vegetable patches, and into chicken coops and cow stalls, where they dug up cabbages, stole chickens or eggs and surreptitiously milked cows. The Germans punished some POWs who had stolen cabbages by tying their hands behind their backs and hanging cabbages around their necks.

Worried about how reports of this pilfering would look on his record, the Hauptmann commanding the march summoned the officers before him. "I have always believed that the English army was well disciplined. I must, unhappily, change my opinion," he yelled.[251]

Desnoyers watched as the hungry English major struck back. "Captain, six months in one of your concentration camps is enough for a soldier to lose all sense of discipline, and most of our men have been detained for four or five years. . . . what you call 'theft' is not. Our men are starving to death because you do not give them a quarter of the food that they need." Both officers knew the end of the war was coming soon, so the English major took a legalistic tone: "You should know in any case, that since the beginning of this forced march, absolutely everything has been noted, from the amount of food given to the way our men have been treated, and this report will count"—his next words echoing both the New Testament and the prophet Jeremiah—"in the day of judgment that will come." The white-faced Hauptmann found the will only to dismiss the officers.

LATE FEBRUARY 1945, HALBERSTADT, GERMANY

CARSWELL STARES DEATH IN THE FACE

The spasm of vomiting that woke Carswell told him he was sicker than he had been when he was struck with dysentery. Nevertheless, his gaunt face and the yellowed whites of his eyes broken by brownish-orange veins that he saw in the metal mirror shocked him. Yet he had to march, so he changed his wet socks for his dry ones (remembering to put the wet ones against his stomach to dry) and joined the column. Soon, his strength gave out, and he sat, soaked, in the slush by the side of the road with other played-out men. A German NCO told them that if they could make just three more miles, he would do what he could to get them on a railcar. How the 200 sick men made it, Carswell did not know, though he recalled stopping repeatedly to vomit or void himself. The next day, as the train slowly chugged to the northwest, he managed to keep some food down.

Near 2 p.m., shortly after the train stopped at Halberstadt, 150 miles southwest of Berlin, an air-raid siren began to wail. "Sick or not, none of us wanted to be on that train, on an open siding, during an air raid. We dived for the door, and in seconds the car was cleared."[252] Then six RAF Mustangs swooped down, firing their cannon at the train. The locomotive blew up, showering the POWs with shards of white-hot steel. Other shells and bullets hit more pitiful targets, POWs, killing about two dozen men.

Even in his weakened state, Carswell owed it to the quick (though wounded) and the dead to help gather them in. In the field adjacent to the siding, he saw a body and walked toward it. He was stunned by "his sightless eyes staring unblinkingly at the sun now emerging from behind the clouds; his face the yellow, drained colour of death; a jagged hole in his belly the size of a bowling ball; that familiar, unmistakable smell of death." Carswell knew the face well, for it had once been that of "Andrew Carswell." And once he had been that man. The living Carswell's face showed the first tears for the dead man, the Canadian's first swapover partner, who was buried under his own name, Dennis Reeves.

MARCH 1945, MILAG UND MARLAG NORD, NEAR BREMEN, GERMANY

Robert Buckham Notes How Hunger Leads to Inflation

The lack of food—the bread ration now being one-seventh and not one-fifth of a small loaf per man per day—competed with the damp cold to make life in Milag Nord miserable. The margarine ration was also cut and "the sausage ration," Buckham noted in his diary, "will only cover one slice of bread every ten days."[253] Chilled by 48 hours of snow and rain and now a deep freeze, not even the report that 50,000 food parcels had arrived in nearby Lübeck lifted the men's spirits; though, once again, the inexorable laws of economics could not be denied as the price of a chocolate bar jumped from 65 cigarettes to 101 on the black market. What did make the men feel better—as they seemingly turned the screws on themselves by recalling favourite meals and dishes—was the decision to raid their almost-depleted Red Cross supplies to produce a treat: two biscuits covered with a mixture of Klim and "goon jam."

EARLY MARCH 1945, MELLINGEN, NEAR WEIMAR, GERMANY

FATHER DESNOYERS ACCOMPANIES SICK MEN TO A LAZARETTO

Even before Hitler became chancellor of Germany in 1933, the people of Mellingen made Heinrich Berndl, a card-carrying Nazi, their *Bürgermeister.* On an early March day, however, their actions were not defined by their fidelity to the Nazi Party, still less by any memory that, four centuries earlier, Christoph Schappeler, the village's pastor, and Sebastian Lotzer, a furrier, drafted one of the first human rights documents in history.[254] Rather, what seized them was the fear that the ragged, stinking column of emaciated men—some, with sunken eyes and pallid skin, obviously sick—harboured the plague of cholera, which killed almost 9,000 people in Hamburg in 1892. As they would have for lepers in the Middle Ages, the people of Mellingen refused to provide refuge for these desperate men.

A short time later, an SS doctor came to examine the men camped in a field outside Mellingen. Shocked at their condition, he ordered 48 of the sickest, accompanied by Father Desnoyers, who would act as their interpreter, to a lazaretto (a hospital that treats contagious diseases) in nearby Bad Sulza. Over the next few days, 18 of these men died, while the column that had been marching for more than a month continued deeper into Germany. By the time it reached Weimar a few weeks later, of the 4,000 men who marched away from Lamsdorf, more than1,200 had died and most remained unburied.

MID-MARCH 1945, DUDERSTAT, LOWER SAXONY, GERMANY

Poolton Trades His Father's Ring to Survive

It is a measure of how arduous the conditions on the Hunger Marches were (and the healing power of a dry place to sleep) that, even though rations continued to be inadequate, Carswell's health improved after he arrived at Stalag XI-B at Fallingbostel. The stories other recently captured airmen told of advances by the American, British and Canadian armies, of the almost nightly progresses of bomber streams, and of the sight of short-range aircraft making strafing runs were also tonics.

Thanks to intrepid truck drivers (among them several Canadians who feared strafing by Allied fighter bombers less than they did starvation), Red Cross supplies continued to arrive at several camps, including Stalag VII-A (Mossburg) and Stalag XI-B. At Milag Nord, though one of the best-supplied camps, the meat ration dropped from 1.25 ounces per man per day in January to 1 ounce in mid-March. The potato ration fell from almost 14 ounces to 6.6 ounces per man. The despised German bread loaf shrank from just over 11 ounces per day to be shared among six men to just under 7.8 ounces to be shared among eight men.

At Stalag IX-C, where Prouse had not seen a Red Cross parcel in months, the bread ration fell to one 4½-pound loaf per day for nine men, or 220 grams (8 ounces) or one piece of hard, dry, sawdust-filled German black bread. By the end of March, the 200 men who suffered along with Poolton as they were marched into the Harz Mountains north of Weimar were eating rotten turnips and sugar beets revealed by the melting snows. In a brick factory in Duderstat, Poolton fell to his lowest point, trading the ring his father had worn in the First World War and that he had hidden from the victors at Dieppe for a quarter of a loaf of bread, which briefly relieved his and his buddies' hunger pangs.

CHAPTER FIFTEEN

April–May 1945

Free at last! Free at last!
Thank God Almighty, we are free at last!

—MARTIN LUTHER KING JR.

1 APRIL 1945, IN A BARN NEAR SPANGENBERG, GERMANY

Father Desnoyers Says Mass in a Barn

The clandestine radio confirmed what Father Desnoyers surmised after the Germans handed out Red Cross parcels and hustled the POWs back onto a road heading east: the Allies had jumped the Rhine and were closing in on Oflag IX-A/Z, near Bad Sulza. While the deep snows of January had been replaced by shoots of green, every mile remained some 2,500 steps, each one part of a 60-mile forced march deeper into the ever-shrinking Reich. The hungry remnants of Hitler's *Volk*—women, many now widows; men too decrepit or boys too young to be dragooned into ersatz battalions; and children whose sallow skin and thin and tired bodies resembled the Kriegies'—clogged the roads.

On 1 April in a nondescript barn where he and the other POWs spent the night, the German guards allowed Desnoyers to set up the altar that weighed down his backpack. Had they been in a proper church, though the priest's Latin would have meant nothing to them, the older guards would have recognized the Lumen Christi, which was one of the few Catholic acts retained by the Lutheran Church. However, instead of the "Light of Christ" growing ever stronger as the fire of paschal candles lit others, on this Easter Sunday morning, hundreds of spiderwebs shimmered by the light produced by an old three-inch candle. Beneath the words that celebrated the Crucified's triumph over death rumbled the sound of guns. Those that were coming closer belonged to General Patton's army, which three days later, on 4 April, would free and feed the prisoners, a modern-day version of the miracle commemorated in Psalm 78, that day's reading, recalling the gift of manna from heaven.

6–9 APRIL 1945, ON A FIELD NEAR WEIMAR, GERMANY

ROBERT PROUSE MANAGES TO MAINTAIN PROPRIETY

The Polish women prisoners were in even more desperate shape than the POWs who would, over the space of four days, march over 60 miles. The Kriegies were footsore and bent from the weight of their rucksacks or backpacks. But they were wearing greatcoats, tunics and pants. The women, herded by baton-wielding "large man-like Nazi women guards," wore rags.[255] The blisters on Robert Prouse's feet testified to the leather of his infantry boots (and the years since his last route march), while the burlap wound around the women's feet testified to their desperation. Prouse was so terribly hungry that, on the night of 6 April, he snuck out of the encampment and to a nearby house, where he traded cigarettes and cocoa for food. When he returned, he saw that even as the time of their Hobbesian state grew short, the guards remained brutish, pushing the women away from the wire and gathering up the food and cigarettes and soap (these last two amounting to currency) that the POWs had thrown to the women, who offered the only thing they still had for food, a "Jig-a-Jig."

The food Prouse bartered for at the farm did not fill his stomach for long. For the next day, like many who'd been reduced to drinking ditch water, he was racked by violent spasms of vomiting and diarrhea. Some found the strength to make their way out of the barn before soiling themselves; most were too weak and lay in their own filth. Prouse belonged to the former group and used the pages of the novel *The Robe* to try to maintain his propriety.

On the 8th, the guards prodded the desperate column of sick men deeper into the Reich. Allied planes were not absent from the sky for long, their strength a counterpoint to the ever-weakening state of the now dehydrated men who had not kept anything down in days. Late in the afternoon, the sickest, Prouse included, were detached from the column and marched another painful three miles to the main camp at Bad Sulza. The Scottish medics forced Prouse to vomit up the last remnants of the feces-contaminated water he had drunk from the ditches. The next day, a revived and cleaned Prouse felt almost guilty when he saw the conditions of the Russian POWs in the neighbouring compound. He had landed at Dieppe weighing more than 175 pounds; now he weighed 130, much more than many Russian POWs.

EARLY APRIL 1945, STALAG III-A, AT A RAIL YARD BETWEEN LUCKENWALDE AND BERLIN, GERMANY

Kingsley Brown Hears a Nursery Rhyme

His joy at having gone to a mass conducted in front of an altar built of "old bits of lumber and wooden boxes" draped with a clean white sheet by a Polish Catholic priest would not have sat well with the author of the only reading material Kingsley Brown could find at Stalag III-A. The Nazi overlords at the subcamp to which Brown and several others from Stalag Luft III were sent (the remainder were sent to Milag und Marlag Nord) would certainly not have approved of the thoughts expressed in the beat-up copy of *Aereopagitica*, John Milton's 1644 pamphlet that argues for the "Liberty of Unlicenc'd Printing," that is, against censorship.[256]

The move from Stalag III-A raised the spectre of being held as hostages but it improved their living conditions. Instead of sleeping three men to a shelf on a three-decked bunk, Brown and the others slept on the floor of the boxcars. In an effort to delay the impending transfer, Brown and his companions aped crippled men well enough to fool the Germans. Depending on where he looked, from the railroad enclosure Brown could see the last spasms of the war—in the acrobatics of the P-47 fighter bombers swooping low to attack emplacements, or in the song "Baa Baa Black Sheep" sung by the 10-year-old schoolgirls who stopped by the fence and which embodied the promise of peace.

8–10 APRIL 1945, MILAG UND MARLAG NORD, NEAR BREMEN, GERMANY

THE EVACUATION OF NAVAL PERSONNEL AND *LES RELIGIEUX*

The Allied officers considered the order for the naval and air force prisoners to undertake a forced march to Lübeck 25 miles to the east to be "criminal." Harry Hurwitz recalls that the officers warned Kommandant Schmidt that, since the air forces were strafing everything that moved, the roads were too dangerous. But even the threat that Schmidt would have to answer to Allied authorities if any of the POWs were killed on the road failed to move him. And so, on the morning of 9 August, a large number of the 6,000 naval ratings and officers took matters into their own hands. Some, thinking they would be better off entirely on their own, disappeared under the wire. Others, including Paul Gallant and Stuart Kettles, hid among the merchant sailors, who were to remain in the camp.

The order to evacuate the main camp, where John Harvie, Edward Carter-Edwards and most of the other Stalag Luft III Kriegies had been for about ten weeks, was issued late in the afternoon on 9 April; Harvie's barracks cleared the gate near 9 p.m. The night was uncomfortable chilly and damp, so despite wearing a greatcoat and army boots, since the line of men was moving slowly, Harvie found himself swinging his arms and stomping his feet to warm up.

Harvie was not much cheered by the sound of what he took to be a Mosquito fighter bomber. How could the pilot know that hundreds of feet below him was a column of defenceless Allied airmen? After two ominously close crumps of exploding bombs, the German guards thought better of marching through the night and led the men back into the camp. Any record of Schmidt's reaction has been lost, but he could not have been happy about this or news that even though the march began again near dawn, it made little progress. Following the "Go Slow" order issued by the Senior British Officer, RCAF Group Captain Lawrence Wray (who had been shot down on 3 May 1944), to keep them near the camp, the men ambled along slowly and stopped to openly barter with civilians. They started their hourly breaks early and "when it was time to continue, studiously ignoring the postens' shouts of "'*Raus! Raus!*'"[257]

EARLY APRIL 1945, CENTRAL GERMANY

Sapper Russ Burrows and Private Pat Ireland Have Some Home Cooking

The order for some of the prisoners to evacuate the camp near Fallingbostel on 8 April meant that Ian MacDonald and thousands of other POWs, including hundreds who had survived Dieppe, would now join tens of thousands of POWs and millions of civilians and German troops already fleeing west on the soggy roads of Germany, away from the Red Army.

The first 12 miles all but broke many men, who were buttressed by others, perhaps bolstered by a turnip or potato picked up while crossing a field. MacDonald remembers the Germans distributing a little cheese and the reviled *Brot*, and behaviour that shifted from intimidating to something approaching ingratiating. The juicy sugar beet MacDonald picked up from a field and ate caused a blister that blocked his throat; he would have died of asphyxiation had he not shoved two fingers down his throat fast and far enough to break the blister. The beating from a guard who used his rifle as a club after catching Andrew Cox stealing several bags of oats hurt all the more since the 100-pound Canadian "had very little flesh to cushion" the blows.[258]

A few days into the march, the Germans distributed Red Cross parcels. These, together with Pat Ireland's woodcraft skills honed in Alberta's Peace River District, emboldened Ireland, Russ Burrows and a British POW to slip away from the march that in the sleet and rain had become so arduous that the German guards had to be relieved often. To get the energy to keep going and fight off chills, they quickly dug through their Red Cross parcels.

"We were getting pretty hungry," recalls Burrows, "when one morning I was woken by a screeching metal sound. I crept around the tree and saw a woman at a well getting some water."

Ireland's trained eye had kept them hidden and running parallel to the autobahn; now Burrows cashed in the many hours he had spent learning German. When he stepped from behind a tree, Burrows knew it was not only the fact that he was dirty that caused the fright he saw in the woman's eyes; he was a man, obviously an escaped prisoner, and she was alone and belonged to what they both knew was soon to be a defeated people—and history spoke loudly of the "rights" claimed by soldiers. "She was terrified," he recounts, "so I quickly and softly I said '*Guten Morgen*' and told her I was hungry. After she motioned and told me to come with her, I told her there were two other men with me."

Although Burrows trusted her, as they approached the house, he became leery. She led them around the side of the building to a door that led into the kitchen. They had been prisoners for three and a half years, and had eaten a thousand pieces of sour, German black bread. Now, before them in a heavy black frying pan, a hausfrau who, he would later learn, had lost a son in the war and did not know where her husband or other two sons were, broke eggs into a bowl, grated potatoes and proceeded to fry up potato pancakes.

11 APRIL 1945, IN A WOOD NEAR FALLINGBOSTEL, GERMANY

MacDonald Escapes from the March

Like Harry Hurwitz and his buddy, who took advantage of the confusion at Milag und Marlag Nord after the order for the forced march was issued to slip under the wire and make a run for the Allied lines, and George Reid, who had escaped with a few other men from a field near Fallingbostel, MacDonald and his crewmate Walter Reed were now on the run. They escaped from the thousands marching from Fallingbostel during the night by hiding in a clump of bushes.

Figuring that he would appear less threatening to anyone they approached for help were he shaved, before they set out toward the west the next morning, Reed opened his kit and set up a metal mirror on a branch. Before he could take the first swipe, a soldier some distance away, likely having seen the glint of sun coming from the bushes, fired at them. "Wally grabbed the mirror and we both started running as fast as we could," recalls MacDonald.

11 APRIL 1945, BAD SULZA, NEAR WEIMAR, GERMANY

Robert Prouse Sees More Death

His liberators were close. So close, actually, that until he saw the plane that peeled off from the squadron and dove toward the train tracks that ran beside Bad Sulza wiggle its wing, Robert Prouse thought that he'd become a friendly-fire casualty.

Early on the 11th, with General Patton's army a scant five miles away, the German guards sought again to march their prisoners away. They started in the Russian compound. When shouting, fixed bayonets and painful blows failed to move the starving Russians, the Germans squeezed their triggers and lunged their bayonets forward. As the surviving Russians were marched away, the guards entered Prouse's compound.

Prouse believed the threat that the Allied POWs would be shot if they did not immediately begin marching. But, like his comrades, he refused to move. The ominous silence that reigned for a few moments was broken by the sound of tanks. Prouse and his comrades all but liberated themselves, for by the time the American Sherman tanks clanked into view at 5:05 p.m., the Germans, reacting to the men's "thunderous cheer," had turned tail and run through the gate.[259] An American tank trooper took one look at the rags cladding Prouse's thinned body, stripped off his battle jacket and handed it to the now free man.

12 APRIL 1945, DITFURT, NORTH-CENTRAL GERMANY

Jack Poolton Is Liberated

The word from the guards was not surprising: another town where there would be no bread. The weather was warmer, so the march, now more of a shuffle, of exhausted men across a blasted and picked-clean landscape was easier than the winter Hunger Marches had been. The rations, a small piece of black bread every four days, did terrible things to the men's digestion and to their sense of propriety.

The British soldier who broke the Kriegies' code of honour by stealing another man's scant ration was distressing enough. More horrifying was the rough justice meted out by the troops who beat the Tommy to a bloody pulp before officers moved him to the barn where Jack Poolton was. Terrified by the men in his barn now also turning on the soldier, Poolton stepped forward and shouted, "Stop! Don't anyone lay a hand on him. He has had enough. . . . You've all been tempted to steal at some time, but never had the guts."[260]

Days later, Poolton offered his RAF sweater to a German soldier in exchange for bread, only to stay hungry, as the representative of the Reich that had marched him halfway across central

Europe and forced him to sleep in fields and dirty barns refused to make a deal because the sweater was "lousy." Later, he hopped the low wall enclosing the field where the Germans were keeping them for the night and found a granary.

On 12 April, the crowing of the cock at 6 a.m. all but merged with the POW who called out from the barnyard, "There's a Jeep out there. There's a Jeep out there!" The Americans were clearly surprised to find the POWs, for within a few moments they radioed back to regimental headquarters: "Do not fire on this town. I repeat, do not fire on this town. There are Yanks and Tommies here."

MID-APRIL 1945, ON A ROAD LEADING TO LÜBECK, GERMANY

Father Bergeron Knows That Because of His Redeemer, He Liveth

Fathers Goudreau and Bergeron could have stayed with the merchant seamen in Milag Nord. They believed, however, that their place was with the men on the road where death from the American and British planes or German shells stalked the columns of terrified men being marched toward Lübeck and, more importantly, across the Elbe River, which would then form one more obstacle between them and the advancing forces of their liberation. The news that President Franklin Roosevelt had died on 12 April saddened the POWs even as the green fields they marched past seemed to promise their freedom.

Day after day they witnessed the awesome power of the Hawker Typhoon fighter bomber that had not even flown when the war began. The sharp bank and 180-degree turn of one plane told Harvie that they'd been mistaken for Germans. As the men dove to the ground, the "Typhoons screamed down, guns blazing, then climbed back up and disappeared," leaving behind stunned, demoralized and dead POWs.[261]

Seventy-eight POWs, including three from Cox's hut who had survived the beaches of Dieppe, and 12 guards were ripped apart by the plane's rockets and four-inch shells. Father Bergeron knew the infantryman's saying that you're safe from bombs except for the one that "has your number on it." And he would have agreed that the immediate reason for his survival was that, just a few minutes earlier, he had noticed men further up the column who had need of his strong back and comforting words. But what mattered to him was the ultimate cause. His *sauveur* had saved him, showing him the want of the men further up the line.

The senselessness of these men's deaths all but destroyed the Kriegies' morale. As the dust cleared, one cried out, "Kill us now if you want. We'd rather die at your hands than be cut apart by our allies."[262] The guards could not call off the march. However, knowing that they too could be shot up by a pilot thinking he was strafing a German army column, after sheathing their bayonets, they allowed the POWs to break ranks and walk in the field, which all hoped would be seen as a signal that they were not German soldiers.

MID-APRIL 1945, ON A FIELD OF HEATHER

MacDonald Survives a Friendly-Fire Incident

Like John Harvie, MacDonald had seen Wehrmacht troops marching to the front. Unlike Harvie, however, who as part of a column being led by German soldiers could savour the moments of coming face to face with the enemy all knew would soon be defeated, each time MacDonald and Reed saw or heard the boots, they had to hide, usually in bushes beside the road.

The underbrush, MacDonald learned a few nights later when a Typhoon bombed a nearby installation, was no more constant an ally than a mountain in the Pyrenees had been. For suddenly the field of heather that ran up to the clump of trees in which he and Reed planned to spend the night was aflame.

"A few moments after the explosions," recalls MacDonald, "we noticed that a wall of fire about a half mile wide was advancing very quickly toward us. We didn't have time to run away, so we thought that if we pulled up the heather around where we were, the fire might just go around us."

The two airmen managed to get back into their little oasis just before the firestorm closed in. As heat from the flames and smoke made each breath more difficult, the psalmist's words "Yea, though I walk through the valley of the shadow of death, I shall fear no evil" came unbidden to MacDonald and gave him hope that he'd survive. At length, the light began to move off, the heat lessened and the crackling wasn't as close, and MacDonald found that, two years and one week after they had survived a fire in a bomber over France, he and Reed had survived a fire on a field in Germany.

MID-APRIL 1945, IN A LUMBER CAMP EAST OF LÜBECK, GERMANY

Stan Darch Is Liberated by a Russian Female Commander Packing a Pistol—and Vodka

Even at this late date, the Reich demanded obedience from what conquered peoples it still controlled. "I couldn't have weighed more than 120 pounds, but they had me and other men swinging axes chopping down trees, cutting them up and then hauling the heavy logs," says Stan Darch. "Breakfast, when we had it, consisted of a piece of bread or fried potatoes, so rousing ourselves in the morning wasn't easy. That morning, however, it took only a few moments to realize something was different. There were no guards; we knew what that meant but didn't really have much idea of what we were supposed to do, when suddenly we heard a tank."

In the excitement, Darch took the star on the front of the tank to signify the United States. "Imagine our surprise," he says, "when the turret opened and we started hearing Russian—and saw that the crew commander was a woman with an automatic weapon slung over her shoulder, a revolver on each hip and a knife stuck in each boot top—and a bottle of vodka in her tunic! We found out later that her husband was the tank's driver."

It took a few moments to sort things out. But with the help of a few prisoners the Russians had taken, the Canadians who spoke German were able to communicate with the Russians, who told them where the British were. Darch does not remember paying much attention to the sound of a Jeep approaching from the other direction until it was close enough to see the white star on it. "It stopped and out climbed an Allied officer, who wanted to speak to the Russians about their respective sectors. So there we found ourselves in the first minutes after liberation listening to Russian being translated into German and then translating it to English and around again," says Darch. The next day, the Russian commander allowed the Canadians to harness a horse to a cart and set off for the British lines.

MID-APRIL 1945, IN A FOREST IN CENTRAL GERMANY

George "Speed" Reid Is Liberated

Several days after they escaped from a makeshift camp near Fallingbostel, and after long hours of walking in a reforested area under a leaden sky, Joe Cronan, another POW, pointed to a smudge of orange in sky and asked, "Speed, have you ever seen the sun come up from the west?"[263] The question seemed comical but signalled that they had spent the better part of the morning heading in the wrong direction.

A few hours later, several Germans in a truck they were passing were too busy talking to take notice of the POWs who slipped quietly by. The same could not be said of the three teenagers who, because they were carrying rifles, were able to stop the escapers on a road in a wood. As Reid tried to convince still-too-young-to-shave "soldiers" that he and Cronan were foreign workers, a car arrived. The driver, a doctor, spoke English and assured the teens that he would take their prisoners to the local jail.

After hearing how long it had been since Reid and Cronan had eaten a real meal and of the conditions they had laboured under in the salt mine, instead of taking them to the jail, the doctor took them to his cabin in the wood, where his wife cooked them a good meal. When a German soldier knocked on the door, the escapers hid, Reid wielding a two-foot-long piece of firewood. A few moments later they saw a self-propelled 88-mm gun clank by as the Germans pulled back behind a bend in the road. The doctor's wife then kept watch, soon calling out, "George, George. This is them."

Reid may have spent the last year and a half as a prisoner of war, but it took only those words to turn him again into an active soldier. To prevent the American Jeeps from heading straight into an ambush, he ran down a road and then across an open field, timing his dives to the ground perfectly each time the Germans to his rear opened up. When he rose from a ditch, he found himself looking at the business end of an American machine gun. "For God's sake, don't shoot," he cried. A young man with lieutenant stripes said, "Who are you and what is all the shooting?" Unable to suppress his sense of humour, Reid told him that he'd taken a shortcut from the Canadian Front in Italy, then said, "But the point is, there is an 88 set up down the road." Not long after he explained he was an escaped POW, five tanks lumbered down the road and made short work of the anti-tank gun.

MID-APRIL 1945, STALAG XI-B, FALLINGBOSTEL, GERMANY

ANDREW CARSWELL IS FREED

The Allies were not far away. The pilots in the planes just above treetop level were the closest, though the pilots of the bombers were closest to Andrew Carswell's heart. He could hear and feel the rumble of their exploding payloads. It is a mark of Carswell's humanity that, even though he knew that each of the explosions opened a little bit further the gate holding him prisoner, his thought was, "It must [be] unendurable for any intelligent German to see the destruction of his or her homeland continuing while Hitler rave[s] like a lunatic about secret weapons."[264]

But still the war dragged on—until the morning following the night when he and his barracks mates heard the sound of a Sten gun, which told them that British troops were nearby. Then, as they waited for the morning rations to arrive, an army POW rushed into their hut, saying between deep breaths, "I just saw a Churchill tank."

MID-APRIL 1945, NEAR LÜBECK, GERMANY

FATHER GOUDREAU FEARS HE AND THE OTHERS WON'T SURVIVE THE WAR

By day, the marchers kept near ditches. They bartered cigarettes for food and saw at least one V2 rocket. When the ground quaked from nearby bombings, Father Goudreau and his congregants could not help but feel that the mass he said that morning or the evening before was "the last he'd celebrate in his life and the last they'd hear."[265] By night, the increasingly tired POWs slept in barns or in fields under the firmament, lit by the flashes of flares and artillery fire. The priest laid his head on a pillow of wood and in place of the sound of cicadas, their ears were filled with the staccato chirp of machine guns.

17 APRIL 1945, 25 MILES WEST OF FALLINGBOSTEL, GERMANY

MacDonald Avoids Friendly Fire and Meets Some Royal Commandos

The small-arms and mortar fire that kept them pinned down signalled that they were close to the Allied lines. "It only lasted for an hour or two," recalls MacDonald. "But the explosions were a little too close, and the machine guns cut the grass above us. My mother wouldn't have been happy with my language, but I couldn't help thinking, 'Damn. If I'm not careful, I'm going to get myself killed by friendly fire just before I get to our lines.'"

The next day, MacDonald and Reed saw two men walking toward them. "They weren't very close, but we could make out that one looked to be wearing American coveralls. Once they got closer, I could tell he was an airman. He'd been shot down and was on the run, and the other fellow was an escaped Russian POW. While the American caught us up with the news, including that President Roosevelt had died, the Russian went into a field to find us some food.

"The next morning, the Russian again went to find food. He returned to tell us that he'd met a German farmer who'd told him the German troops had left. We immediately began to walk toward where we thought the Americans were and soon ran into another farmer, who confirmed that the troops had left. A few hundred feet down the road, we heard singing and then, much to our surprise, there appeared a number of Russian POWs who were well fortified with vodka and were walking back toward Russia. The Russian who was with us joined them, while Wally and I walked toward the west.

"About a quarter mile further down the road, we saw a convoy. The first car stopped when the driver saw us. They were Royal Marine commandos, and we were washed over by a feeling of pure joy and elation," recalls MacDonald.

20 APRIL 1945, WESTERTIMKE SUBCAMP OF MILAG UND MARLAG NORD

LES RELIGIEUX UNDER FIRE

Kommandant Rogge's decision to keep some of the Oblates and Sacred Heart Brothers in the subcamp at Westertimke should have given them a measure of protection. But as part of its defence of the village of Westertimke (and in violation of the Geneva Convention), the Wehrmacht placed a six-barrelled Nebelwerfer mortar and two tanks next to the camp. *Les religieux* had never seen anything like the Nebelwerfer, which shook their barracks, causing the men of the cloth to spend the fourth anniversary of their capture digging a series of trenches in which they could take cover during the day and sleep at night; the Allied shells killed 6 and wounded 14 of the POWs that night.

22 APRIL 1945, STALAG III-A, LUCKENWALDE, NEAR BERLIN

KINGSLEY BROWN WRITES A NOTE FOR A FORMER GERMAN GUARD

From the enclosure at Stalag III-A, to which he had been moved back a few weeks earlier, Brown could not tell whether the explosions that shook the ground came from Canadian, British or American bombers, which had been pummelling Berlin, or from the tens of thousands of Russian heavy guns and rocket launchers ringed around the city's north, west and south. Though none of the shells appeared aimed at the camp, as their tempo built, one by one the guards disappeared on the run.

Around noon, a guard named Paul Reemt-Heeren, who had been with Brown's group since Stalag Luft III, found Kingsley Brown in a dingy corner of his hut. The destruction Brown had witnessed had dampened his wrath, for as he looked upon the man, he "tried to imagine what it must be like for a proud German in this hour of such crushing defeat and chaos."[266]

Reemt-Heeren told Brown that he was going to try to make it through the American lines to Magdeburg, where his wife and children were. He then pulled a pen and card from his pocket, saying, "You could help me . . . I don't know what I might run up against . . . I tried to do the right thing by the prisoners, you know that." Using the German word *vielleicht*, which in this context has a meaning closer to "beseeching" than to "perhaps," he asked if Brown could put in a good word for him. Brown took the card and, in the same hand that he had once compiled the database from which was produced his ill-fated identity as a Bulgarian steelworker, wrote that Reemt-Heeren "had done the best he could do to make life more comfortable for the prisoners in his charge." He signed it, adding his rank, service number and Canadian address.

Two days later, the advance guard of the Third Guards Tank Regiment of the First Ukrainian Front liberated the camp.

24 APRIL 1945, ON AN ESTATE NEAR LÜBECK, GERMANY

Harvie Makes Himself Comfortable and Awaits the End of the War

Power had shifted.

RAF Sergeant "Dixie" Deans, the Senior British Officer, had been to the camp at Lübeck and declared that, since it was overcrowded, unsanitary and short on food, he would not order the 12,000 men who had marched out of Milag und Marlag Nord to take one further step. And the Germans, who knew that Stalin's troops were within a couple of thousand yards of Hitler's chancellery and, more to the point, that the British were 40 miles to the east, realized there was nothing they could do about it. Instead, Deans gave his word that the men would stay at the estate a few miles outside Lübeck that they had stopped at the day before. Over the next week, as the war continued around them and hundreds of soldiers and untold numbers of civilians died, Harvie and the other marchers fairly set up housekeeping and slept in clean straw.

Meanwhile, Robert Buckham, who had left Milag und Marlag Nord with another group of men, was spending his second day at a former artillery school barracks near Lübeck, and in significantly more salubrious conditions than they had experienced during their first night on the road when they had spent the night in a pig-sty. Among the stranger aspects of life in the faux castle was that the POWs and German guards shared the washroom, where they shaved standing next to each other.

26 APRIL 1945, ON A ROAD 25 MILES SOUTH OF HAMBURG

Survivors of Dieppe Are Strafed by RAF Planes

The guards, some of whom had summarily executed men who had fallen out of the line of march that had begun at Fallingbostel, moved quickly to reassert their authority after Stan Darch and the Kriegies erupted into cheers when an RAF plane wiggled its wings. First, they reversed the column; after about a mile's march, they turned it onto a road heading north. For few moments, the tree-lined road elicited the hope of spring. And the roar of the RAF planes swooping toward them promised another wing salute.

This time, however, there were no cheers. Instead, the pilots, having mistaken the column for a troop of German soldiers, fired their machine guns as they roared by just above the budding trees. The pilots realized their mistake almost immediately. But at 150 miles per hour and firing more than 300 rounds per minute, their fire quickly ran down the length of the column. Some men, Darch included, had time to jump into a nearby ditch. Many who couldn't get off the road were lucky as the bullets fired from machine guns from different planes staggered from left to right to produce what amounted to a dead zone running down the road. Scores died, including Lance Corporal Thomas R. Gage, who had survived the First World War, only to be one of the 89 Allied corpses the Germans ordered their comrades to leave by the side of the road.

28 APRIL 1945, MILAG UND MARLAG NORD, NEAR BREMEN, GERMANY

Les Religieux, the Survivors of *A.D. Huff* and HMCS *Athabaskan* Are Liberated

Five days earlier, they were in a dangerous location. Save for a small corridor that connected the camp to Lübeck, Milag und Marlag Nord was encircled by different Western armies, any of which, of course, were eagerly awaited by the Kriegies. The more pessimistic prisoners realized that they could be hit by friendly fire at any moment. The setting up of a forward observation post for a nearby artillery piece confirmed that that the Germans had pulled back and that Milag und Marlag Nord and its subcamp at Westertimke were now, in Stuart Kettles's words, "right in no-man's land." Soon "shells and mortars whined right over the camp. When they quieted down, moanin' Minnies [Nebelwerfer] would start up, and the sound they make would send shivers up and down the spine of a skeleton," recalled the officer who had seen his warship blasted apart.

Though not a soldier, Kettles was not surprised that after the shells and mortars, the "machine guns start[ed] talking." With an American buddy, he dug a slit trench, which ensured they would be below the line of fire and better protected from falling flak.

At 11:30 p.m., the noise lessened, and Brother Georges-Aimé Lavallée prepared for another night of sleeping in his three-foot-wide gash in the ground. Minute gave way to minute without a blast, or the whine or ripping sound of a machine gun. The unaccustomed silence prompted the men to peek over their trenches. Ten minutes before Kettles and the other survivors of *Athabaskan* would have begun their second full year of captivity, a tank belonging to the Scots Guards, which had shared battle honours with the Canadians during the last 100 days of the last war, rumbled through the main gate and liberated the camp.

29 APRIL 1945, STALAG VII-A, MOOSBURG, GERMANY

Father Larivière Is Liberated

Despite his Teutonic name, Charles H. Karlstad was an American brigadier general, tasked with pursuing the remnants of the 17th SS Panzer Grenadier and 719th Infantry Divisions that were falling back toward a bridge over the Iser River. Earlier on the 29th, a car travelling under a flag of truce and carrying a Swiss Red Cross official, an SS officer and two POWs—one an American, the other a British officer—arrived at Karlstad's headquarters in Puttenhausen to tell him that between his men and the bridge was Stalag VII-A, which held more than 100,000 prisoners, including 30,000 Americans.

Freeing the captured Americans and other Allied troops was important. But the German proposal to create a neutral zone that encompassed the bridge was unacceptable because it would allow all the Germans to withdraw across it unmolested. Worse, were the Germans to be playing by anything less than the Marquess of Queensberry's rules, they could take the POWs with them as human shields. Accordingly, Karlstad rejected the proposal and instead demand the unconditional surrender of Moosburg.

When the surrender was not forthcoming, American armour overwhelmed in quick succession first an SS stand on the banks of the Amper, then dug-in positions in the field between the river and the town. The Americans raced through the town for the bridge over the Iser, which the Germans blew up just before they reached it. As other Americans neared the camp, the SS peppered their armour with small-arms fire, which was answered with shells and machine-gun fire.

Father Larivière was liberated by US lieutenants Joseph P. Luby and William J. Hodges, whose heaviest gun was a .30 calibre machine gun mounted on their Universal Carrier. As the soldiers approached the gate of Stalag VII-A, they saw 250 armed guards between the inner and outer wire. "Without slackening speed but with both hands on the business end of his machine gun, [Luby] rolled into the middle of the German formation, brought his jeep to a sudden halt and called '*Achtung*'."[267] He then ordered the Germans to line up and drop their weapons. And thus, for the first time in almost three years, hundreds of those who had been captured at Dieppe could look around and not see a German soldier ready to take a bead on them.

2 MAY 1945, NEAR LÜBECK, GERMANY

Father Bergeron Knows Fear

The order to board the train that was to take the wounded and sick men the final 36 miles to Lübeck gave Father Bergeron pause. Since leaving Milag und Marlag Nord, he'd seen dozens of burned-out trains.

But the contents of the small, tan cardboard suitcase he insisted on carrying himself assured him. The value of the chalice inside the suitcase was so different from the silver ones used even at the small church in Jonquière, Quebec, where he had served as an altar boy, and from the ones used by Father Deschâtelets at the ceremony on 21 July 1940 in Cap-de-la-Madeleine (near Trois-Rivières, Quebec), where the Oblates received their mission. Silver in colour, though not in substance, the largest and most important item showed the marks of the tin bashing that turned a couple of Klim cans into a chalice, the holy cup wherein wine is transformed into the blood that Catholics believe affirms life—so different from that which when spilled on the ground soon turns the brown of death. The monstrance, which holds the Host, was also of beaten tin, an incised Cross on its ill-fitting cover. The velvet bag that seemed a reliquary protected a glass pipette that measures out the four drops of wine. The suitcase also contained a carefully folded white chasuble that a Kriegie had made for the priest to wear during mass.

Bergeron's faith gave him the strength to give succour to the wounded and sick men loaded onto the train, and to hear of stories told by men and women who had survived the horrors of Dachau. Bergeron's faith tamped down his fears during the 36 hours it took the train to chug to Lübeck and the three days it served as his barracks until late in the afternoon on 2 May when British troops liberated him, a few hours after Harvie, Goudreau and Tommy Thompson were also freed. Three days later, the Tommies caught up with the column of men that included Edward Carter-Edwards and several other RCAF men who had been in Buchenwald.

2 MAY 1945, A TOWN IN THE SUDETENLAND, CZECHOSLOVAKIA

John Grogan Is Liberated

The day before, John Grogan and four other men took advantage of the disorder caused by a strafing attack to escape from their column of POWs. Now they were holed up in the rubble of a village that the Germans had a tenuous hold on until, moments after, several T-34 tanks clanged into view and "the ground seemed to explode around where the Germans were."[268]

Worried that the Russians might have itchy trigger fingers—and surprised by the sight of a woman climbing out of the first tank and then directing traffic—Grogan and the others waited. They saw an officer "with bits of red on the collar of his tunic and on his peaked cap" get out of his car and spread out his map on the hood. Then they saw more soldiers and armed civilians, who a New Zealand soldier thought were probably partisans, carrying soup kettles. At that point, they figured that the village was secure and fingers somewhat less itchy.

They were wrong. As soon as he stepped out the door, a sniper fired just over Grogan's head, causing Grogan to duck back into the wrecked house he and the others had been hiding in. Another soldier, who had found the universal sign of surrender, lowered a white sheet from an upstairs window. "Here goes," the New Zealand soldier said as he and his Allied comrades walked out of the house with their hands up. Luckily, one of them spoke Russian and yelled, "English prisoners of war. Don't shoot!"

3 MAY 1945, NEAR LÜNEBERG, GERMANY

Russ Burrows Finds Himself Under Allied Orders Again

They had been camping in the field for days. Before that, they'd been at a farm where, amazingly, each man had been given several Red Cross parcels. So Russ Burrows and Pat Ireland, who a few days after feasting on potato pancakes joined a shuffling band of POWs that included several Canadians, were not hungry. The German guards were nothing like those who had shackled Burrows and his comrades. Gone was their swagger. Gone too was their Führer, who had committed suicide three days earlier; now their shrunken state's commander was Reichspräsident Karl Dönitz, who, in order to give thousands more Germans the chance to cross into American or British lines, was dragging his feet in the surrender negotiations. Some five hours earlier, his writ ended on a patch of ground in Lübeck close to where Robert Buckham's group had been encamped for more than a week when one of General Bernard Montgomery's columns emerged from the mist and smoke. The explosion of a shell fired from the lead tank silenced a machine gun in a nearby house, serving as a coda to Buckham's war.

A few hours earlier, three British Bren gun carriers rumbled into Burrows's view. "The British were in hot pursuit of an SS detachment. After asking us if we had food, they said they'd inform the proper authorities about our location and that we were to disarm the guards. What really surprised us, however, was the officer who then said that we were to go into a small town built around a man-made lake and secure it," says Burrows, who armed himself by appropriating a guard's rifle and bayonet. "If anything, the townspeople were just as happy as we were to hear that the war was over."

7 MAY 1945, STALAG XVIII-C, MARKT PONGAU, NEAR SALZBURG

Father Juneau Is Liberated by the Russian Army

It had taken almost two weeks of marching, but on 23 April, Father Juneau and some 13,000 other POWs evacuated from Stalag XVIII-A in Wolfsberg had reached Stalag XVIII-C. Conditions at the camp at Markt Pongau, which already held 5,000 more men than it was designed to, were deplorable. In the overcrowded hospital, "sick men [were] lying in every corner."[269] More worrisome was the food situation, which despite the presence of Red Cross officials soon became dire.

On 2 May, even though the Wehrmacht units nearby were still fighting the Americans, the camp's Kommandant ordered the guards to leave, effectively leaving the camp in control of the senior Allied officers. By 6 May, their control was stretched to the breaking point when several hundred hungry men broke out of the camp and looted a German goods train. Order was restored, but the incident convinced the officers to send a medical officer to Salzburg, which they knew was in American hands. The following day, a party of American troops arrived and formally liberated the camp and arranged for supplies to be delivered.

8 MAY 1945, ON A FARM 16 MILES SOUTH OF LÜBECK, GERMANY

Brian Hodgkinson Is Liberated by Canadian Paratroopers

No one in the part of the farm where Brian Hodgkinson was being held knew that a day earlier at Rennes, France, Dönitz had signed the surrender agreement ending the war in Europe. What they did know was that the guards had vanished, and that Polish POWs and dragooned Russian farm labourers who had tended the purebred Jersey cows had also vanished. A few moments of explanation by a Scottish soldier with the relevant experience, trial and error, and some good-natured razzing telling the pilot to "Steer the bloody thing, Hodge," resulted in first a wet pants leg and then some milk in a pail.[270] By the time his comrades realized that the teats could be used as pistols, the floors, walls and remnants of the Kriegies' uniforms were doused.

Shortly after noon, as the cows lowed peacefully, Hodgkinson looked toward the entrance of the farm and saw the uniforms of the Canadian paratroopers, and his war too was over.

Chapter Sixteen

Homecoming

I pass, like night, from land to land;
I have strange power of speech;
That moment that his face I see,
I know the man that must hear me:
To him my tale I teach.

—Samuel Taylor Coleridge,
"Rime of the Ancient Mariner"

For some, the moment of liberation was quickly followed by truck rides to airfields and flights to Britain. Barely a day passed between when Royal Marines slapped Ian MacDonald's back and showered him with cigarettes and chocolate bars and when he climbed down from the Stirling bomber in an airport in England, where, within minutes, he went through what amounted to the ex-POW's baptism. "They took us to an outdoor area and put small pipes in our pants legs and the arms of our jackets and blew in DDT to kill the fleas and lice." Having washed and donned a new uniform, he and some other men climbed into a truck heading for the Canadian base at Bournemouth. "For weeks I'd had only the haziest idea where I was. And then, on the truck that took us from the airport, I saw through the wet windshield the unmistakable landmark of England, Big Ben, and I knew exactly where I was," says MacDonald.

Andrew Carswell was back in England on 19 April, just days after feasting on a loaf of white bread still warm from the oven and a disconcerting encounter with two British soldiers in a Jeep who urged Carswell and another POW to kick down the door of any German's house and "pick up some souvenirs." When Carswell pointed out that looting was illegal, the soldier asked, "And who's going to report us?"[271] Honoured by the co-pilot who offered the ex-Lancaster pilot his seat, Carswell's first glimpse of England was of the cliffs of Dover standing against the setting sun. In his tattered clothes, he felt bashful when, upon landing, a pretty young woman wearing the stylish uniform of the Women's Auxiliary Air Force led him to table and supplied him with tea and cakes as she explained the delousing and bureaucratic procedures to follow. Then he was assigned to a sergeant's room, where he found clean towels, soap and a razor, as well as a pair of RAF-issue pyjamas. Sitting on the bed, with its clean, starched white sheets, Carswell savoured his freedom.

Jack Poolton arrived in England on the 22nd. In the ten days since he'd been liberated when an American Jeep arrived at the barnyard near Ditfurt and a German guard handed over his rifle with the words "*Ich bin jetzt der Gefangene* (sic)" (I am the prisoner now), much had happened.[272] A week earlier, as the former POWs awaited transportation to Britain, a delegation of Ditfurt's older women came to the Senior British Officer and asked him to billet British or American "*kommraden*" in their homes to protect them against marauding Poles. Poolton volunteered and understood the mother of the family he was assigned to when said she had always "despised Hitler," though he did not believe her. And he understood what she was offering when she said she would sleep on the couch and he would sleep in the bed with the young woman. The man who had survived a sniper's bullet at Dieppe, who had been so thirsty at Envermeu that he tried to suck water from the damp earth beneath a factory floor, who had been shackled like a common criminal, turned down the offer by saying he would sleep on the couch.

A few days later, while walking back to the town, Poolton and several other men were surprised when a soldier stepped from behind a hedgerow, Tommy gun at the ready, and said, "Who the hell are you guys?" Poolton's explanation brought a deluge of cigarettes and chocolate bars from American troops, who, despite the radio message sent on the 12th, had not known there were any POWs there. At Halberstadt, Poolton's and the other British POWs' haggard looks stunned the "beautiful American Red Cross women" and sickened the "black American attendants" charged with delousing.[273] On the 21st, after he realized RAF planes would not be soon arriving, an American pilot welcomed Poolton and his British comrades aboard his plane for a flight to Brussels. A day later, Poolton walked into an office at Waterloo Station and sent a telegram to his family before travelling to the Fourth Canadian General Hospital in Farnborough.

Late the previous week, the SS *Duchess of Richmond* tied up in London and Father Boulanger disembarked. His journey back to England began, as did Jacques Nadeau's and that of the men the Russians liberated with him, with a trek east. Nadeau's liberators had allowed the Canadians to take a horse and cart, and their encounters with suspicious units to the rear eased (though their watches not saved) by a pass signed by none other than Marshal Zhukov, who upon meeting the former Kriegies insisted on toasting them with vodka. By contrast, a Russian officer told Father Boulanger and the men with him, "The road is there . . . March!" Over the 28-day, 200-mile arduous march across the devastated Polish countryside, the priest came to see his small, almost always hungry party as a gathering of Cains, frightened and fleeing "the land of sin."[274]

Somewhere south of the ruins of Warsaw, Nadeau's group boarded the same Katowice-Odessa train Boulanger had boarded a day or two earlier after praying before the famed Black Madonna, in Częstochowa, Poland. Perhaps because Boulanger was a priest or because he had crossed Poland with British POWs, whom the Soviets assumed to either have received aid from or been sympathetic to the Polish nationalists loyal to the exiled government in London and not the Communist puppets Stalin was in the process of installing in Poland, the Russians herded Boulanger's group into an overcrowded cattle car the priest likened to "a library of humanity." In Nadeau's car, in contrast, the five Canadians could stretch out and sleep. None of the Canadians was injured when several trains jumped the tracks. Instead of helping the wounded and respecting the dead, the Russian troops and trainmen looted the broken bodies. Boulanger wrote in disgust, "You'll have to convince someone else other than me that these are civilized people . . . But I forget . . . they are our allies! *Vive* Stalin! *Vive* the Russian paradise."[275]

Of the few days he spent in the Black Sea port before boarding the SS *Duchess of Bedford*, Nadeau's most difficult moment occurred while he and his comrades were being deloused. The women who came into the room to pick up the basket filled with their flea-ridden clothes pointed at their penises, laughing at each other's running commentary. Though spared this mortification, Boulanger was interned in a makeshift camp where armed guards patrolled and once again Red Cross parcels staved off hunger. On 22 March, Boulanger stepped aboard the SS *Duchess of Richmond*, and since she, like the *Duchess of Bedford*, belonged to Canada Steamship Lines, like Jacques Nadeau, the priest was actually on sovereign Canadian territory almost a month before reaching London.

By 8 May, Victory in Europe Day—immortalized for most North Americans by the image of a sailor kissing a woman in Times Square—more men, including John Harvie, were back in England; years later he recalled enjoying the difference between the second-class hotel he had been billeted in when he was a fledgling airman and the turreted Royal Bath Hotel he stayed in in 1945, and rued the fact that his stomach was not quite up to the rich food available from the kitchen more used to serving royalty. Though liberated by the Russians, Stan Darch was lucky that he was not, as were Kingsley Brown and hundreds of other men from Stalag Luft III, still in a POW camp, this time under Russian control.

The well-armed female tank commander likely knew nothing of the growing tensions between the Russians and the Western Allies over Stalin's demand that Soviet POWs who had fought for the Germans be forcibly repatriated to Russia. These tensions had resulted in Russian soldiers firing over the heads of ex-POWs who had climbed into American trucks arriving in Luckenwalde, thus forcing the men back into the prison camp.[276] Instead, the tank commander gave Darch and the other POWs a team of horses and a wagon that allowed them to cover the 40 miles to the American lines in time to eat supper at a proper hour on 5 May. Darch arrived in England on the 10th, three days after the crew of HMCS *Athabaskan* arrived in the belly of a Lancaster bomber and three days before Robert Brooks and his crewmates arrived in England; they had been liberated by the Russians on 23 April.

Hitler had been dead for almost a month, and the war in Europe had been over for nine days when a plane carrying most of the Oblates and Sacred Heart Brothers touched down at Stanmore, just outside London. Since they were not soldiers, after being deloused they were sent to Canada House. There, *les religieux* were given identity papers and money. The Knights of Columbus arranged for rooms at a reasonably priced hotel. Despite years of living *dans la langue des anglais*, the priests and brothers soon discovered that cockney was for all intents and purposes another language and that its speakers could not understand their pronunciation of "Trafalgar Square," "Pall Mall" or even "the Thames." Saddened by the devastation wrought by the Blitz, by the V1s and V2s, one of which destroyed the transept of the Catholic church closest to their hotel, the Oblates and brothers soon had reason to thank Jesus again, for Fathers Goudreau and Bergeron had joined them. By the end of the month, their ranks had grown to 14 with the arrival of Fathers Larivière and Juneau.

Among the last Canadian POWs to leave war-shattered Europe was Kingsley Brown, who along with hundreds of other Allied airmen, including many who had been in Buchenwald, waited with increasing impatience in Luckenwalde. The end of the war did nothing to improve the appalling conditions at Luckenwalde, though the local commander, Major Ledbedev, moved quickly to improve the food situation by making available to the Allied soldiers stores captured a few miles away. The wine the Russian drivers shared with Brown was welcome and, in his inebriated state, the show they put on blasting the empties and then carving their initials into the concrete supports of an overpass with their automatic weapons was impressive. However, what meant more to him was the surplus of beans. For about a week before the Russians drove Brown and the other Allied airmen to a Bailey bridge that spanned the Elbe, and thus the American lines, the airman who had spent years being hungry brought pails of bean soup to a German family that lived in Weinberge, "a little row of charming middle-class homes nestled on a wooded slope overlooking Luckenwalde."[277] At one time the facility held 45,000 men, in a space designed for less than a quarter of that number. Five thousand men died there, including thousands of Russian POWs killed by typhus, and were buried in unmarked mass graves.

* * *

By the time Brown and the men with him were feasting on hot white bread, Fathers Desnoyers and Boulanger were already back in Canada, as Carswell and John Harvie soon would be. Within a week, Ian MacDonald walked up the gangplank leading to the RMS *Aquitania*, still painted battleship grey; before heading across the Irish Sea, the ship berthed in Greenock, Scotland, where Stuart Kettles and most of the survivors of HMCS *Athabaskan* boarded the ship that had taken 400,000 men to war. Stan Darch walked up the gangplank of SS *Ile de France* on 8 June. A week later, RMS *Scythia*, which survived being hit by an aerial torpedo during the invasion of North Africa, steamed into Montreal's harbour carrying most of the Oblates and Christian brothers; by then the last missing *religieux*, Father Pellerin, who after being liberated had been sent to Rome, where he met with Pope Pius XII, had made his way to London.

The Canadian government's decision to repatriate the POWs as quickly as possible, and because they were scattered in different places and reached Britain in a piecemeal manner, meant that men from the same unit were not necessarily on the same ships that steamed into Halifax or Montreal, or the same trains arriving in Montreal from New York. Thus, their welcome back to Canada tended to be a low-key, personal affair. Almost certainly the exception to this occurred just after 8 a.m. on 29 May when the bulk of *Athabaskan's* survivors walked out of Montreal's Windsor Station to find that the band that had serenaded them as they stepped onto the platform was now playing in the street in front of a crowd of 3,000 cheering civilians. Though he welcomed the warmth of their sentiments, mindful of the loss of 120 shipmates and his ship, Stuart Kettles felt that the cheers were misplaced.

Poolton spent these weeks—during which the survivors of SS *A.D. Huff*, Edward Carter-Edwards and thousands of other Canadian POWs, arrived in Canada—in a hospital, which he had entered shortly after VE Day. He was so thin and sickly looking that his Uncle Bill did not recognize him at a party until he asked Poolton's brother who his "friend" was. Weeks of being injected with liver did little but damage his extremely thin skin. The infection that affected his ears and throat caused days of delirium and could have killed him had doctors at the No. 19 Canadian General Hospital not turned to the new wonder drug, penicillin. By late July, he too was back in Canada.

On the journey north from Toronto, Poolton, like many other former Kriegies, rehearsed what he would say to his mother and wondered if he would simply smile or cry. To his surprise, his mother and siblings boarded the train at Moonbeam, the stop before Kapuskasing, so that they'd have a little private time before the train arrived in what everyone involved called "Kap," where some 200 people were waiting under a huge sign that read "Welcome home, Jack." Poolton found himself as if in a dream unable to say even hello and, more ominously, unable to say how he felt. Perhaps after years of dreaming of it, his first night home could only be a disappointment. An uninvited couple plied him with questions about being a POW, when all he wanted to do was sit at the kitchen table and thank his family for the parcels they'd sent him.

In 1945, nothing was known about what today we call post-traumatic stress disorder; indeed, the Red Cross went so far as to advise families not to talk about the war, and to rapidly change the subject if it came up. On Poolton's second night home, his father, acting as he might have had the war never occurred, took his son to see the film *Drums*. The scenes of a Scottish regiment being destroyed in India's North-West frontier left the survivor of Dieppe traumatized. Like Stan Darch and other Kriegies, he had had nightmares while being a prisoner, but now they came more often. "I'd had a few nightmares in the camps, but once I got home they became more common. I'd be back on the beaches of Dieppe and men would be dying and crying out around me. I'd scream out in the middle of the night and scare the hell out of my mother," says Darch, who also remembers being wound up so tight that for about a year the sound of a roofer's construction gun caused him to flatten himself by a building and the sight of an airplane doing stunts over his backyard caused him to dive to the ground in expectation of a strafing run.

Wracked by survivor's guilt and separated by a gulf from the victorious soldiers now coming home, Poolton's thoughts turned darker. The horrible memories of the battle he had been in, the humiliation of being shackled, the pain of the Hunger March combined now in a different way than they had in the POW camp, where, no matter how hungry, cold and lousy they were, the POW's urge to survive was paramount. In the safety of northern Ontario, where his mother's home cooking was before him three times a day, he started to consider suicide.

As Poolton struggled, reproaching himself for every promise he had made in Germany but now found himself unable to keep, *les religieux* fulfilled a promise they had made to themselves and the Virgin. On 15 August, after having spent a few weeks with their families, they gathered at the Oblate basilica at Cap-de-la-Madeleine, near Quebec City, for a mass of thanksgiving. As he had so often behind the barbed wire, Father Pâquet led the priests and brothers: "We come to say 'Thank You,' kind Mother, in the joy of our liberation and the profound happiness of our return. We thank you for having kept us alive when so many of our companions of exile and captivity have died, and by doing so, you have spared inexpressible sorrow to those we love."[278]

Religion too helped Ian MacDonald, who met his first cousin on the ship that brought him home. Their fathers picked them up at the train station in Truro, Nova Scotia. As MacDonald walked into his kitchen in Lourdes, his mother said, "My prayers have brought him home," recalls Rita MacDonald, Ian's sister. He drank a bottle of milk, with cream floating on the top, afterward explaining to his mother that the only milk he had had since leaving home had been bluish and burned your stomach.

"When I came home, I had some nightmares and for a while the summer thunderstorms brought back memories of air raids. But, as I had during the war when I'd had those scrapes with eternity in France and Germany, I had faith in my Maker, who had brought me home," says MacDonald. Hours later, after catching up on the news of his family, he knelt beside the bed he had slept in the night before going to war and said his prayers with the same rosary the SS officer had insulted two years earlier.

Faith and the strong Jewish community in Montreal helped ease Harry Hurwitz's way back to civilian life. Not long after walking into the family's apartment in an area Mordecai Richler would later make famous, Hurwitz heard how every morning for five or six months his sister would go down the stairs as soon as the mail had been delivered to check for a letter from him. As his father looked on, his sister told of the arrival of the letter in which Harry informed his family that he was a prisoner in Germany. She ran to the synagogue where her father was praying. Although females were supposed to stay to one side, she approached her father anyway, and as the elder Hurwitz davened, she said, "Papa, Harry's alive." He finished his prayer, then took the letter to the rabbi, who announced that their prayers had been answered.

That night, his first back home, the prayers said before dinner, which Harry had said hundreds of times in a Jewish version of a *messe blanche*, dated back millennia and linked him to his bar mitzvah when, in the eyes of the Jewish community, he became a man.

* * *

In the fall, MacDonald headed off to St. Francis Xavier University in Antigonish, Nova Scotia, to study first-year science (a year later he entered the pharmacy program), Hurwitz got a job with the Lionel company, makers of model trains, and Darch went to trade school to study to become a machinist. Poolton struggled, working first laying hardwood floors and roofing, and then in a paper mill. During the early fall, he pinned his hopes on a three-ton Ford pickup truck that friends persuaded him to buy so he could fulfill his promise of working for himself. By mid-fall, he had decided to enroll in a mechanics course sponsored by the Department of Veterans Affairs. Since wartime production restrictions had not yet been fully lifted, the truck did not arrive at the Ford dealership until January 1946. By then, Poolton was halfway through the course and "starting to get on with my life."[279]

* * *

Still in a state of shock from what he'd been through in Buchenwald and on the Hunger March, Carter-Edwards cried when his mother and brother picked him up at the train station in downtown Hamilton and took him home to the low bungalow, a stone's throw from the railway tracks that still run past the Dofasco plant, which during the war stamped out millions of armour plates used in ships, tanks and armoured personnel carriers. And he knows he cried when he saw his sick father. Much else of those early months home is still buried, save for the nightmares and the pain of being disbelieved.

The nightmares, Carter-Edwards recalls, were all so similar. There was a building made of red brick. It was filled with people standing almost shoulder to shoulder but, like on the *Appellplatz* at Buchenwald, there was enough room for them to collapse. "I didn't see them on the ground, but I knew they were dead," he says. At times the nightmares were of a woman in tattered clothes holding a baby. "It was obviously her child," Carter-Edwards says. "And as I watched, its eyes would slowly close." They were being gassed, and when the baby's eyes closed, they were all dead. "I knew what the smoke from the crematorium would look and smell like." For months he would escape by going on late-night walks on the streets of Hamilton with his mother.

His parents, and later Lois, whom he married in 1946, believed the stories of his experiences. But many others, including well-meaning friends, did not. "I'd tell people I'd been in Buchenwald. Some responded by saying I had a severe problem, that I'd mixed up being a POW and being in Buchenwald. They'd ask, 'Are you Jewish?' or 'Do you have a number tattooed on your arm?' They were right that I was in psychological trouble, but they were wrong that I'd made anything up"—Carter-Edwards's tone as he says these last words registering the still-present pain of conversations he had with young men now long dead. What was more painful and, Carter-Edwards believes, more damaging were those who pretended to believe him but behind his back expressed their doubts. "My circle in Hamilton wasn't large, and I soon heard what people were saying about me. Despite the pain and rage in me, the things people were saying kept my emotions frozen, and I kept silent."

In the early 1950s, Carter-Edwards, who had returned to his job at Westinghouse, joined an amateur theatre troop. "I'd always liked plays, and I joined for fun. I had no idea that learning to become a character, learning his emotions, acting on stage and even singing would begin to free up my emotions," he says. "I still could not remember much of what happened, but at least I no longer felt emotionally dead about those years. My wife's warm family also helped, and gradually I began to feel normal again."

Like so many others veterans of the war, for decades Carter-Edwards did not speak out about his experiences. "It was a strange phenomenon," says MacDonald. "As we got on with our lives, none of us wanted to talk about our past. Even early on, when I was studying to be a pharmacist, I knew other men who had been in the air force, and we didn't speak about our experiences. Later I even met men who I knew were POWs, but they didn't know I had been one, and it wasn't ever brought up." In the late 1980s as the 50th anniversary of the end of the war approached, a renewed interest in the veterans and their experiences prompted many to break their silence. Carter-Edwards can date the recovery of his voice almost to the day.

In the early 1950s, the Canadian government recognized via a sentence on his service record and his disability pension that he had indeed been in Buchenwald. In late April 1988, Carter-Edwards received a letter from the International Tracing Service, an arm of the International Committee of the Red Cross in Geneva. The letter confirmed that, according to German records, Carter-Edwards was committed to Concentration Camp Buchenwald by the Paris office of the SS (the order, presumably, also committed the Allied airmen in Fresnes Prison to Buchenwald). The letter, the Red Cross emblem stamped on its upper-left-hand corner now faded, goes on to say that "prisoner number 78361 was treated several times in the infirmary of Concentration Camp Buchenwald in the period from 11th of September 1944 to 14th of October 1944 (diagnosis pneumonia BTS) and from 15 October 1944 to 9th of November 1944 (diagnosis, pneumonia BTS, grippe, bronchitis) [and] was transferred to Stalag [Luft III] Sagan on 28th November 1944."[280]

EPILOGUE

Over the course of 40 bombing missions, Norman Reid's training in astral navigation and map reading had served his crews well. On their 28th mission, the sum total of the triangles and lines he drew ensured that when they had to bail out of their Wellington bomber after being hit while bombing German positions north of Anzio, they were close enough to the Allied lines to walk to safety. These same skills ensured that they'd find the bridge at Turnu Severin and, later, allow him to radio his coordinates to Allied forces in Italy. In between, when judging whether to reveal himself to the four rough-looking men, knowing how to use a sextant and about sines and cosines was useless. In a strange and foreign land, peopled by figures that even then seemed to him as coming from a B-grade western, Reid relied on gut instincts. His escape from the maize field seemed the kind of story he'd read in *Boy's Own Annual.*

At Dieppe, six hours of battle exhausted everything learned in two years of training, which included neither how to suborn guards with cigarettes nor the art of jumping from a moving train. The Fusiliers Mont-Royal who jumped from the trains destined for POW camps in Germany trusted that their mother tongue would ease their way through Occupied France. Neither the reading of civilians nor the intrepid confidence needed to reveal themselves to those who would have been handsomely paid to betray them was taught in the drill halls of Montreal or the training camps of Britain.

Ian MacDonald's high school French helped, but, as Edward Carter-Edwards's story shows, it alone doesn't explain how an evader could survive for weeks on the run. Nor does what the Air Ministry called Escape and Evasion training, which consisted mainly of being told how to put on a parachute and count to ten before pulling the rip cord, and of an explanation of the contents of the Escape and Evasion kit. Evading the Gestapo required the dauntlessness that, perhaps, only men still in or barely out of their teens can have. It also required a sixth sense, luck, and the imagination to see one's self as a latter day Scarlet Pimpernel, the era's James Bond, whom they knew from the film starring Raymond Massey.

Not even years of garrison duty in England could prepare men like Stan Darch—who in the moments before raising his arms in surrender experienced the exhilaration and terror of battle—for the sheer boredom of life in a POW camp. Coming to terms with the humiliation of being defeated, the degradation of being kept filthy, hunger and the enforced idleness vexed Lieutenant Colonel Cecil Merritt, who earned Victoria Cross before being captured at Dieppe, to the point that after being liberated he spat that being a POW "cannot be translated into virtue."[281] And yet, as shown by his own career, which included an escape attempt that earned him assignment to the forbidding Colditz Castle, being a POW—or better, surviving being a POW—required its own type of mettle. For men like John Grogan and Andrew Cox, that mettle included the sang-froid to swap over.

None of the members of the Escape Committee at Stalag Luft III could have known that the Great Escape would tie up some 70,000 men or that the Germans would murder 50 escapers in cold blood. But, like similar committees in other camps, they knew that escapes cost the Germans something and that trying to thwart them was also a drain on the Reich's resources. Wally Floody and his comrades had no doubt that even had they never been used, the digging of tunnels and the making of compasses and other escape gear maintained morale, and thus acted like a thumb in the eye of the goons. Despite their shock and humiliation, the survivors of Dieppe did what they could to mock the Germans for shackling them and so reaffirmed their status as free men, something the German guards were not.

Soldiers, sailors and airmen may not have believed they would end up "rotting in a POW camp," but at least intellectually they knew it was a possibility. By contrast, whatever concerns the Oblates and Sacred Heart Brothers may have had as they boarded the SS *Zamzam*, spending years behind *les barbelés* was not one of their imagined futures. Their evangelical calling gave *les religieux* a mission, albeit one very far from Basutoland. Alone among the Kriegies, the fathers and brothers were able to openly apply their training to their lives in the barren lands of Stalag VIII-B, Milag und Marlag Nord, Stalag Luft III and a dozen other camps. Yet, as Father Charbonneau's secret communication with Oblates in Posen and Father Goudreau's smuggling of letters shows, theirs was not "a cloistered virtue, unexercised and unbreathed"; rather, the Oblates sallied out, albeit in secret, against their adversary, to paraphrase John Milton.[282]

King and country mattered. Andrew Carswell, Russ Burrows and Stuart Kettles may not have known about the Nazis' worst sins when they climbed onto their plane, landing craft or warship, but they knew the answer to the question posed by a wounded flyer on Brian Hodgkinson's ward during the airmen's debate with Dr. Meinhoff: "How long before you try to gobble up North and South America and the rest of Africa and Australia?"[283] As the war continued and the Canadians saw Germany's disregard for the Geneva Convention, so starkly evident in the Reich's murder of more than 150 Canadians in Normandy, the inhumane treatment of the Russians, and the indications of the killings of millions of Jews, Roma, Poles and others, it took on greater meaning. Forced to watch from the sidelines, Kriegies sabotaged when they could. One of the few arrows in their quiver stung: Canadians would light a Sweet Caporal or a Player's cigarette, smoke it halfway and then, in front of the guards who had access to much inferior cigarettes, throw the half-smoked fag on the ground and ostentatiously grind it into the dirt.

Central to both to servicemen and *les religieux* were their ties to their families. Especially because of the delay of ten or so weeks, if it brought news of illness, mail could raise concerns. The absence of mail, however, threatened to undermine the men's equilibrium. Reading that one's mother had made jam, father and uncle had painted a garage, or wife or girlfriend had cried upon receiving one's letter rebalanced the men. Giving advice, as Father Bergeron did; jesting with his mother, as MacDonald did; telling Jacqueline how much he loved her, as Jacques Nadeau did hardly appear as defiant acts. Yet they were. For each time a soldier, sailor, airmen, priest or brother did so, he affirmed his independence from the German carceral, and his life back in Canada.

Merritt was right to honour the men who fought from the "landings in Sicily to the very end." The vice formed by the Canadian, British and US Armies (and air forces and navies), and the Russian army in the field, crushed Nazi Germany. However, the officer who earned a VC at Dieppe was too hard on himself—and by extension the thousands of other POWs—when he said that his "war lasted six hours." Whether or not they evaded for weeks or swapped over and escaped (only to be recaptured), the Kriegies remained men at war. For them, the derring-do of battle was replaced by perseverance. Like the character of Mankind in the 15th-century morality play *The Castle of Perseverance*, men like Ian MacDonald, Edward Carter-Edwards, Andrew Carswell, George Reid, Russ Burrows, Stuart Kettles, Stan Darch, John Grogan, Stan Dutka, Tommy Thompson and Jack Poolton; Fathers Goudreau, Charbonneau, Juneau, Paquet, Desroyers and Barsalou; and Brothers Georges-Aimée, Antoine Lavallée and Roland Counayer . . . defended themselves daily against despair brought on by insults, violations of their Geneva rights, debilitating hunger and, in the winter of 1944–45, the misery of the Hunger Marches. Their resoluteness in the face all that their Nazi overlords meted out, and their love for each other—and the Allied cause—should not be forgotten.

The Men

Name	Rank/Service/Religious Order	Date*
Alfred Burke Thompson	RAF Pilot Officer	9 September 1939
Vernon Howland	Captain (British) Fleet Air Arm	13 June 1940
Andrew Cox	RAF Warrant Officer 1st Class	8 September 1940
Preston Ross	Merchant Mariner/*A.D. Huff*	22 February 1941
George Shaker	Merchant Mariner/*A.D. Huff*	22 February 1941
Dr. Charles Fisher	Surgeon Lieutenant/RCN/RN	4 April 1941
Robert Barsalou, OMI	Oblates of Mary Immaculate	17 April 1941
Raoul Bergeron, OMI	Oblates of Mary Immaculate	17 April 1941
Gérard Boulanger, OMI	Oblates of Mary Immaculate	17 April 1941
Herménégilde Charbonneau, OMI	Oblates of Mary Immaculate	17 April 1941
Roland Cournoyer, OMI	Oblates of Mary Immaculate	17 April 1941
Bernard Desnoyers, OMI	Oblates of Mary Immaculate	17 April 1941
Philippe Goudreau, OMI	Oblates of Mary Immaculate	17 April 1941

* *The date is the day when each of these men enter our story.*

Name	Rank/Service/Religious Order	Date*
Paul Juneau, OMI	Oblates of Mary Immaculate	17 April 1941
Louis Larivière, OMI	Oblates of Mary Immaculate	17 April 1941
Gérard Pâquet, OMI	Oblates of Mary Immaculate	17 April 1941
Léo Parent, OMI	Oblates of Mary Immaculate	17 April 1941
Pierre-Paul Pellerin, OMI	Oblates of Mary Immaculate	17 April 1941
Antoine Lavallée, SC	Brothers of the Sacred Heart	17 April 1941
Georges-Aimé Lavallée, SC	Brothers of the Sacred Heart	17 April 1941
Maurice Nadeau, SC	Brothers of the Sacred Heart	17 April 1941
Brian Hodgkinson	Pilot Officer/ RCAF	27 October 1941
Kingsley Brown	Pilot Officer/RCAF	3 July 1942
George A. Browne	Artillery Officer/Canadian Army	19 August 1942
Russ Burrows	Sapper/Canadian Army	19 August 1942
Stan Darch	Private/Canadian Army	19 August 1942
Lucien Dumais	Company Sergeant Major/ Canadian Army	19 August 1942
John Grogan	Private/Canadian Army	19 August 1942
Guy Joly	Private/Canadian Army	19 August 1942
Conrad Lafleur	Private/Canadian Army	19 August 1942
Antoine Masson	Captain/Canadian Army	19 August 1942
Jacques Nadeau	Private/Canadian Army	19 August 1942
Jack Poolton	Private/Canadian Army	19 August 1942
A. Robert Prouse	Private/Canadian Army	19 August 1942
John Runcie	Captain/Canadian Army	19 August 1942
Robert Vanier	Private/Canadian Army	19 August 1942

NAME	RANK/SERVICE/RELIGIOUS ORDER	DATE*
Vincent McAuley	Acting Squadron Leader/RCAF	11 December 1942
Sydney P. Smith	Pilot Officer/RCAF	12 December 1942
Andrew Carswell	Pilot Officer/RAF	17 January 1943
Ian R. MacDonald	Sergeant/RCAF	15 April 1943
Stewart Cowan	Wing Commander/RCAF	29 July 1943
Robert Brooks	Sergeant/RCAF	24 August 1943
Roy McLernon	Squadron Leader/RCAF	24 August 1943
George Reid	Corporal/Canadian Army	13 October 1943
Ken Woodhouse	Pilot Officer/RCAF	19 March 1944
Harry Hurwitz	Able Seaman/HMCS *Athabaskan*	29 April 1944
Stuart Kettles	Leading Writer/HMCS *Athabaskan*	29 April 1944
Harry Liznick	Able Seaman/HMCS *Athabaskan*	29 April 1944
Norman Reid	Flight Officer/RCAF	8 May 1944
Stan Dutka	Lance Sergeant/Canadian Army	7 June 1944
Edward Carter-Edwards	Wireless Operator/RCAF	8 June 1944
John Harvie	Flight Officer/RCAF	8 June 1944
C.B. Morris	Sergeant/Canadian Army	8 June 1944
Kenneth Macalister	Special Operations Executive	21 August 1944
Frank Pickersgill	Special Operations Executive	21 August 1944
Romeo Sabourin	Special Operations Executive	21 August 1944
James G. Young	Squadron Leader/RCAF	25 August 1944
Edward Blenkinsop	Squadron Leader/RCAF	28 October 1944
Robert Buckham	Flight Lieutenant/RCAF	28 January 1945

Acknowledgements

One of the pleasures of being a military historian is getting to know such men as Ian R. MacDonald of Halifax, Nova Scotia; Norman Reid of Sidney, British Columbia; Stan Darch of Hamilton, Ontario; and Edward Carter-Edwards of Smithville, Ontario.

For his friendship and the hundreds of hours of telephone interviews over a number of years and for arranging with his brother to lend me the family's collection of his and their wartime letters, I owe Ian a debt that the telling of his story of evasion, betrayal and imprisonment by the Gestapo and survival of the Hunger March can only partially repay. Norman's story of his escape from Yugoslavia is only part of what I owe him; his engineer's precision cleared up many technical mysteries for me. Telling of the horrors of Dieppe, of the humiliation of free men being shackled, of the deprivation of the POW camps and the misery of the Hunger March caused Stan to choke up, a testament to both the pain that had survived across seven decades and to his comrades. Ed, whose story runs from being shot down to evasion to a Gestapo prison in Paris and, along with 26 other Canadians, to Buchenwald, where, while he was there, three Canadian SOE (Special Operations Executive) agents were among 16 executed, took courage and fortitude to tell a stranger over the phone. For this I thank the man with the gentle voice who, when he visits schools to tell students about what he saw and suffered through in Konzentrationslager Buchenwald, carries with him a rail spike that once held the track that took him and hundreds of thousands more into the camp nestled in the gentle hills of Thuringia.

I must also thank Ron Beal, a medical corpsman who, like his fellow Torontonian, Leo Panatelo, was captured along with 1,900 other Canadians at Dieppe. Harry Hurwitz of Montreal shared with me his unique story of being the only Jewish member of the Royal Canadian Navy to be captured. For sharing with me the story of his father, Surgeon Lieutenant Charles Fisher of Waterloo, Ontario, I thank Dr. Hugh Fisher (Albany, New York).

Father André Dubois, director of the Archives Deschâtelets at Saint Paul University in Ottawa, did more than simply provide me with access to the hundreds of letters and memoirs written by the Oblates and Sacred Heart Brothers captured in April 1941. The dozens of questions he answered with good humour about the priests and brothers—many of whom he knew—made it seem, as I read the words they wrote on flimsy paper and postcards, that I was conversing with these brave and honourable men. *Père André m'a donné une entrée dans une vision du monde depuis longtemps oublié, celui qui enrichit notre compréhension du temps derrière les barbelés.*

Both my dean at Algonquin College in Ottawa, Russell Mills, and my chair, Robyn Heaten, support my writing endeavours outside the college, and for this, and their friendship over many years, I thank them.

Few writers could wish for more help from his colleagues than I have received from my fellow military historians over the years. Jonathan Vance, whose writing on prisoners of war is a model of scholarship, has helped me clarify my ideas. Dr. Tim Cook of the Canadian War Museum is both a friend and inspiration. Dr. Jeff Noakes, also at the Canadian War Museum, pointed me in the right direction at the beginning of this project. Jane Nesbitt, director of the museum's research library, and Carol Reid and Maggie Arbour-Doucette have, as always, been extremely helpful.

I owe special thanks to two historians. The first is Dr. Bill Rawling, who guided me through understanding Dieppe and who I am collaborating with on an edition of the Oblates' letters. The second is Dr. W.A.B. Douglas, whose wealth of knowledge about the Canadian military is an inspiration and who, despite all that he had contributed to our military history over decades, was like a kid in a candy shop when I told him about discovering the Oblates' and Sacred Heart Brothers' story.

Historians overseas have also helped me immeasurably. Sandra Sigmund, the director of the Buchenwald archives, graciously came in on her day off and opened the archives to me. The day my wife and I spent touring the P.O.W. Camps Museum, Stalag Luft III in Żagań (formerly Sagan), Poland, with its director, Marek Łazarz, was as perfect a day as an historian can imagine. As well, let me thank the various members of the SOE Yahoo! discussion group and especially Steven Kippax.

Father Kupka, OMI, an octogenarian Oblate priest in Poznań, Poland, who knew the two Oblates that Father Charbonneau met with secretly, was not only a gracious host and riveting raconteur, he also explained how the occupation of his part of Poland worked and the terrible costs the Polish people and the Oblates paid. *Dobry ojciec, bardzo dzi kuj.*

David Johnston, my agent, allowed me to get on with the work of research and writing.

Jim Gifford, my editor, embraced this project from the beginning, wielded Track Changes like a scalpel, and joined me in the joy of uncovering these forgotten stories. Allegra Robinson, Judy Phillips, Tilman Lewis and the HarperCollins production team did the yeoman's work, making this difficult book attractive and easily readable.

Finally, as always, I must thank my children, Pascale and Nicolas, as well as Tyson Lowrie, who together transcribed the Oblates' letters and know the pleasures of putting words together to make meaning.

Endnotes

1. It is not possible to determine whether the words "Pau, Bourdeaux and Fresnes Prison in Paris" were obliterated by a German or a Canadian censor.

2. In addition to the Oblates, the Sacred Heart Brothers and the American missionaries and their families, *Zamzam* carried some 20 members of a shadowy group called the British-American Ambulance Corps; and seven Canadian women, one of whom, Mrs. Kathleen Levitt, was travelling with her children, Wendy and Peter.

3. Grogan, 92.

4. Vance, *Gallant Company*, 4.

5. Thompson's postwar account actually says "sumptuous report." However, the context makes clear that "report" should have been "repast."

6. At that meeting, Göring thanked Mackenzie King for the two bison that Canada had sent the Berlin Zoo, before turning to more substantive matters, including how much wheat Canada could export to Germany and Germany's complaint that it felt constricted by Great Britain.

7. Cox, 28–29. By the time Cox was captured, the Germans held some two dozen Canadian POWs.

8. North, 202.

9. Cox, 32.

10. As translated by G.-A. Lavallée.

11. Quoted in Parker, 297.

12. E. Nadeau, 57, 61.

13. The translation "Wandering missionaries of the Atlantic" does not do justice to the line written by Father Gérard Pâquet. As we will see below, the word "*errant*" (lost/wanderer) had a special meaning for French Canadians.

14. Murray, "The Sinking of the 'Zamzam,'" *Life* 10, 25: 70.

15. Quoted in E. Nadeau, 40.

16. See Vance, *Objects of Concern*, 103–25, for a discussion of the halting development of Canada's POW apparatus.

17. The Canadian Ernest Shackleton (no relation to the Antarctic explorer) and Briton Sebastian Coe (father of Lord Coe, organizer of the 2012 London Olympics) escaped from the train. The details of their adventure-filled trip to Spain are lost because the report they filed with the Admiralty upon reaching England has gone missing and the article Shackleton published in the *Toronto Star* on 4 October 1941 was doctored so as to prevent the Germans from following their route. All that is certain is that the two intrepid men escaped and reported what they had seen to British authorities.

18. Cox, 49. One novel that caused so much interest that it had to be divided into ten-page segments was D.H. Lawrence's *Lady Chatterley's Lover*, which had been banned in Britain and the United States for obscenity.

19. David Shavit, "'The Greatest Morale Factor Next to the Red Army': Books and Libraries in American and British Prisoners of War Camps in Germany during World War II," *Libraries & Culture* 34, 2 (Spring 1999), http://sentra.ischool.utexas.edu/~lcr/archive/fulltext/LandC_34_2_Shavit.pdf.

20. By the end of the war, more than 6,000 Allied soldiers had taken final exams, with a pass rate of almost 80 per cent. In Canada, not only did professors from Queen's University proctor exams for U-boat officers held in Fort Henry and Bowmanville, Ontario, but on at least one occasion a U-boat officer in full uniform crossed the stage at Queen's to pick up his BA diploma.

21. Cox, 56–58.

22. As we will see below, such baiting of their German captors was not always popular. For many, however, small acts of rebellion were vital to Kriegies' sense of themselves as men at war.

23. The term "Babylonian captivity" refers two periods. In 597 B.C., after winning the siege of Jerusalem, King Nebuchadnezzar II deported tens of thousands of Jews to Babylon (modern-day Iraq). They were held captive there for 80 years,

until Cyrus the Great defeated the Babylonians and allowed willing Jews to return to Jerusalem. The term was then applied to the period during the fourteenth century when the papacy resided in France. In 1309, to avoid political turmoil in Rome, the French pope Clement V moved the papacy from Rome to Avignon, where it remained until 1378.

24. Quoted in E. Nadeau, 134.

25. Ibid., 136. It is a measure of the brothers' erudition and Lavalée's sense of humour that the poem is a dithyramb, which, according to Plato, originated in the cult of Dionysus, the god of wine, fertility and ecstacy.

26. Ibid., 146.

27. Ibid., 171.

28. Goudreau's confrere and fellow Canadian, Father Luc Miville, who was stranded at an Oblate seminary near La Brosse-Montceaux after the fall of France in June 1940, also risked his life for the Allied cause. Because he was bilingual, he was able to run a clandestine radio station, which was used to plan drops of guns and munitions destined for the Resistance. Miville was one of the few at the seminary to survive a massacre of priests and brothers perpetrated by the Germans on 24 July 1944.

29. Quoted in Hodgkinson, 31, 34, 56.

30. Hodgkinson, 39, 61.

31. Ibid., 36, 63.

32. Ibid., quoted in 64–65.

33. The General Roman Calendar (of the Saints) in use today is not the same one that was in place in the 1940s. Then, the Fête de Saint Jean de la Croix fell on 24 November.

34. St. John of the Cross, "Dark Night of the Soul."

35. Cox, 63.

36. Quoted in Hodgkinson, 47, 48, 83.

37. Ibid., 98.

38. The Kriegies erroneously took this to mean that the United States was at war against Nazi Germany. In fact, the United States did not declare war against Germany until after Hitler declared war against the United States on 11 December.

Interestingly, none of the POWs' letters, diaries or memoirs that I have read record this fact.

39. Since neither Cox's nor any of the other POWs' memoirs I've read mention it, none appeared to know that, with the attack on Hong Kong, almost 2,000 of their countrymen belonging to the Royal Rifles of Canada and the Winnipeg Grenadiers were now fighting Canada's first land battle of the Second World War.

40. E. Nadeau, 114.

41. Hodgkinson and quoted in 107–8.

42. Quoted in Hodgkinson, 117.

43. Cox, 71.

44. Allister, 76.

45. "Canadian Missionaries Behind Barbed Wire," part 1, *P.O.W. Journal*, April, May, June 1980: 41.

46. Quoted in E. Nadeau, 168.

47. Hodgkinson, 130.

48. Quoted in Hodgkinson, 132.

49. Another 88 German Oblates were imprisoned in regular prisons for varying periods.

50. A.J. Barker, quoted in Mackenzie, 176.

51. Quoted in E. Nadeau, 164–65.

52. Charbonneau, "Fraternité oblate en pays de captivité," 14.

53. Quoted in Brown, 108.

54. Quoted in Atkin, 118.

55. Poolton, 43.

56. Atkin, 231.

57. Quoted in and Dumais, 46, 27.

58. Ibid., 47.

59. The most seriously wounded—and there were hundreds—were taken first to Hôtel-Dieu Hospital in Dieppe. The casual way the Germans treated the wounded Canadians shocked the nuns. The wounded were then sent to the Dieppe train station and on to Rouen.

60. Poolton, 45.

61. Quoted in Atkin, 247.

62. Ibid., 249.

63. Dumais, 51.

64. Although Mackenzie King told Hitler that, were Britain to be attacked, Canada would come to its aid, it cannot be said that Mackenzie King's diary entry for 29 June 1937 was his finest hour. The following quote comes from page 10 of King's entry for this day:"His [Schmidt's] eyes impressed me most of all. There was a liquid quality about them which indicated keen perception and profound sympathy. . . . He was very nice, sweet and, one could see, how particularly humble folk would come to have a profound love for the man. He never once became the least bit restless during the talk of an hour and a quarter which we had together. . . . It seems to me that in this he was eminently wise. . . . As I talked to him, I could not but think of Joan of Arc. He is distinctly a mystic. He was telling me that the German people, many of them, begin to feel that he was on a mission from God, and some of them would seek to reverence him almost as a God. He said Hitler himself tries to avoid that kind of thing. He dislikes any of them thinking of him as anything but a humble citizen who is trying to serve his country well."

Mackenzie King's reaction to Hitler is perhaps even more surprising given that (though neither Hitler nor Schmidt seemed to be aware of it) the prime minister spoke fluent German; he owed his first electoral victory to the fact that he could speak the language of the farmers around his home town of Berlin (Kitchener), Ontario. Available at www.collectionscanada.ca.

65. Schmidt, 250.

66. Mellor, 98, 99.

67. Since immigration from France was cut off after the British defeated the French at the Battle of the Plains of Abraham in 1759, Dumais's Quebec dialect did not develop the way the dialect of the French of Île-de-France (Paris) did. Dumais's accent and many of the words he would have used bore similarities to the regional French of Upper Normandy. In addition, French farmers in the provinces tended to hold the governments in Paris or Vichy with equal disdain.

68. Dumais, 70.

69. Ibid., 76.

70. Ibid., 77, 78.

71. Quoted in and Dumais, 79.

72. Quoted in Ousby, 161.

73. Ninetta Jucker, quoted in Glass, 218.

74. Quoted in Todorov, 66.

75. Quoted in Roland, 13.

76. Mellor, 102.

77. Poolton, 55.

78. *Apologia Pro Vita Sua* is Cardinal John Henry Newman's autobiography, which charts his spiritual journey from Anglicanism to Catholicism.

79. Larivière's use of "conscript" is incorrect and likely stems from the fact that French Canadians had traditionally opposed conscription (as they did in the 1917 Conscription Crisis and again in the Conscription Referendum in April 1942) as well as service in the armed forces. There is no indication that Larivière knew of the Conscription Referendum.

80. Quoted in Dumais, 88.

81. Quoted in and Dumais, 87, 87–88.

82. Quoted in Grogan, 23.

83. Quoted in Mellor, 112.

84. Quoted in Grogan, 27. The next morning, Canadian officers at Oflag VII-B, in Eichstätt, were shackled, as they were the following day and the one after that. Subsequently, each day, guards choose 20 officers to shackle. As Jonathan Vance explains in "Men in Manacles," as soon as the British started arranging with Canada for a retaliatory shackling of German POWs in the Dominion, the Germans upped the ante by shackling an additional 4,128 prisoners, a third of whom were Canadian.

85. Dumais, 92, 93.

86. Ibid., 95.

87. Prouse, 31.

88. The debate about retaliatory shacklings also involved the government of Australia, which was alarmed, lest its own POWs be shackled. Such luminaries as the 87-year-old George Bernard Shaw and famed classicist Dr. Gilbert Murray, both of whose works were sent by the Red Cross and other organizations to the men in the camps, also opposed Churchill's request that Canada increase the number of Germans being shackled.

89. Poolton, 60, 61.

90. Quoted in S.P. Smith, 119.

91. S.P. Smith, 132.

92. Quoted in ibid., 147.

93. Prouse, 41.

94. S.P. Smith, 147.

95. Poolton, 61.

96. Quoted in E. Nadeau, 236.

97. Ibid.

98. E. Nadeau, 236.

99. None of the Kriegies knew that as their stomachs growled and they lived from Red Cross parcel to Red Cross parcel, German POWs in Canada were fed so well that some Canadians complained that the prisoners ate better than they did.

100. Over the course of the war, more than 40 million Red Cross parcels were sent to Europe, 16.5 million from Canada. Since the parcels were sent to a central distribution point, the men could receive either an American, a Canadian or a British parcel. Although Geneva and the Red Cross intended for each man to receive one parcel per week, or 2,070 calories per day, very few POWs received parcels this often. Unlike American and British parcels, Canadian ones did not contain cigarettes; these were sent by families and various patriotic funds. *Les religieux* received cigarettes from such diverse groups as the Order of the Daughters of the Empire and the Ontario Chinese Patriotic Fund.

101. Carswell, 12.

102. This same mixture of pride and concern was felt by the families of the thousands of women who served in war zones with the Canadian Women's Army Corps (CWACs), the Women's Royal Canadian Naval Service (WRENS) and the Royal Canadian Air Force (RCAF) Women's Division.

103. Carswell, 39, 41, 43–46.

104. Recent work by neuroscientists using MRI to study the brain while reading shows that Darch and other POWs were not being hyperbolic when they said that reading transported them back home. Reading always involves two parts of the brain: the language centre and, depending on what is being read, another part of the brain. Reading the word "kick," for example, activates the part of the brain associated with the leg muscles in conjunction with the language centre. This means, says Professor Raymond Mar of York University, that "in a very real sense, especially given the extreme situation they were in, when prisoners read letters from home they were transported into a familiar zone created by their minds that was in an emotional sense tied to being 'home.'" Personal interview with the author and email, 13 April 2013.

105. Carswell, 58.

106. Quoted in ibid., 67. Other POWs report similar outbursts, as did Errol Flynn and David Niven recalling a particularly upset director named Michael Curtiz; see TCM.com, "Michael Curtiz," http://www.tcm.com/tcmdb/person/42547%7C111394/Michael-Curtiz/notes.html.

107. Prouse, 44.

108. Quoted in Dancocks, 107.

109. Interestingly, rather than name homosexuality as an offence, the regulations governing the RCAF, RCN and Canadian Army spoke of "bringing scandal on the service" or "any other disgraceful conduct of a cruel, indecent or unnatural kind." However, according to Paul Jackson, the notes to the *Manual of Military Law* "made it clear that the legislation was intended to prosecute" homosexuals. P. Jackson, 81.

110. Determining the rate of either homosexual longing or activity is at this late stage impossible. One Australian pilot at Stalag Luft III estimated the occurrence at 0.33 per cent. Many who wrote about it—Geoffrey Broom, a merchant mariner at Milag Nord, wrote that by end of 1944, a "hell of a lot of men seem to be affected here . . . some of them were quite obvious. . . . and quite out of control"—were outraged at the idea. Roger Coward, who was at an *Arbeitskommando* connected to Stalag Luft VIII, claims that Senior British Officers and padres "did everything possible to keep youngsters from the older perverts" and that the POWs themselves asked the Germans to break up couples.

The fact that other men, including *les religieux*, did not refer to homosexuality does not testify to its absence, for most men did not mention it in their postwar interviews, memoirs or even in interviews undertaken more recently by the Imperial War Museums. Others, like A.D. St. Clair, a British soldier captured at Tobruk who moved to Canada after the war, notes that although the Kriegies were for the most part at the age which under normal circumstances would have seen "the height of our sexual energies," food was usually much more important. Whether he is correct about sexuality in civilian prisons is less important than the cautionary note: "Do not make the mistake of comparing a POW camp with a modern maximum-security prison where, I understand, homosexual rape by 'boss' prisoners of young newcomers is quite common. We . . . were all under military discipline." Brown and Coward quoted in Mackenzie, 213; St. Clair, 255. These angry denunciations are, however, exceptions to the general silence about homosexual activity in the camps. This silence itself is, perhaps, a better indicator of a general tolerance that also went all but uncommented upon in memoirs.

111. Presumably the medical corpsmen to whom Fisher refers were able to engage in homosexual acts more easily because they had access to more private locations. As Eric Newby, a British soldier in an Italian POW camp, wrote of masturbation, or, as it was derisively known at the time, "self-abuse," it was difficult to "perform the operation while lying cheek by jowl with 26 other people in a room illuminated by searchlights, [it] required a degree of stealth which had deserted most of us since leaving school," referring, of course, to British boarding schools. Quoted in Gilbert, 119.

112. Prouse, 113. Toward the end of his study of homosexuality in the military during the Second World War, Paul Jackson notes that the phenomenon of "male marriages" that Pierre Berton wrote about in his memoir *Starting Out* also occurred in POW camps, where men became emotionally dependent on each other for years. These "marriages," which were recognized by camp argot, were seen by some as violating the notion that men should be strong and independent, and as interfering "with the looser relationships that were transferable from comrade to comrade." Nevertheless, they were prevalent enough to develop a nomenclature. Further, the close emotional attachments, Jackson concludes, were not always sexual (nor, of course, were assignations necessarily emotional). P. Jackson, 263–64.

113. Quoted in Dancocks, 107.

114. Carswell, 77.

115. Quoted in Brown, 68, 67.

116. Carswell, 84, 88.

117. Brown, 69.

118. Harry Jay in *Britain at War*, 41 (September 2010): 65.

119. The line from Shakespeare's *Julius Caesar* (Act 2, Scene 2) is Caesar's: "Cowards die many times before their deaths; / The valiant never taste of death but once." If anything, the escaper is an avatar of the valiance. Later, Prouse appears to misremember Falstaff's famous line (*Henry VI*, Part 1: Act 5, Scene 4) "The better part of valour is discretion," which is more popularly remembered as "Discretion is the better part of valour." No one can remotely consider Prouse and his companions as acting cowardly.

120. Prouse, 60, 61.

121. Grogan, 38, 39, 40.

122. Prouse, 67.

123. Grogan, 41, 42, 49.

124. Carswell, 113, 115.

125. Quoted in Glass, 311.

126. Grogan, 46, 53.

127. Earlier that day, Vincent McAuley and his escape partners landed in Barcelona, in neutral Spain. To travel from Vatican City to Ciampino airport—that is, through Rome, an enemy capital—they were likely taken in cars registered to the Holy See onto the tarmac. Once aboard the Spanish plane, they were technically on Spanish soil.

Also on a home run were nine Canadian officers who, along with 47 others, had climbed out of a tunnel that ended in a chicken coop a short distance from Oflag VII-B, in Eichstätt, Germany. Most of the escapers, including Lieutenant Colonel Cecil Merritt, who commanded the South Saskatchewan Regiment and earned a Victoria Cross at Dieppe, headed southeast toward Switzerland, 150 miles away. All nine were recaptured but, as historian Jonathan Vance notes, "unchastened by the experience; a few weeks later, two of the Canadians escaped from their punishment cell by cutting the window bars and lowering themselves on stolen ropes to the ground below" (*Objects of Concern*, 158–59). For their troubles, the Canadians were sent to the forbidding POW camp in Colditz Castle.

128. Prouse, 77.

129. Brown, 142. One can only imagine what Kipp and his partner would have said had they known that German POWs being held in Canada had access to the Eaton's catalogue and were able to send such items as stockings and underwear back to Germany in parcels paid for by the Canadian government.

130. Brown, 143.

131. Later in the year, inflation almost ruined Brian Hodgkinson's distillery business. When he started it, a box of prunes cost 7 cigarettes and one of raisins 20. After two other combines joined the moonshine-making business, demand for "raw materials" doubled their prices. One of his competitors dismissed the Canadian's complaint blithely: "The market is simply responding to demand." Quoted in Hodgkinson, 161.

132. Brown, 144.

133. G. Smith, 27.

134. Ibid., 59.

135. According to Church historian Professor Michael Attridge at St. Michael's College at the University of Toronto, "Father Juneau's actions would have certainly shocked most present and would have symbolized important theological and pastoral considerations. Theologically, in this period, the Church was understood to be represented in its hierarchy, especially in its priesthood. Having the priest face the congregants in this most solemn encounter between Church and people—indeed, for many, between God and people—would have shown them that the Church is with them in these horrific times. Instead of feeling isolated and detached from the Church, people would have felt themselves to be a part of a single community." Personal interview with the author and email, 20 November 2012.

136. Søren C. Flensted, "Halifax V DK261 crashed near the island of Mandø on 24/8 1943," *Airwar over Denmark*, www.flensted.eu.com/19430084.shtml.

137. G. Smith, 70, 69, 70.

138. Quoted in Vance, *Gallant Company*, 164.

139. Quoted in G. Smith, 84.

140. Plenderleith and Welters, who were captured almost immediately, were already at Stalag IV-B. Unlike most pilots who escaped after being shot down over Europe, McLernon went on to fly over Occupied Europe again, completing 31 missions, earning a Distinguished Flying Cross and promotion to wing commander of RCAF's 408 "Goose" Squadron.

141. Prouse, 86, 89.

142. G. Smith, 105, 108, 109, 111.

143. Because of the shackling of the Dieppe POWs, there were no repatriations in 1942 and most of 1943. Two groups, one of 42, the other of 48, were repatriated in 1944. In early 1945, 81 prisoners (not including, as will be seen below, *les religieux*) were repatriated.

144. Reid, 30, 33, 35, 36.

145. G. Smith, 115, 135, 140, 154.

146. Ibid., 167, 172, 182, 184.

147. In *And No Birds Sang*, Mowat writes admiringly of Giovanni's skills and honour: "If he could not find one of our people to rescue, he would bring a captured German instead. . . . He asked nothing from us and would accept nothing except food, most of which I suspected he gave away to needy peasants behind the German lines" (188–89).

148. Reid, 45.

149. Quoted in Dumais, 116.

150. Quoted in E. Nadeau, 186.

151. Quoted in Greenhous et al., 737.

152. Dumais, 126.

153. Aided by two members of the Resistance he'd turned, Pierre Napoleon Poinsot, the commissioner of the Paris police, spent 1942 patiently putting together a file of what to do to break *les femmes dans la Résistance*. In early 1943, 180 (including, it seems likely, the women in the *Pat Line* who had helped Dumais 15 months earlier) were arrested. Beatings did not elicit the desired information, nor did months of imprisonment or malnutrition that caused their stomachs to balloon. In 1943, the women were transferred to Auschwitz, where a number died almost immediately in a forced race through the January snows. Others died as a result of forced labour in draining marshes. By mid-April, only 80 of these brave women were left alive.

154. Dumais, 129, 132, 133.

155. Quoted in and Brown, 157, 159, 158. "Joe Ricks" was a Czech officer named Josef Bryks, who served in the British Army.

156. Reid, 49, 48.

157. Quoted in and Brown, 162, 163, 164.

158. Quoted in and Dumais, 144, 145.

159. Brown, 172.

160. Ibid., 173.

161. Parole tools included saws, hammers and other building equipment that would be given to the POWs on their "word of honour" (*parole*) that they would not be used in escape attempts.

162. Dumais, 147, 149.

163. Ibid., 156.

164. Barsalou did not know that, since May 1942, when the first U-boats entered the St. Lawrence River, a "dim-out" regimen (which everyone called a "black-out") had been in place for Canada's east coast, including Quebec's North Shore and Gaspé coast.

165. Dumais, 159, 160.

166. Quoted in Mellor, 137–8.

167. Dumais, 165.

168. Quoted in Lavender and Sheffe, 98, 99, 101.

169. Ibid., 107.

170. Ibid., 109. Unless Dumais sent two reports, there is some confusion about when this report was sent to MI9. Dumais recalls sending it with Bonaparte I, while Woodhouse recalls it being sent with him on what was Bonaparte III or IV, though the details about having to sink it rather than letting it fall into German hands are the same. Unfortunately, a search of the British National Archives at Kew has produced only the file folder in which the report should have been; the folder does not indicate the date the missing report was written.

171. From a Canadian point of view, the film's greatest offence is not Steve McQueen's famed motorcycle ride but the total absence of Canadians. Wally Floody, who served as a consultant on the film, is transmuted into American Danny Velinski, played by Charles Bronson.

172. Quoted in Vance, *Gallant Company*, 231.

173. Bullet Decree and keeping numbers. De Bello, "The Bullet Decree," http://ww2.debello.ca/library/440304.html.

174. Quoted in Vance, *Gallant Company*, 195.

175. Ibid., 246.

176. Ibid., 247.

177. Quoted in Vance, *Objects of Concern*, 157.

178. Quoted in Vance, *Gallant Company*, 261.

179. Ibid., 255, 264, 265.

180. Ibid., 286.

181. From 1793 until 1919, Posen, as the city is known to Germans, was part of Germany. Despite the Treaty of Versailles, which granted the region called Greater Poland to the newly reformed Polish state, many Germans never stopped considering Posen as part of Germany. After defeating Poland in September 1939, Hitler incorporated Poznań, as it is known to Poles, into the Reich. Companies such as Telefunken and Focke-Wulf, whose famous Condor dive bomber terrorized Spain and Warsaw, rushed to take advantage of the well-educated—and largely German-speaking—workforce. In November 1942, Heinrich Himmler told a select crowd of SS officials gathered in Posen about the "Extermination of the Jewish People" and crowed about working 10,000 Russian women to death if it meant one more anti-tank trap.

182. Quoted in Vance, *Gallant Company*, 288.

183. Quoted in Carswell, 177.

184. The Nazis were nothing if not consistent, as can be seen from the decree that Germans could not accept blood donations from POWs, "since the possibility of a prisoner of war of Jewish origin being used as a donor cannot be excluded with certainty." Cohen, *Soldiers and Slaves*, 71–72.

185. Quoted in E. Nadeau, 234.

186. Quoted in *The Enterprise*, Iroquois Falls, 2 November 1988, B1.

187. Poolton, 93.

188. Carswell, 209.

189. Quoted in Dumais, 185. The invasion of Normandy brought with it the order to suspend the *Shelburn Line* and the instructions to await the Allied advance. Dumais did the former but ignored the latter when he joined with a *Maquis* who

attacked Germans and bombed German positions in what was still Occupied France. Shortly after the Allies liberated Paris, Dumais, who was still officially attached to MI9, returned to his apartment to find a British officer, a Canadian provost marshal and a number of other well-armed men intent on arresting the man the concierge had reported as an imposter and black market operator. Even though Dumais's belt buckle read *"Gott mit uns"* (God is with us) and he wore a mishmash of French, American, British and Canadian uniforms, the Canadian lieutenant believed Dumais's story. He returned to England a few days later.

190. Carswell, 218, 226.

191. Soldiers in battle are not Boy Scouts. While admittedly slight, the difference between the Hitlerjugend's actions and those of the Canadians who, during the bitter fight for Caen, fired on "the Jerries [who] came in with their hands up shouting '*Kamerad*'" (quoted in Stafford, 126) is due to the fact that the battle was still raging around the Canadians and their blood was still up.

192. Quoted in Margolian, 60.

193. Ibid., 69.

194. Ibid., 72. Meyer was convicted and sentenced to death. The sentence was commuted by Canadian major general Christopher Vokes, who said while considering Meyer's request for clemency, "There isn't a general or colonel on the allied side that I know of who hasn't said, 'Well, this time we don't want any prisoners'" (quoted in Brode, 105). Meyer served a five-year sentence in Dorchester Penitentiary before being transferred to a British military prison in West Germany. He was released in September 1954. He became a major figure in HIAG, the Waffen-SS's veteran's organization and in 1957 published a memoir entitled *Grenadier* that praised the SS's—and his—role in the war. For a full discussion of Kurt Meyer's trial see Brode.

195. Ibid., 114.

196. Today, in countries like Canada, where there are not enough priests, Larivière's question has taken on a new urgency. In some places, such as in the far north, deacons are allowed to administer (previously blessed) communion wafers. Both Larivière and Ducharme would have recognized the revolutionary aspect of an affirmative answer to the question about distributing the priests' sacerdotal power. If being a member of the "faithful living in the world" is enough to qualify someone to give the sacraments, then the entire structure of the Catholic Church from the priest up to the pope can be called into question. Indeed, it is not going too far to suggest the trajectory of Larivière points to something resembling Lutheranism.

197. During the war, Pope Pius XII had other concerns, but he and his theological

advisors must have begun considering the "school of Darwin" in a way that would have surprised Charbonneau. In 1950 the pope issued the encyclical *Humani Generis*, which says that the "Church does not forbid that . . . research and discussions, on the part of men experienced in both fields, take place with regard to the doctrine of evolution, in as far as it inquires into the origin of the human body as coming from pre-existent and living matter." In his 1996 address to the Pontifical Academy of Sciences, Pope John Paul II added, "New findings lead us toward the recognition of evolution as more than a hypothesis." http://www.ewtn.com/library/papaldoc/jp961022.htm.

198. Carswell, 231.

199. Stalag IX-B is also known as Stalag 357.

200. In late July, a month after Dr. Peter Brownless, who worked with Charles Fisher, offered the Canadian surgeon lieutenant his place on a repatriation list (because Fisher was married and had a young daughter, while Brownless was a bachelor), Fisher boarded a train that took him from Milag Nord onto a ferry bound for Göteborg, Sweden. A few days later, he arrived in Liverpool on the SS *Gripsholm*, which soon sailed for New York, where he and a number of wounded Canadian soldiers boarded a train for Montreal.

201. The censor who stamped *Geprüft* 67 almost certainly did not catch MacDonald's irony here. In Britain, the Senior Service is the Royal Navy. The Royal Canadian Navy, by contrast, dated only to 1910; the Dominion's "senior service" is the militia.

202. Harvie, 39.

203. Quoted in ibid., 40.

204. Ibid., 52.

205. Childers, 239.

206. With the help of the *Maquis*, Stevenson reached England on 4 September 1944. His report was the first by a Canadian detailing the airmen's treatment in Fresnes Prison.

207. Quoted in Childers, 244.

208. Harvie, 65.

209. Quoted in Childers, 247.

210. Harvie, 67.

211. Quoted in Prouse, 124.

212. Just after Christmas 1943, when Jack Pickersgill was in London with Prime Minister Mackenzie King, he arranged for a message to be sent to Frank saying, "Jack says mother is well." The fake "Pickersgill" answered, "Thank Uncle Jack for his message," which Kay Moore, a junior member of the SOE communications staff who knew Frank Pickersgill well disbelieved, since she'd never heard of an "Uncle Jack." SOE missed, therefore, a central piece of evidence showing that Pickersgill and Macalister had been arrested and, curiously, forwarded the following message to the Pickersgill family: "All the best to Jack. Thanks for the personal message from mother. Please send her all my love and tell her I hope to be back soon." Quoted in Vance, *Unlikely Soldiers*, 230.

213. Vance, *Unlikely Soldiers*, 247.

214. Harvie, 83.

215. Kogon, 116.

216. Harvie, 99.

217. Ibid., 106.

218. http://www.lyricsmania.com/peat_bog_soldiers_lyrics_pete_seeger.html

219. There is some controversy about the dates the SOE men were executed. I am following Jonathan Vance's *Unlikely Soldiers* here.

220. In a visit a few years ago to Buchenwald, Edward Carter-Edwards and other surviving members of the KLB (*Konzentrationslager Buchenwald*) Buchenwald Concentration Camp Club were taken on a tour of this factory. "The visit was sombre," he told me. "But the hair on the back of my neck stood on end when we entered the director's office, and we saw that all the director had to do was look out his window to see the smokestack above the ovens he made—and the smoke from the fires that burned men and women."

221. In *Soldaten: On Fighting, Killing, and Dying; The Secret WWII Transcripts of German POWs*, Sönke Neitzel and Harald Welzer go beyond the well-rehearsed argument that the Germans on the Eastern Front fought tooth and nail because they feared (correctly) that the Russians would wreak terrible revenge for the rape and rapine that the Wehrmacht unleashed on Russia. The transcripts of conversations that were surreptitiously recorded show that while the average soldier may not have been "Nazified," he was certainly "Hitlerfied," having invested an inordinate amount of his self-identity in the idea of the Führer and his notion of struggle (*Kampf*).

222. Quoted in Herzog, 173.

223. Such are the fortunes of war that, but for taking a right at a fork in the road instead of a left, like his comrades who had also bailed out, Carter-Edwards would have soon fallen in with a *Maquis* cell that connected them to MI9, which arranged for his crewmates to return to Britain.

224. Quoted in Kogon, 138.

225. Harvie, 114. On their first day in Buchenwald, Squadron Leader Phil Lamason, the Senior British Officer present, who had been shot down on 8 June while on a bombing raid near Paris, told the airmen, "Gentlemen, we have ourselves a very fine fix indeed. The goons have completely violated the Geneva Convention and are treating us as common thieves and criminals. However, we are soldiers! From this time on, we will also conduct ourselves as our training has taught us and as our countries would expect from us." Quoted in Moser.

226. Reid, 69, 75.

227. J. Nadeau, 111.

228. The survivors of Buchenwald resented both what they saw as the comfort of Stalag Luft III and the fact that the men there were uninterested in hearing about the horrors of Buchenwald.

229. Quoted in Celis, 230.

230. Harvie, 163, 166.

231. Prouse, 128.

232. Harvie, 175.

233. Quoted in E. Nadeau, 252.

234. Harvie, 176. At New Year's, Harvie gave way to a certain bitterness for those back in Canada with "safe cushy war jobs" who would never have to face enemy fire or know what it was to serve their country when hungry, cold and without prospects for shelter, and who could enjoy the night by getting drunk (177).

235. Quoted in Leasor, 115.

236. None knew, of course, that the Germans wanted to hold on to their prisoners for two reasons. Since the Reich was being crushed between millions of Russians coming from the east and the Americans, British and Canadians coming from the west, to say nothing of the thousands of bombers laying waste to German towns, cities and transportation infrastructure, the first reason, to deny some 250,000 men to the Western Allies, makes little sense. Given the POWs' condition, they

would not be battle-ready for many months. The second reason, to use POWs as bargaining chips for some future negotiation, was hopelessly naïve and violated Geneva.

237. Grogan, 95

238. Carswell, 247.

239. As it happens, there was another Canadian at Neuengamme Concentration Camp. George Rodrigues, who had been born in Montreal and had served in the Canadian Army's Corps of Signals before joining MI9, had arrived there in May 1944. He had been inserted into France in August 1943 and captured two months later. Rodrigues was evacuated to Ravensbrück Concentration Camp in April 1944. He survived the war only to die two weeks after it ended from tuberculosis. Rodrigues's MI9 records in the British Archives remain sealed.

240. J. Nadeau, 114.

241. Quoted in Brown, 197.

242. Harvie, 192.

243. Carswell, 250.

244. Poolton, 107.

245. Harvie, 193.

246. Buckham's group won the lottery this time, being billeted in a château in Muskau, where there was food, water to heat and a bath, along with a well-equipped woodworking shop, where the POWs repaired their jury-rigged sleds and wagons.

247. Grogan, 96.

248. Poolton, 105.

249. Prouse, 129.

250. Quoted in E. Nadeau, 275.

251. Quoted in ibid., 276.

252. Carswell, 254, 255.

253. Buckham, 52.

254. *The Twelve Articles: The Just and Fundamental Articles of All the Peasantry and Tenants of Spiritual and Temporal Powers by Whom They Think Themselves Oppressed.*

255. Prouse, 145.

256. Brown, 213. Ironically, the one group in England that Milton did not believe should have freedom of speech was Brown's Catholic co-religionists.

257. Harvie, 210.

258. Cox, 103.

259. Prouse, 148.

260. Poolton, 112, 116.

261. Harvie, 212–13.

262. Quoted in E. Nadeau, 288.

263. Reid, 80, 84–85.

264. Carswell, 258, 261.

265. Quoted in E. Nadeau, 287.

266. Brown, 224, 225

267. Jim Lankford, "Stalag VII: The Liberation," Moosburg online, http://www.moosburg.org/info/stalag/14theng/html.

268. Grogan, 108–9.

269. Ian Brown, "Prisoner of War," http://www.stalag18a.org.uk.

270. Hodgkinson, p. 235.

271. Carswell, 265.

272. Poolton, 117, 120.

273. Ibid., 121.

274. Quoted in E. Nadeau, 281, 282,

275. Quoted in E. Nadeau, 283.

276. Once returned to Russia, most of these thousands of Russians were promptly sent to penal colonies.

277. Brown, p. 248.

278. Quoted in E. Nadeau, p. 302.

279. Poolton, 139.

280. BTS stands for British Thoracic Society.

281. Quoted in *London Times*, 17 July 2000, Merritt obituary.

282. "Aeropagitica: A Speech of Mr. John Milton for the Liberty of Unlicenc'd Printing," http://www.dartmouth.edu/~milton/reading_room/areopagitica/text .shtml.

283. Quoted in Hodgkinson, 48.

Bibliography

Allister, William. *Where Life and Death Hold Hands*. Toronto: Stoddard, 1989.

Amyot, Éric. *Le Québec entre Pétain et De Gaulle: Vichy, La France Libre and Les Canadiens Français 1940–1945*. Montreal: Fides, 1999.

Atkin, Ronald. *Dieppe, 1942: The Jubilee Disaster*. London: Macmillan, 1980.

Beaudoin, Emile. "Canadian Missionaries Who Served as Padres in P.O.W. Camps." *Veterans Journal*, Winter 1978: 28–30.

Berger, Doris L. *Twisted Cross: The German Christian Movements in the Third Reich*. Chapel Hill: University of North Carolina Press, 1996.

Blatman, Daniel. *The Death Marches: The Final Phase of Nazi Genocide*. Translated by Chaya Galai. Cambridge, MA: Harvard University Press, 2011.

Britain at War. "Some You Win, Some You Lose." *Britain at War* 41 (September 2010): 62–66.

Brode, Patrick. *Casual Slaughters and Accidental Judgments: Canadian War Crimes Prosecutions, 1944–1948*. Toronto: University of Toronto Press, 1997.

Brown, Kingsley. *Bonds of Wire: A Memoir*. Toronto: Collins, 1989.

Buckham, Robert. *Forced March to Freedom: An Illustrated Diary of Two Forced Marches and the Interval between January to May 1945*. Stittsville, ON: Canada's Wings, 1990.

Burns, Patricia. *Life on the Home Front: Montreal, 1939–1945*. Montreal: Véhicule Press, 2013.

Campbell, Ian J. *Murder at the Abbaye: The True Story of Twenty Canadian Soldiers Murdered at the Abbaye d'Ardenne.* Ottawa: Golden Dog Press, 1996.

Carswell, Andrew. *Over the Wire: A Canadian Pilot's Memoir of War and Survival as a POW.* Toronto: Wiley and Sons, 2011.

Celis, Peter. *One Who Almost Made It Back: The Remarkable Story of One of World War Two's Unsung Heros, Sqn Ldr Edward "Teddy" Blenkinsop, DFC, CdeG (Belge), RCAF.* London: Grub Street, 2008.

Chancellor, Henry. *Colditz: The Definitive History.* New York: HarperCollins, 2002.

Charbonneau, Herménégilde. "*Fraternité* oblate en pays de captivité." *L'Apostolat des Missionnaires Oblats de Marie Immaculée* 16, 2 (December 1945): 12–14.

———. *Mon nom est Eugène de Mazenod.* Montreal: Missionnaires Oblates de Marie Immaculée, 1975.

Childers, Thomas. *In the Shadows of War: An American Pilot's Odyssey through Occupied France and Camps of Nazi Germany.* New York: Henry Holt, 2002.

Ciardi, Fabio, ed. *Dictionary of Oblate Values.* Rome: Association for Oblate Studies and Research, 2000.

Cohen, Roger. *Soldiers and Slaves: American POWs Trapped by the Nazis' Final Gamble.* New York: Knopf, 2005.

Cox, Andrew B. *Our Spirit Unbroken: Memoirs of a Prisoner of War.* Port Elgin, ON: Brucedale Press, 1999.

Dancocks, Daniel G. *In Enemy Hands: Canadian Prisoners of War, 1939–45.* Toronto: McClelland and Stewart, 1990.

Dear, Ian. *Escape and Evasion: Prisoner of War Breakouts and Routes to Safety in World War Two.* London: Arms & Armour, 1997.

Douglas, Tom. *Canadian Spies: Tales of Espionage in Nazi-Occupied Europe during World War II.* Canmore, AB: Altitude, 2003.

Doyle, Peter. *Prisoners of War in Germany.* Oxford: Shire Library, 2008.

Dumais, Lucien, with Hugh Popham. *The Man Who Went Back.* London: Leo Cooper, 1975.

Durflinger, Serge. *Fighting from Home: The Second World War in Quebec.* Vancouver: UBC Press, 2006.

Foot, M.R.D., and J.M. Langley. *MI9: Escape and Evasion, 1939–1945*. Boston: Little, Brown, 1980.

Gilbert, Adrian. *POW: Allied Prisoners of War in Europe, 1939–1945*. London: John Murray, 2006.

Glass, Charles. *Americans in Paris: Life & Death under Nazi Occupation*. New York: Penguin, 2010.

Gossage, Carolyn. *The Accidental Captives: The Story of Seven Women Alone in Nazi Germany*. Toronto: Dundurn, 2012.

Goudreau, Philippe. "Quelques tribulations d'un 'embarbelé." *L'Apostolat des Missionnaires Oblats de Marie Immaculée* 17, 1 (January 1946): 6–8.

Green, Peter. *The March East 1945: The Final Days of Oflag IX A/H and A/Z*. Stroud, UK: History Press, 2012.

Greenfield, Nathan. *The Damned: The Canadians at the Battle of Hong Kong and the POW Experience, 1941–45*. Toronto: HarperCollins, 2010.

Greenhous, Brereton, Stephen J. Harris, William C. Johnston, and William G.P. Rawling. *The Crucible of War 1939–1945: The Official History of the Royal Canadian Air Force*. Vol. 3. Toronto: University of Toronto Press, 1994.

Grogan, John Patrick. *Dieppe and Beyond for a Dollar and a Half a Day*. Renfrew, ON: Juniper, 1982.

Halliday, Hugh A. "Relief Amid Chaos: The Story of the Canadian POWS Driving Red Cross Trucks." *Canadian Military History* 11, 2 (Spring 2002): 61–65.

Harvie, John D. *Missing in Action: An RCAF Navigator's Story*. Montreal: McGill-Queen's University Press, 1995.

Herf, Jeffrey. *The Jewish Enemy: Nazi Propaganda in World War II and the Holocaust*. Cambridge, MA: Harvard University Press, 2006.

Herzog, Rudolph. *Dead Funny: Humor in Hitler's Germany*. Translated by Jefferson Chase. Brooklyn, NY: Melville House, 2011.

Hodgkinson, Brian. *Spitfire Down: The POW Story*. Edited by George E. Condon. Newcastle, ON: Penumbra Press, 2000.

Hoever, Dom Hugo, ed. *Missel Quotidien Saint-Joseph*. New York: Catholic Book Publishing, 1956.

Intelligence Team of the Psychological Warfare Division of the Supreme Headquarters of the Allied Forces. *The Buchenwald Report.* Translated by David A. Hackett. Foreword by Frederick A. Praeger. San Francisco: Westview Press, 1995.

Jackson, Bill. *The Lone Survivor.* North Battleford, SK: Turner-Warwick, 1993.

Jackson, Paul. *One of the Boys: Homosexuality in the Military during World War II.* Montreal: McGill-Queen's University Press, 2004.

Jones, Elwood. "Young Pilot's Life Well Documented." *Peterborough Examiner.* 3 October 2010. http://www.militarian.com/threads/murdered-pilots-life-well-documented.2035/.

King, David. *Death in the City of Light: The Serial Killer of Nazi-Occupied Paris.* New York: Crown, 2011.

Kogon, Eugen. *The Theory and Practice of Hell: German Concentration Camps and the System Behind Them.* Translated by Heinz Norden. New York: Farrar, Straus and Giroux, 2006.

Lagrandeur, Philip. *We Flew, We Fell, We Lived: Stories from RCAF Prisoners of War and Evaders.* St. Catharines, ON: Vanwell, 2006.

Lavender, Emerson, and Norman Sheffe. *The Evaders: True Stories of Downed Canadian Airmen and Their Helpers in World War II.* Toronto: McGraw-Hill Ryerson, 1992.

Leasor, James. *Green Beach.* London: Corgi, 1976.

Levasseur, Donat. *Histoire des Missionnaires Oblats de Marie Immaculée: Essai de synthèse.* Vol 1. Montreal: Maison Provinciale, 1983.

———. *A History of the Missionary Oblates of Mary Immaculate: Toward a Synthesis.* Translated by John Rheidt and Aloysius Kedl. Rome: General House, 1989.

Levitt, Peter. *A Memoir of the Sinking of the "Zamzam."* Toronto: Lugus, 2011.

Mackenzie, S.P. *The Colditz Myth: The Real Story of POW Life in Nazi Germany.* Oxford: Oxford University Press, 2004.

MacLaren, Roy. *Canadians Behind Enemy Lines, 1939–1945.* Vancouver: UBC Press, 2004.

Margolian, Howard. *Conduct Unbecoming: The Story of the Murder of Canadian Prisoners of War in Normandy.* Toronto: University of Toronto Press, 2000.

Mellor, John. *Dieppe, Canada's Forgotten Heroes: The Horrifying Story of the D-Day Rehearsal That Went Wrong.* Alma, ON: Maple Leaf Route, 1985.

Moore, Bob, and Kent Federowich, eds. *Prisoners of War and Their Captors in World War II.* Washington, DC: Berg, 1996.

Moorhead, Caroline. *A Train in Winter: An Extraordinary Story of Women, Friendship and Survival in World War Two.* Toronto: Random House, 2011.

Moorhouse, Roger. *Berlin at War.* New York: Basic Books, 2010.

Moser, Joe. "Joe Moser—Buchenwald Flyboy," http://buchenwaldflyboy.wordpress.com/about-joe-moser/.

Mowat, Farley. *And No Birds Sang.* Vancouver: Douglas & McIntyre, 2012.

Nadeau, Eugéne. *La Perle au Fond du Gouffre: "Zam-Zam" et Barbelés.* 5th ed. Montreal: Fides 1953.

Nadeau, Jacques. *Dieppe, ma prison: Récit de guerre de Jacques Nadeau.* Outremont, QC: Athéna Éditions, 2008.

Nadeau, Jean-Benoît, and Julie Barlow. *The Story of French.* New York: St. Martin's, 2006.

Nichol, John, and Tony Rennel. *Home Run: Escape from Nazi Europe.* London: Penguin, 2008.

North, Richard. *The Many Not the Few: The Stolen History of the Battle of Britain.* London: Bloomsbury, 2012.

Ousby, Ian. *Occupation: The Ordeal of France, 1940–1944.* New York: Cooper Square Press, 2000.

Parker, Mike. *Running the Gauntlet: An Oral History of Canadian Merchant Seamen in World War II.* Halifax: Nimbus, 1994.

Poolton, Jack A., with Jayne Poolton-Turvey. *Destined to Survive: A Dieppe Veteran's Story.* Toronto: Dundurn, 1998.

Pringle, Sherry J. *All the Ship's Men: HMCS* Athabaskan's *Untold Stories.* St. Catharines, ON: Vanwell, 2010.

Prouse, A. Robert. *Ticket to Hell via Dieppe: From a Prisoner's Wartime Log, 1942–1945.* Toronto: Van Nostrand Reinhold, 1982.

Reid, George A. *Speed's War: A Canadian Soldier's Memoir of World War II.* Seattle: Madrona, 2007.

Riding, Alan. *And the Show Went On: Cultural Life in Nazi-Occupied Paris.* New York: Knopf, 2010.

Roland, Charles G. "On the Beach and in the Bag: The Fate of the Dieppe Casualties Left Behind." *Canadian Military History* 9, 4 (Autumn 2000): 6–25.

Schmidt, Dr. Paul. *Hitler's Interpreter.* New York: MacMillan, 1951.

Shackleton, Ernest. "Escape Story." *Toronto Star.* 4 October 1941.

Shavit, David. "'The Greatest Moral Factor Next to the Red Army' Books and Libraries in American and British Prisoner of War Camps in Germany during World War II." *Libraries & Culture* 34, 2 (Spring 1999).

Smith, Gladys E. *Forty Nights to Freedom: The True Prisoner of War Escape Story of Wing Commander Stewart F. Cowan (Ret.).* Winnipeg: Queenston House, 1984.

Smith, Sydney Percival, with David S. Smith. *Lifting the Silence: A World War II RCAF Bomber Pilot Reunites with His Past.* Toronto: Dundurn, 2010.

Snyder, Timothy. *Bloodlands: Europe between Hitler and Stalin.* New York: Basic Books, 2010.

Speer, Nicole, Jeremy R. Reynolds, Khena M. Swallow, and Jeffrey M. Zacks. "Reading Stories Activates Neural Representations of Visual and Motor Experiences. *Psychological Science* 20, 8: 989–99. http://dcl.wustl.edu/PDFs/Speer09.pdf.

St. Clair, A.D. (Sandy). *The Endless War.* North Battleford, SK: Turner-Warwick, 1987.

St. John of the Cross. "Dark Night of the Soul." *The Collected Works of St. John of the Cross.* Rev. ed. Translated by Kieran Kavanaugh and Otilio Rodriguez. Washington, DC: ICS Productions, 1991. http://www.catholictreasury.info/books/dark_night/dn1.php.

Stafford, David. *Endgame, 1945: The Missing Final Chapter of World War II.* Boston: Little, Brown, 2007.

Thompson, Douglas (Padre). *Captives to Freedom.* London: Epworth Press, 1955.

Todorov, Tzvetan. *Facing the Extreme: Moral Life in the Concentration Camps.* Translated by Arthur Denner and Abigail Pollack. London: Weidenfeld and Nicolson, 1999.

Vance, Jonathan F. *A Gallant Company: The Men of the Great Escape.* Pacifica, CA: Pacific Military History, 2000.

———. "Men in Manacles: The Shackling of Prisoners of War, 1942–1945." *Journal of Military History* 59 (July 1995): 483–504.

———. *Objects of Concern: Canadian Prisoners of War through the Twentieth Century.* Vancouver: UBC Press, 1994.

———. *Unlikely Soldiers: How Two Canadians Fought the Secret War against Nazi Occupation.* Toronto: HarperCollins, 2008.

Walker, Stephen. *Hide and Seek: The Irish Priest in the Vatican Who Defied the Nazi Command.* Guilford, CT: Lyons Press, 2011.

Witt, John W. *Lincoln's Code: The Laws of War in American History.* New York: The Free Press, 2012.

UNPUBLISHED MEMOIRS AND DIARIES*

Booker, Stanley. *The Royal Air Force KL Buchenwald.* Buchenwald Archives.

Miller Fisher, Charles. *Memoirs of a Neurologist.* Library of Congress cat. no. 92–072067.

Lavallée, Antoine. *L'Afrique chez les boches: première partie; mon voyage en Afrique.* Archives Deschâtelets.

———. *L'Afrique chez les boches: deuxième partie; ma captivité en Allemagne.* Archives Deschâtelets.

Lavallée, Georges-Aime, SC. *Marking Time behind Barbed Wire: Four Years of Captivity in Germany, 1941–1945.* Archives Deschâtelets.

Olmstead, Gordon. *Memoir.*

Shaker, George. *Wartime Log, 29 August 1944 to 23 April 1945.*

Sturgeon, Neil Mosher. *My WWII POW Diary.*

* *Copies of these memoirs and diaries are in the possession of the author.*

Oblate Letters*

There are two sources for the letters written by the Oblate fathers and brothers. The first is the Archives Deschâtelets at Saint Paul University in Ottawa. The second is the Oblate journal *L'Apostolat.*

Archives Deschâtelets holds letters by:

Father Robert Barsalou
Father Raoul Bergeron
Father Gérard Boulanger
Father Herménégilde Charbonneau
Brother Roland Cournoyer
Father Bernard Desnoyers
Father Philippe Goudreau
Father Paul Juneau
Father Louis Larivière
Father Gérard Pâquet
Brother Léo Parent
Father Pierre-Paul Pellerin

Between July 1941 and December 1944, *L'Apostolat* published 15 articles containing extracts from letters written by the fathers and brothers. Below is a list of the years, months and pages where these articles can be found:

1941	
July	pp. 206–14
October	pp. 261–66
November	pp. 306–8
1942	
April	pp. 5, 10–16
June	pp. 10–16
July/August	pp. 5–8
September	pp. 12–14
October	pp. 5–7
November	pp. 15–16
December	pp. 6–9
1943	
February	pp. 13–17
May	pp. 6–7
1944	
March	pp. 4–5
June	pp. 8–9
December	pp. 14–18

* *Copies of these letters are in the possession of the author.*

Interviews

Ron Beal
Beverly Brooks (on her father, Robert Brooks)
Edward Carter-Edwards
Stan Darch
Father André Dubois, OMI
Harry Hurwitz
Father K.S. Kupka, OMI (Poznań, Poland)
Marek Łazarz (director of P.O.W. Camps Museum, Stalag Luft III, Żagań, Poland)
Ian MacDonald
Dr. Raymond Mar
Dr. Keith Oatley
Leo Panatelo
Norman Reid

Reports and Interviews with the Department of National Defence, History Secretariat

George A. Browne
Stan Darch
Rev. John Foote
Vernon Howland
Ken Hyde
Stuart Kettles
Vincent McAuley
Leslie S.G. Moore
Roger J. Teillet
Alfred Burke "Tommy" Thompson
Hauptmann Richard Schnösenberg (Dieppe Report)
James Griffith Young (Report of Murder)
Report No. 1 War Crimes Investigation Unit

Reports and Interviews with Library and Archives Canada

Lucien Dumais
Stanley Dutka
Joly Lafleur and Robert Vanier
J.M. MacDonald
J.B. Morris
John Runcie
Derek M. Warner

Index

ABOUT THE AUTHOR

Nathan M. Greenfield, PhD, is the Canadian correspondent for *The Times Educational Supplement* and a contributor to *Maclean's*, *Canadian Geographic* and *The Times Literary Supplement*. He is the author of *The Damned*, a finalist for the Governor General's Award for Non-Fiction; *Baptism of Fire*, a finalist for the Edna Staebler Prize for Creative Non-Fiction; and the widely praised *The Battle of the St. Lawrence*. Nathan Greenfield lives in Ottawa.